CONSUMER BEHAVIOR

CONSUMER BEHAVIOR

Ayalla Ruvio
Eli Broad College of Business, Michigan State University

and

Dawn Iacobucci
Owen Graduate School of Management, Vanderbilt University

VP	Nancy Gerome
Director, Portfolio Management	Lise Johnson
EDITOR	Jennifer Manias
EDITORIAL ASSISTANT	Campbell McDonald
SENIOR MANAGING EDITOR	Judy Howarth
PRODUCTION EDITOR	Umamaheswari Gnanamani
MARKETING COORDINATOR	Jessica Spettoli
COVER PHOTO CREDIT	d3sign/Getty Images; © Prostock-studio/Shutterstock; © filadendron/Getty Images; © SDI Productions/Getty Images; © eclipse_images/Getty Images; © Tom Werner/Getty Images

This book was set in 9.5/12 STIX Two Text by Straive™.

Founded in 1807, John Wiley & Sons, Inc. has been a valued source of knowledge and understanding for more than 200 years, helping people around the world meet their needs and fulfill their aspirations. Our company is built on a foundation of principles that include responsibility to the communities we serve and where we live and work. In 2008, we launched a Corporate Citizenship Initiative, a global effort to address the environmental, social, economic, and ethical challenges we face in our business. Among the issues we are addressing are carbon impact, paper specifications and procurement, ethical conduct within our business and among our vendors, and community and charitable support. For more information, please visit our website: www.wiley.com/go/citizenship.

ISBN: 978-1-119-91241-5 (PBK)
ISBN: 978-1-119-91242-2 (EVALC)

Library of Congress Cataloging-in-Publication Data

LCCN number: 2022049701

The inside back cover will contain printing identification and country of origin if omitted from this page. In addition, if the ISBN on the back cover differs from the ISBN on this page, the one on the back cover is correct.

SKY10041121_011123

ACKNOWLEDGMENTS

The authors wish to thank the many people at Wiley who have helped to make this *Consumer Behavior* book possible! They include Jennifer Manias, Editor; Campbell McDonald, Editorial Assistant; Jessica Spettoli, Assistant Marketing Manager; Judy Howarth, Senior Managing Editor; and, Umamaheswari Gnanamani, Content Refinement Specialists.

We are also grateful to Rich S., Rick B., and Sidney L.

PREFACE

The intention of this textbook is to provide a contemporary, fresh voice for *Consumer Behavior* for undergraduates, MBAs, and Executives. Consumer behavior is a course that students usually like, in part because they can relate to it – we are all consumers, after all. Our book is positioned to help professors edutain their students. We want this book to be the one that students actually choose to read! We created this *Consumer Behavior* book to be informative and at least a little bit fun.

The Table of Contents follows this preface. In short, the chapters are organized as follows:

- Part I (Chapters 1–3) introduces and provides an overview of consumer behavior – what it is, why it is important to the brand and to the company, how and why companies need to listen to consumers to obtain insights to help develop and revise strategies. We take a strategic view of consumer behavior and highlight the importance of consumers' insights as a driving force for companies' survival and success.

- Part II (Chapters 4–6) delves into the process of a consumer buying behavior. This decision process encompasses consumers' recognition of a need or want to buy something, how those decisions unfold, how they evaluate the purchase afterward, and what kind of factors marketers should be aware of that affect the entire process. We also discuss consumers' post-purchase behavior and biases in decision-making, including topics drawn from behavioral economics.

- Part III (Chapters 7–12) cover concepts that help unpack the factors that impact consumer behavior decision-making and buying processes. These factors include getting the readers-students—to understand better how consumers think about themselves, what the consumers' various motivations that they're trying to address with their purchases are, how consumers learn, such as from marketing communications and advertising but also through their own online searches or talking with friends, as well as an understanding of consumer perception. If a company or brand thinks it is talking to its target customers, it needs to assess whether the consumers see the brand and messaging as it is intended. This part closes with a consideration of how to think about different target consumers (e.g. varying in age, socioeconomic status).

- Part IV (Chapters 13–15) covers some important contemporary issues, with a chapter each on global consumers, how to use social media effectively, and ethical aspects of consumer behavior, or what we're calling "do good" consumption. We believe in exposing students to these issues so we also have "box inserts" on each topic in each chapter throughout the book.

For Instructors

Each chapter includes the following features:

- The chapters are written in an approachable style (i.e. not boring!) to gain and retain the reader's attention.

- Each chapter contains several types of box inserts:
  - Global issues
  - Ethics issues
  - Social media

- Each chapter opens with learning objectives and a motivating story or vignette, and the chapters close with discussion questions and a list of key terms.

- The publisher can provide professors adopting this book for their classes with Instructors' Materials, including a test bank, computerized test bank, instructor's manual, chapter outlines, and PowerPoint slides. The instructor website is www.wiley.com/go/ruvio/consumer behavior1e.

For Students

The enhanced e-text includes self-check concept check questions and Bloomberg Quicktake videos for each chapter with associated study questions.

BRIEF CONTENTS

CONTENTS

About the Authors

Dr. Ayalla Ruvio is an Associate Professor of Marketing at Michigan State University. She is the Academic Director of the Master of Science in Marketing Research. She is an applied consumer behavior researcher who focuses on issues such as identity and consumption, material versus experiential consumption, consumer arrogance, and cross-cultural consumer behavior. Her research has been published in refereed journals including the *Journal of Academy of Marketing Science, International Journal of Research in Marketing, Journal of Product Innovation Management,* and *Leadership Quarterly.* She is the coeditor of the volume on *Consumer Behavior* in the International Encyclopedia of Marketing and the book *Identity and Consumption.* Dr. Ruvio's research has been featured in numerous media outlets all over the world, including the CNN, TODAY show, Good Morning America, *Time* magazine, *The New York Times, Forbes, Consumer Reports, The Daily Telegraph, The Atlantic, The Telegraph,* and the *Toronto STAR.* https://broad.msu.edu/profile/aruvio

Dawn Iacobucci is the E. Bronson Ingram Professor of Marketing at the Owen Graduate School of Management, Vanderbilt University. She was Senior Associate Dean for Owen (2008–2010), Professor of Marketing at the Kellogg School of Management, Northwestern University (1987–2004), the Coca-Cola Distinguished Professor of Marketing, Professor of Psychology and Head of the Marketing Department of the University of Arizona (2001–2002), and the John Pomerantz Professor of Marketing at Wharton, the University of Pennsylvania (2004–2007). She received her M.S. in Statistics, and M.A. and Ph.D. in Quantitative Psychology from the University of Illinois at Urbana–Champaign.

Her research focuses on social networks and methodological questions. She has published in the *Journal of Consumer Psychology*, *Journal of Marketing*, *Journal of Marketing Research, Journal of Service Research, Harvard Business Review, Marketing Science, International Journal of Research in Marketing, Psychometrika, Psychological Bulletin*, and *Social Networks.* Iacobucci teaches Marketing Management, Marketing Research, Marketing Analytics, and Services Marketing to MBA and executive MBA students, and multivariate statistics and methodological topics in Ph.D. seminars. She was editor of both the *Journal of Consumer Research* and *Journal of Consumer Psychology.* She edited *Networks in Marketing, Handbook of Services Marketing and Management, Kellogg on Marketing,* and coedited with Bobby Calder, *Kellogg on Integrated Marketing.* Iacobucci authored *Marketing Models: Multivariate Statistics and Modeling Analytics,* 4th ed., *Mediation Analysis, Analysis of Variance,* 2nd ed., *MM1-4,* and *Marketing Management,* 6th ed. https://business.vanderbilt.edu/bio/dawn-iacobucci

Introduction: Consumer Behavior Insights

PART I

1

Introduction: Consumers are Key to a Company's Success

LEARNING OBJECTIVES

After studying this chapter, you should be able to:

- Understand why learning about consumer behavior is key to an organization's survival, growth, and success.

- Understand that consumer behavior is important to anyone in business but especially to marketers.

- Appreciate how marketers can help organizations meet consumers' needs, wants, and demands.

- Understand why consumers' behavior is so challenging.

Imagine that you have a great idea for a product. Something really cool and completely new. It's a product that has yet to be introduced to the market – it's going to be the first of its kind! You are ready to jump right in and invest in this idea. But hold on – Do you know if there is a real need for such a product? Do you know if consumers would prefer this product to other options they have? Do you know if consumers will be willing to pay for such a product and how much they would be willing to pay?

Despite modernization, technology, and sophisticated research tools, the question that has intrigued sellers and buyers from the dawn of human history – What do consumers want? – remains as enigmatic today as it was thousands of years ago. However, the insights gathered by researching consumers' behavior can provide answers to such questions.

Consumer behavior refers to *how* buyers (individuals, groups, or organizations) make decisions prior to, during, and after acquiring a product (goods, services, experiences, etc.) to satisfy their needs, wants, and demands.

Who is the consumer? Is it the person who pays for products and services? Or is it the person who uses these products and services? Can a company or nonprofit organization be a consumer? In a broad sense, consumers can be individuals, households, groups, companies, or organizations that acquire goods or services for the purpose of direct use or ownership. This does not necessarily mean that the person or organization that pays for the product is the actual end user or end consumer. For example, when parents buy something for their kids, the parents pay for the product, but the children are the end users. Likewise, the purchasing department can pay for software that will be used by each worker in the company.

Consumer behavior refers to *how* buyers (individuals, groups, or organizations) make decisions prior to, during, and after acquiring a product (goods, services, experiences, etc.) to satisfy their needs, wants, and demands. It encompasses all of the cognitive and psychological processes, behaviors, motivations, beliefs, emotions, and values that are associated with the acquisition, use, and disposal of products.[1] Acquisition of a product can occur in multiple ways – through purchasing, renting, sharing, borrowing, trading, and/or gifting – and all of these behaviors interest markets. Understanding consumer behavior is critical to any company or organization, regardless of size, type, or industry and whether they are nonprofit or for-profit, because the organization's survival, growth, and success are built on its customers. The knowledge derived by studying consumers' behavior is called **consumer insights**.[2]

> *"Consumer insights should guide the strategic decision-making of companies in attracting and retaining their customers!."*
>
> *Merrill Dubrow, CEO of M/A/R/C Research*

Consumer insights the knowledge derived by studying consumers' behavior.

The study of consumer behavior and the insights it generates is beneficial not just to marketers and businesses; consumer insights also help policy makers, regulators, and legislators develop and implement policies and laws that protect consumers' rights, ensure ethical and truthful advertising as well as establish safe and fair marketing practices. Advocacy groups can also benefit from consumer behavior insights because they lobby and promote consumers' rights. Finally, even consumers themselves can benefit from learning more about their behavior and habits – especially habits that are detrimental to their health and well-being (compulsive and impulsive buying behaviors, hoarding, consumption of addictive substances, etc.).

In this book, we take you on a journey to understand consumer behavior and relate it to marketing practices. As such, this book will help you in two ways.

1. First, it will provide you with insights into how consumers behave in the marketplace that will help you perform better as a businessperson. Regardless of your major or where you will eventually work, the success of your company (for-profit or nonprofit) will ultimately depend on your understanding of your consumers and your ability to convert this understanding into actionable strategies. Have you ever seen a successful company without customers?

2. Second, this book will provide you with insights into your own behavior as a consumer. While you still may fall for some "great deals" and wishful promises, at least you will know why you are doing so.

Consumer Behavior as a Multifaceted Phenomenon

Consumer behavior is multifaceted and goes beyond the purchase of products. It's a complex process that involves multiple decisions and sometimes multiple people, as well as multiple actions and behaviors. Figure 1.1 presents a framework of consumer behavior and serves as a road map for this book.

The figure shows that the individual consumer decision-making process (Chapter 4) prior to, during, and after (Chapter 5) the acquisition of a product is the heart of the framework. It encompasses everything that happens prior to the acquisition phase, including all of the decisions about what to get, when to do it, how to do it, how much to acquire, how to pay for it, and how much to pay. Marketers can influence consumers' decision-making going into the purchase, and the post-purchase period is important for marketers as an opportunity to further build relationships with their consumers.

Multiple factors can affect this process, which makes it rather complex. Overall, we can divide them into internal and external factors.

- **Internal factors** refer to factors that are intrinsic to the consumer. These include the motivation for acquiring a product, the learning process, perceptions, attitudes, and beliefs that influence consumers' decision-making. These factors are normally unobservable. Companies and marketers can learn about them only by conducting market research.

Internal factors factors that are intrinsic to the consumer.

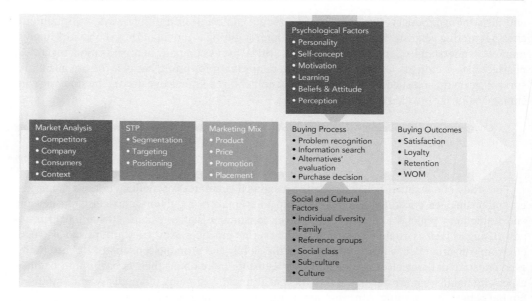

FIGURE 1.1 Consumer Behavior and Insights Framework

External factors
factors such as the consumers' sociocultural environment, their family and friends, their reference groups, and the people they interact with online and offline.

- **External factors** are factors such as the consumers' sociocultural environment, their family and friends, their reference groups, and the people they interact with online and offline, all of which will have an effect on their decision-making.

These factors make consumers similar to or different from each other. For example, many students in your class have a similar motivation when it comes to achieving their degree. But, you are also very different from other students when it comes to your personality, background, and even future aspirations. As we will see in the next chapter, marketers can group consumers with similar characteristics to address their needs more efficiently. Note, however, that companies will group (segment) consumers based on criteria that are relevant to their product. For example, the fact that you are all students may be important to companies that are selling textbooks or other college supplies, but this will not be relevant for other companies that don't target students. This is another key reason why studying consumers' behavior and consumer insights is so critical to all companies and organizations. Companies must understand what criteria help to differentiate between who their consumer is and who is not. Sometimes those criteria are obvious – such as in the example of the textbook. But they are not always that obvious, or there may be multiple criteria that are relevant to a company or a product. After we explain all these factors in the following chapters, you'll come to appreciate that the marketer's job is challenging!

Marketing mix
strategies related to their product, price, placement, and promotion.

Figure 1.1 also includes other factors that are related to marketers' efforts to influence consumers' decision-making process. Companies and organizations can (and should) influence this process through the implementation of a **marketing mix**,[3] a term used to describe the strategies related to their product, price, placement, and promotion (Chapter 2). These strategies are guided by consumer insights gleaned from market analysis (Chapter 3) as well as segmentation, targeting, and positioning strategies (Chapter 2). As you can see, the consumers' decision-making process is the focal point of the buyer–seller interaction.

Consumers
or buyers – those who acquire products to satisfy their needs.

The Buyer–Seller Interaction

Products
can be goods, services, experiences, activities, ideas, information, or anything offered to a market to satisfy a need.

The buyer–seller interaction is the heart of studying consumer behavior.[4] As we noted above, **consumers**, or buyers, are those who acquire **products** that can be goods, services, experiences, activities, ideas, information, or anything offered to a market to satisfy a need. Consumers can be individuals or businesses. These products can be for the consumer's use or for the use of others, be the individuals or companies. **Sellers**, or marketers, are individuals or organizations that offer such goods or services. If you have a pair of sneakers that you are not using, and you post them on Facebook Marketplace, you are the seller. When you are buying textbooks, you are the buyer or the consumer. The interaction between buyers and sellers happens in the **marketplace**, the environment – physical or non-physical – where buyers and sellers engage in the process of exchange.[5] Figure 1.2 illustrates the interaction between buyers and sellers, so let's delve into all its pieces.

Needs

The first step in the buyer–seller interaction is consumers' **needs**.[6] Needs are basic human requirements that are essential for an individual to survive, to function in a social context, and to achieve complete development and self-actualization. According to Abraham Maslow, needs are the motivating forces behind any action we take.[7] We'll see more in Chapter 7 about consumer motivation. All individuals share some needs, but they vary in terms of their intensity and the ways in which they are fulfilled. For example, some people have a strong need for social interaction; they enjoy meeting and interacting with many people. Others, however, may only need a good friend or two to fulfill their social needs.

Consumers are driven to acquire goods and services to fulfill their needs. These needs give marketers the opportunity to offer products. In Chapter 2, we will see that linking products to consumers' needs is essential to the success of the products and the companies selling them.

One topic that is often discussed in the context of the buyer–seller interaction is whether marketers can create needs. It sounds reasonable that if needs motivate consumers to buy products, then creating those needs will help companies sell more products. Marketers don't really *create* needs, but marketers *can* influence and shape those needs.[8]

- For example, marketers can make consumers' needs salient ("Are you hungry now?"). They can remind consumers of their future needs ("What will you have for dinner?").

Marketers can also make consumers feel as if they need a specific product.

Sellers
or marketers – individuals or organizations that offer such goods or services.

Marketplace
the environment – physical or non-physical – where buyers and sellers engage in the process of exchange.

Needs
basic human requirements that are essential for an individual to survive, to function in a social context, and to achieve complete development and self-actualization.

FIGURE 1.2 Buyer–Seller Interaction

- For example, they may ask, "Do you need a car?" Most people will answer "yes" to this question, because how can you function in our world without a car? But do you really "need" that fancy car? Furthermore, it is not the car you need – your need is for transportation. Millions of people around the world don't own a car and use other forms of transportation. In big cities, many people use public transportation, ride-share services, and even bicycles to get where they need to go.

Wants

Wants
specific products and brands consumers choose to satisfy their needs based on their culture and individual personality.

Wants reflect the way consumers fulfill their needs. The term refers to the specific products and brands consumers choose to satisfy their needs based on their culture and individual personality.[9] While most basic needs do not change over time, the *way* in which consumers fulfill them does. The choices that consumers make depend on their culture and their personal preferences. For example, consider your breakfast options. You might have cereal, eggs, bacon, pancakes, doughnuts, or muffins, all of which are very common breakfast options for Americans. For the same reason, your consideration set will not include fried rice or fried noodles, which are very common breakfast options for Asians. However, if you are a vegetarian, for instance, your consideration set will not include bacon. Regardless of your culture, it's a personal preference.

The Global Mindset

American vs. Asian breakfast

Marketers can offer products that answer consumers' personal preferences; they can also help consumers develop new preferences or help them become more receptive to new offerings. For example, marketers help educate consumers about eco-friendly products and healthy food options and convince their companies to offer new products that meet these new preferences. We will discuss ways marketers educate consumers in the context of consumer learning.

DON'T TEXT AND DRIVE.

You can't count on a text message to reveal what's happening on the road in front of you. That's why, each year, an estimated 100,000 crashes have been tied to texting and driving, while an additional 1.2 million crashes involve other cell phone use.

DON'T TXT & DRIVE

Marketers also help with societal messaging such as "don't text and drive!" campaign of BMW.

Demand

Demand is an economic principle reflecting consumers' willingness and ability to pay a certain price for the desired product. A consumer's decision about whether or not to purchase a product will consist of these two considerations. For example, would you pay ten dollars for a can of Coke? Probably not. Even though you could afford to pay ten dollars, you would probably refuse to do so. In contrast, you might want to drive a brand-new Ferrari. However, being a college student probably means that you cannot afford this car (yet!).

Marketers constantly invest time and money into forecasting the demand for their products, and, of course, marketers try to promote the product to increase demand. Marketers can increase the demand for their products in several ways.

- They can make products more attractive to consumers in terms of quality, price, image, innovativeness, or any other desirable product attribute. Doing so will increase the value of the product in the eyes of the consumer and their willingness to pay for it.

- Marketers can also run promotions that make products more affordable for consumers, motivating them to purchase products that they otherwise probably would not buy.

Exchange

Exchange is the process by which buyers and sellers negotiate over something of value (i.e. a product). Decades ago, Richard Bagozzi (1975) noted that "any exchange is marketing."[10] This statement still holds today. Both buyers and sellers can initiate an exchange process. Buyers

Demand
an economic principle reflecting consumers' willingness and ability to pay a certain price for the desired product.

Exchange
the process by which buyers and sellers negotiate over something of value (i.e., a product).

normally initiate an exchange process if they need or want to buy something. For example, if you run out of gas, you will stop at the gas station to fill up your car. Alternatively, the exchange process can be initiated by the seller, normally in the form of marketing messages such as advertisements, commercials, salespeople, and promotions. Promotions sent by email or pop-ups are attempts by sellers to engage you in an exchange process. Regardless of who initiated the exchange process, consumers are the buyers, and they normally have more control over it. They can terminate the exchange process at any point. In fact, there are laws that give consumers control even after the sale was made. For example, in most states in the United States, consumers have the right to cancel any transaction within three days if the purchase was made at a facility other than the seller's place of business (e.g. consumers' residence, hotels, convention centers).

Figure 1.3 shows that a marketing exchange requires five conditions[11]:

1. Any exchange process should include two or more parties with unsatisfied needs. It's the starting point of every consumption process. When you are browsing the internet for a product that you want to buy, you are starting an exchange process. When a company sends you a promotional text message, it is trying to engage you in an exchange process. But, if you stop browsing the internet or do not respond to the promotional text message, the exchange process will end because one of the parties (you) terminated the exchange process.

2. Both parties must be looking to fulfill their needs through the acquisition or sale of a product or a service. As we will see in Chapter 7, consumers have a variety of needs (e.g. physiological, social, psychological) and will consider multiple options to fulfill these needs. Companies also have needs such as increasing revenue, expanding brand recognition, and building a good reputation. An exchange process must address the needs of all parties involved.

3. The product or service that is at the center of the exchange process must have value for both parties. Note that this does not mean that the product will have the same value. Occasionally, you may be interested in a product but not buy it because you think it is overpriced. Other times, you may find a product that you want at a price that you are willing to pay or even lower (a bargain!).

Two or more parties with unsatisfied needs.

A desire and ability to satisfy these needs.

A way for the parties to communicate.

Something of value to be exchange between parties.

Freedom of each party to accept or reject.

FIGURE 1.3   Conditions for Exchange

4. Both parties must have the ability to communicate with each other. This communication may be transactional (i.e. negotiating over a price) or informational (i.e. discussing a product or an upcoming promotion). In either case, an offer must be communicated.

5. Finally, each of the parties should have the right and the ability to reject offers from the other side. Exchange is not a binding process. Buyers and sellers should have the option to walk away from the deal. Picture this: You see a product you like on Facebook Marketplace. You message the seller to negotiate a price. At any given moment, you can walk away from the deal and so can the seller. But the process of exchange still took place.

The main goal of marketers is to initiate an exchange process. How? Any marketing message, whether a commercial, a magazine ad, a social media ad, a promotional mailing, an in-store display or promotion, is an attempt to engage consumers in an exchange process. Some marketing gurus estimate that we are exposed to four thousand to ten thousand marketing messages a day.[12] Of course, not all exchange processes end successfully – that is, not all exchange processes result in a sale. How many times have you put an item in your virtual cart and never purchased the item? Or deleted a promotional email? Regardless of the end results, the process of exchange took place, similar to the marketplace example above.[13]

Transaction

The end result of a successful exchange process is a **transaction**, when the buyer pays the seller and in return receives the desired product. While transactions normally entail a monetary exchange, anything of value can be transacted. For example, some housing programs offer students the opportunity to live for free with an elderly person in return for companionship.[14]

Transactions can trigger both good and bad feelings. Studies show that when consumers shop or see something that they would like to purchase, the area in their brain that is in charge of feeling physical pleasure is activated. By contrast, marketing researchers have found that when consumers pay, the area in their brain that is in charge of feeling physical pain is activated, causing **pain of paying** – paying hurts! Since we are programmed to avoid pain, one would think that the pain of paying would help us resist the temptation of shopping because it will reduce the pleasure we derive from it. However, marketers constantly develop ways to ease our pain of paying.[15] For example, giving consumers the option to "buy now and pay later" is designed to ease the pain of payment by temporarily removing the painful aspect of the purchase and creating a gap between the purchase and the payment.

The most "painful" way to pay is by using cash. It draws consumers' attention to the price of the product and the amount of money they need to spend on it. Using a credit card, on the other hand, is much less painful because it distances consumers from the act of paying.[16] Using cell phones is even less painful, making transactions much smoother and enjoyable for consumers. Some argue that in the future we will use biometrics to pay for our purchases, and the "pain of paying" will become a thing of the past.

A marketer's job doesn't end with the purchase. During transactions, or shortly thereafter, consumers need to be reassured that they made the right choice. They want to be rewarded for choosing this specific brand of product rather than other options. They also often want to know that companies care about their opinions and experiences when using their products. Marketers can take the opportunity to offer consumers something that will encourage them to come back and shop again. For example, many retailers such as Kohl's and Macy's offer cash back on current purchases to be used toward future shopping. Such methods help companies foster long-lasting relationships with their consumers (we'll say more about this in Chapter 5).

Transaction
the end result of a successful exchange process, when the buyer pays the seller and in return receives the desired product.

Pain of paying
a feeling experienced by consumers when they pay for a product.

Post-purchase Behavior

Post-purchase behavior
all the behaviors consumers engage in after a transaction is completed.

Some people think that "consumer behavior" ends after a transaction is completed. However, think about what happens after you buy something – that is, **post-purchase behavior**. Does your relationship with the seller end once you've paid? Probably not. If you are happy with the product, you are more likely to return to the store for future purchases. You might even tell others about your positive experience, generating "word of mouth." If you are unhappy with the product you purchased, you might contact the seller for an opportunity to amend the situation. In fact, marketing studies show that you are most likely to tell others about your bad experience and go on social media and share the details about it.[17] Chapter 5 focuses on this post-purchase stage of consumer behavior.

Marketers have learned that selling products is important. But what happens after the customer leaves the store is also important.[18] The exchange process and the transaction give marketers the opportunity to start developing a relationship with their customers. These relationships should be nurtured and cultivated after the transaction. Marketers use different strategies to do this. Examples include offering consumers the opportunity to join their loyalty rewards program or sending consumers coupons for their birthday. However, the most common tactic marketers use to make sure that their consumers are happy with their purchases is sending them a customer satisfaction survey.

Another critical element that is associated with this phase of the decision-making process is the disposal of products.[19] Consumers have various ways of doing so. The obvious way is to throw the product away once the consumer is done using it. But consumers can also resell their unneeded products through a variety of outlets such as garage sales, Craigslist, Facebook Marketplace, and eBay. They can also donate them or give them away. And, of course, consumers can just store their unused and unneeded products. All of these options provide marketers with opportunities to develop their business, offer new products, and create a competitive advantage. (This topic involves the roles of consumers and companies with regard to sustainability, and we'll talk about it more throughout the book.)

For Patagonia sustainability is so important that it encourages its customers to repair their products instead of buying new ones. The company even offers store credit for used items returned to them.

Just as Patagonia encourages the repair, reuse, and recycling model,[20] we also care about ethics and values of marketing and consumer behavior. We discuss ethical frameworks in Chapter 15, and we describe marketing examples in most chapters in a feature we call "Do the Right Thing!" For example, there are ethical concerns when conducting marketing research (Chapter 3) and even in how marketers construct their messages when they're trying to persuade consumers to buy their products (Chapter 6). Here's an example.

Do the Right Thing!

Marketers sometimes hear the following criticism: "Marketers make people buy stuff they don't want, they don't need, and they can't afford." Do you believe this is true? Have you ever bought something you didn't want, need, or couldn't afford, and if so, do you recall why you did so? Was an ad, a social media endorsement, or a set of product reviews and ratings so compelling that it controlled your mind and sent you to make the purchase? Consumer behavior is more complicated than that – and it's what makes consumers so interesting to study!

Why Is Consumer Behavior So Challenging?

While consumers' basic needs are constant across individuals and time, how consumers get their needs met can vary. Consumer behavior is very dynamic, constantly changing, even affecting the marketplace where buyers and sellers interact.[21] Marketers are always looking for new products, new trends, and new ways to satisfy consumers' needs. In some cases, this task is very challenging.

Take, for example, the introduction of the iPad in 2010,[22] the first tablet ever to be introduced to the market. How do you think Apple decided if there was a real need for such a product or if consumers would prefer this product to other options they had? How did the company decide whether and how much consumers would be willing to pay for the iPad? These challenges are real. Companies face them every day. To deal with these challenges, companies monitor changes in consumer behavior constantly.[23] We can identify several areas whose dynamics have proven challenging for marketers.[24]

The Way Consumers Shop Keeps Changing

It used to be very simple. If you wanted a product, you would go to a nearby store and purchase it. Of course, today, you can buy any product from any store and from any place in the world without leaving your home, and the product will be delivered to you. Consumers today have infinite products available to them at any time on their computers, cell phones, and tablets. In addition, they expect their shopping experience to be enjoyable and consistent across devices. Consumers also have all the information they need to make smart decisions about products. As a result, the balance of power between buyers and sellers has shifted even more toward buyers. With more options and more knowledge, consumers are driving the buyer–seller interaction. This power imbalance challenges marketers because they often find themselves following consumer trends instead of leading them.

The Way Consumers Fulfill Their Needs Keeps Changing

To stay ahead in the fight for consumers' interest and attention, marketers must constantly come up with new ways and new options to satisfy consumers' needs. Indeed, sometimes it is the consumers who come up with new ways to satisfy their needs. The sharing economy is a good example. Uber and Airbnb are alternatives that have developed to answer consumers' needs in ways that are different from what had been available. More than ever before, consumers want convenience, simplicity, speed, and good value. Their loyalty is much more fluid and can easily be influenced by every new product or product alternative introduced to the market. As a result, marketers struggle not just to attract new consumers but also to retain the ones they have.

The Way Consumers Communicate with Other Consumers Keeps Changing

Just as going to the store is no longer the only way to shop, meeting people in person in order to communicate with them is no longer the only option. Consumers have multiple ways in which they can learn about each other's experiences and opinions about products and services. For every product that consumers consider, there are hundreds of others who have rated it, reviewed it, YouTubed about it, or posted about it on other social media. Consumers can post their own questions about where to buy a product, how much to pay for it, how to use it, what other options they have, what the new products and trends are, and any other questions they might have – and get answers immediately.

This abundant availability of information also means that consumers can form their opinions about a product or service without any interaction with the seller. In fact, information from marketers is considered less trustworthy than that from friends and other consumers. This situation challenges marketers and pushes them to find creative ways to communicate with consumers that will be perceived as more trustworthy. Marketers have met these challenges by using influencers and opinion leaders.

Social media changes rapidly (e.g. What are the "cool" websites and for which age groups?), so it is very challenging but, seen in a positive light, that means the marketing environment is dynamic and exciting! Social media is so important to marketers that we devote an entire chapter to discussing how marketers can use social media effectively and smartly (Chapter 14). In addition, we provide a social media story in almost every chapter and ask questions such as "How does social media facilitate customer satisfaction?"(Chapter 5) and "How does a consumer learn from social media?" (Chapter 9).

Those with Whom Consumers Communicate Keeps Changing

The variety of ways in which consumers communicate also means that they interact with a wide range of people, some of whom they will never meet. Rather than interacting just with people in their own village, consumers now interact with those in the global village. Consumers' social networks have expanded in directions far beyond location and time. Social media has enabled consumers to develop interest groups and communities centered on shared interests in products or brands.

Brand communities a group of consumers with a common bond around a brand.

Brand communities are not about geography, but instead are based on a group of consumers with a common bond around a brand. Members in brand communities provide consumers with more in-depth knowledge about the products and brands that interest them. They also provide a side benefit: consumers can participate in social relationships with other consumers and feel a sense of belonging over a common interest. These communities indicate the strength of the brand and provide companies with an opportunity to create meaningful bonds with their consumers.[25]

BRAND COMMUNITIES ON SOCIAL MEDIA

Harley-Davidson has an enthusiastic, well-connected brand community.

SUMMARY

Studying consumer behavior is important for any individual pursuing a business career in two ways: First, it provides insights into how consumers behave in the market so a businessperson can make better strategic decisions. Second, it provides insights into one's personal experience as a consumer, which helps one understand and relate better to other consumers.

Consumers' needs drive them to acquire goods and services to fulfill those needs, which provide marketers with the opportunity to offer such products. The specific products and brands that consumers choose to satisfy their needs reflect their wants and are affected by their culture and personal preference. Optimally, marketers would offer products that answer these personal preferences, help consumers develop new preferences, or become more receptive to new offerings.

While consumers can initiate the exchange process if they need or want to buy something, marketers can initiate the exchange process of negotiating over something of value by distributing communication messages such as ads, commercials, and promotions. A successful exchange process results in a transaction. The buyer pays the seller and in return receives the desired product. The exchange process and the transaction give marketers the opportunity to start developing a relationship with their customers that should be nurtured and cultivated to build trust and brand loyalty.

Consumers' basic needs are constant across individuals and time, but their behavior is dynamic. First, the way consumers shop has changed. With more options and more knowledge, consumers are driving the buyer–seller interaction. Second, the way consumers fulfill their needs has changed, and they readily switch between brands depending on who offers the most convenience, simplicity, speed, or good value. Third, how consumers communicate with others has changed. There are multiple ways in which they can learn about each other's experiences and opinions about products and services. The availability of information means buyers do not have to interact with the seller. Finally, who consumers communicate with has changed. Brand communities are an example of how consumers seek more in-depth knowledge about the products and brands that interest them without having to interact with the seller.

KEY TERMS

Consumer behavior	Marketing mix	Marketplace	Demand	Pain of paying
Consumer insights	Consumers	Needs	Exchange	Post-purchase behavior
Internal factors	Products	Wants	Transaction	Brand communities
External factors	Sellers			

EXERCISES

1. Needs, wants, and demands – How do you define these terms and how they differ from each other. For example, is your cell phone a need?

2. In pairs or small groups, discuss how something could be either a need or a want. For example, when dressing for an interview, is nice business attire a want? Or is it really a need, to signal one's serious interest in fitting in with the interviewing organization? As another example, when taking a friend to a restaurant to celebrate a success, is the notion of going to a nice restaurant merely a "want" that any restaurant could fulfill? Or should the restaurant "need" to be nice to signal to the friend a level of caring and support?

3. In pairs or small groups, discuss a recent purchase where you, as a consumer, initiated the exchange. What did the process look like? Did you seek information online? Go to a store or purchase online? Did you provide the company with any feedback in person or on social media? Alternatively, discuss a recent purchase you made that was greatly influenced by marketing. In other words, as much as we believe that we ignore pop-up ads, commercials during streaming TV shows that we can't click through, or driving past billboards, think of a time when an ad seemed to put a thought in your head that you later investigated and that eventually triggered you to purchase the product.

4. In pairs or small groups, discuss times you've posted information on social media saying something about a recent purchase. Did you do so because you were satisfied or dissatisfied? What made you post? What did you say about the product?

5. When you are in class, look around you. List all the marketing messages that you are exposed to. How many are there? Did you notice them all?

ENDNOTES

1. American Marketing Association, "Consumer Behavior," https://www.ama.org/topics/consumer-behavior/.

2. Flora Frichou, "What Are Consumer Insights and How Do I Use Them? An Introduction," *Trustpilot* (blog), July 5, 2020, https://business.trustpilot.com/reviews/learn-from-customers/what-are-consumer-insights-and-how-do-i-use-them.

3. E. Jerome McCarthy, *Basic Marketing: A Managerial Approach* (Homewood, IL: Irwin, 1960).

4. American Marketing Association, "Guides and eBooks," https://www.ama.org/topics/white-paper.

5. Jagdish N. Sheth, "Buyer–Seller Interaction: A Conceptual Framework," in Beverlee B. Anderson, ed., *Advances in Consumer Research*, Vol. 3 (Cincinnati, OH: Association for Consumer Research, 1976), 382–86.

6. Sumit Saurav, "Understanding Needs, Wants and Demands in the Marketing World," LinkedIn post, April 2, 2020, https://www.linkedin.com/pulse/understanding-needs-wants-demands-marketing-world-sumit-saurav/?articleId=6651412915658252288/.

7. Abraham H. Maslow, *Motivation and Personality* (New York: Harper & Row, 1970).

8. Jonathan R. Ferrer, "The Great Controversy: Does Marketing Create or Satisfy Needs?" *LinkedIn post, May* 25, 2015, https://www.linkedin.com/pulse/great-controversy-does-marketing-create-satisfy-needs-r-ferrer-mba-5/.

9. Geraldine Fennell, "Consumers' Perceptions of the Product—Use Situation: A Conceptual Framework for Identifying Consumer Wants and Formulating Positioning Options," *Journal of Marketing* 42, no. 2 (1978): 38–47.

10. R. P. Bagozzi, "Marketing as Exchange," *Journal of Marketing* 39, no. 4 (1975): 32–39.

11. http://www.ekerk.com/.

12. https://www.forbes.com/sites/forbesagencycouncil/2017/08/25/finding-brand-success-in-the-digital-world/?sh=d151083626e2.

13. F. S. Houston and J. B. Gassenheimer, "Marketing and Exchange," *Journal of Marketing* 51, no. 4 (1987): 3–18.

14. J. T. Gourville, "Pennies-a-day: The Effect of Temporal Reframing on Transaction Evaluation," *Journal of Consumer Research* 24, no. 4 (1998): 395–408.

15. E.Y. Chan, "The Consumer in Physical Pain: Implications for the Pain-of-paying and Pricing," *Journal of the Association for Consumer Research*, 6, no. 1 (2021).

16. A. M. Shah, N. Eisenkraft, J. R. Bettman, et al., "'Paper or Plastic?': How We Pay Influences Post-transaction Connection," *Journal of Consumer Research* 42 (February 2016): 688–708.

17. M. C. Gilly and B. D. Gelb, "Post-purchase Consumer Processes and the Complaining Consumer," *Journal of Consumer Research* 9, no. 3 (1982): 323–28.

18. R. Mugge, H. N. Schifferstein, and J. P. Schoormans, "Product Attachment and Satisfaction: Understanding Consumers' Post-purchase Behavior," *Journal of Consumer Marketing* 27, no. 3 (2010): 271–82.

19. R. Trudel, J. J. Argo, and M. D. Meng, "The Recycled Self: Consumers' Disposal Decisions of Identity-linked Products," *Journal of Consumer Research* 43, no. 2 (2016): 246–64.

20. Patagonia, https://www.patagonia.com/stories/dont-buy-this-jacket-black-friday-and-the-new-york-times/story-18615.html; and https://justtradeplnu.wordpress.com/2014/04/17/dont-buy-our-jacket/.

21. S. P. Douglas and C. S. Craig, "The Changing Dynamic of Consumer Behavior: Implications for Cross-cultural Research," *International Journal of Research in Marketing* 14, no. 4 (1997): 379–95.

22. https://www.apple.com/newsroom/2010/01/27Apple-Launches-iPad/.

23. https://www.mckinsey.com/business-functions/marketing-and-sales/our-insights/understanding-and-shaping-consumer-behavior-in-the-next-normal.

24. https://www2.deloitte.com/us/en/insights/industry/retail-distribution/the-consumer-is-changing.html.

25. A. M. Muniz, and T. C. O'Guinn, "Brand Community," *Journal of Consumer Research* 27, no. 4 (2001): 412–32.

CREDITS

2

Consumers' Insights as Drivers of Marketing Strategies

LEARNING OBJECTIVES

After studying this chapter, you should be able to:

- Understand the important role consumer behavior and insights play in the strategic decision-making of companies and organizations.

- Help your company develop consumer-centric strategies to address your consumers' needs more effectively and efficiently.

- Help articulate your company's unique value proposition, which includes consumers (for relevancy), the company (for deliverability), and competitors (for differentiation).

- Understand that marketing strategy involves STP: segmentation, targeting, and positioning.

- Understand that companies deliver their products to consumers via the marketing mix of the four Ps: product, price, place, and promotion.

Some years back, John Antioco, the CEO of Blockbuster, the leader in home movie and video game rental services at the time, was considering an offer he had recently received. The offer came from a young, still struggling company that operated a DVD-by-mail rental service. The cofounders of the new company, Reed Hastings and Marc Randolph, offered Antioco the opportunity to acquire their company for $50 million dollars. Antioco decided to pass on this offer. His reasoning was that Blockbuster was in the "movie and video game rental industry," not the "mailing industry."

Facepalm! Ten years later, Blockbuster went bankrupt, and that other company you know to be Netflix is now a multi-billion company, leaving Blockbuster in the dust.[1] Well done, Netflix!

Marketing myopia defining the company's business in terms of a product instead of a need or a solution to a problem.

Successful Businesses Provide Solutions

The moral of the story is that a company should never define its business in terms of a product or function rather than as a solution to a problem. Defining the company's business in terms of a product reflects a shortsighted strategy and indicates that the company suffers from what's been called **marketing myopia**.[2] Instead, companies should take a marketing-oriented view and define their business as a solution to their consumers' problems, which reflects a long-term view of the business. **Marketing orientation**[3,4] perspective focuses on the needs and wants of consumers as a focal point of the company operation. Companies with a marketing orientation are often referred to as **customer-centric companies**. These companies prioritize their consumers' needs as the driving force for all strategic decisions in the company. They aim to delivering greater value to their consumers and address their needs throughout the entire customer journey.

The case of Blockbuster and Netflix also demonstrates the importance of consumer behavior and insights to the strategic definition and operation of any company. While often discussed and studied independently, consumers' problems, needs, and wants are the heart of the unique value of every company. Products come and go, but the benefits they had provided persist. If Blockbuster had defined its business as "family entertainment providers," buying Netflix would have fit this value proposition (we define this shortly).

In contrast, Netflix defined its business as "media and entertainment services." This business definition allowed Netflix to offer a wide range of services, including creating original content. This flexible business definition also enabled Netflix to transition smoothly from a DVD-by-mail rental service company to a streaming company and to keep its value proposition relevant to consumers' needs.

The definition of the business is closely related to a company's unique value proposition. If this unique value proposition becomes obsolete due to changes in consumers' preferences, technological changes, or lack of differentiation, the company will cease to exist.

Consumers are the key to a company's success. Imagine the company as a ship, the market as an ocean, and the consumer as the ship's destination. In order for the ship to reach its destination, it needs to know where it is and the best course to get there. Every action that every person on the ship takes should be designed to get the ship to its destination. The smallest error in judgment will cause the ship to miss its destination. Similarly, for a company to succeed, it needs to identify who its consumers are, the best way to reach them, and what is needed to do so successfully. Consumers' insights are critical for these tasks and drive this process. Any insight gathered from the market should serve one purpose: to help the ship reach its destination. In this chapter, we will focus on the important role of consumer behavior and consumer insights as drivers of marketing strategy.

Consumer-Centric Strategy

Clearly, marketers should center their strategic planning on their consumers. But how exactly should they do so? Figure 2.1 outlines the marketing strategic planning process. **Marketing strategy** is the process by which companies create and deliver unique value to their consumers. As noted above, many companies today implement a customer-centric strategy, which centers on consumers' needs and attempts to provide them with optimal solutions and greater value. These companies understand that there is no such thing as "a consumer." There are different segments of consumers who have different needs.

This process encompasses three main elements that lead to firm outcomes:

1. A company's unique value proposition
2. A segmentation, targeting, and positioning (STP) process
3. Marketing mix strategies

Marketing orientation defines the company's business as a solution to their consumers' problems, which reflects a long-term view of the business.

Customer-centric companies companies with a marketing orientation view.

Marketing strategy the process by which companies create and deliver unique value to their consumers.

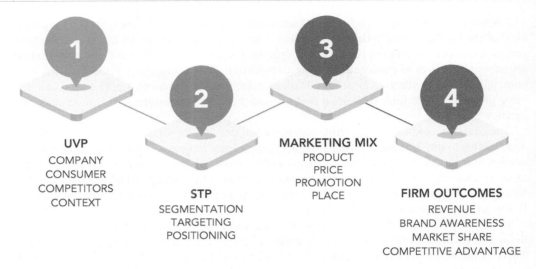

FIGURE 2.1 The Marketing Strategy Process

What to Offer Consumers: A Unique Value Proposition

Unique value proposition (UVP) a statement that articulates the promise the company makes to its customers to be delivered in a unique and differentiated way.

A **unique value proposition (UVP)** reflects the basis for the existence of any company. It's essentially a statement that articulates the promise the company makes to its customers to be delivered in a unique and differentiated way. The starting point of the marketing strategy process, not surprisingly, is the consumer.

Let's take a closer look at the elements of a UVP, as presented in Figure 2.2:

- From the *consumers*' perspective, "relevancy": How do the company's offerings solve consumers' problems or improve their current state?

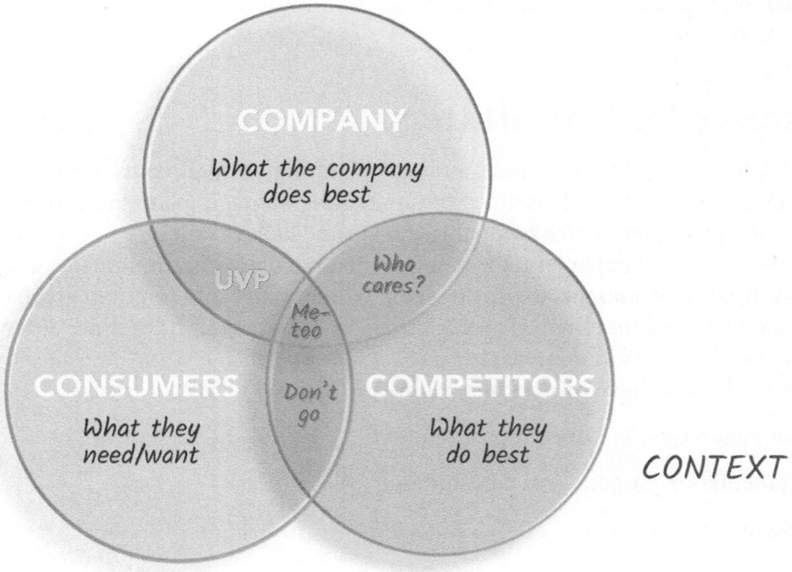

COMPANY
What the company
does best

UVP

Who
cares?

Me-
too

CONSUMERS
What they
need/want

Don't
go

COMPETITORS
What they
do best

CONTEXT

FIGURE 2.2 Unique Value Proposition

- From the *company's* perspective, "deliverability": What specific benefits do the company's offerings deliver?

- From the *competitors*' perspective, "differentiation": In what way are the benefits offered by the company different from those of the competitors? Why should customers buy the company's offerings and not those of the competitors?

The interaction among these three elements – the consumer, the company, and the company's competitors – creates four zones of intersection:

The ***unique value proposition zone*** includes the overlap between the company's offerings and consumers' needs. It excludes any overlap with the competitors. The UVP zone reflects the company's ability to provide consumers with desirable offerings that address their needs in a way that is distinct from the company's competitors.

This zone reflects the company's **Points of Difference (PODs)**. These are benefits that the company offers that are desirable to its consumers, and are NOT being offered by its competitors. This is what makes the company unique and different in the eyes of the consumers. They will choose this company over its competitors and will be willing to pay more for its offerings. Well-established PODs provide the company with a competitive advantage and secure its position in the market.

The ***me too zone*** is where there is overlap between the company's offerings, consumers' needs, and its competitors' offerings. This zone reflects the company's ability to provide consumers with desirable offerings that address their needs, but not in a way that is clearly differentiated from the company's competitors.

This zone reflects the company's **points of parity (POPs)**. These are benefits that the company offers that are desirable to consumers, but they are also offered by competitors. Consumers can get these benefits from any company, and they can easily switch between brands due to the companies' lack of differentiation. The choice of purchase, then, is typically influenced by promotions and sales. The ***who cares? zone*** reflects the overlap between the company's offerings and those of its competitors. Notice that this zone is outside the sphere of consumers. In other words, all of the players in this zone offer undifferentiated products that are not desirable in the eyes of consumers. Consumers don't care – the offerings don't address any of their needs or problems. This zone is also referred to as **points of irrelevance (POIs)**. Companies that operate in this zone risk failure.

The ***don't go zone*** indicates the overlap between the competitors' offerings and consumers' needs. The focal company does not operate in this zone. There are two ways to interpret this situation. The first is that competitors might offer something that the focal company should not offer in order to maintain its differentiation. In this case, the company has determined that it would be best not to compete in this zone. The second is that the company is overlooking a potential opportunity. In this case, the company needs to explore this opportunity and decide if it's worth pursuing.

The context that the company operates in will determine the effect of each of these elements as well as the dynamic between them. They will change from industry to industry, product to product, and company to company based on its position in the market.

Points of difference (PODs) these are benefits that the company offers that are desirable to its consumers, and are NOT being offered by its competitors.

Points of parity (POPs) these are benefits that the company offers that are desirable to consumers, but they are also offered by competitors.

Points of irrelevance (POIs) these are offerings that do not address any of the needs or problems the consumers have.

How to Craft a Successful Unique Value Proposition

While having a unique value proposition is critical to any company, crafting one can be extremely challenging. Figure 2.3 illustrates a simple template of a unique value proposition. Note that it starts with consumers and their needs – while you might already have a sense of the consumers and their needs, you are still advised to use marketing research to help to identify those in a more rigorous way (as we'll see in Chapter 3).

For *(target market)*

Who wants/needs *(the problem the company solves)*

The offering *(what the company does)*

Which provides *(the company's solution to the problem)*

Unlike *(other competitors)*

Only the company of offers *(key differentiator)*

FIGURE 2.3 Value Proposition Template

Target market is a group of consumers with similar characteristics or needs that the company can serve successfully with its products or services.

Notice that a precise definition of the **target market** and those consumers' needs is key for the success of the process. A target market is a group of consumers with similar characteristics or needs that the company can serve successfully with its products or services. Thus, companies get this part of the unique value proposition wrong, their entire planning process will be off target, similar to a ship that is using the wrong coordinates.

For example, Lyft defined its target market as serving "people who need a simple method for getting from Point A to Point B."[5] Uber, on the other hand, defined its target market as "people who need low-cost, on-demand transportation." Despite the difference in the definitions of their target markets, both companies are perceived as quite similar and risk losing their differentiation. Both of these companies are operating in the me too zone. They are both offering a desirable product but with very little differentiation.

After defining the target market and identifying its needs, companies need to be very clear about the offerings and benefits they provide to their consumers. They need to state clearly how their brand addresses their consumers' needs and solves their problems. Companies cannot assume that consumers will figure this out. They need to state it explicitly. And smart companies build in some flexibility.

For example, we all know Zoom through online classes, but that's not how the company defines itself. According to the company, its UVP is that it offers online accessibility. Many elements of the company's operation, such as videoconferencing, group meetings, simple online meetings, and teaching platforms, fit under the umbrella of accessibility. By defining its offerings as accessibility, Zoom leaves room for further development and growth over and above what the company is doing now.

The final elements of the unique value proposition address the idea of differentiation. Most companies know the first two pieces – they tell you what it is that they have to offer, and they tell you what consumer needs they are addressing. Nevertheless, most of them will have a hard time pinpointing what it is that makes them different from another company that claims to be doing the same thing.

Yet some distinctiveness is extremely important. In today's business reality, in which consumers have access to infinite options with a click of a mouse, differentiation is everything.

And it's not that difficult – almost every element of the business can serve as a point of differentiation: the product's features, performance, style, price, brand image, customization, durability, quality, and convenience, as well as the company's expertise, experience, and service. Marketing research can be used to identify those points that are the most attractive to your company's customers.

What Value Proposition Should Companies Choose?

A company's choice of which unique values propositions to highlight should be guided by the factors that are most desirable in the eyes of consumers and what the company can deliver. A desirable value proposition offers consumers attractive and relevant benefits. These should be an element that consumers will be willing to pay for and will make them choose the company over its competitors. Consumers must regard the company's value proposition as distinct and superior to that of its competitors. The UVP also needs to be credible and authentic to the brand.

For example, Lush (https://www.lushusa.com/stories/article_our-fresh-handmade-story.html) offers "fresh handmade cosmetics."[6] While the cosmetic industry focuses on mass production and often uses artificial ingredients in their products, Lush has positioned itself as an authentic alternative to traditional cosmetic products. The company offers "handmade, vegetarian, cruelty free products." All of its products are made with ethically sourced ingredients. This value proposition makes the brand stand out and differentiates it from competitors. Yet even Lush must stay relevant to consumers. If consumers no longer view handmade cosmetic products as desirable, Lush's differentiation and value proposition it offers its consumers will be at risk.

From the company's perspective, a unique value proposition needs to be feasible, profitable, and difficult for the competition to replicate:

Feasible – Companies must be true to the promise they make to their consumers. Lush does that brilliantly, which makes their value proposition extremely powerful. From a strategic perspective, companies are better off under-promising and overdelivering than overpromising and underdelivering. The online shoe and clothing retailer Zappos, for example, offers four-day delivery.

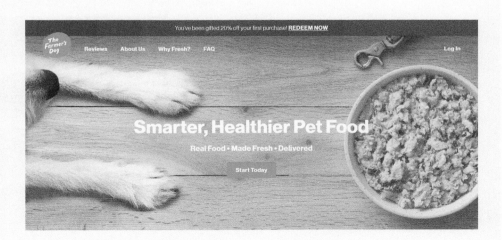

The Farmer's Dog's UVP is – 'healthy pet food'

But in many cases, the company manages to deliver orders the next day. By underpromising and overdelivering, Zappos delights its consumers.

Profitable – Obviously, a company's source of differentiation should be profitable. For example, if the cost of materials for Lush increases, it might pose a threat to its profitability. During the COVID-19 pandemic, many companies struggled with reopening their businesses because their fixed costs such as electricity, heat, and salaries increased overnight due to the measures they had to take to ensure social distancing and a safe environment for both consumers and employees. At the same time, they were unable to serve the same number of consumers because of the need to maintain social distancing. Restaurants, for example, could operate only at 25 percent capacity in many areas or had to close for extended periods. Many businesses lost money by being operational again.

Difficult to replicate – Companies adopt the successful practices of other companies all the time. When one company adopts the source of differentiation of another company, that point of differentiation changes to a point of parity. Losing differentiation thus means losing the unique value proposition and benefits the company has to offer to its consumers. In 2020 Walmart launched its Walmart+ program, which was in direct competition with Amazon Prime. While Walmart's e-commerce business wasn't nearly as large as Amazon's, it did have the advantage of its extensive brick-and-mortar presence to support the program. And, of course, we know that during the COVID-19 pandemic, more people than ever turned to shopping online just because they had no other choice. That included Walmart's traditional shoppers, so it was very good for Walmart to make this strategic move. If Walmart+ proves to be a successful strategic move, Amazon will lose this aspect of its differentiation and unique value. What do you think: would you shop at Amazon or Walmart+, or both?

Figure 2.4 presents sources of differentiation and competitive advantage for different companies.

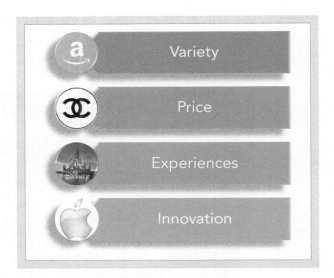

FIGURE 2.4   Different Bases of Consumers' Value

Finding the Right Consumer: Segmentation, Targeting, and Positioning

After crafting a unique value proposition, companies need to communicate it to their target market. A target market consists of a segment or segments of the market (i.e., a group or groups of consumers) toward which the company aims its marketing efforts to deliver its value.

Specifically, marketing strategies involve **segmentation, targeting, and positioning (STP)**.[7] We will take a look at each of these S, T, and P elements in more detail shortly, but as a brief introduction, STP is a three-step process that enables companies to be more effective and efficient in delivering their value through their offerings. First, the market is segmented, or divided into smaller groups of consumers (e.g., consumers who are younger versus older, and affluent versus less well-off) with shared characteristics or needs. Second, each segment is targeted based on its specific needs and preferences. Third, the company positions its value and offerings according to each identified segment. Dividing the market into smaller segments enables companies to be efficient with their resources. It also makes it easier for them to develop a specific, tailored approach for each segment to connect and engage with potential customers instead of using a generic marketing strategy that would not be as appealing or as effective. A company can also focus its efforts on a single group as its target segment (e.g., young and affluent consumers). Now let's take a closer look at the elements of the STP model presented in Figure 2.5.

> **Segmentation, targeting, and positioning (STP)** a three-step process that enables companies to be more effective and efficient in delivering their value through their offerings.

Segmentation

Market segmentation is the first step in the STP process. **Segmentation** refers to the division of the broader consumer market into subgroups of consumers based on shared characteristics or needs.[8] In this stage, the company identifies the segments in the market to which it can deliver its value successfully and build profitable customer relationships.

It is impossible for any company to provide value to the entire market. Consumers have diverse needs, and they are looking for diverse solutions for their problems. Companies must identify the segments in the market that they can serve in the best way possible in order to address this diversity successfully, be efficient with their resources, and be more effective in delivering their value.

Companies should also avoid those segments to which they cannot provide real value. In today's competitive market where consumers have more options than ever before, reaching the right consumer the right way is critical to a company's survival and success.

Being able to correctly identify the segmentation base that will ensure that the company targets the segment of consumers most suited to the value it is offering is key to creating a competitive advantage and strategic position in the marketplace. Companies should use its marketing

> **Segmentation** division of the broader consumer market into subgroups of consumers based on shared characteristics or needs.

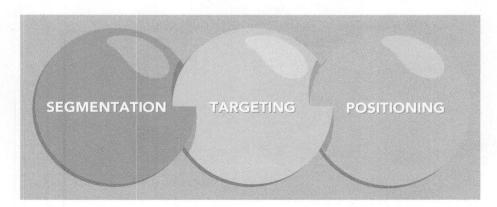

SEGMENTATION   TARGETING   POSITIONING

FIGURE 2.5 The STP Process

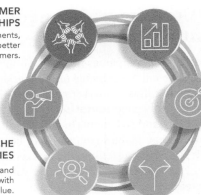

BETTER CUSTOMER RELATIONSHIPS
By focusing on one or a few segments, companies can form better relationships with their consumers.

STRONG MARKETING MESSAGES
Firms can develop strong marketing messages that resonate with the needs of the selected segments.

IDENTIFY NICHE OPPORTUNITIES
Identify underserved and untapped niche markets fit with the company's value.

BEING FOCUSED WITH RESOURCES
Companies' resources can be invested in those segments that are expected to generate the highest return.

EFFECTIVE MARKETING TACTICS
By focusing on specific segments, companies can be more effective in employing their marketing tactics.

STRONGER BRAND DIFFERENTIATION
A more focused UVP can address the needs of consumers in specific segments resulting a stronger brand.

FIGURE 2.6   Benefits of Market Segmentation

research and consumers' insights to identify the segments of consumers whose specific needs or problems they can address effectively and on whom they will have the strongest impact.

Figure 2.6 summarizes the benefits of market segmentation for companies.

How can companies segment the market? Recall that the strategic marketing process starts with a unique value proposition. The UVP should clearly define the consumers whose needs and problems the company's value addresses. This definition should drive the selection of the segmentation criteria or bases and should be based on extensive marketing research. Figure 2.7 shows the different bases of segmentation.

Geographic segmentation – For this type of segmentation, marketers use the geographic location of customers. In other words, consumers living in a specific area are presumed to have different needs or purchasing behaviors than those living in another area (e.g., in the United States, people in the North need snowblowers, while those in the South like sweet tea).

Geographic segmentation can be based on region, country, state, neighborhood, climate zones, level of area density, postal code, or any other geographical criteria that are relevant to the value

> **Geographic segmentation** dividing the market based on the geographic location of the consumer.

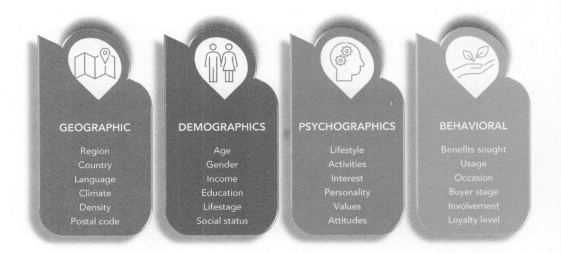

GEOGRAPHIC	DEMOGRAPHICS	PSYCHOGRAPHICS	BEHAVIORAL
Region	Age	Lifestyle	Benefits sought
Country	Gender	Activities	Usage
Language	Income	Interest	Occasion
Climate	Education	Personality	Buyer stage
Density	Lifestage	Values	Involvement
Postal code	Social status	Attitudes	Loyalty level

FIGURE 2.7   Bases of Segmentation

the company has to offer its consumers. Geography can also include factors like different consumer languages, climate differences, and density of living spaces. When using country-based geographic segmentation, companies consider cultural differences and the need to make greater adaptation to their marketing mix to target the consumers in these countries (see Chapter 12). For example, L'Oréal uses geo-segmentation extensively across its brands. It adapts its product portfolio, marketing messages, celebrities used, and other elements of the marketing mix to target consumers in different cultures and countries.

Global Mindset – Geographic Segmentation
L'Oréal targets women in countries across the world!

Demographic Segmentation
Dove targets men!

Demographic segmentation dividing the market based on the demographic characteristics of the consumer.

Demographic segmentation – Demographics are descriptions of consumers in terms of their age, gender, ethnicity, race, education, income, occupation, marital status, social status, life stage, and size of family. Demographics are the most commonly used basis for segmentation, because they are easy to obtain, cheap to collect, and very predictable over time. Marketers use demographics as the basis of segmentation because they assume that consumers with similar demographics will have similar needs and exhibit similar behaviors.

For example, consumers of your age have different needs than consumers who are much younger or much older than you. The different age groups are interested in different products, want different product benefits, and are loyal to different brands. Demographics also help marketers monitor and predict any future changes in the population, such as generational cohort sizes and aging markets.

Marketers normally will focus on just one or a few demographic characteristics to keep things manageable. Like any basis of segmentation, marketers' choice of which demographics to use depends on their relevance to the value they have to offer consumers and whether or not a demographic segment produces distinct behavior.

For example, it would make no sense for Coca-Cola to use gender as a basis for segmentation, because it is unlikely that men and women will exhibit different patterns of consumption when it comes to Coca-Cola beverages. But it does make sense for Gillette to target its Venus razors to women. In addition, even when shopping for the same product, men and women differ when it comes to their motivations for shopping, their shopping style, the product features sought, their information processing, and their preferences for the tone of ads. Marketers should take all of these differences into account when using gender-based segmentation.

As useful as demographic segmentation is, it has its limitations. Not all young people, for example, behave the same, not all men behave the same, and so on. Because of this, demographic segmentation is often used in conjunction with other bases of segmentation, such as lifestyle, that capture other aspects of consumer behavior, such as brand and media choices.

Psychographic segmentation – Psychographics include elements such as lifestyle, personality, attitude, and values, all of which we will explore in depth in the subsequent chapters. Psychographic profiles are constructed based on consumers' activities, interests, and options.

Given that consumers with similar demographics can have different psychographic profiles and thus exhibit different consumption behaviors, psychographic segmentation integrates psychology and demographics to get a fuller and richer picture of consumers and the market and to produce more meaningful segments. For example, think about yourself and your friends. You all might be about the same age, but you each have slightly different lifestyles – one likes the outdoors, one likes video games, one likes to travel more than the others. These different lifestyles result in different purchases, brand preferences, and websites as sources of information.

Psychographic segmentation is especially useful for marketers of high-end products that express consumers' self-image. Yet getting these kinds of data is typically more costly. In addition, it can change quickly over time and must be updated to stay relevant.

Lifestyle – In marketing research, the term **lifestyle** broadly covers how consumers live, particularly how they spend their time and money. A helpful tool in lifestyle psychographic segmentation is the **Activities, Interests, and Opinions (AIO)** model (see Figure 2.8) – the AIO factors are not about a consumer's demographics or where they live – it's about what they do, how they think, and what they care about.[9] Using surveys and other feedback, researchers can construct individual consumers' psychographic profiles, which can help marketers assess and reach their target markets. Naturally, brands, products, and consumption play an important role in shaping lifestyle. Marketers find lifestyle a very useful aspect of segmentation because much of it is consumption based. Think about it: What do you spend money on? Probably some college-related expenses, some social events and sporting events, and all of these have products associated with it.

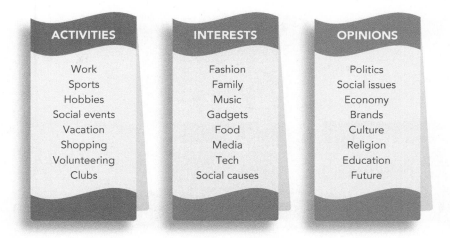

FIGURE 2.8 The AIO Model

Marketers use lifestyle segmentation to execute all elements of the marketing mix. They will develop and offer products for different lifestyles (product strategy). They will use lifestyle to better position their offerings and target their consumers (communication strategy), to price their products appropriately (price strategy), and to choose the right distribution channels and partners (channel strategy). Lifestyle is also a powerful segmentation tool, especially when combined with other segmentation bases such as demographics and personality. Psychographic segmentation involves segmenting the market based on consumers' personality, traits, lifestyle, and values. As such, marketers invest much time in researching their consumers' lifestyle, and employ a variety of techniques and to collect information. Some of these tools we will cover in Chapter 3. Here we are going to focus on one of the most prominent tools that were developed especially to identify segments of consumers with different lifestyles: VALS.

VALS (Values, Attitudes, and Lifestyles), **presented in Figure** 2.9. owned by Strategic Business Insights, is one of the most widely used psychographic tools.[10] Originally, VALS was developed to profile US consumers based on two factors. The first was consumers' primary motivation: ideals, achievement, and self-expression. As a primary motivation, ideals reflect knowledge and principles that guide consumer behavior. Achievement reflects what drives consumers: an aspiration for success. Self-expression refers to the motivation to express one's self-identity via a variety of activities.

The second factor is resources, and it reflects several psychological traits in conjunction with key demographics: novelty seeking, innovativeness, self-confidence, energy, vanity, intellectualism, impulsiveness, and leadership. The differences in consumers' level of resources will enhance or constrain their ability to express their primary motivation.

Together these two factors create eight lifestyle profiles. Figure 2.9 offers details about each profile.

The consumer segments represented in VALS are very useful to marketers. What's helpful about this way of thinking is that it goes beyond demographics. As important as demographics are, take any group, say, men ages twenty to thirty. Now, think about the group: are all men ages twenty to thirty the same? Do they like the same music, buy the same brands of athletic shoes, prefer the same drinks, and so on? No, any group is heterogeneous, or made up of different kinds

VALS (Values, Attitudes, and Lifestyles)
one of the most widely used psychographic tools. It profiles US consumers based on their motivations and their recourses.

Successful, sophisticated consumers. They enjoy the finer things in life and new products. Skeptical of advertising.

Thinkers

Information seekers. Conservative and practical consumers. They focus on the value of the product and not on its image. Like educational, public media.

Achievers

Have goal-oriented lifestyles and a deep commitment to career and family. Like conspicuous permium products. Interested in business, news, and self-help publications.

Experiencers

Young, variety seeking and impulsive. Follow fashions and fads. Interested in social activities. Like products that make them look "cool". Heavy users of social media.

Believers

Conservative and traditional consumers, with beliefs reflecting family, religion, community, and the nation. Prefer domestic products and are highly loyal. Seek bargains and watch a lot of TV.

Strivers

Image conscious, trendy and fun-loving consumers. Struggle financially and view shopping as a social activity. Like stylish products that signal higher social status. Prefer TV over reading.

Makers

Express who they are by what they do. Highly self-sufficient and seek physical recreation. But basic and functional products, with comfort, durability and value. Unimpressed by luxuries. Prefer TV over reading.

HIGH

RESOURCES AND MOTIVATION

LOW

Survivors

Older consumers with very few resources. Focus on meeting needs rather than fulfil desires. Brand loyal, love coupons and sales and trust advertising.

FIGURE 2.9   The VALS Framework

of people with different likes and dislikes. VALS thinks about the consumers values, attitudes, and elements of their lifestyles. These help predict consumer decisions – partly because more information is better, but also because, in using VALS, marketers are already focusing on a group of people, say the "strivers" segment, who are known to have some similar ways of thinking about their world.

Lifestyle – what you want to look like, what you want to drive.

Behavioral segmentation – This type of segmentation categorizes consumers based on behavioral patterns of interaction with the company or the brand. This approach doesn't look at who consumers are or what they say or do; it looks at what consumers do, when they do it, in what way, or how often (see Figure 2.10).

Marketers constantly monitor our behavior as consumers – at least, they should. Companies collect, store, and analyze data on every aspect of our interactions with them on a regular basis, including offline and online. Think of your grocery loyalty card – you're getting discounts, and

Behavioral segmentation refers to categorizing consumers based on behavioral patterns of interaction with the company or the brand.

PURCHASING BEHAVIOR

Differences in consumers' behavior during the process of purchase decision making

BENEFITS SOUGHT

Which benefits, features, or values, drive consumers purchasing decision.

USAGE RATE

Frequency and amount of purchasing used to identify light, average and heavy users.

OCCASION OR TIMING

When consumers make a purchase: day, time or special occasion.

CUSTOMER SATISFACTION

Lever of satisfaction with the product or the brand: low, neutral or high.

ENGAGEMENT LEVEL

Level of engagement that consumers have with the brand: low, neutral or high.

USER STATUS

Status of a consumer: nonuser, prospect, first-time buyer, regular, or defector.

CONSUMER JOURNEY STAGE

The stage of the consumer journey that consumers are in; how fast or slow they progress.

FIGURE 2.10 Behavioral Segmentation Methods

the company is getting data. (Sometimes companies sell their information to a third party, a practice that has been criticized repeatedly due to privacy concerns.)

An increasingly popular use of behavioral segmentation is employing artificial intelligence to provide consumers with a more personalized experience based on their past patterns of behavior. Netflix, for example, offers movie recommendations based on individualized preferences. Netflix leverages its data to gain an understanding of its viewers and provide them with exactly what they are looking for.

Targeting
identifying which segment or segments provide the company with the best business opportunity.

Targeting

Once a company has decided how to segment the market, it needs to identify which segment or segments provide the company with the best business opportunity. The attractiveness of a segment will be determined by the characteristics of the segment, the company's competencies and resources to address the segment's needs, the level of competition (current and future), and the ability of the company to compete in this segment. The following criteria need to be evaluated and met in order for a company to use its marketing mix with a given segment:

Measurable – Companies need to measure the potential sales value or volume of the segment they are targeting. How large is the specific segment? Without being able to estimate the size of the targeted segment, companies cannot be certain that the segment is worth pursuing.

Substantial – An attractive segment should be sufficiently large and have significant spending power (together leading to profitability). It needs to support the cost of a separate marketing mix. If the size of the targeted segment is too small to support the cost of the tailored marketing activities, such an investment cannot be justified.

Accessible – Companies should be able to access and serve the consumers they are targeting with their marketing activities. Most importantly, companies need to be certain that they can serve the consumers in this segment in a way that matches the company's abilities and strengths.

Differentiable – Consumers in a specific target market must have needs or characteristics that are different from those of consumers in other segments. Marketers talk about the targeted segment being internally homogeneous (consumers in the segment are similar), yet externally heterogeneous (across segments, consumers are different). Without clear differences between segments, companies cannot target their marketing mix efficiently and without risking any overlap with their operations in other segments.

Stable – The targeted segment must be stable so that the company can predict the behavior of its consumers in the future with a sufficient degree of confidence. No company should focus on an unstable customer segment that is likely to disappear or change beyond recognition in the near future.

Congruent with the company's value – Companies should target segments that are aligned with their offered value. In other words, companies should serve those target markets whose value addresses the needs or characteristics of its consumers.

Do the Right Thing!

Segmentation and targeting have always presented challenges. Do people who live in different countries or regions within a country vary in their likes and dislikes? Yes. Is it acceptable to target people who live in different locations with different products and advertisements? Yes. What about segmentation and targeting based on demographics? Do people who are male or female or older or younger or one race or ethnicity or another have different preferences? Yes, sometimes. Is it acceptable to use that information for strategic targeting? Yes, but it needs to be done while respecting the dignity of any individual or group.

Social media's strengths have proven to be especially useful in developing good strategic targeting. For example, social media are measurable – we will say more in Chapter 13, but social media analytics can capture valence, such as the numbers of likes or positive text postings, as well as other content, such as stories about consumers using a particular brand. The volume and speed of social media posts and endorsements can help a brand team decide if a marketing opportunity is in fact substantial. As for accessibility, marketing communications that draw from social media and then are posted to those social media sites are an extremely cost-efficient and audience-effective way of reaching the target group of consumers.

To summarize, the purpose of targeting is to identify the best market opportunities for the company. Targeting must use the consumer data and insights that were obtained during the segmentation stage. Then, based on the company's value and the analysis of the "consumer journey" (from "thinking about it" to "looking at brand choices" to "buying it" to "being satisfied as a customer), the company can target the marketing mix successfully with a minimum of waste (not spend on uninterested consumers, not spend on consumers who aren't ready yet).

> *"Positioning is an art. Great positioning tells a compelling, attention-grabbing story – a story that resonates with your audience!"*
>
> *Rebel Brown, Consultant and marketing strategist*

Positioning

The last stage of the STP process is positioning. **Positioning**[11] reflects the effort of a company to shape consumers' perceptions about its brand or product relative to its competitors. In this stage, the company focuses on forming a distinct image or identity for its brand in a way that resonates with the needs of the targeted segment. While the company should build on its value, the communication of this value must be tailored to the specific target market and stress the needs or the problems that are relevant to the consumer segment the company is targeting. By utilizing a positioning strategy, a company can have a much stronger impact on its target market. Positioning of the brand or the product should be based on the data and insights obtained in the previous stages of the STP process. A company's positioning can be based on the following elements.

Product characteristics* or *customer benefits–based positioning – Positioning can be based on the product's features or benefits, especially if they are unique and differentiated. For example, the ad from YETI shown here highlights the durability of the product that can stand up to lions, tigers, and bears. (Yes, it was tested using these animals.) Companies are advised to highlight only one significant characteristic of the product in their messages. They are often tempted to feature more than one characteristic, but doing so may confuse consumers. This approach is unlikely to be very effective and may hurt the effectiveness of the message. Keep it simple!

Price-based positioning – Companies can use price to position their brand or product. Price affects consumers' perceptions about the brand or product because they often use it as a signal of quality. Because of this, companies can position themselves based on low prices (e.g., the Walmart ad) or high prices, if the company wants to promote itself as having a premium brand or product (e.g., Louis Vuitton or other expensive designers).

Positioning the utilization of the marketing mix to influence consumer perceptions regarding a brand or product relative to competitors.

Customer benefits–based positioning positioning that is based on the product's features or benefits, especially if they are unique and differentiated.

Price-based positioning positioning that is based on the product's price.

Benefits-based Positioning
YETI is offering a playful challenge. If it can resist these fierce beasts, one of its "benefits" is toughness!

Price-based Positioning
five BELOW company's name makes their price-positioning clear.

Quality-based positioning – Similar to price, quality can be used as a source of positioning. High-end products will highlight this element in their messages. But even products that are not high-end might underscore their quality in messages such as "Best value for money." For example, in this ad, Kapiti, the ice-cream company, associates its product with a luxury item to signal quality. Using the word *designer* also sends a message of quality.

Quality-based positioning positioning that is based on the product's quality.

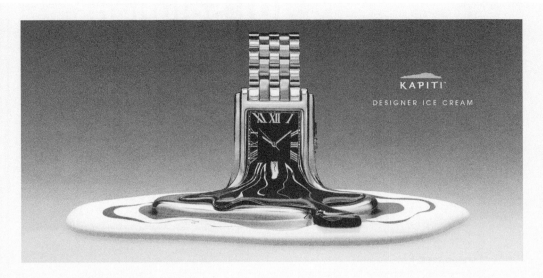

Quality-based Positioning
Kapiti tries to explain its quality by showing high design (watch) with the flow of ice-cream melting.

Product use–based positioning – This type of positioning associates the product with a specific use. It reminds or educates consumers of what they can do with the product and when they can do it. In many cases, this type of positioning is used to present consumers with new ways of using the product and thus helps to expand the market. In the Arm & Hammer ad here, the company presents consumers with 101 ways to use its product that go beyond the typical use of baking soda.

Product use-based positioning positioning that associates the product with a specific use.

Competitor-based positioning – Companies that use this type of positioning make an implicit or explicit reference to their competitors.[12] The purpose of this strategy is to say their brand is better than the competition with regard to a feature that is important to consumers. This strategy is effective but also risky. The company's competitors can retaliate and respond to such an unfavorable comparison. Campbell's ad showcases their "Select Harvest" soup and compares it to Progresso. The differentiator is MSG (monosodium glutamate), which Campbell's product does not contain. The assumption behind this ad is that not having MSG in the product is relevant to consumers who are interested in canned soup.

Competitor-based positioning positioning that makes an implicit or explicit reference to the company's competitors.

Product Use-based Positioning
Arm & Hammer says there are 101 different ways to use the product – great "product-use" positioning.

Competitor-based Positioning
Competitor-based positioning is exemplified by advertisements that feature not only the main brand, but a competitor, to make the case: We are better than them!"

Culture-based positioning – In some cases, highlighting the country of origin of the product or brand or relating it to a cultural symbol enhances its value. Indeed, some countries are associated with a specific type of product, such as in the case of the TAG Heuer ad that emphasizes the Swiss origin of the watch. Switzerland is well-known for its excellent watches, and highlighting this fact in the ad gives the brand a competitive advantage. Patriotism is another cultural aspect that plays an important role in positioning. In America "Made in the USA" is a feature that consumers favor.

To summarize, the STP process is a very powerful and useful approach to build and execute strategy for companies. Making data-based decisions is better than simply relying on instincts, so identifying the segment or segments of consumers that present companies with the most promising business opportunities, targeting the right segment, and crafting the right positioning for the target segment require data collection to understand consumer needs and preferences. Without consumer insight data, companies will not be able to execute an STP strategy successfully.

Note that consumer data gathering is an ongoing, dynamic process that requires companies to constantly monitor the market to detect changes in consumers' needs, the entry of new competitors, and the development of new business opportunities. All of these factors can have an effect on a company's unique value proposition.

Culture-based positioning positioning that highlights the country of origin of the product or brand or relating it to a cultural symbol enhances its value.

How to Get the Product to the Consumer: The Marketing Mix

Once a company has chosen and defined its value to the consumer and identified the right segment(s) to operate in, the next step is to actually deliver the product or the service to the consumer. For that purpose, companies employ a **marketing mix**, a set of strategies that companies use to sell products or services to their target customers. The mix has four components – **product**, **price**, **place**, and **promotion** – known as the four Ps (Figure 2.11). The concept was introduced in the 1960s by marketing professor E. Jerome McCarthy and has been widely used by

The marketing mix a set of strategies that companies use to sell products or services to their target customers, including product, price, place, and promotion strategies.

FIGURE 2.11 The Marketing Mix

companies since then to develop a profit-yielding strategy.[13] Developing strategies using the right combination of the four Ps will help companies:

- maximize their strengths and minimize their weaknesses.
- strengthen their competitive advantage.
- be more agile and responsive to market changes.
- improve the efficiency and effectiveness of internal processes.

For the marketing mix to be successful, all four Ps need to work together.[14] We begin by looking at the four Ps individually.

Product Strategy

Product strategy refers to what the company is selling.

The product element of the marketing mix refers to what the company is selling. It can be a tangible product, a service, an experience, a person, or a place, basically anything that has a value and can be sold. An effective product strategy depends on extensive research and development to craft its value, understand how it meets consumers' needs, develop a product launch plan and timeline, train the sales force, and educate consumers about it. This strategy will be adjusted according to the target market, product life cycle, level of competition, and market conditions.

For example, when a new product is introduced to the market, the company will engage in an extensive effort to educate consumers about it. However, when the product reaches maturity, the market is well developed, and the company's efforts will focus on differentiating the product from the competition. When Apple introduced the first iPad in 2010,[15] consumers were not familiar with the concept of a tablet. Apple invested a great deal of time and effort to educate consumers about the benefits of the product. Today there are more players in the tablet market. Consumers are familiar with the product, so companies focus on differentiating their tablets from those offered by their competitors.

Price Strategy

Price strategy refers to the cost of purchase for consumers.

Price refers to the cost of purchase for consumers. Price depends on multiple variables including the cost of the materials, transportation, sales, and advertising, as well as the desired profit margins. Most importantly, the price strategy needs to reflect the value of the product in the eyes of the consumers and its positioning in the market.[16]

Setting the product's price requires consideration of multiple pricing strategies, analysis of similarly priced products in the market, and insights from consumers through surveys and focus groups to assess the value of the product. As we will see in Chapter 11, consumers' perceptions about the price are often more critical than the actual, real price. The more valuable the product is considered, the more consumers will be willing to pay for it.

For example, the cost of a pair of running shoes might be the same for Nike and FILA. However, you might be more willing to pay more for one than the other. Similarly, the cost of a bottle of Coke will be cheaper at your local supermarket and more expensive at a vending machine – the latter price builds in the fact that you're paying for a Coke and convenience.

Placement Strategy

Placement strategy refers to the way the product will be provided to the customer, or the point of sale or service.

This element of the marketing mix refers to the way the product will be provided to the customer, or the point of sale or service. This strategy helps companies determine what retail channel is the most suited to a product, based on the value they aim to provide. For tangible products, this consideration will include physical locations as well as online platforms. Services can be provided in multiple places, such as at a specific location or at the consumers' home. Safelite,[17] for example, centers its value on the fact that their employees will go anywhere at any time to fix a customer's windshield.

The point of sale should fit the brand's overall value. You can find Maybelline products in any drugstore, but you will not find them in Saks Fifth Avenue. Similarly, you will find La Prairie in Saks Fifth Avenue but not in any drugstore. This choice of placement is based on the brand's value. Prestige brands will choose prestige placements, while more affordable brands will be found in affordable placements such as drugstores.

Place also includes the placement of the product in a store. Companies will pay a premium for more visible and accessible placements.

Promotion Strategy

Promotion strategy includes any activity designed to connect with a company's target market.[18] It refers to the message itself, the way it is communicated, who it is communicated to, how that audience is reached, what means of communication is used, and how often the promotion happens.

Companies utilize a wide range of techniques and means to communicate with consumers. They use advertising, sales promotions, public relations, social media campaigns, and loyalty rewards programs. Figure 2.12 presents examples of the promotion mix.[19]

Whatever method of promotion a company uses to connect with its consumers, it must be aligned with the product's value, the targeted consumers, and the rest of the marketing mix. The figure below[20] shows that men and women prefer different social media platforms. Targeting them efficiently should take that difference into consideration.

Promotion strategy includes any activity designed to connect with a company's target market.

FIGURE 2.12 The Promotion Mix

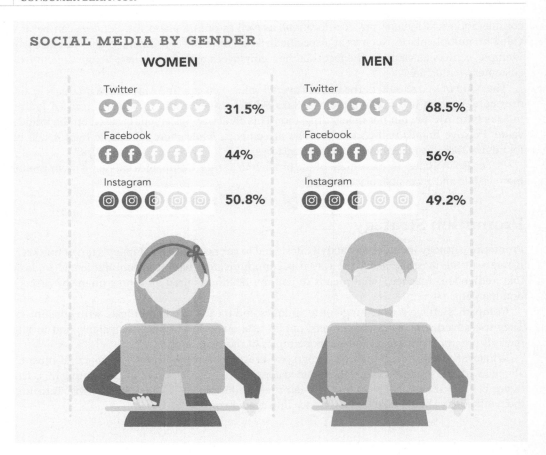

Beyond the Four Ps: The Four Cs of the Marketing Mix

While the four Ps are widely used, some marketing gurus say that the framework focuses too much on the company and not enough on the consumer. To remedy this, some have added the four Cs – consumer, cost, convenience, and communication – to reflect a more consumer-centric view of marketing.[21] The four Cs are also easily adapted to a digital marketing mix. As more businesses go online, adjusting the marketing mix accordingly is critical.

Shifting from a product strategy to a *consumer strategy* – Aligned with a value-based view of the company's offering, this element of the marketing mix focuses on the wants and needs of consumers.[22] Companies should not sell products; instead they should solve consumers' problems. Such a strategy requires extensive market research and consumers' insights to direct the company's strategy.

Shifting from a price strategy to a *cost strategy* – This strategy takes a broader view of the cost of acquiring a product or service, which goes beyond the price tag.[23] It includes all of the time and effort that consumers invest prior to a purchase. It also includes the cost of switching and the cost of missing out on other options.

Shifting from a place strategy to a *convenience strategy* – Consumers appreciate when companies make it easy for them to obtain the product or service.[24] Think about the percentage of your purchases that you make online. It's just more convenient.

Shifting from a promotion strategy to a *communication strategy* – Consumers are very leery of traditional marketing messages. We know that consumers actively block marketing messages and ads. Yet they do look for information about the products that they are interested in. They trust recommendations from other consumers, bloggers, and YouTube influencers, all of which can be used by companies to communicate their message.

SUMMARY

Defining a company's business in terms of a product or a function should be a thing of the past. In order to succeed, a company should have a strategic definition of its business as a solution to consumers' problems and needs; that way the company can maintain relevancy when adversity hits or the market shifts.

Marketing strategy is what drives a company by creating and delivering value to consumers. This requires leveraging three main elements: a unique value proposition (UVP); a segmentation, targeting, and positioning (STP) process; and marketing mix (four Ps) strategies.

Once a company has determined its UVP, it must then develop and implement marketing mix strategies. These strategies reflect the way a product or service is being offered, its price, and the way its value is being communicated to the company's different target markets.

This approach with enable a company to strengthen its competitive advantage, be more agile in response to market changes, and improve the efficiency and effectiveness of internal processes. How much time and effort a business puts into crafting a thoughtful consumer-centric marketing strategic plan will determine its long-term success in the market.

KEY TERMS

Marketing myopia
Marketing orientation
Customer-centric companies
Marketing strategy
Unique value proposition (UVP)
Points of difference (PODs)
Points of parity (POPs)
Points of irrelevance (POIs)

Target market
Segmentation, targeting, and positioning (STP)
Segmentation
Geographic segmentation
Demographic segmentation
Psychographic segmentation
Lifestyle
Activities, Interests, and Opinions (AIO)

VALS (Values, Attitudes, and Lifestyles)
Behavioral segmentation
Targeting
Positioning
Customer benefits–based positioning
Price-based positioning
Quality-based positioning
Product use-based positioning

Competitor-based positioning
Culture-based positioning
Marketing mix
Product strategy
Price strategy
Placement strategy
Promotion strategy

EXERCISES

1. With a class teammate, think of two or three companies that are well-known and two or three companies that may be less familiar. Imagine consulting with each company: how would you describe their business in terms of a product and in terms of a solution to a problem?

2. You can do this alone, but get feedback from a friend in class who knows you reasonably well: How would you describe yourself as a brand? What is your (personal) value proposition?

3. In pairs or small groups, pick a brand that you are all familiar with and write its value proposition. What elements of the value proposition were easy to write? What elements were harder?

4. Start thinking about the different customer segments you are in, for phones, computers, cars, clothing, hair styles, restaurant

preferences. While your demographic and geographic factors might not vary across those product categories, think about how your preferences vary across those products. Which ones do you buy more frequently? Which ones are you more price sensitive about? Which ones do you have more brand loyalty for? You'll see that these attributes (psychographics and behavioral) will be important throughout this book.

5. Go to the VALS website: http://www.strategicbusinessinsights. com/vals/presurvey.shtml. Take the survey. What is your primary segment? What is your secondary segment? How similar or different they are from other students in your class?

6. In pairs or small groups, pick a brand or a product that you are all familiar with and try to identify different segments of this brand or product as outlined by on the segmentation bases reviewed in this chapter.

ENDNOTES

1. Minda Zetlin, "Blockbuster Could Have Bought Netflix for $50 Million, but the CEO Thought It Was a Joke," *Inc.*, September 20, 2019, https://www.inc.com/minda-zetlin/netflix-blockbuster-meeting-marc-randolph-reed-hastings-john-antioco.html.

2. T. Levitt, "Marketing Myopia," *Harvard Business Review* 82, no. 7/8 (2004): 138–149.

3. A. K. Kohli and B. J. Jaworski, "Market Orientation: The Construct, Research Propositions, and Managerial Implications," *Journal of Marketing* 54, no. 2 (1990): 1–18.

4. J. C. Narver and S.F. Slater, "The Effect of a Market Orientation on Business Profitability," *Journal of Marketing* 54, no. 4 (1990): 20–34.

5. https://optinmonster.com/32-value-propositions-that-are-impossible-to-resist/.

6. Lush, https://www.lushusa.com/stories; https://justtradeplnu.wordpress.com/2014/04/17/dont-buy-our-jacket/.

7. P. Kotler and K. L. Keller, *Marketing Management,* 15th ed. (Pearson, 2016).

8. https://www.ama.org/marketing-news/better-segmentation-for-better-insights/.

9. William D. Wells and Douglas J. Tigert, "Activities, Interest, and Opinions," *Journal of Advertising Research* (August 1971): 27—35.

10. http://www.strategicbusinessinsights.com/vals/; L. R. Kahle, S. E. Beatty, and P. Homer, "Alternative Measurement Approaches to Consumer Values: The List of Values (LOV) and Values and Life Style (VALS)," *Journal of Consumer Research* 13 (1986): 405—9; A. Mitchell, *The Nine American Life Styles (New York: Warner,* 1986).

11. John P. Maggard, "Positioning Revisited," *Journal of Marketing* 40 (January 1976): 63—6.

12. G. J. Gorn and C. B. Weinberg, "The Impact of Comparative Advertising on Perception and Attitude: Some Positive Findings," *Journal of Consumer Research* 11, no. 2 (1984): 719—27.

13. E. J. McCarthy, *Basic Marketing: A Managerial Approach* (Homewood, IL: Irwin, 1960); Neil H. Borden, "The Concept of the Marketing Mix," *Journal of Advertising Research* 4, no. 2 (1964): 2—7.

14. Ahmad Kare, "Evolution of the Four Ps: Revisiting the Marketing Mix," *Forbes,* January 3, 2018, https://www.forbes.com/sites/forbesagencycouncil/2018/01/03/evolution-of-the-four-ps-revisiting-the-marketing-mix/?sh=192a49be1120.

15. https://www.apple.com/newsroom/2010/01/27Apple-Launches-iPad/.

16. G. J. Tellis, "Beyond the Many Faces of Price: An Integration of Pricing Strategies," *Journal of Marketing* 50, no. 4 (1986): 146—60.

17. https://www.safelite.com/.

18. C. N. Leonidou, C. S. Katsikeas, and N. A. Morgan, Greening" the Marketing Mix: Do Firms Do It and Does It Pay Off?," *Journal of the Academy of Marketing Science* 41, no. 2 (2013): 151—70.

19. M. Chaudhuri, R. J. Calantone, C. M. Voorhees, and S. Cockrell, "Disentangling the Effects of Promotion Mix on New Product Sales: An Examination of Disaggregated Drivers and the Moderating Effect of Product Class," *Journal of Business Research* 90 (September 2018): 286—94.

20. https://www.statista.com/statistics/274828/gender-distribution-of-active-social-media-users-worldwide-by-platform.

21. A. Payne, P. Frow, and A. Eggert, "The Customer Value Proposition: Evolution, Development, and Application in Marketing." *Journal of the Academy of Marketing Science* 45, no. 4 (2017): 467—89.

22. R. Hamilton, "Consumer-based Strategy: Using Multiple Methods to Generate Consumer Insights that Inform Strategy," *Journal of the Academy of Marketing Science* 44 (2016): 281—5.

23. C. W. Craighead, G. T. M. Hult, and D. J. Ketchen Jr, "The Effects of Innovation—Cost Strategy, Knowledge, and Action in the Supply Chain on Firm Performance," *Journal of Operations Management* 27, no. 5 (2009): 405—21.

24. K. Seiders, L. L. Berry, and L. G. Gresham, "Attention, Retailers! How Convenient Is Your Convenience Strategy?," *MIT Sloan Management Review* 41, no. 3 (2000): 79.

CREDITS

How (and Why) to Listen to Consumers

3

LEARNING OBJECTIVES

After studying this chapter, you should be able to:

- Understand the difference between marketing research and consumers insights.
- Appreciate why marketing managers can benefit tremendously from trying to understand consumers – marketers gain useful insights, and consumers feel as if the company cares.
- Understand the marketing research process.
- Understand the variety of ways to listen to consumers, from monitoring social media to running surveys to conducting A/B tests, and more.

Imagine being on a brand team of a fabulous, tried-and-true brand. The brand has had tremendous consumer loyalty for a very long time, and the brand team members are sure that, with all their collective experience, they understand consumers. The thing is, a competitor was starting to score higher on a consumer preference test, so the brand team decided it was time to tweak. They did. Unfortunately, the brand team completely underestimated consumer loyalty – consumers were really ticked that the company would mess with their beloved brand. The company was embarrassed and had to relaunch the old, pre-tweaked brand. Couldn't happen, right? Hello, Coke Classic.[1]

How did the brand team mess up? By not asking the right questions.

Listening to Consumers as a Marketing Strategy

Understanding consumers' needs and wants is critical to the survival, growth, and success of any organization. To develop such understanding, marketers must rely heavily on continuous marketing research.[2] **Marketing research** is a systematic multistage effort of collecting, analyzing, and interpreting information about the consumers, the market, a product, or any other marketing-related element. Marketing research provides the brand team with the knowledge about the industry trends and other developments in the market that might indicate missed opportunities for the company or potential threats. The process of marketing research and its stages are presented in Figure 3.1.

Marketing research a systematic multistage effort of collecting, analyzing, and interpreting information about the consumers, the market, a product, or any other marketing-related element.

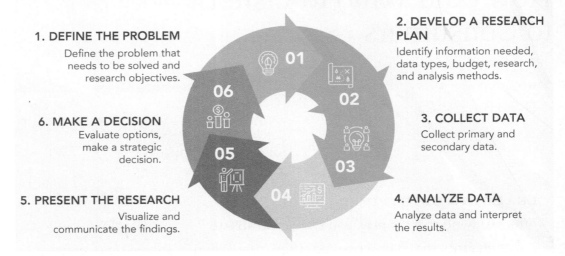

FIGURE 3.1 The Marketing Research Process. Adapted from Iacobucci, D. & Churchill, G. A. (2018). Marketing research: methodological foundations. Published by CreateSpace Independent Publis.

Consumer insights
the knowledge derived by studying consumers' behavior. It builds on the data gathered via marketing research and analyze and interpret it in a way that guides companies' strategic decisions.

As Figure 3.1 indicates, the end result of marketing research (done correctly) is to have sound data on which to draw conclusions.[3] **Consumer insights** build on the data gathered via marketing research and analyze and interpret it in a way that guides companies' strategic decisions.[4] The purpose of consumer insights research is to transform the data into actionable information relevant to the brand, such as insights about their attitudes, perception, level of stratification for segmentation, preferences, and opinions about new offerings. In other words, marketing research helps companies to understand *what* is happening in the market, while consumer insights research helps companies to understand *why* it's happening and how they should adjust their strategies in order to continue providing real value to their consumers successfully and to maintain a competitive advantage. Specific benefits of consumer insights research are presented in Figure 3.2.

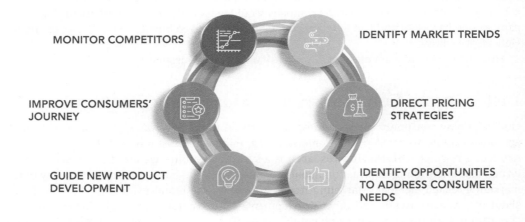

FIGURE 3.2 The Role of Consumer Insights. Adapted from Iacobucci, D. & Churchill, G. A. (2018). Marketing research: methodological foundations. Published by CreateSpace Independent Publis

Kinds of Marketing Research Data

There are many techniques marketers use to collect consumer information, such as focus groups, surveys, big data, and A/B tests. In this chapter, we'll discuss these and many others. One way to distinguish among methods of marketing research is to note whether they involve secondary or primary data (Figure 3.3).[5] **Secondary data** are data that already exist that might be useful in shedding light on the current marketing questions facing the brand team. **Primary data** are data the brand team decides it must go out and collect. Many factors enter into this decision, such as whether to run a focus group or survey. As we proceed, we'll see there are some guidelines.

Secondary data
data that already exist that might be useful in shedding light on the current marketing questions facing the brand team.

Primary data
data the brand team decides it must go out and collect.

Secondary Data

There are significant differences between secondary and primary data, which are summarized in Figure 3.4. In this section, we will discuss secondary data.[6] Secondary data might be accessible online or perhaps in the organization, such as data that had been collected for a previous project that might be useful now. Accordingly, secondary data are often classified as either *internal* (data that the company collected and kept) or *external* (data that someone else collected, such as the government or trade organizations, and has made available to other users).

Common sources of internal secondary data include past company projects, certainly, but also think about how useful it can be to tap into the firm's customer relationship management (CRM) database. CRM includes contact information about customers, their purchase histories, information about a customer's responsiveness to past promotions and price sensitivity, and much more. The information can be extracted from barcodes, those omnipresent machine-readable visual data generators that are found on everything from basic packaged goods to cars. All of these market transactions yield useful data that can be stored and accessed to try to understand what drives consumers and what preferences they've shown thus far.

Common sources of external secondary data include macro databases, such as household income distribution information by zip code, available through the US Census Bureau at data.census.gov, or comparable international data, available at www.cia.gov.[7] For brand teams looking to expand to new markets or launch new products, these basic demographic

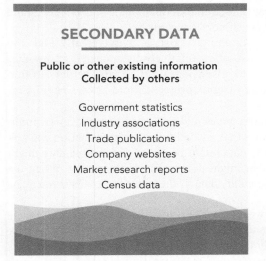
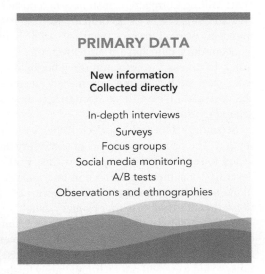

SECONDARY DATA

Public or other existing information
Collected by others

Government statistics
Industry associations
Trade publications
Company websites
Market research reports
Census data

PRIMARY DATA

New information
Collected directly

In-depth interviews
Surveys
Focus groups
Social media monitoring
A/B tests
Observations and ethnographies

FIGURE 3.3 Characteristics of Secondary Versus Primary Data

CRITERIA	SECONDARY RESEARCH		PRIMARY RESEARCH	
SOURCE	−	Collected by others	+	Collected by the researcher
CONTROL	−	Less control over data	+	High control over data
RELEVANCY	−	Not specific to the research question	+	Specific to the research question
COST AND TIME	+	Less costly and not time consuming to obtain	−	Expensive and time consuming to obtain
ACCESSIBILITY	−	Publicly available, including to competitors	+	Not freely or easily available to the public
RESEARCHER BIAS	+	Less likely to be biased	−	Possibility of bias exist
TIME	−	Past data	+	Real-time data

FIGURE 3.4   Secondary Versus Primary Research. Adapted from Iacobucci, D. & Churchill, G. A. (2018). Marketing research: methodological foundations. Published by CreateSpace Independent Publis

databases can help forecast market size potential. In addition, the barcode scanner data just referred to as a source of internal data can be expanded to include consumers' purchase actions on competitor brands, if the organization is willing to pay the owner of the combined dataset, typically a marketing research firm, such as A. C. Nielsen, or sometimes a retailer, such as a large chain like Walmart or Target. These data allow marketers to answer such questions as "When our competitor ran a promotion, did we lose many customers, and shortly thereafter, did they return to purchase our brand again when the competitor's promotion ended?"

Social media can be a source of secondary data as well. Companies can watch social media postings that sometimes reveal consumers' sensitivities to various brands in the context of their lives. In a recent move, PepsiCo announced that the brand Aunt Jemima was being renamed as Pearl Milling Company. Consumers had posted opinions about the previous brand name, and its logo and imagery, and the company realized it was time (well past time!) for a change.[8] The brand managers wanted to show that they cared about consumers' concerns.

Secondary data have many strengths. The data already exist, so it is typically easy and quick to access the information. The data are also often relatively inexpensive, sometimes even free, such as when one merely needs to look elsewhere on the firm's servers to find the past data. Given these strengths, a consumer insights project should always begin with secondary data.

Secondary data aren't perfect; if they were, marketers would never need to collect new information. The primary weakness of secondary data is that, by definition, the information was collected to serve another purpose. At this point, the data might be out of date, or the data might describe consumer preferences in one market that might not generalize to another. When the marketer runs up against this shortcoming of secondary data, if there remain unanswered questions, then it's time to gather primary data.

Not surprisingly, the profile of strengths and weaknesses of primary data is the reverse image of secondary data. Primary data allow marketers to answer the questions they've posed because the data collection project was created purposely to do so. On the other hand, any project takes time, so answers will not be immediately forthcoming, and of course, time is money, that is, primary data projects costs money.

PepsiCo rebranded
Aunt Jemima
to Pearl Milling
Company.

Types of Primary Data Collection

There are numerous types of primary data collection methods. They tend to be characterized as exploratory, descriptive, or causal. **Exploratory research**[9] methods are those used when the marketing question is still being formed. For example, if sales are falling off, is it because our customers are aging, because our brand is too expensive, or because there are new, good, alternative brands as options? When the questions are themselves a bit uncertain, there is no point in running a **survey** (list of questions used for collecting data from a predefined group of respondents about a specific topic of interest), because it's not clear what questions should be asked on it.

Exploratory methods include such approaches as focus groups and interviews. In a focus group, a moderator interacts with several consumers; in an interview, the interviewer asks questions of an individual consumer. The verbal responses are captured either by recording or in the marketer's notes. Marketing researchers might also ask consumers to use storytelling, keep a consumer diary, or submit photographs, or the marketer might observe a consumer making shopping decisions. Let's examine these options in greater detail.

Marketing researchers used to call consumers and conduct phone interviews (e.g. "Which brand do you use? Have you ever tried this brand?"). These days no one wants to be bothered by phone calls, certainly not from a company that claims to simply want their opinions. As there is a well-founded suspicion that a sales pitch will follow. However, the interview method is not dead. Sometimes customers are solicited via email or Facebook, or sometimes on site, such as at a grocery store or car dealership. Customers are asked to participate in a quick, five- to ten- minute, **interview**,[10] during which the interviewer asks them about their buying habits and preferences. The interviewer has a scripted list of questions to ask, but the strength of the interviewing technique is to let respondents go off script and say whatever they want. Those unanticipated comments are often a goldmine of insights for the brand team. Marketers who thought their

Exploratory research
methods used when the marketing question is still being formed.

Survey
a list of questions used for collecting data from a predefined group of respondents about a specific topic of interest.

Interview
a data collection method aimed to obtain information via a list of questions or unstructured conversation.

brand didn't appeal or was too expensive could be surprised to learn, for example, that older respondents didn't purchase their brand simply because it was on the top grocery shelf and they couldn't reach it.

In a **focus group**, eight to ten consumers gather for one to two hours at a central location (e.g. an office near an airport) to discuss a brand.[11] These consumers are sampled from a company's database or a marketing research firm's panel (large group of consumers who are getting paid for their participation), or they're recruited through online ads or in stores. As in an interview, a moderator has a list of scripted questions to pose to participants for a group discussion. Here, too, the moderator allows a free-flowing interaction among participants, until the discussion goes too off topic, when the moderator can pose the next question to bring the group back on track.

The reports from interviews and focus groups are usually audio and video recordings as well as text transcriptions, which may be read or analyzed via text analytics to look for frequencies of words or certain buzz words. In addition, in both interviews and focus groups, the marketer might ask respondents to tell stories about what the brand has meant to them, or make a collage of photographs comprising Google images or clipped from magazines about how they perceive the brand image. Note that all of these findings are **qualitative data**[12]; that is, the nature of the information is in the form of text or pictures. Qualitative data are deeply rich in information and different from and complementary to quantitative data that are numbers-based, such as ratings on a survey that lend themselves to certain kinds of statistical analysis.

Get deep insights with focus groups and interviews.

Another form of qualitative data collection is simple **observation**. This type of data collection is labor intensive, but it usually yields tremendous insights and is thus quite cost effective. Rather than intercepting a shopper at a local grocery store and asking, "Why are you buying that brand?" the researcher would be disguised as another shopper and walk up and down the aisles simply watching customers' brand choices and their decision-making. For example, in the brand category of interest, do consumers just consult their shopping lists, look at the store shelves, grab one brand, and move on? Or do they deliberate, begin to choose one brand, but ultimately choose another, taking the time to read labels?

A combination of interviewing and observing is called **ethnography**.[13] For example, after observing a consumer's natural brand predilections, the marketer might then approach the consumer and ask about his or her preferences and reasoning. With a household's permission, some ethnographers have even ventured into a consumer's home to watch the family dynamics as a dinner is prepared, or as laundry is being done, or as kids run around grabbing snacks. One way of conducting an ethnography is as a **participant-observer**.[14] In this approach, the marketer studies consumers in the consumption setting – if you want to understand Harley Davidson riders, ride with them; if you want to understand women getting hair extensions, hang out in the beauty salon and get your hair done; if you want to see what is consumed at tailgate parties, attend one every weekend and participate and observe.

At this point, the exploratory methods have yielded some insights, so there is better clarity as to what information the brand team seeks. Sometimes after a focus group is run, a manager has heard a consumer say something that really rings true, so the manager is ready to put the insight into action. The problem is, as rich and insightful as exploratory methods are, they bring the concern that the results have been derived based on small samples. Thus, no matter how authentic the voices of the consumers sounded in the interviews or focus groups or ethnographies, before taking marketing action, the brand team needs a little more confirmation on a larger scale.

Descriptive research[15] methods take the insights drawn from the exploratory phase and test them out on a larger, random, more representative sample of consumers. A typical descriptive method is a survey of at least one hundred consumers (usually many more), with the resultant data being analyzed by descriptive statistics (means, standard deviations) and correlations and regressions. If a focus group had found that one of the participants wanted red toothpaste, now the survey can confirm that the majority of consumers wanted red toothpaste or find that, although there may be a small segment of consumers who like red toothpaste, most prefer white or aqua.

A survey is a list of questions for consumers about their purchasing decisions, for example, of pasta sauces. The questions might revolve around current buying habits, which brands, what size jars, what flavors, and so on, and may include speculative questions about possible future buying (e.g. "Would you consider a pesto-tomato-mushroom sauce?"). Surveys should begin with the most interesting questions to help engage the survey takers and reinforce their willingness to participate. Surveys usually end with demographic questions (e.g. when applicable, gender, household income, and number of adults and children in the home).[16]

Surveys are useful because they allow marketers to ask consumers questions about virtually anything. Yet, as with any consumer insights technique, they have some weaknesses. For example, response rates typically aren't much higher than about 2 percent; one very clear correlate is that the longer the survey, the lower the response rate (which falls off with every new screen of questions). Marketing researchers also try very short surveys (two or three questions) sent to consumers' as text messages es, but the brevity of these surveys render them not particularly useful for data analysis (more on that later). In addition, it is important to avoid questions based on memory (e.g. asking consumers about a favorite brand is likely to produce reliable results, but asking how much that jar of pasta cost the last time they bought it is likely to be quite error-prone). Questions that seem clear to the brand team can be ambiguous to the consumer, so pre-testing is important.

Observation
directly watching the behavior and interaction of consumers in their natural environment.

Ethnography
a combination of interviews and observations to study a specific phenomenon.

Participant-observer
a way of conducting an ethnographic research.

Descriptive research
a research method that take the insights drawn from the exploratory phase and test them out on a larger, random, more representative sample of consumers.

Netnography
observing the online
behaviors and inter-
actions of consumers
mostly on social media.

Causal research
a research method
in which the mar-
keter aims to identify
a cause-and-effect
relationship bet-
ween two variables
by manipulating the
independent variable.

Experiment
a research method
that provides sights
into cause-and-effect
by demonstrating
what response occurs
when a particular var-
iable is manipulated.

Independent variable
the variable that is
being manipulated.

Dependent variable
the measured response.

A/B testing
a type of an experiment
in which participants
are exposed to one of
two conditions.

Test market
a research method
used by companies
to explore consumers
response to their new
products or marketing
campaigns, by testing
it on a small group
of consumers before
launching it to the
general market.

An increasingly important descriptive method is scraping social media for brand mentions. In a way, the social media postings are like secondary data in that they already exist, but they are primary data for the marketer who must find them, organize them, and begin to study and analyze them. These postings are unsolicited consumer opinions and typically represent the bimodalities of ardent consumer fans and brand haters. The opinions of brand fans obviously make for happier reading, but negative opinions can be informative as well. When marketers read consumers' online dialogues and contribute to the online discussion as a fellow fan, they are participating in an online form of ethnography called **netnography**.[17]

Once a posted survey window is completed, or the social media comments over a set duration have been obtained, marketers can begin analyzing data. Means certainly are important, but beyond that, usually marketers are interested in what correlates with or predicts (via regression) consumers' interest in a brand: Was it an advertisement they've seen, or chatter on social media, or a coupon promotion that got them to try it? Or are they brand loyal? Do consumers just repeat their brand selections from past purchases?

Descriptive methods are extremely useful to marketers. But there are some questions these techniques are not well-suited to answer. For example, most consumers don't want to be known as cheapskates, but in fact most consumers are price sensitive in product categories they don't care much about. Marketers could analyze frequencies of scanner purchases and try to correlate them with brand prices versus competitor brands. But causal methods for obtaining consumer insights might yield clearer results.

Causal research[18] methods are those in which the marketer aims to identify a cause-and-effect relationship between two variables by manipulating the independent variable; for example, the marketer manipulates the price by setting it high for one group of consumers and low for another group of consumers, then watches consumer responses, do they buy or not. This attempt to investigate causal relationships requires **experiments**,[19] a type of research in which consumers are randomly assigned to groups, thus, at the moment, making the groups essentially equal. The marketer then introduces the manipulation, such as different price points, and measures the participants' responses. If the different groups of consumers respond differently, the different responses may be cleanly attributable to the manipulated factor. The factor being manipulated is called an **independent variable**, and the measured response is called a **dependent variable**.

A popular form of experiment is **A/B testing**. In this causal research method, an experiment is designed in which participants are exposed to one of two versions, "A" and "B", of whatever is being tested – a website or a product advertisement, for example and their responses are compared. Figure 3.5 shows two kinds of A/B tests.[20] In the first, companies frequently wonder how appealing and effective their emails are in propelling consumers to clickthrough and head online to purchase their products, half of the email recipients are randomly chosen to receive an email with a generic salutation ("Dear Valued Customer"), and the other half receive a personalized email with their name. If personalization is more effective, then the company would see more click-throughs by the recipients in the second group.

A/B tests are often used for researching ad designs online. Figure 3.5 shows two versions of a shampoo ad on the company's website: a standard approach with a photo of a model with lustrous hair, and another version with an image of a happy couple on a beautiful beach. The first emphasizes the effectiveness of the shampoo; the second invokes a lifestyle. Consumers response to these versions will determine which version the company will use in its website.

There are many kinds of A/B tests. The experiments might be run in the real world, such as a **test market**. A test market is a research method used by companies to explore consumers response to their new products or marketing campaigns, by testing it on a small group of consumers before launching it to the general market. For example, to test how a newly introduced product

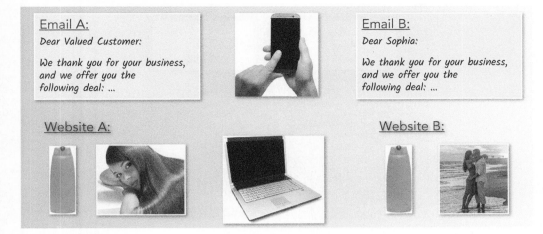

Email A:
Dear Valued Customer:

We thank you for your business, and we offer you the following deal: ...

Email B:
Dear Sophia:

We thank you for your business, and we offer you the following deal: ...

Website A:

Website B:

FIGURE 3.5   A/B Tests

sells in different regions of the country, market researchers could compare sales in Atlanta (group A) and San Diego (group B). Or they could test in one market only, say, Atlanta, and compare sales of product A, available in certain stores, and product B, available only in others.

Marketers are always interested in new ways to learn from consumers. A relatively new form of investigation that shows promise is consumer neuroscience, or **neuromarketing**, which uses the tools of neuroscience – eye tracking and electroencephalography (which measures brain cell activity) are especially popular – to study the behavior of consumers and their decision-making processes. In this type of research, test participants' psychophysiological reactions are monitored as they are shown images and videos of ads and brands. These measurements would be complementary to interview or survey data – a consumer might not want to admit being interested in a product featured in an ad, for example, but the neurologic signs might tell another story.

Neuromarketing research uses the tools of neuroscience to study the behavior of consumers and their decision-making processes.

Big Data

Marketers are taking advantage of **big data**. What are big data? Imagine a giant spreadsheet with many consumer households represented in the rows, and the columns are brands and products. The entries in the table might be 0s and 1s, indicating items (columns) a consumer (row) had bought (1) or not (0), or they could be dollar values (how much was spent on this product this quarter) or dates (how recently the consumer bought this product), for example. There are also usually additional variables, such as the consumer's or household's income level, the average price of goods bought during the past year, and so on. Big data are so much fun to analyze! See Figure 3.6 for pros and cons of big data.

Big data are characterized by the three Vs: volume, velocity, and variety.[21]

Big data a large, hard-to-manage volumes of structured or unstructured data.

- *Volume* refers to the large number of data points, in terms of the number of consumers (the rows in the spreadsheet), and the number of variables, such as items bought or available for purchase (columns). Amazon, Walmart, and eBay, to name just a few of the large companies mining information, have data on tens of millions of consumers (rows), and billions of products (columns). Now that's big data!

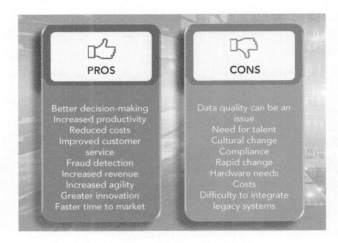

FIGURE 3.6   Pros and Cons of Big Data

- **Velocity** refers to the speed at which the data are collected and updated. As much data as Walmart processes, it gets updated hourly. Can you imagine being a brand manager and getting hourly market shares?

- **Variety** refers to the many kinds of data. Some data are numeric, such as scanner sales data. But big data also refers to social media posts about a brand, photos uploaded on Instagram or Facebook, positive and negative comments, likes, and so on. The variety of types of big data can be especially challenging.

  - But not everyone knows how to "scrape" data from social media sites to find out if people "like" their brand.

Database marketing, or direct marketing – using CRM data to reach out to consumers.

  - Text analytics are still developing, and marketers have to deal with ambiguities, such as when a consumer posts, "Oh yeah, the service was great, eye roll" obviously indicating sarcasm, yet text analyses have to be trained to not pick up on "service was great" as if it was a positive endorsement.

Recency
the most recent time a consumer purchased the company's product or services.

  - And if likes or texts are hard, business people struggle even more with how to "analyze" online images (e.g. photos of a consumer using your brand) or video clips.

The label big data also describes a lot of data that firms already have, including their CRM data sets mentioned previously as a type of secondary data. When marketers use these CRM data to reach out to consumers, it's called **database marketing**, or direct marketing.[22] Database marketers care about RFM: **recency, frequency,** and **monetary value.** Recency refers to the most recent time a consumer purchased the company's product or services – a few weeks ago or more than six months ago? Frequency refers to the number of items that consumer buys in a typical year. Monetary value refers to the worth or price points of the items the consumer typically buys: does the consumer buy high-end products or just cheaper items when they're on sale?

Frequency
the number of items that consumer buys in a specific time frame.

Monetary value
the worth or price points of the items the consumer typically buys.

The use of big data in marketing analytics is exciting, but smart marketers have always known that data (of any size) helps teach them about their customers. What are consumers buying, or not, and why? With the proliferation of big data, opportunities for consumer insights is greater than ever. If the label of marketing research sounds boring to you, think of it instead as "consumer insights" or "market analysis" (sounds tough!) or even: "Ok team, here's how I can defend our marketing strategy because I know what our consumers want!"

Do the Right Thing!

It's important to respect people's choices and their "space" when conducting marketing research and obtaining consumer insights. For example, most surveys are opt-in, so consumers are not being forced to yield data or opinions. (Indeed, most consumers do not opt in; response rates of around 10 to 15 percent are considered reasonable.) Focus groups and interviews are similarly opt-in. But what about observations? Some experts would say it is proper to inform consumers that the marketer wishes to watch them (e.g., when choosing among soups on a shelf at the grocery store). Other experts say that if you inform people, they may behave differently because they know that their actions are on display. Yet marketers with experience in observing consumers (even behind one-way mirrors at a focus group) learn that consumers forget about the marketer's presence very quickly and behave essentially as they would naturally.

Marketing Analytics

With all of these kinds of data available, how does the brand team extract consumer insights? It is perhaps not surprising that there are also many ways to analyze these data sources. To keep things simple, let's focus on three of the most commonly used techniques of marketing analytics: cross-tabs, regression, and conjoint analysis.

Cross-tabs are simply tables of numbers displayed to examine the relationship between rows and columns.[23] The table rows might be men versus women, and the columns might be brand A versus brand B. The brand team is looking at these numbers to see whether there are gender differences in the category of brand preferences.

Cross-tabs are tables of numbers displayed to examine the relationship between rows and columns.

A popular use of cross-tabs is to examine brand loyalty and brand switching. Suppose the company has purchased scanner data for cookies, which are bought in most households multiple times a year. In such scanner data, the purchases would show when consumers bought which brands, what the price was when they bought it, whether a coupon was used or not, whether the consumer had been exposed to an online advertisement in the last few days or not, and so forth. The series of cookie purchases for a brand-loyal household might look like this: first time measured – t_1 = Oreo; second time measured – t_2 = Oreo, third time measured – t = Oreo, where t stands for time. A household switching brands (for variety, price sensitivity, or other reasons) might show purchases like this:

$$t_1 = \text{Chips Ahoy}, t_2 = \text{Oreo}, t_3 = \text{Pepperidge Farms}.$$

Marketers would gather the sequential data for times "t" and "t+1" (so t_1 and t_2, then t_2 and t_3, etc.) and form a cross-tab like that in Figure 3.7. In this form, it's easy to see that brand A (Oreos) enjoys a great deal of loyalty – the diagonal value depicting t to $t+1$ repeat purchasing is high. Brands B (Chips Ahoy) and C (Pepperidge Farms) enjoy some loyalty, but actually, they are seen as substitutable competitors in the eyes of consumers, because consumers go back and forth between the two brands.

Regression is a statistical model in which the marketer tries to predict some outcome (dependent variable), such as, How likely is it that the consumer will buy brand A? as a function of some independent variables (a variable that is independent of the outcome) that can range from measures of previous attitudes, demographic variables, advertising exposures, current prices of brand A and its competitors, and so on.[24] An example model would look like this:

Regression a statistical model in which the marketer tries to predict an outcome (dependent variable), as a function of an independent variables (a variable that is independent of the outcome).

$$\text{might buy } A = b_0 + b_1 (\text{bought } A \text{ last time}) + b_2 (\text{female}) + b_3 (\text{high income}) + e.$$

CROSS-TABS ON SCANNER DATA

TIME *t+1*

		BRAND A	BRAND B	BRAND C
	BRAND A	50	30	30
TIME *t* BRAND B		30	40	40
	BRAND C	30	40	40

FIGURE 3.7   Consumer Loyalty and Brand Switching

That equation is read as follows: "We predict that the likelihood with which consumers would buy brand A increases when they've bought A last time, and for rich women." The *b* terms are called regression coefficients, and they can be positive or negative (the previous interpretation assumed they were all positive). The first term, b_0, is called an intercept, and it's the starting point from which the estimates are then adjusted upward if the other *b*'s are positive, or downward, for negative *b*'s. The last term, *e*, represents error, an acknowledgment that no model is perfect, it's just making the best prediction that it can.

Regression is a very useful and rather straightforward model that most business people are at least somewhat aware of. As a result, regression is a very popular technique in marketing analytics.

Conjoint analysis is a technique that allows a marketer to test trade-offs that consumers are willing to make when considering brand choices.[25] The marketer presents study participants with options such as (a) a pack of twenty gel capsules of Tylenol for $2.99, (b) a pack of twenty gel capsules of Tylenol for $3.99, (c) a pack of twenty gel capsules of store brand pain reliever for $2.99, or (d) a pack of twenty gel capsules of store brand pain reliever for $3.99.

> **Conjoint analysis** is a technique that allows a marketer to test trade-offs that consumers are willing to make when considering brand choices.

CONSIDER THESE 20 GEL CAP PACKS

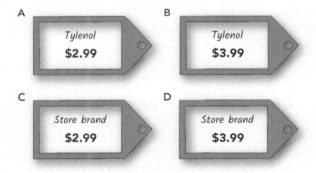

In that set-up, the consumer is asked, "Rate these four options from 1 to 10, where 10 is the option you most prefer." Naturally, most consumers would seek to maximize on familiar brands and do so at the cheapest price possible, so they'd go for choice a. Most consumers conversely try to avoid the nonbrand at the expensive price, so they would not opt for choice d. The question is, if choice a is unavailable, who are the brand-loyal consumers who would stick with Tylenol but pay more (choice b), and who are the price-sensitive consumers who would choose the store brand to save money (choice c)?

In this data table, we see that both types of consumers want the name brand, Tylenol, and they want to pay the lowest price. Very sensible! We can see that consumer A is more brand loyal because they still rate the more expensive Tylenol option better than the store brands. By comparison, consumer B would prefer the store brand (again, at the lower price), and then the more expensive options are rated lower regardless of brand.

	BRAND CODE	PRICE	PRICE CODE	CONSUMER A	CONSUMER B
Tylenol	1	$2.99	1	10	1
Tylenol	1	$3.99	2	9	5
Store Brand	2	$2.99	1	4	8
Store Brand	2	$3.99	2	2	3

Conjoint analysis is run via a regression on that data table. The ratings of the attractiveness of the four options serve as the dependent variable, and the predictor variables are brand and price. The regression would look like this:

$$\text{Predicted preference} = b_0 + b_1\,(\text{brand}) + b_2\,(\text{price}).$$

For consumer A, the conjoint regression model results are

$$\text{Predicted preference} = 18.25 - 6.5\,(\text{brand}) - 1.5\,(\text{price}).$$

For consumer B, the conjoint results indicate

$$\text{Predicted preference} = 17.00 - 2.0\,(\text{brand}) - 5.0\,(\text{price}).$$

These results support our observations in the table that consumer A is brand loyal (the b weight for brand is bigger), whereas consumer B is more price sensitive (the b weight for price is bigger). As the brand code changes from 1 (Tylenol) to 2 (store brand), preference drops (the b weights are negative). As the price code changes from 1 ($2.99) to 2 ($3.99), preference drops.

When the brand teams gets results like this from a good sized sample of consumers, they can determine how large the segments are of brand-loyal versus price-sensitive consumers. Information like this is very helpful in strategic planning.

> *Consumer data will be the biggest differentiator in the next two to three years. Whoever unlocks the reams of data and uses it strategically will win.*
> *Angela Ahrendts, former SVP of retail at Apple, former CEO at Burberry*

Consumer Insights Partners

Brand teams have many options of where to turn for help with consumer insights. In large firms, there is typically some in-house marketing research function or experts. But when that is lacking, or when the project seems larger than normal, help can be obtained by consulting with marketing research firms. Some of those firms compile and offer syndicated data services and are also capable of designing and executing primary research projects. These firms often have a panel of consumers who they can tap for a sample project, who could serve on focus groups or keep diaries, or their loyalty cards and purchase data may be captures. Advertising agencies also usually have some insights experts (granted, their focus will be mostly on developing and testing ad copy or media planning). Some industries have research foundations that designed to answer questions that may affect multiple providers, and some government agencies can help with insights, particularly in nonprofit applications more than commercial ventures.

SUMMARY

Understanding what consumers do by drawing conclusions from their actions is important, yet knowing why they behave the way they do gives marketers more than just a surface-level insight into their target consumer. The marketing research process builds the foundation on which to draw sound consumer insights. Marketing research and consumer insights work hand in hand to better inform strategic decisions.

Consumer information can come from two common sources: primary and secondary data. Typically, marketing researchers will use both types of data to better inform their recommendations to the brand team and to corporate leadership. The trade-offs for collecting either type of data come down to cost and time. Secondary data can be quick and low cost, but they may not answer the research questions, whereas primary data takes time and money but directly answer research questions. The business needs and the resources available determine the kind of data to be collected.

There are three common techniques used to collect primary data: exploratory research, descriptive research, and causal research. Each builds on one another; exploratory research is used when the precise nature of the business question is still being formed; descriptive research takes those insights from the exploratory phase and tests them out on a representative sample of consumers; finally, causal research allows marketers to answer some "if-then" questions (e.g. If we raise prices, then how much will sales volume drop off?) by manipulating specific variables.

With the technological advances that have taken place over the past few decades, marketers have more access to consumer information than ever before. Big data allow marketers to tap into consumers insights from multiple touchpoints and do so rapidly. Customer relationships management data are another source for marketers to gain insights.

Large-scale research studies don't have to be done in-house, and typically, companies will seek additional help from consumer insights partners to execute such extensive research. These partners will run marketing analytics, such as the most common techniques: cross-tabs, regressions, and conjoint analyses. The partnership will help provide answers to business questions that could potentially alter or further support the companies' strategic direction.

KEY TERMS

Marketing research	Qualitative data	Independent variable	Frequency
Consumer insights	Observation	Dependent variable	Monetary value
Secondary data	Ethnography	A/B testing	Cross-tabs
Primary data	Participant-observer	Test market	Regression
Exploratory research	Descriptive research	Neuromarketing research	Conjoint analysis
Survey	Netnography	Big data	
Interview	Causal research	Database marketing	
Focus group	Experiment	Recency	

EXERCISES

1. Here is a demo so you can see why no member of a brand team should act as a focus group moderator or interviewer – the brand team is just not objective enough, and if the research isn't going to be objective, there is no point in doing it. Think of a brand you love (or hate). Ask a classmate what he or she thinks about that brand. Watch yourself and your reactions – it's so hard to stay neutral. If you love the brand and your neighbor doesn't like it or is neutral, it's human nature to try to jump in and persuade them to change their opinion. If the brand was one you don't like, and your classmate does, it's tempting to jump in and explain why they're wrong. You can't do that in marketing research, so you have to hire a moderator or interviewer. They aren't as passionate about the brand as you, as a brand team member, are, because it's your life and work.

2. This is also a demo of sorts; here the lesson to learn is why it's helpful to ask an expert (in-house is fine, or hire a marketing researcher) to write a survey. It doesn't seem hard but check this out: Think about a local restaurant and write a short (one-page) survey about it. Write questions to ask about the location,

the ambience, the quality of the food and menu variety, the prices, and so on. Tweak the survey until you think it's reasonably good, then give it to a person in class (not a friend), and ask them to try to answer the questions and comment aloud to you as they go along. Their comments may indicate that there are questions that are ambiguous or overly complicated, as well as other problems. That's why pretesting is helpful before launching a full survey.

3. Go to Google and try out the trend analysis their analytics let you do. Type in a search term, for example, a recent news item or a sports team or particular athlete. See how easy it is to watch the trend line grow, and see if you can explain when it goes up or down. In particular, what was happening when the searches picked up?

4. A vitamin company plans to introduce a new product that targets kids. The company wants to know what factors would affect kids' consumption of vitamins. Would you recommend the company to conduct primary or secondary research? Explain your recommendation. What type of questions would you ask? What is the biggest challenge you identify in researching kids' consumption?

5. COVID-19 has challenged many traditional marketing research methods. As a small-group class project, identify the different ways that COVID-19 has changed marketing research methods. Which of these changes do you think will continue in the future?

ENDNOTES

1. https://www.history.com/news/why-coca-cola-new-coke-flopped.

2. General marketing research and consumer insights books: Alvin, Burns, Ann Veeck, & Ronald Bush, *Marketing Research*, 8th ed. (New York: Pearson, 2016); Dawn Iacobucci & Gilbert A. Churchill Jr., *Marketing Research: Methodological Foundations*, 12th ed. (Nashville, TN: Earlie Lite Books, 2018).

3. Iacobucci & Churchill, *Marketing Research*.

4. R. Hamilton, "Consumer-based Strategy: Using Multiple Methods to Generate Consumer Insights that Inform Strategy," *Journal of the Academy of Marketing Science* 44, no. 3 (2016): 281–8.

5. Iacobucci and Churchill, *Marketing Research*.

6. Iacobucci and Churchill, *Marketing Research*.

7. https://data.census.gov/cedsci/; https://www.cia.gov/the-world-factbook/.

8. https://contact.pepsico.com/pearlmillingcompany/article/what-is-the-history-of-pearl-milling-company.

9. https://research-methodology.net/research-methodology/research-design/exploratory-research/.

10. A. E. Goldman, "The Group Depth Interview," *Journal of Marketing* 26, no. 3 (1962): 61–8.

11. Focus groups: David L. Morgan, *Basic and Advanced Focus Groups* (Los Angeles: Sage, 2018).

12. https://www.simplypsychology.org/qualitative-quantitative.html.

13. Ethnography: David Fetterman, *Ethnography: Step-by-Step*, 4th ed. (Los Angeles: Sage, 2019).

14. C. J. Calhoun, *Dictionary of the Social Sciences* (New York: Oxford University Press, 2002).

15. V. Mittal, "Descriptive Research," *Wiley International Encyclopedia of Marketing* (Chichester, UK: Wiley-Blackwell, 2010).

16. Survey Design: Sheila B. Robinson & Kimberly Firth Leonard, *Designing Quality Survey Questions* (Los Angeles: Sage, 2018).

17. Robert V. Kozinets, *Netnography: Redefined* (London: Sage, 2015).

18. H. Oppewal, "Causal Research," *Wiley International Encyclopedia of Marketing* (Chichester, UK: Wiley-Blackwell, 2010).

19. B. J. Calder, L. W. Phillips, and A. M. Tybout, "Designing Research for Application," *Journal of Consumer Research* 8, no. 2 (1981): 197–207.

20. Cellphone with freest usage rights on Google: https://www.google.com/search?as_st=y&tbm=isch&hl=en&as_q=cellphone&as_epq=&as_oq=&as_eq=&cr=&as_sitesearch=&safe=images&tbs=sur:fmc#imgrc=NGSR_QiK8wFfEM.

    Laptops with freest usage rights on Google: https://www.google.com/search?as_st=y&tbm=isch&hl=en&as_q=laptop&as_epq=&as_oq=&as_eq=&cr=&as_sitesearch=&safe=images&tbs=sur:fmc.

    Shampoo bottle: https://www.google.com/search?as_st=y&tbm=isch&hl=en&as_q=shampoo+bottle&as_epq=&as_oq=&as_eq=&cr=&as_sitesearch=&safe=images&tbs=sur:fmc#imgrc=a2nOHWz-6-EjaM.

    Couple on beach: https://www.google.com/search?as_st=y&tbm=isch&hl=en&as_q=couple+on+beach&as_epq=&as_oq=&as_eq=&cr=&as_sitesearch=&safe=images&tbs=sur:fmc#imgrc=VAPPa8qj39SPHM.

    Hair: https://www.google.com/search?as_st=y&tbm=isch&hl=en&as_q=hair&as_epq=&as_oq=&as_eq=&cr=&as_sitesearch=&safe=images&tbs=sur:fmc#imgrc=5t0ghsnLKOYmdM.

21. Big Data: Mayer-Schönberger, Viktor and Kenneth Cukier (2014), *Big Data: A Revolution That Will Transform How We Live, Work, and Think*, London: Eamon Dolan/Mariner Books; Provost, Foster (2013), *Data Science for Business: What You Need to Know about Data Mining and Data-Analytic Thinking*, Sepastopol, CA: O'Reilly Media; Stephens-Davidowitz, Seth (2017), *Everybody Lies: Big Data, New Data, and What the Internet Can Tell Us About Who We Really Are*, New York: Dey Street Books.

22. Arora, N., Dreze, X., Ghose, A., Hess, J. D., Iyengar, R., Jing, B., Joshi, Y., Kumar, V., Lurie, N., Neslin, S., Sajeesh, S., Su, M., Syam, N., Thomas, J., and Zhang, Z. J. (2008), "Putting One-to-One Marketing to Work: Personalization, Customization, and Choice," *Marketing Letters*, 19 (Sept.), 305–321.

23. https://humansofdata.atlan.com/2016/01/cross-tabulation-how-why/.

24. Lewis-Beck, C., & Lewis-Beck, M. (2015), *Applied Regression: An Introduction*, 2nd ed., Sage.

25. https://sawtoothsoftware.com/conjoint-analysis.

CREDITS

Iacobucci, D. & Churchill, G. A. (2018). Marketing research: methodological foundations. Published by CreateSpace Independent Publis.

https://www.pepsico.com/news/press-release/aunt-jemima-rebrands-as-pearl-milling-company02092021

https://www.shutterstock.com/image-photo/group-executives-working-together-office-670819636

https://www.google.com/search?as_st=y&tbm=isch&hl=en&as_q=cellphone&as_epq=&as_oq=&as_eq=&cr=&as_sitesearch=&safe=images&tbs=sur:fmc#imgrc=NGSR_QiK8wFfEM:

https://www.google.com/search?as_st=y&tbm=isch&hl=en&as_q=laptop&as_epq=&as_oq=&as_eq=&cr=&as_sitesearch=&safe=images&tbs=sur:fmc

https://www.google.com/search?as_st=y&tbm=isch&hl=en&as_q=shampoo+bottle&as_epq=&as_oq=&as_eq=&cr=&as_sitesearch=&safe=images&tbs=sur:fmc#imgrc=a2nOHWz-6-EjaM:

Couple on beach: https://www.google.com/search?as_st=y&tbm=isch&hl=en&as_q=couple+on+beach&as_epq=&as_oq=&as_eq=&cr=&as_sitesearch=&safe=images&tbs=sur:fmc#imgrc=VAPPa8qj39SPHM:

hair: https://www.google.com/search?as_st=y&tbm=isch&hl=en&as_q=hair&as_epq=&as_oq=&as_eq=&cr=&as_sitesearch=&safe=images&tbs=sur:fmc#imgrc=5t0ghsnLKOYmdM:

Bob Parsons GoDaddy quote from: https://www.lifehack.org/articles/lifehack/bob-parsons-on-his-16-rules-for-survival.html#:~:text=Anything%20that%20is%20measured%20and,you%20problems%20will%20be%20there

Figure 3.5: niekverlaan/Free Photos - Free Images/CC0; Marco Verch Professional Photographer/Flickr; Betsy Jons/Flickr; Petr Kratochvil/CC0; Marco Verch Professional Photographer/Flickr; Pickpik

Image p. 45: The Quaker Oats Company

Image p. 46: Lucky Business/Shutterstock

CONSUMER BUYING PROCESS

PART II

How Consumers Make Decisions

LEARNING OBJECTIVES

After studying this chapter, you should be able to:

• Understand how consumers make decisions.

• Understand that decision-making unfolds as a process.

• Appreciate that marketers can actively influence consumer decision-making at different touch points or stages of that decision-making.

• Understand how consumers' decision processes operate during innovation and in response to new products.

You want to buy a new car. What are the stages you'll go through from the moment you realized that you need a new car to the moment you purchase one? How many models or brands will you consider? What are the most important criteria for you in a car? Appearance? Reliability? Fuel efficiency? Warranty? Cost of repairs? Resale value? Where would you get the information that you need? Friends? Family? Online? There are so many decisions to make for one simple action.

Consumer Decision-Making

Consumer's decision-making process reflects the stages that consumers go through before, during, and after they purchase a product or service.

Consumers make decisions every day, sometimes multiple times a day, about the products they want (or do not want) to purchase. A **consumer's decision-making process**, or the buyer's journey, reflects the stages that consumers go through before, during, and after they purchase a product or service. In other words, it's the process consumers undertake between recognizing a need and satisfying it. This process can be simple or complex depending on product-related factors (e.g. the risk of purchasing it, options available) or consumer-related factors (e.g. expertise or knowledge, level of involvement).[1]

A simple view of consumers' buying behavior is illustrated in Figure 4.1. Marketers try to map this process, yet a large part of it is not explicit. That's why it is often referred to as a black box. We can only observe and document the outcomes, such as what brands and products consumers buy, how much money they spend, and when they spend it. Nevertheless, marketers can take strategic actions by implementing the marketing mix, to influence consumers throughout the process.

Understanding this process is critical for companies.[2] Mapping and monitoring it via extensive data collection, such as scanner data, can inform marketers about some of the pain points that consumers experience during the process. Marketers can then use this information to identify

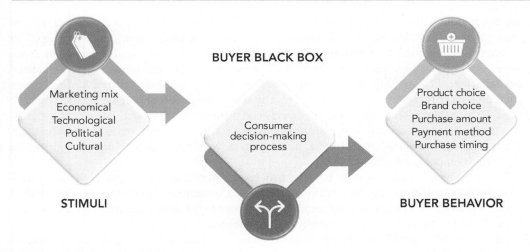

BUYER BLACK BOX

FIGURE 4.1 Basic Model of Buying Behavior

market opportunities and potential challenges. Furthermore, marketing efforts should be aligned with the process of consumers' decision-making and should guide and direct their purchasing behaviors, as we will discuss next.

Inside the Black Box

Figure 4.2 shows a five-step, rational consumer decision-making process. (We'll see in Chapter 6 that sometimes the process gets modified, but what we're discussing in this chapter is the typical process.) It also shows the actions that marketers can and should take at each step. Each provides marketers with the opportunity to interact with consumers. Understanding this helps marketer to design an effective marketing mix and create real value for their consumers. We will review the first steps in this chapter, and the final step, post-purchase behavior, in the next chapter.

Problem Recognition

The starting point of the consumers' decision-making process is their recognition that they have an unfulfilled need or problem. **Problem recognition** occurs when consumers realize that they

> **Problem recognition** is a discrepancy between consumers' current state and a desired future state.

FIGURE 4.2 A Strategic View of the Consumer Decision-Making Process

Actual state
is the state that consumers are currently experiencing.

Desired state
is a future state consumers want to achieve, that will motivate them to seek a product that will satisfy their need or solve their problem.

Consumers' involvement
is the extent to which a product or a purchase is relevant and of interest to the individual consumer.

Extensive problem-solving
a situation where consumers have little or no information about or experience with the product or brand options that can solve their problem.

High-involvement purchases
are those that are infrequent, costly, very important to consumers, and regarded as risky.

Routinized purchases
are purchases that consumers have made multiple times.

are not content with their current state, they want to change it and satisfy their need or address their problem (e.g. "My phone is dropping a lot of calls and data – I need a new phone!" or "I don't really need this, but that messenger bag would look impressive as I walk into an interview," or "My coworker has new earbuds, and I want a pair.") The tension between consumers' **actual state**, the state that they are currently experiencing, and their **desired state,** a future state they want to achieve, will motivate them to seek a product that will satisfy their need or solve their problem. Recall the concept of needs and wants from Chapter 1. Recognizing a problem at the "needs" level will drive consumers to find solutions at the "wants" level. Their personal preferences and culture will affect the solution they choose, even for simple things such as deciding what to have for breakfast.

The problems consumers want to solve may have different levels of complexity and intensity, resulting in different decision-making processes.[3] **Consumers' involvement,** the extent to which a product or a purchase is relevant and of interest to the individual consumer, will determine the level of complexity and intensity of their decision-making process.

In an **extensive problem-solving** situation, consumers have little or no information about or experience with the product or brand options that can solve their problem. In such situations, the options are typically difficult to evaluate and compare. They involve problems that are completely new to consumers, requiring them to invest significant effort to solve them. An extensive problem-solving situation normally typifies **high-involvement purchases**[4] – those that are infrequent, costly, very important to consumers, and regarded as risky. Choosing the right college to attend, for example, is a high-involvement purchase that requires extensive problem-solving. Think about all the time and effort you invested in learning about different colleges to be able to decide which one to attend; it is a big decision, with major consequences, so it feels like a decision with a lot of risk.

Of course, not all decision-making processes are extensive. Most purchases involve **routinized response behavior,** or routine problem-solving, purchases that consumers have made multiple times. In such cases, consumers typically choose the same product or brand, or choose from a limited group of acceptable products or brands.[5] They make such purchases without investing much effort.

ROUTINE PROBLEM-SOLVING involves situations like ordering your favorite Starbucks coffee.

ROUTINE PROBLEM-SOLVING	LIMITED PROBLEM-SOLVING	EXTENSIVE PROBLEM-SOLVING
❖ Skip some of the stages of the decision-making process ❖ Low-cost products ❖ Low risk ❖ Frequent purchasing ❖ Low consumer involvement ❖ Familiar product class and brands ❖ Little/no search for information ❖ Few brands considered ❖ Few product attributes evaluated ❖ Limited shopping time		❖ Going through all the stages of the decision-making process ❖ More expensive products ❖ High risk ❖ Infrequent purchasing ❖ High consumer involvement ❖ Unfamiliar product class and brands ❖ Extensive search for information ❖ Many brands considered ❖ Many product attributes evaluated ❖ Extensive shopping time

FIGURE 4.3 Problem-solving Characteristics

Think about buying a cup of coffee. You probably order your usual favorite coffee or one of your preferred drinks and will make a routine decision. Now imagine that the store ran out of one of the ingredients necessary for making your favorite coffee. The barista offers you several other options, which are variants of your favorite. In this case, you will engage in **limited problem-solving** to make your choice. In limited problem-solving situations, consumers have prior experience with the product or brand options that can solve their problem but are unfamiliar with different variants of the product. In such situations, consumers have limited time or resources to spend on the search for alternative options. In addition, they normally have no interest in investing much effort in solving their problem, so they are likely to make their choices on the spot.

Both routinized response behavior and limited problem-solving involve **low-involvement purchases** – those that are frequent, inexpensive, relatively unimportant to consumers, and regarded as having minimal risk. Consumers are not interested in finding the absolute best solution to their problem, because making the wrong choice does not have major repercussions. A choice that is "good enough" will be fine (this is also called satisficing). Figure 4.3 present the characteristics of the different problem-solving types.

Problem recognition can be the first touch point between marketers and consumers.[6] At this stage, marketers can make consumers' unfulfilled needs or problems salient to them, such as in this McDonald's ad that encourages consumers to think about a lunch solution. Marketers can also raise consumers' awareness about options that they did not consider initially. For example, Beyond Meat[7] educates consumers about plant-based protein that can be an alternative to meat. And, of course, marketers can help consumers recognize problems that they didn't think of initially or that are relevant to them but might not affect consumers directly. For example, green products address environmental problems that are relevant to all consumers, but consumers differ in the extent to which they are aware of or concerned about such issues.

One of the most effective tools that marketers have to connect with consumers is mobile technology and mobile marketing. Indeed, m-commerce, or mobile-based commerce, is on the rise. Last year, m-commerce accounted for 50 percent of all retail e-commerce.[8] Mobile technology

Limited problem-solving are situations where consumers have prior experience with the product or brand options that can solve their problem but are unfamiliar with different variants of the product.

Low-involvement purchases small, mundane, routine purchases, inexpensive, relatively unimportant to consumers, those are made automatically without really thinking about them and those that carry very low risk.

Are you hungry?
Recognizing a need is the
first step in the consumer
decision-making process.

offers benefits to both consumers and marketers. Mobile devices enable consumers to receive and access information anytime, anywhere. They help consumers to save time, effort, and money; make shopping more convenient; and can enhance the overall purchasing experience.

Mobile technology can be leveraged by marketers throughout the consumer decision-making process. As you can see in Figure 4.4, in the problem recognition stage, sending consumers

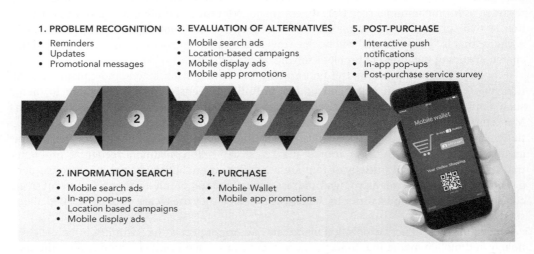

FIGURE 4.4 Mobile Marketing and Consumer Decision-Making Process

mobile marketing messages can act as an external driver or cue, helping consumers recognize their need and motivating them to start the buying process.[9] The product or service should be positioned as a solution to a problem the consumer is facing.

The mobile marketing tools that are relevant to this stage are

- Reminders of a sale or a promotion or a product that the consumer was interested in

- Updates about new arrivals, upgrades, or extensions of sales

- Promotional items, such as coupons and discounts

Information Search

Once consumers realize that they have an unfulfilled need or problem, they will start to obtain the information they need to address it. In other words, they will engage in a **prepurchase search**,[10] a search that is directly related to the recognition of the need or problem, to find the optimal product or service.

What information are they looking for?

1. What are their options? Consumers look for information about different ways or different brands that can address the need or problem.

2. What are the different characteristics of each option? Consumers evaluate mainly the performance and price of the different options.

3. What are the criteria that differentiate these options? Consumers consider other relevant criteria that can help them choose one option over the others.

In general, there are two types of information searches.[11] The first in an **internal search,** which refers to the retrieval of information from long-term memory. In such cases, consumers rely on their own experience with the product or brand as a source of information.

Consumers also use an **external search**[12] to acquire information that is beyond their direct experience with the product or brand. Consumers often conduct an external search about a product or brand even if they have previous experience with it.

Today, more than ever before, consumers have access to a wide range of information sources. In searching for a new car, you might begin by looking at the manufacturers' websites and specialized car websites. You will probably watch informational YouTube videos, ask friends and family about their opinions, then stop at a dealership to get more information and experience your options firsthand.

Internal and external information searches complement each other. Each of these sources provides different benefits. In the search for a new car, for example, the manufacturer's website offers a breadth of information. YouTube and other online sites can provide different views and opinions about the options of the car you're considering. Friends and family are your most trusted source. And visiting the dealerships will provide you with an opportunity to form your own opinion based on your judgment and experience. Overall, as Figure 4.5 shows, consumers trust the information that is provided by friends and family and review websites the most (for all kinds of products, not just cars).

Mobile phones play a critical role in the information search stage. Today over half of consumers (58 percent) in the United States search for information on their mobile devices, double the number from five years ago.[13] This trend is expected to grow in the next few years and is attributed to the convenience and accessibility that mobile devices offer. This gives mobile marketing

Prepurchase search is a search that is directly related to the recognition of the need or problem, to find the optimal product or service.

Internal search refers to the retrieval of information from long-term memory.

External search refers to acquiring information that is beyond consumers' direct experience with the product or brand.

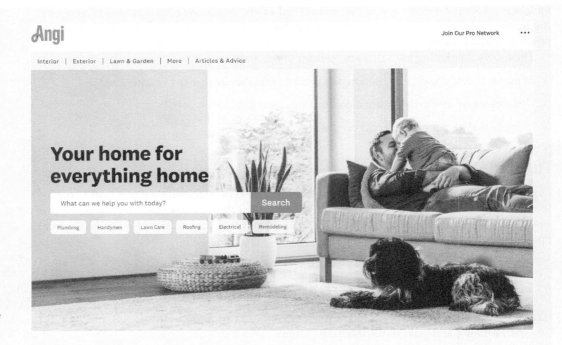

Angi is an example of an external source of information.

FIGURE 4.5 Sources of Information

an advantage over other forms of communication channels, such as print ads and TV and radio commercials. Mobile devices also have the advantage of enabling marketers to customize their messages and the type of information that they are sharing to different target markets. It helps marketers provide the right information to the right consumers. In this stage, marketers also need to highlight points of differentiation from their competitors. In other words, they need to provide consumers with the information that will help them choose their brand and product over the competitors.

The mobile marketing tools that are relevant to this stage are

- Mobile search ads, such as click to locate ads, text ads, or product listings ads.

- In-app pop-ups, which are triggered by consumers' actions in an app. For example, if you are looking for a backpack in an app, you might see an in-app pop-up offer about backpacks that might direct your search.

- Location-based campaigns direct ads to consumers relevant to their specific location.

- Mobile display ads – or mobile banner ads appear on different websites that might affect consumers information search and decision-making.

ADVERTISING ON SOCIAL MEDIA

MOBILE DISPLAY ADS

Level of Engagement in the Information Search

The level of consumer engagement in an external search can be measured in different ways, such as the number of websites visited, the number of people consumers talk with, and the number and length of the online searches. There are product-, consumer-, and situation-related factors that affect consumer engagement in an external search for information.

Product-related Factors

Number of alternatives: The more alternatives consumers have, the more time and effort they will invest in searching for information. Specifically, consumers search for information about the criteria that differentiate between the options they are considering. Decisions with many options can feel overwhelming, so consumers often will use selection criteria to reduce the number of options (e.g. "There are so many cars to choose from, but here are the ones I can afford").

Perceived risk: Consumers will invest more time and effort in information searches if they regard the purchase as risky. The motivation for the search for information is to reduce or minimize the risk associated with the purchase. Risk can be financial (e.g. "If I choose badly, I'll feel like I've wasted money") or risky in other ways (e.g. socially risky: "If I choose a restaurant to take a friend to, and the food or service is bad, I'll be embarrassed").

Price: Price can be regarded as an aspect of consumers' perceptions about the risk involved in the purchase. Another aspect of price is the cost or effort of switching products. Consumers will search for more information about products that are expensive or involve high costs for switching to other choices. Even if one's current preferred brand isn't perfect, sometimes it's "good enough," considering the effort it would take to look into switching to another brand.

Perceived differentiation: If consumers regard the alternatives they are considering as similar to each other with very little differentiation, they will not invest a great deal of time and effort in searching for information. In this case, there will be no added value to obtaining more information. If consumers think that all of the brands are pretty much the same, they'll feel that their choice isn't particularly important, and it won't feel risky. So, they will not spend much time or effort into "choosing wisely."

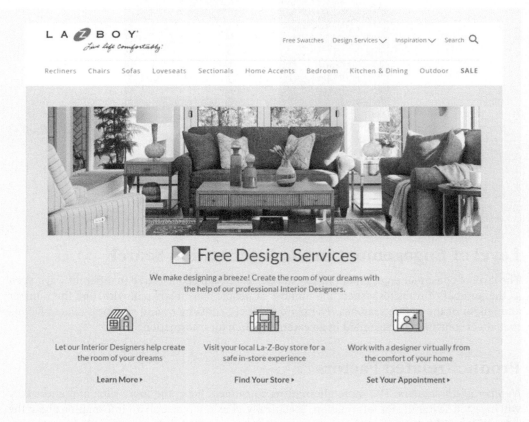

La-Z-Boy helps consumers minimize the perceived risk of making the wrong decision by offering free design services.

Consumer-related Factors

Prior experience: Research shows that consumers with a moderate level of prior experience will search for more information than those who have no experience or a lot of experience. A possible explanation for this nonlinear relationship between prior experience and the amount of information searched for is that consumers with limited prior experience are most likely to discount or even ignore products or brands that they are not familiar with. In contrast, very experienced consumers do not need more information in order to make a purchasing decision. So neither of these segments invest in as much time or effort in making the purchasing decision as the customers who are neither total novices or total experts.

Involvement: High levels of purchasing involvement will be associated with more information searches – it's natural to spend more time looking at products you care about. If the product is important to consumers, they will invest more time to make sure they make the right choice. We all want to think of ourselves as smart shoppers but maybe not for every product. For example, we will think, "There are only twenty-four hours in a day, and which brand of [product category I don't care about] doesn't matter much."

Perceived expertise: Consumers who see themselves as experts in a certain product category are more likely to invest more time and effort in information searches. Consumers will use the acquired information not just for purchasing purposes, but also to establish their expertise in the eyes of others. Even if a consumer expert isn't blogging and bragging about a recent purchase, people can and will notice, and they'll assume the consumer expert made a good choice.

Personal characteristics: Studies show that consumers who are more educated, have a higher income and are younger will engage in more information searches. Of course, these qualities are correlated with people who are online a lot, so they're savvy about where to go to find solid information.

Situation-related Factors

Time availability: If consumers feel that they need to make a rushed purchasing decision, they will do very little searching for information or might even skip this stage all together. Time constraints also increase the perceived riskiness of the purchase. Time is money!

Purchase recipient: When consumers plan to purchase a product for someone else (e.g. a gift), they are more likely to search for more information about the product. The purpose of the information search is to minimize the likelihood that the purchase will reflect negatively on the giver, indicating that he or she made a bad choice.

Availability of information: Readily available information might have opposite effects on consumers' search for information. On the one hand, a wealth of information might encourage consumers to invest time and effort in searching. On the other hand, it might have an overwhelming effect and discourage consumers from searching.

As you can see, consumers are motivated by different reasons when searching for information. As Figure 4.6 shows, purchases can vary according to the consumers' level of involvement and the frequency with which the item is bought. Marketers can impact all of these purchases using different strategies. Marketers should take these reasons into consideration and address them in their marketing messages and the information they provide to consumers.

- For example, when it comes to large, expensive purchases, marketers should highlight those elements that address consumers' perceptions about risk, such as warranties and the option to return the product.

- In the case of products with little differentiation, marketers should focus on those elements that provide consumers with added value to persuade them to choose their offerings.

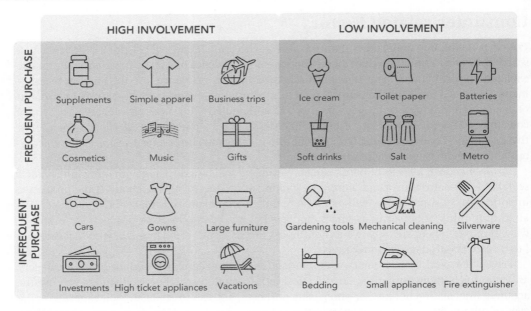

FIGURE 4.6   Level of Involvement and Frequency of Purchase

At this stage, it is imperative that marketers provide as much information as they can using both offline and online sources. A marketer's goal should be educating consumers about the available solutions to their problems, while highlighting the decision criteria that work in their favor.

In some cases, consumers engage in an ongoing search. This type of search normally is motivated by curiosity or the desire to stay up-to-date with the latest news. It's typically independent of a problem or a specific need. We are most likely to search for information about topics we are interested in, such as our hobbies (remember: high involvement).

Evaluation of alternatives is consumers' assessment of the all the product and brand options in terms of their ability to deliver the benefits that they are looking for.

Awareness set a set of brands that consumers are familiar with and are able to recall or recognize.

Total set a broader set of brands that include options that consumers are not aware of.

Do the Right Thing!

Is it "fair" to consumers or other companies when a company pays search engines, such as Google and Yahoo, to appear early in a search? The consumer decision-making process begins with problem recognition and an information search. As consumers evaluate their options, the process resembles a funnel, with the number of purchase options reduced to a few. Thus, an ad or favorable search placement presumably influences the early stages of the decision-making process in that it may persuade consumers to include, or exclude, certain brands that they might not normally have considered. Or is it "All's fair in love and branding," in that paying for a good search placement is simply enhancing consumer awareness?

Evaluation of Alternatives

How do consumers choose which brand or product to buy? Based on the information gathered in the previous stage, they evaluate all the product and brand options in terms of their ability to deliver the benefit that they are looking for.[14] Most consumers start with an **awareness set** of brands they are familiar with and are able to recall or recognize. The awareness set is normally a subset of a **total set**, a broader group of brands that include options that consumers are not aware

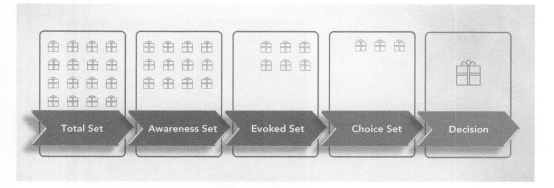

FIGURE 4.7 Alternative Consideration Process

of. They then narrow their awareness set of brands to an **evoked set** (or consideration set), which refers to all of the specific brands that consumers will consider purchasing. The evoked set typically includes very few brands, normally three to five. Consumers narrow the evoked set further to a **choice set,** which often includes two or three best options. This is the final set of brands from which consumers make a purchase decision.[15] Figure 4.7 illustrates consumers' considerations when making a choice.

Marketers need to know what it takes to get into a consumer's decision set. The kinds of factors that make consumers exclude a brand from consideration are these:

1. _Level of familiarity:_ Consumers tend to exclude or ignore brands they don't know.

2. _Prior impression:_ If consumers had a bad experience in the past with a brand, or if they formed a negative opinion about a brand (poor performance or quality), they won't consider it as an option.

3. _Brands with no special benefits:_ If consumers believe that a brand does not offer any particularly useful benefit, they'll exclude it.

4. _Poor positioning:_ Some brands are overlooked due to poor positioning and marketing messages that do not align with the consumers' shopping criteria.

5. _Social image:_ Consumers exclude brands that don't reflect who they are or how they want others to see them. They want their brand choices to be acceptable to their social groups.

These reasons for exclusion highlight how important it is for companies to be very diligent and targeted with the information they provide consumers. Lack of information or poor positioning will push consumers away.

Evaluative Criteria

What will make consumers choose one brand over another? They base their choices on one or more evaluative criteria, meaning the factors, features, or benefits consumers look for when considering a solution to their problem. A **feature** is a characteristic of the brand or product that is related to its performance. A **benefit** is a favorable outcome that is the result of the feature. It is closely related to the value the product provides consumers. For example, an office chair can be ergonomic, which is a feature of the chair. The benefit of this feature is comfort.

Evoked set
set of the specific brands that consumers are familiar with and will consider purchasing.

Choice set
often includes two or three best brand options.

Feature
a characteristic of the brand or product that is related to its performance.

Benefit
a favorable outcome that is the result of the feature. It is closely related to the value the product provides consumers.

Orion telescopes are so powerful, they let you see the stitching on the flag on the moon!

In general, evaluative criteria can be[16]

1. *Functional:* A product attribute that relates to its performance. An example is in the ad for Orion telescopes.

2. *Emotional:* What emotions does the brand evoke? Subaru, for example, relates its brand to love.

3. *Social:* This criterion is relevant for brands whose products are used publicly. For example, a TUMI briefcase is on display – is it particularly a better briefcase, or is it that the brand signals that the consumer is cool and successful?

Evaluative criteria typically reflect benefits that consumers view as desirable. They are concerned with product features only in relation to the benefits they provide. Companies will add features to enhance a product's benefits to increase its value in the eyes of consumers and make them include it in their evoke set. It is imperative for marketers to communicate the benefits of their products in relation to consumers' evaluative criteria. Furthermore, they need to highlight those criteria that work in their favor.

Normally, consumers have one or a few evaluative criteria for simple or low-involvement products, such as toilet paper, batteries, and soft drinks. However, for high-involvement products, such as cars, houses, and cell phones, consumers will employ multiple evaluative criteria. These criteria aren't weighted equally – some will be more important than others in affecting the purchase decisions.

Marketers must gather information about

1. Which evaluative criteria consumers use

2. How these criteria affect the options they consider

3. The relative importance of each criterion

Such information can direct marketers' communication strategies as to which criteria they should focus on. Information about consumers' evaluative criteria can be measured directly by asking consumers about the criteria that affect their decision-making. In some cases, these methods might not be accurate, especially when social considerations or emotions are involved. Sometimes, even when direct methods are employed and a critical criterion is identified, companies will have a hard time convincing consumers to purchase their product.

A classic example of such a situation is the long rivalry between Pepsi and Coca-Cola. Since 1975 Pepsi has held the "Pepsi Challenge," a blind taste test that is performed in public places (and recently on social media), in which consumers are presented with two cups, one with Pepsi and one with Coca-Cola. After tasting the drinks, they indicate which of them they prefer. The results tend to be in favor of Pepsi over Coca-Cola. However, despite these repetitive results, Coca-Cola sales continue to outperform those of Pepsi around the world. For Coke consumers, Pepsi is not even an option due to their loyalty to Coca-Cola.[17]

As in the previous stages, mobile technology plays an important role in the evaluation of alternatives stage and has distinct advantages over other communication channels. This technology enables consumers to evaluate alternatives anywhere at any time. How often did you see a product you wanted in a store, then you checked it out on your cell phone to make sure that you are getting the best option at the best price? Indeed, mobile technology helps consumers to enjoy the best of both in-store and online shopping experiences. In-store shopping has limitations, such as the number of product alternatives available in the store and very limited comparison of possible alternatives. Online shopping also has drawbacks. You cannot touch, feel, or try products. Mobile technology offers consumers a way to overcome these limitations and enjoy the benefits of both shopping experiences.

Mobile technology enables marketers to reach consumers both online and in store for a stronger effect. In this stage, marketers should highlight those decision criteria that will lead consumers to choose their brand and product over the competitors. As with these messages can be tailored and customized to highlight different criteria that are relevant to different target markets.

The mobile marketing tools that are relevant to this stage are

- Mobile search ads that are triggered the consumer's search and appear in search results.

- Location-based ads that enable marketers to reach consumers when they are in or near the store.

- Mobile display ads.

- Mobile app promotions that can be tailored to specific stores.

Purchase Decision

When consumers finally make a purchase decision, they use different rules to help them simplify that decision (see Figure 4.8). This figure illustrates a number of features for several cars, and explains what criteria a consumer would use to choose among the cars if they followed each of the different decision making rules. These rules are overarching guidelines that help consumers evaluate and compare product attributes and brand alternatives.

Compensatory decision rule. When consumers evaluate a brand or a product, they list all the attributes that they are interested in, and for each option they rate the brand on each of the attributes. The brand option that gets the highest score is the one the consumer will purchase. This type of decision rule allows one high-scoring attribute to compensate for or balance out a low-scoring attribute of the same brand or product.[18]

Noncompensatory decision rule. In contrast, using non-compensatory decision rules means that a high score on one attribute will not offset a low score on another attribute of the

Compensatory decision rule choosing the brand option that gets the highest score.

Noncompensatory decision rule a high score on one attribute will not offset a low score on another attribute of the brand or product.

Features				Decision Rules				
				Compensatory ##	Non-compensatory			
Brand	Price (rated high # = better value)	Good for environment? (10 = excellent)	Reliable quality? (10 = excellent)	Weights: price .5, environment .2, reliable .3	Disjunctive (e.g., price must be ≤ $30k)	Conjunctive (e.g., price < $30 AND good for environment, 7+)	Lexicographic (rate on price, then reliability)	Elimination-by-aspects (e.g., first cut is environment, then reliable)
Chevrolet Camaro	$30,995 (3)	5	5	4.0	No	No	3, not reliable No	First pass: no
Ford Mustang	$33,505 (2)	7	5	3.9	No	No	2, not reliable No	First pass: yes Second: no
Honda Accord	$27,785 (7)	7	7	7.0 Winner	Possible	Possible	7, & reliable	First pass: yes Second: yes Possible
Jeep Wrangler	$29,790 (4)	5	6	4.8	Possible	No	4, less reliable No	First pass: no
Mercedes A	$33,795 (1)	6	7	3.8	No	No	1, & reliable Possible	First pass: no
Toyota 86	$29,745 (5)	6	7	5.8	Possible	No	5, & reliable Possible	First pass: no
VW Golf	$28,595 (6)	7	7	6.5	Possible	Possible	6, & reliable Possible	First pass: yes Second: yes Possible

Compensatory = (.5 x price rating) + (.2 x environment) + (.3 x reliablity)
e.g., Camaro = (.5 x 3) + (.2 x 5) + (.3 x 5) = 4.0

FIGURE 4.8 Examples of Decision Rules

brand or product.[19] For example, if it is important to you to buy an American-made car, the fact that the foreign cars on your list of choices have better mileage per gallon or specific desirable features or benefits will not compensate for the fact that they are not made by an American company.

There are four types of non-compensatory decision rules. The first is the **conjunctive rule,** which sets up a minimum acceptable cutoff level for each criterion. Consumers will choose a product only if its attributes are equal to or exceed the minimum cutoff level of all criteria. This is the most commonly used decision rule, because it helps to manage the amount of information that consumers need to consider when making a decision. Note that this rule might result in several acceptable options. In this case, consumers will need to apply additional rules to make a final choice. A conjunctive rule is commonly used to eliminate options that are out of the individual consumer's price range, are not available in the consumer's geographic location, or are just not desirable. This rule is often employed in low-involvement purchases, where consumers are aiming for the first "good enough" option.

When companies target consumers who are using this rule, they must ensure that their products will outperform the minimum requirement for each criterion. The product does not necessarily need to have exceptional performance. It only needs to pass the cutoff level to be considered.

The second type of non-compensatory decision rule is the **disjunctive rule,**[20] which establishes a minimum level for each criterion, similar to the conjunctive rule. With the disjunctive rule, consumers will choose a product with the attribute that is equal to or exceed the minimum cutoff level of at least one criterion. For example, they will reject a computer that does not meet their minimum requirements for memory or speed.

When the target market uses the disjunctive decision rule, it is critical to surpass the consumers' requirements on at least one of the key criteria. This point should be stressed in advertising messages and on the product's package. Since the first brand a consumer evaluates that exceeds one of the requirements is often purchased, extensive distribution and dominant shelf space are important, as is understanding how consumers "break ties" if the first satisfactory option is not chosen.

The third type of noncompensatory decision rule is the **lexicographic rule,**[21] which ranks the importance of each criterion. Consumers will select the brand that performs the best based on that most important criterion. However, if two brands perform similarly based on that criterion, they will move to the second-ranked criterion to evaluate and compare them. They will continue

Conjunctive rule choosing a product only if its attributes are equal to or exceed the minimum cutoff level of all criteria.

Disjunctive rule choosing a product with the attribute that is equal to or exceed the minimum cutoff level of at least one criterion.

Lexicographic rule choosing a product based on ranked criteria from the most to the least important criterion.

down their ranking, until one brand performs significantly better than the others. This decision-making rule requires the product to perform better than its competitors on the most important criteria and requires marketers to communicate that point to consumers.

A fourth (and similar) rule is the **elimination-by-aspects rule**.[22] As with the lexicographic rule, consumers rank the importance of the criteria. In addition, they set up cutoff levels for each criterion. For a brand to be considered, it must pass the cutoff level, starting with the most important criterion and going down the ranked criteria. The rationale in this process is that consumers end up with the brand that has all of their important criteria, as well as one more. The difference between this rule and the lexicographic rule is that when using a lexicographic decision rule, consumers seek the brand that outperforms other brands. In contrast, when utilizing the elimination-by-aspects rule, they seek the brand that outperforms their threshold on the important criteria.

When targeting consumers who are using the elimination by aspects rule, companies have two options. The first is to provide superior performance in relation to consumers' requirements for their important criteria and communicate that point in their marketing messages. The second is to try to influence the ranking of the criteria, making the area in which a marketer's product excels the most important.

One of the greatest advancements over the past few years has been the development of mobile payment options available to consumers. Indeed, whether they are shopping online or in store, consumers are shifting away from cash and credit cards and taking advantage of the convenience that mobile technology provides. From 2018 to 2020, the number of mobile users doubled, reaching 800 million worldwide.[23] But not only payment options were digitalized. Cryptocurrencies, such as Bitcoin, Ether (the cryptocurrency of the Ethereum blockchain platform), and Dogecoin, are on the rise. There are now over 4000 different cybercurrencies in existence today.[24] These currencies are being adopted by companies and banks, as well as private consumers. The uses of these currencies as payment and transactional methods are evolving at a fast pace. For example, you can buy tickets to the Dallas Mavericks games using Dogecoin.

Marketers can use these digital and cyber options to make the purchase process easy and enjoyable for consumers. The mobile marketing tools that are relevant are

- Mobile wallet: a virtual wallet that stores payment card information on a mobile device.

- Mobile app promotions: incentive consumers to complete their purchase, reminding them of products left in their cart.

Consumers do not buy products. They buy product benefits.
David Ogilvy, the "Father of Advertising"

Making Decisions About a New Product

Do you like new products? Are you one of those who buys the latest model of a cell phone or computer? An exciting time for marketers is when they're launching a new product. Hopefully, good marketing research has been done to show there is a need or demand for a product, and the internal research and development team has integrated its innovative ideas with consumer feedback to create an excellent product for the marketplace. The term **diffusion of innovation** refers to the rate at which consumers adopt innovations and their spread within the market over time. A successful product is one that most consumers eventually adopt. **Adoption** reflects the level of receptiveness consumers have to new ideas, behaviors, or products.

Figure 4.9 presents the process of diffusion of innovation.[25]

Diffusion marketing researchers consider the set of consumers as roughly a normal distribution. Very few (2.5%) will be innovators, looking to buy a new product as soon as they can.

Elimination-by-aspects rule choosing a product based on ranked criteria as well as a cutoff level.

Diffusion of innovation refers to the rate at which consumers adopt innovations and their spread within the market over time.

Adoption of innovation reflects the level of receptiveness consumers have to new ideas, behaviors, or products.

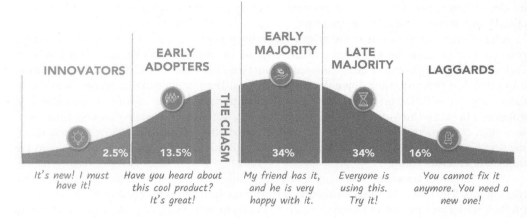

FIGURE 4.9   Diffusion of Innovation. Adapted from Rogers, E. (1962), Diffusion of Innovations, The Free Press, New York, NY. Moore, G. A. (2002). Crossing the Chasm (Revised ed.). New York: Harper Collins

Another segment (13.5% of consumers) will buy shortly thereafter, etc. The majority (early and late) form the bulk of any market, and finally some consumers (about 16%) may never show an interest or buy the new product.

Even within a target segment, there are differences among consumers in their openness to new products and ideas. Think about the different kinds of things you buy – for some product categories, you might keep an eye on what's new, say, new cell phone features, new laptop capabilities, or new fashionable haircuts. In contrast, there are plenty of things you buy for which you don't care about innovation.

When consumers are actively searching for the next new product, they are said to be **innovators** in that they're the first to buy the product and try it out. In terms of the decision-making process, they hit the problem recognition phase long before other consumers even think about such options. These consumers are motivated by the excitement that is involved in experimenting with a new product, and they are not afraid to take risks. As Figure 4.9 indicates, these consumers, also known as lead users or beta testers, are the first to adopt or buy a product. Consumer researchers find it especially helpful to identify early adopters because they can be helpful in providing feedback to the brand team to perhaps tweak the new product before a large-scale product launch to enhance the chances of success. As such, innovators are not concerned about how well a product functions. They like to be in a position where they can examine every new spec and feature of the product and provide useful feedback that will help marketers improve their product. They are also not price sensitive. On the other hand, these consumers are more "techy" in nature. Their focus is on the innovative aspects of the product and its features. They normally don't invest much effort in spreading the word about it.

Early adopters, on the other hand, provide marketers with social benefits. These consumers are also risk oriented, but not to the degree that innovators are. They will typically wait for a more finalized and reliable version of the product before purchasing it. Early adopters have the highest degree of opinion leadership relative to other categories of consumers. Their motivation to buy a new product is to establish their expertise. They will share their opinion about the product with a wide range of consumers, normally, online through social media. The opinion of early adopters is key for the new product to reach a critical mass. Early adopters can help the company cross the chasm.

The chasm is the strategic challenge companies face when trying to move from a small segment of the market (innovators and early adopters) to the mainstream and broader segments

Innovators
are consumers who are actively searching for the next new product.

Early adopters
are consumers who will typically wait for a more finalized and reliable version of the product before purchasing it.

The chasm
is the strategic challenge companies face when trying to move from a small segment of the market (innovators and early adopters) to the mainstream and broader segments of the market.

of the market. In order to do so, they need to cross the chasm between early adopters and the early majority.

Crossing the chasm is challenging because early adopters and the early majority are motivated by different needs. Early adopters are looking for "coolness" and cutting-edge features, whereas the early majority is looking for a better product, not a new product.

This means that marketers must target these two segments of the market differently. Early adopters will respond well to positioning that highlights uniqueness and coolness. The early majority will respond to positioning that demonstrates how this new product is better than other options that are currently on the market. For a product to cross the chasm, it needs to offer consumers real value – a good product that has something that consumers desire and that is significantly different from that of competitors and other options (see Chapter 2).

Early majority consumers might try the product after they see whether or not the early adopters like it. It takes consumers in this category longer to adopt a new product. While they do love new products, these consumers are risk averse and price sensitive. They want to make sure that if they spend their money on a product, it will function properly. These consumers are more followers than influencers. They will turn to early adopters to learn from their experience and opinion. If the early majority adopts the new product, it has a good chance of reaching maturity and being adopted by the late majority and eventually by laggards.

Late majority consumers are very skeptical when it comes to new products and ideas. They will be open to adopting them only after the average consumer has adopted them. Their motivation to adopt a new product may be due to social pressure or out of necessity. They must be convinced not just by the utility of the product but also by its acceptance by the larger market. This group of consumers is also very price sensitive. Deals and promotions work well with them. Marketers see this group of consumers as an opportunity to dispose of excess inventory.

Finally, there are some consumers, the so-called **laggards,** who either come to the marketplace late or might not ever buy in to a trend. Laggards are traditionalists by nature. Their motto is "Why change it if it's not broken?" They really do not like change and will often reject new products and ideas. By the time they adopt a new product, most other consumers will probably regard it as obsolete. Marketers should not invest resources in targeting this group of consumers.

Sometimes the speed of innovation can be somewhat controlled by a marketer. Figure 4.10 lists the factors that can speed up diffusion:

- *Relative advantage.* When a new product is clearly better than current products, it has an obvious relative advantage, and sales will be quick and strong.

Early majority are consumers who want to make sure that if they spend their money on a product, it will function properly.

Late majority consumers are very skeptical when it comes to new products and ideas and will adopt new products only after average consumer has adopted them.

Laggards are consumers who either come to the marketplace late or might not ever buy in to a trend.

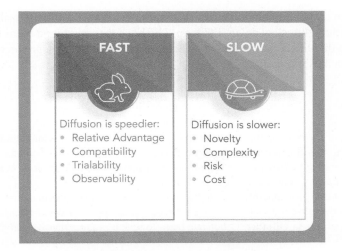

FIGURE 4.10 Product Factors Influencing Diffusion Speed

- *Compatibility.* When the new product is compatible with the behaviors, values and other products consumers currently use. For example, some electronics can easily be plugged into existing electronics (e.g. computers, phones, and music and entertainment devices), making them compatible with the user's lifestyle.

- *Trialability.* Is there an opportunity to try the new product before committing to purchasing? Test-driving a new car or sampling foods in a supermarket are two examples. Having the ability to experiment with the new product before committing to it reduces the risk in adopting it.

- *Observability.* If consumers can't try out the new product directly themselves, can they observe someone else using it? When a friend buys a new bike or tablet, you can see it (and, if the friend allows, try it out). When a friend buys a new pillow for her home, that's less observable.

There are also factors known to slow down diffusion:

- *Novelty.* Strangely enough, consumers are reluctant to adopt products or ideas that are too new, that is, those that are too remote or different from what they are using now. This is especially problematic when introducing disruptive innovations, meaning innovations that create a whole new market or product category. When Steve Jobs introduced the iPad, there was no such product on the market. To make it easier for consumers to understand this product, he created an image of it as something between a cell phone and a computer. This presentation helped consumers visualize the value of the new product and understand it.

- *Complexity.* To what degree is it difficult to understand or operate the innovation? If the item being purchased is complex, consumers won't just rush to buy it. Especially today most consumers are looking for simple, intuitive-to-operate products. Consumers do more online research when they commit to their next phone or laptop than they do when they consider a new condiment, like ketchup. If a new product is simple, it will be adopted (purchased) more quickly than if a new product is complex.

- *Risk.* If there is risk involved in the purchase, that slows down its adoption. Risk can take different forms, such as social risk. For example, you might like that style of shirt, but you're worried what your friends might think of it.

- *Cost.* How much a new product costs is important, but for a new product it's critical. So new products that are expensive (e.g. that laptop) don't fly off the shelves as fast as cheaper goods (e.g. that ketchup).

Marketers can try to highlight the factors that speed up diffusion and try to allay the fears surrounding the factors that slow down diffusion. The hope is that a brand team has thought of a good innovation that the target customers will appreciate, that the new product sales are strong, and that the launch is successful.

SUMMARY

The consumer decision-making process is one of the most important concepts in marketing. Consumers go through this process every time a need or problem is recognized, looking to satisfy or solve it by buying a product or service. As marketers, our role is to be readily available during every stage and at every touchpoint, communicating how our offering best provides the value and solution to consumers' need or problem in comparison to all other competitors" products – best features and best benefits. There are five main stages of this process that consumers complete: problem recognition, information search, alternative evaluation, purchase, and post-purchase.

In the problem recognition stage, consumers feel a tension between their actual state and their desired state. This tension will motivate them to seek a product that will satisfy their needs and solve their problems. Marketers can craft marketing messages that make such problems salient and build awareness for their products or services and how they solve such problems.

In the information search stage, consumers actively seek information, internally or externally, that will better inform their purchase decision. This stage can be influenced by product-, consumer-, and situation-related factors. Marketers should provide resources that educate consumers on how their products or offerings differentiate from competitors.

In the alternatives evaluation stage, consumers consider the many brands that are on the market. The process of narrowing down their options from a consideration set to a choice set can be influenced by evaluative criteria, such as what features and benefits each product or service offers that are most important to consumers. Marketers should highlight the critical decision criteria and emphasize the ideal placement of their product or service.

The purchase decision can be influenced by a set of rules that describe how consumers make their decisions. Compensatory decision rules can be offset by a high-scoring attribute compensating for a low-scoring attribute. A non-compensatory decision rules strategy is the opposite and does not allow for one attribute to offset another. Three variants of this concept are the conjunctive rule, disjunctive rule, and lexicographic rule. Marketers can best support consumers by communicating incentives, reassuring consumers, and connecting on a brand level.

The postpurchase stage is covered in more detail in chapter 5, but the intent for marketers is to provide customer satisfaction, so as to build and strengthen relationships with consumers, and to address any issues that occurred in the prior stages.

These purchase decision phases are modified by consumers' self-selection as innovators, early adopters, early or late majority adopters, or laggards. Market researchers like to get feedback from early adopters to enhance the likelihood of success for a product launch.

KEY TERMS

Consumer's decision-making process
Problem recognition
Actual state
Desired state
Consumers' involvement
Extensive problem-solving
High-involvement purchases
Routinized purchases

Limited problem-solving
Low-involvement purchases
Prepurchase search
Internal search
External search
Evaluation of alternatives
Awareness set
Total set
Evoked set

Choice set
Feature
Benefit
Compensatory decision rule
Noncompensatory decision rule
Conjunctive rule
Disjunctive rule
Lexicographic rule

Elimination-by-aspects rule
Diffusion of innovation
Adoption of innovation
Innovators
Early adopters
The chasm
Early majority
Late majority
Laggards

EXERCISES

1 Think about a recent product that you have purchased. Map your decision-making process (or consumer journey). Did you go through all the stages? Did you skip some stages? How long did each stage take? What would have changed your final purchasing decision?

2 Think of two recent shopping experiences you've had, where, for one, you did a reasonable amount of prepurchase information seeking, and for the other, you did very little. Why did those pre-decision or prebuying information search processes vary? How did the nature of what you were looking to buy contribute to whether you wanted to "read more about it" or just "go with it" and buy something?

3 Think of two or three items you buy frequently when you go grocery shopping that you really don't put much thought into. They are routine purchases, and you don't want to revisit the decision every time you buy. Yet what could a marketer do to shake you out of that complacency? What could they do to make you rethink your decision and buy a different brand?

4 When you are thinking about buying something, and you're trying to learn more about it, and the brands, and the options, when (for what kinds of products or services) do you go to friends for advice, versus you look at online ratings and comments posted by strangers? Are there any differences?

5 Think about your dream vacation this summer. Compare it to the dream vacation of one of your friends. What are the differences and similarities in the decision-making process of your chosen vacations? What would make you make a different choice? How can marketers affect your decision-making process and purchasing choice?

ENDNOTES

1. J. Payne, J. R. Bettman, & E. J. Johnson, "Consumer Decision Making," in *Handbook of Consumer Behavior*, ed. T. S. Robertson & H. K. Kassarjian (Englewood Cliffs, NJ: Prentice-Hall, 1991), 50–84.

2. D. Court, D. Elzinga, S. Mulder, & O. J. Vetvik, "The Consumer Decision Journey," *McKinsey Quarterly* 3 (2009), https://www.mckinsey.com/business-functions/marketing-and-sales/our-insights/the-consumer-decision-journey.

3. J. E. Burroughs & D. Glen Mick, "Exploring Antecedents and Consequences of Consumer Creativity in a Problem-solving Context," *Journal of Consumer Research* 31, no. 2 (2004): 402–11.

4. G. Laurent & J. N. Kapferer, "Measuring Consumer Involvement Profiles," *Journal of Marketing Research* 22, no. 1 (1985): 41–53.

5. P. Sharma, & B. Sivakumaran, "Impulse Buying and Variety Seeking: Two Faces of the Same Coin? Or, Maybe Not!" Association for Consumer Research Conference, 31, Toronto, Canada, 260–261.

6. R. Hamilton, & L. L. Price, "Consumer Journeys: Developing Consumer-based Strategy," *Journal of the Academy of Marketing Science* 47 (2019): 187–91.

7. https://www.beyondmeat.com/.

8. https://www.statista.com/statistics/249863/us-mobile-retail-commerce-sales-as-percentage-of-e-commerce-sales/.

9. http://erenkocyigit.com/effects-mobile-marketing-consumer-decision-making-process/.

10. B. Detlor, S. Sproule, & C. Gupta, "Pre-purchase Online Information Seeking: Search versus Browse," *Journal of Electronic Commerce Research* 4, no. 2 (2003): 72–84.

11. J. B. Schmidt, & R. A. Spreng, "A Proposed Model of External Consumer Information Search," *Journal of the Academy of Marketing Science* 24, no. 3 (1996): 246–56.

12. S. E. Beatty & S. M. Smith, "External Search Effort: An Investigation across Several Product Categories," *Journal of Consumer Research* 14, no. 1 (1987): 83–95.

13. S. Singh & J. Swait, "Channels for Search and Purchase: Does Mobile Internet Matter?" *Journal of Retailing and Consumer Services* 39 (November 2017): 123–34.

14. J. R. Hauser, & B. Wernerfelt, "An Evaluation Cost Model of Consideration Sets," *Journal of Consumer Research* 16, no. 4, 393–408.

15. N. H. Abougomaah, J. L. Schlacter, & W. Gaidis, "Elimination and Choice Phases in Evoked Set Formation," *Journal of Consumer Marketing* 4, no. 4 (1987): 67–72.

16. T. Fernandes, & M. Moreira, "Consumer Brand Engagement, Satisfaction and Brand Loyalty: A Comparative Study between Functional and Emotional Brand Relationships," *Journal of Product and Brand Management* 28, no. 2 (2019): 274–86.

17. https://www.businessinsider.com/pepsi-challenge-business-insider-2013-5.

18. N. C. Lago, A. Marcon, J. L. D. Ribeiro, J. F. de Medeiros, V. B. Briao, & V. L. Antoni, "Determinant Attributes and the Compensatory Judgement Rules Applied by Young Consumers to Purchase Environmentally Sustainable Food Products," *Sustainable Production and Consumption* 23 (July 2020): 256–73.

19. A. Aribarg, T. Otter, D. Zantedeschi, et al., "Advancing Noncompensatory Choice Models in Marketing," *Customer Needs and Solutions* 5 (2017): 82–92.

20. P. Smets, "Belief Functions: The Disjunctive Rule of Combination and the Generalized Bayesian Theorem," *International Journal of Approximate Reasoning* 9, no. 1 (1993): 1–35.

21. A. Tversky, "Intransitivity of Preferences," *Psychological Review* 76, no. 1 (1969): 31–48.

22. A. Tversky, "Elimination by Aspects: A Theory of Choice," *Psychological Review* 79, no. 4 (1972): 281.

23. chrome-extension://oemmndcbldboiebfnladdacbdfmadadm/ https://www.gsma.com/r/wp-content/uploads/2020/09/GSMA-State-of-Mobile-Internet-Connectivity-Report-2020.pdf.

24. https://www.statista.com/statistics/863917/number-crypto-coins-tokens/.

25. E. Rogers, *Diffusion of Innovations* (New York: Free Press, 1962); G. A. Moore, *Crossing the Chasm,* rev. ed. (New York: Harper Collins, 2002).

CREDITS

http://www.advertisetips.org/2020/02/morning-heres-to-best-part-of-your-day.html

https://www.adsoftheworld.com/media/print/mcdonalds_einstein

http://erenkocyigit.com/effects-mobile-marketing-consumer-decision-making-process/

https://www.angi.com/

https://appsamurai.com/mobile-banner-ad-design-tips-for-better-conversion-rate/

https://www.la-z-boy.com/

https://www.reddit.com/r/funny/comments/33rh55/this_ad_for_orion_telescopes/

Rogers, E. (1962), *Diffusion of Innovations*, The Free Press, New York, NY.

Moore, G. A. (2002). *Crossing the Chasm* (Revised ed.). New York: Harper Collins.

https://blog.clicksend.com/2017/02/mobile-shopping-give-consumers-experience-want/

Figure 4.4: DenPhoto/Adobe Stock

Image p. 60: Starbucks

Image p. 62: McDonald's Corporation

Image p. 64: AngiClothing

Image p. 65: FunMobility

Image p. 66: La-Z-Boy Incorporated

Image p. 70: OrionTelescopes & Binoculars

Post-Purchase Behavior

5

LEARNING OBJECTIVES

After studying this chapter, you should be able to:

- Understand that how a consumer thinks about your brand after a purchase is as important as the decision-making process that led to the purchase.

- Understand how companies are monitoring consumers' post-purchase behavior.

- Appreciate that marketing managers want repeat purchasing but, even more, loyalty, so they try to build and nurture relationships with customers.

- Understand consumers' behavior post-purchase, including word-of-mouth, complaints, and disposal of product.

You're on a late-night flight to meet up with friends to ski in Denver. Due to extreme weather conditions, the plane is forced to divert and land in New Mexico. It's 10:00 p.m. You and 160 other passengers are tired, hungry, and far away from your destination. This is a very common and frustrating event. What is uncommon is your pilot's reaction to the situation. Using his own money, he orders pizza for the entire plane to ease the situation.[1] How would this act make you feel? Would you fly with this airline again? Would you tell others about your experience?

Understanding Post-Purchase Behavior

The final stage in the consumer buying experience is **post-purchase behavior**.[2] This term refers to any emotions or attitudes that consumers have and additional actions that they may take after paying for their purchase. How customers feel about a purchase will significantly influence whether they will buy the product again or instead consider other brands or product options. By sharing their feelings about the purchase, consumers can influence the purchasing decisions of other consumers. Thus, consumers' experience *after* the purchase is as important as their experience before the purchase.

Marketers often mistakenly believe that if they made a sale, they served a happy consumer, who is more likely to be loyal and return to make another purchase and perhaps share their positive experience with others, in person or on social media. As we will see, these assumptions are not always correct interpretations of consumers' post-purchase behavior.

Post-purchase behavior
refers to any emotions or attitudes that consumers have and additional actions that they may take after paying for their purchase.

Consumer Satisfaction and Dissatisfaction

Satisfaction or dissatisfaction
a subjective assessment of the gap between consumers' initial expectations of the product or the purchasing process (pre-purchase) and their perceptions about the actual performance of the product or their actual purchase experience (post-purchase).

The experience consumers have with the product or service that they purchased, or even with the shopping experience itself, can lead to feelings of **satisfaction** or **dissatisfaction**. Consumers' level of satisfaction or dissatisfaction is a subjective assessment of the gap between their initial expectations of the product or the purchasing process (pre-purchase) and their perceptions about the actual performance of the product or their actual purchase experience (post-purchase).[3]

- Consumers will be satisfied if their purchase meets their expectations, which include the product's performance, looks, quality, and any other aspect they value.

- When the product exceeds consumers' expectations in a significant way, they might even feel delighted.

- Customer dissatisfaction results when the purchase experience falls short of their expectations.

Note that in some cases, even though the product has met consumers' expectations, they will not experience satisfaction. For example, let's say that you purchased an item in a discount store known for selling cheap products. You have realistic expectations about the product's quality and performance, meaning you expect little from it. Indeed, the product that you purchased broke after a short time. In this case, the product has met your expectations, but you will probably not be satisfied with it.

Cognitive Dissonance

Cognitive dissonance
a situation in which consumers question whether their buying decision was the right one.

If a product fails to meet consumers' expectations, they will feel dissatisfied, and that can lead to **cognitive dissonance**.[4] In marketing, cognitive dissonance refers to a situation in which consumers question whether their buying decision was the right one. If they think they made a wrong decision, they will experience an inconsistency between their view of themselves as good shoppers (a belief) and the reality that they made a bad decision (the action).

"Customer service shouldn't just be a department, it should be the entire company."
Tony Hsieh, founder and CEO of Zappos

Regret or buyer's remorse
happens when consumers make unfavorable comparisons between a chosen option and an unchosen option.

Cognitive dissonance might also lead consumers to feel a sense of **regret** or **buyer's remorse**.[5] Regret happens when consumers make unfavorable comparisons between a chosen option and an unchosen option. Imagine that you bought a new car. If you don't like the car, you might regret having chosen it over other car options you considered. You might also regret making the purchase compared to not buying a new car at all. In some cases, consumers can regret not making a certain purchase.

Dissatisfaction doesn't always lead to feelings of cognitive dissonance. It tends to occur in the following situations:

- When the decision is important ("I should have done more research online!")

- When the product purchased is high price, high involvement, or high risk ("It's OK, but I spent so much, I was hoping it would be better.")

- When there are multiple alternatives that offer similar or even better value ("Ugh, I should have gone with that other brand.")

- When consumers cannot back away from their decision, and it's irreversible ("I guess I'll just have to live with this.")

- When consumers have little self-confidence ("I don't know much about this product category. I guess I better ask for more advice next time.")

Since cognitive dissonance is an uncomfortable state, consumers do try to reduce it and restore consistency between their beliefs and actions. They will change whatever is the easiest for them to reduce dissonance. For example, consumers could return the product and choose a different alternative, they could complain about it to the company or to friends, or they could post negative comments about it online.

Cognitive dissonance and its negative consequences make mitigating it especially important for marketers. One proactive step marketers can take is to allow consumers to return the product. Marketers can also increase the value they offer to consumers via their products to make other options less attractive. Or they can boost consumers' self-confidence by reaching out to them after the purchase and reassuring them about their decision.

In fact, reaching out to consumers after the purchase is a good idea. Acquiring consumers is only half of the equation of a successful business. Retaining them is the other half. Building a strong base of loyal consumers is the key for any successful business. Loyal consumers spend more, they share positive word-of-mouth communications with others, and they become brand ambassadors.

Thus, marketers must be proactive in ensuring their consumers' satisfaction both before and after the purchase. Since consumers' level of satisfaction is determined by their assessment of the product in comparison to their expectations, at the pre-purchase stage, marketers need to actively manage consumers' expectations. In fact, marketers can "wow" consumers by implementing a strategy of under-promising and over-delivering with their products and services. Figure 5.1 lists common strategies marketers use to reduce their consumers feelings of dissonance.[6]

Measuring Consumers' Satisfaction

It is critical for marketers to measure and monitor consumers' level of satisfaction; it's been said, "We can't manage what we don't measure!" Nevertheless, consumer satisfaction is a difficult concept to measure. The most common way to measure satisfaction is to use the **Customer Satisfaction Score (CSAT)**.[7] Consumers are usually asked to rate their level of satisfaction on a scale of

Customer Satisfaction Score (CSAT) rates consumers' level of satisfaction on a scale of 1 to 3, 1 to 5, or 1 to 7, ranging from "not satisfied at all" to "completely satisfied," or use a five-star rating system.

01 SETTING CORRECT EXPECTATIONS
Consumers with clear expectations about the product, shipping, service, and price are less likely to experience cognitive dissonance.

02 SENDING REASSURING COMMUNICATIONS
Reassuring consumers that they made the right choice can help reduce feelings of regret and cognitive dissonance.

03 WARRANTY, EXCHANGES, AND SERVICE
Good warranty and exchange policies, as well as good service are key to post-purchase satisfaction and dissonance reduction.

04 OFFERING EASY RETURNS
Offering effortless returns almost guarantees reducing the experience of post-purchase dissonance, as it eliminates potential loss related to the purchase.

05 ASK FOR FEEDBACK
Asking for feedback can signal consumers that their experience truly matters and help reduce dissonance.

FIGURE 5.1 How Can Marketers Reduce Post-purchase Dissonance?

The most common use of CSAT.

Net Promoter Score (NPS) asks consumers to rate their likelihood of recommending the business to others on a scale from 1 to 10.

Promoters (with a rating of 9 or 10) those who give the highest ratings are the most valuable customers.

Passives (with a rating of 7 or 8) satisfied customers who will switch between brands if they find a better deal.

Detractors (with a rating of 0 to 6) the least valuable consumers for a business who may damage the reputation of the business by spreading negative word-of-mouth or writing negative reviews.

1 to 3, 1 to 5, or 1 to 7, ranging from "not satisfied at all" to "completely satisfied," or use a five-star rating system, with one star the lowest rating and five stars the highest. The CSAT measure is best used to measure satisfaction immediately after a specific consumption experience. About 80% of consumers usually report that they are "satisfied" or "completely satisfied." This means that the data are quite skewed. Can marketers really draw conclusions from this feedback about their consumers' level of satisfaction? Can they assume that 80% of their consumers will visit their business again or will spread positive word-of-mouth messages about their product or business?

One way to be more confident in the customer satisfaction score is to compare satisfied and dissatisfied customers. A popular measure of consumer satisfaction called the **Net Promoter Score (NPS)**[8] asks consumers to rate their likelihood of recommending the business to others on a scale from 1 to 10. The NPS is thought to be easy to answer because it's not asking consumers about their feelings; instead, it's asking consumers about the probability that they will take a certain action. The responses can be divided into three categories:

1. **Promoters (with a rating of 9 or 10):** Those who give the highest ratings are the most valuable customers. They are very satisfied with the product, brand, or business, feel involved with it, and are likely to advocate for it. These consumers are easy to retain. They will make more purchases and spend more money than other consumers. Promoters, as their name indicates, will promote the brand or business and refer other consumers to it, generating more revenue for the business.

2. **Passives (with a rating of 7 or 8):** These customers are also satisfied with the product, brand, or business. However, they are more prone to switch between brands if they find a better deal; they have little loyalty. Retaining them is costly, and as their name indicates, they will not promote the brand or business.

3. **Detractors (with a rating of 0 to 6):** These are the least valuable consumers for a business. In fact, they might actively damage the reputation of the brand or business by spreading negative word-of-mouth messages and writing negative reviews.

The NPS is easy to calculate. To do so, subtract the percentage of the consumers in the "Detractors" category from the percentage of the consumers in the "Promoters" category. For example, in Figure 5.2, 61.5% of the consumers fall into the "Promoters" category, and 11.6% of the consumers

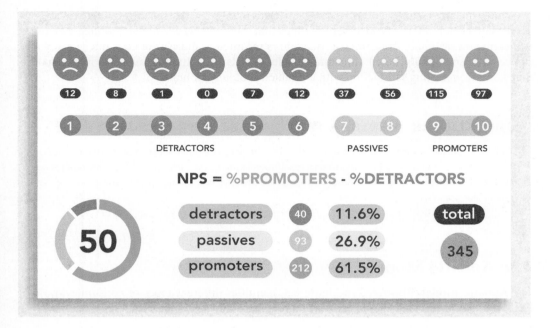

FIGURE 5.2 Net Promoter Score (NPS)

fall into the "Detractors" category. The NPS is about 50 (61.5 − 11.6 = 49.9). The NPS ranges between −100 and +100. Generally, any score above zero is good, anything above +50 is excellent, and over +70 is considered outstanding.[9]

Both CSAT and NPS are single-item measures. Marketers often use multi-item measures to assess satisfaction. The advantages of using such measures are that they provide more information to marketers, for example, not just "Are you satisfied?" but "Are you satisfied with the quality?" and "Are you satisfied with the price?" However, as surveys get longer, 80% of consumers abandon such surveys halfway through, and more than 50% will not complete a survey that takes more than three minutes to complete. This results in a very low response rate (around 9%[10]), which raises questions about the generalizability of the information derived from such surveys, that is, the validity of the takeaway.

Another common practice is to use different measures to get a more reliable picture of the consumers' level of satisfaction.

Consumer Loyalty

Consumer loyalty reflects consumers' attitudes and behaviors that indicate they really like and are loyal to a product, service, brand, or business.[11] Such behaviors include repeat purchases, preferences over other alternatives, being less price sensitive, and hopefully generating positive word-of-mouth messages. Consumer loyalty can result from high levels of satisfaction, consistently positive buying experiences, and the sense that the product or brand provides value. However, just because consumers are very satisfied with a product, service, brand, or business doesn't mean they are loyal to it. You might buy a product, be very satisfied with it, and still prefer a different product to it (it's just that, say, the alternative costs a lot more). Therefore, marketers need to measure consumer loyalty independently from satisfaction and not assume that a purchase indicates loyalty.

Consumer loyalty reflects consumers' attitudes and behaviors that indicate they really like and are loyal to a product, service, brand, or business.

While consumer loyalty and consumer satisfaction are related terms, they are distinct. Consumer satisfaction refers to consumers' feelings that their need is adequately fulfilled by a product, company, or brand. Consumer satisfaction is regarded as a driver of consumer loyalty and can be more emotionally based. Consumer loyalty reflects an attitudinal and behavioral response that stems from feeling satisfaction with a product, company, or brand.

CONSUMERS' SATISFACTION ON SOCIAL MEDIA

Marketers rely heavily on social media to gather insights into customer satisfaction of brands. Social media provides marketers with unparalleled reach to customers. As such, measuring and monitoring customers' satisfaction on social media is an extremely effective way to understand customers' view of a particular brand, product, or service.

The Apostle Model

Apostle model identifies different types of consumer loyalty.

Loyalists or apostles consumers who are very satisfied and very loyal to the brand or business.

Mercenaries consumers who are also satisfied with the brand or business. However, they will switch between brands.

The **Apostle model**, illustrated in Figure 5.3, identifies different types of consumer loyalty.[12] Each segment has its own characteristics and requires a different approach.

Loyalists – Also called apostles, these are consumers who are very satisfied with your products, brand, or business. They make repeat purchases and are loyal to your business. These are your most valuable consumers. They will spend more on your product, share positive word-of mouth messages about it, and be your best promoters. These consumers will ensure the growth and success of your business.

Mercenaries – These consumers are also satisfied with your product, brand, or business. However, they will switch between brands. These consumers are usually price sensitive. They will look for the best offer and bargain. They are also impulse buyers and will pursue trends and fads. They have little attachment to any particular brand, and they would be expensive to attract and difficult to keep.

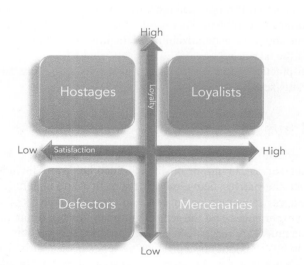

FIGURE 5.3 The Apostle Model

Hostages – These consumers are not satisfied with your product, brand, or business. Even though they might be repeat customers and continue purchasing from you, their behavior does not reflect satisfaction. They probably do so because they have no alternative options or the cost of switching is high. They can easily turn into defectors.

Defectors – These are consumers who either purchased from you once, had a negative experience, and are no longer your consumers or they never purchased from you but still have strong negative opinions about your products. They buy other brands, and they try to convince others to do so by spreading negative word-of-mouth about your products, brand, or business.

Marketers should use different strategies with each of these groups of consumers. By doing so, they can improve the loyalty of their satisfied consumers and sometimes even transform negative complainers into promotors.

- With loyalists a.k.a. apostles, marketers need to build long-term relationships and show their appreciation to these consumers. Apostles who promote your brand by spreading positive word-of-mouth messages deserve special treatment and customer service. Marketers who pay attention to these groups will see a good return on their efforts.

- Since mercenaries are motivated by the desire for good deals, it is important to communicate to this group the value of the brand and its benefits. However, marketers should remember that mercenaries will switch between brands, so they should not invest too much effort in retaining them.

- Regardless of the reasons why hostages are still customers, marketers should try to understand their needs and their source of dissatisfaction, and address them if possible. There is a chance that these consumers could become loyalists or at least mercenaries if their sources of dissatisfaction are addressed. However, for this group, marketers should be mindful of not spending too much effort in improving the satisfaction level of these consumers.

- Defectors are often motivated by a bad experience. Marketers should address such situations promptly and effectively. They should try to understand the source of the bad experience and address it or compensate the consumers if possible. Situations like that also give the company an opportunity to really delight the consumers with their response. While most companies cannot delight or "wow" consumers on a regular basis due to cost considerations, they might be able to do so in cases of service failure. Such actions will not only increase consumer loyalty but also minimize the spread of negative word-of-mouth messages. And, of course, the bad experiences are a learning opportunity for the company – Are there changes that could be made to lessen the probability that the problem will arise again?

Clearly, loyal consumers are the backbone of any successful business. Beyond repeat purchases, more spending, and the sharing of positive word-of-mouth communications, loyal consumers offer a wide range of benefits to any business. They are less susceptible to competitors' messages, more open to new products and services, and more likely to provide honest and helpful feedback that will help improve business practices and even offer ideas for new products. Loyal consumers tend to stay and even defend businesses in bad situations and during scandals. They will also actively counter negative reviews from other consumers. Finally, these consumers are the most cost-effective ones for any business. A Bain & Company study showed that in financial services, for example, 5% increase in consumers' retention leads to at least a 25% increase in profits, given that these retained consumers are likely to spend 67% more on the business's products and services.[13]

Hostages
consumers who are unsatisfied with the brand or business even though they are repeat consumers.

Defectors
unsatisfied consumers who will never purchase from the business again but still have negative opinions about it.

In the United States, 40% of online shopping revenue comes from repeat customers, who make up only 8% of site visitors.

Measuring Consumer Loyalty

Just as it's important to measure consumer satisfaction, it is also critical to measure loyalty. There are several common measures for doing so.[14]

Loyal customer rate
number of repeat consumers divided by the total consumers the business has.

Loyal customer rate (also referred to as the repeat purchase ratio) is the most basic measure of consumer loyalty. The loyal customer rate is calculated by identifying the total number of consumers who visited the business in a certain time period (e.g. a month, a quarter, or a year), then identifying the number of consumers who made more than one purchase during this time period, and dividing the number of repeat consumers by the total number of consumers in that time period. For example, if you have 100 consumers, and 27 of them are repeat customers, your loyal customer rate is 27%. There are many variants to this measure. You can measure the percentage of customers that purchase three times or more from you, for instance. Shoppers who purchase from a business three times or more are 54% more likely to continue shopping there.[15] You can also measure this for any time period, such as yearly, monthly, or weekly.

Customer lifetime value (CLV)
refers to the total revenue that a business can expect a single customer to generate over the entirety of his or her relationship with the business.

$$\text{Loyal Customer Rate} = \frac{\text{Number of Repeat Customers}}{\text{Total Customers}}$$

Customer acquisition cost (CAC)
reflects the cost of acquiring a single consumer.

Customer lifetime value (CLV) refers to the total revenue that a business can expect a single customer to generate over the entirety of his or her relationship with the business.[16] The CLV accounts for **customer acquisition cost (CAC)**, which reflects the cost of acquiring a single consumer, including marketing expenses, operating expenses, and the fixed costs associated with manufacturing and selling the product. (In subsequent years, the company expends customer retention costs, but these tend to be much smaller than acquisition costs, partly because the company can connect directly to known, acquired, customers.)

The ratio between CAC and CLV indicates the return a business should expect from investing to acquire a new consumer. Successful companies normally maintain a 1:3 ratio of CAC to CLV. In other words, for every dollar they invest in acquiring a new consumer, they can expect to earn $3 in return.

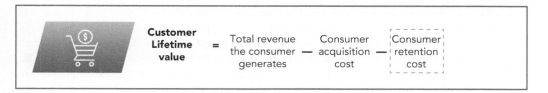

$$\text{Customer Lifetime value} = \text{Total revenue the consumer generates} - \text{Consumer acquisition cost} - \text{Consumer retention cost}$$

The **churn rate** reflects the percentage of consumers that stop purchasing products or services from a business during a certain time period. A churn rate of 5% or less is considered to be good. The formula below indicates how the churn rate is calculated. Companies should monitor their churn rate constantly to proactively address problems if they see the rate begin to inch upward, which indicates that the company is failing to retain its customers. Note that the churn rate can be calculated for any time period.

Churn rate reflects the percentage of consumers that stop purchasing products or services from a business during a certain time period.

For example, if you had 5000 consumers at the beginning of 2021, and 200 of them stopped shopping at the end of that year, then your business churn rate for 2021 is 200/5000 = 0.04, which, when converted to percentage, is 4%.

$$\text{Churn Rate} = \frac{\text{Shoppers at the end of the period}}{\text{Shoppers at the beginning of the period}}$$

Loyalty Rewards Programs

Loyalty rewards programs are a structured marketing tool for fostering long-term relationships with consumers by rewarding them for repeat purchases and loyal buying behavior. A customer loyalty program provides incentives to get customers to buy again and again. These programs are designed to incentivize consumers to make frequent purchases and to show a preference for the company over its competitors by offering consumers discounts, special offers, points toward future rewards, or free products. They make consumers feel appreciated and valued by businesses.

Loyalty rewards programs a structured marketing tool for fostering long-term relationships with consumers by rewarding them for repeat purchases and loyal buying behavior.

It is estimated that the global worth of loyalty programs is over $250 billion in value.[17] A 2017 Accenture study showed that in the United States, about 90% of retail companies use loyalty rewards programs, and 77% of all US consumers participate in them. Loyalty programs are considered a very effective marketing tool for businesses. They increase the companies' profitability, make their consumers feel good about their purchases, and enable brands and businesses to connect better with their customers. In addition, about 73% of consumers who are members of a loyalty program will recommend the business to others, will spend about 5–20% more, and will increase a business's revenue by 5–10% on average. Loyalty rewards programs are so common that consumers expect businesses to offer them, and consumers often determine the value of a brand or a business by the program and the rewards it offers.

Loyalty rewards programs have another important benefit for marketers. They enable businesses to collect important information about their consumers, including their demographics, purchases, frequency of purchases, changes in purchasing habits, and preferences. This information is very valuable to the company and sometimes as a resource to be sold to other companies. Such information helps companies predict market trends and demands, and guides pricing and promotional planning. And when strategically leveraged, it can help businesses earn a larger **share of wallet**,[18] that is, the percentage of disposable income that customers spend with one business.

Finally, loyalty rewards programs provide businesses with direct access to their consumers, making marketing communication much easier – the company knows who the customers are. Using attractive offers and promotions, businesses can target different segments of consumers more effectively and introduce new products or services more easily. Many companies will offer customized promotions and offers to individual consumers based on their purchasing habits and interests. This direct line of communication also helps companies issue recalls if needed.

Of course, nothing is perfect, and loyalty programs have disadvantages for companies as well. We've seen that just because consumers buy a specific brand does not necessarily indicate that they are loyal. Some consumers will enroll in a loyalty rewards program primarily for the rewards. These programs can be very costly for companies. In fact, most companies do not know how to effectively price and utilize them, and they lose money operating the programs. In addition, because loyalty programs are so common, they are undifferentiated and appear identical across brands. Companies struggle to offer unique programs that will enhance their value and provide them with a competitive advantage.

Another disadvantage of loyalty programs is that businesses use them to predict future demand based on historical purchasing behavior. However, consumers' lifestyles, needs, interests, preferences, and shopping behavior change over time. Making strategic decisions based on historical data may prove detrimental. In addition, loyalty rewards programs are affiliated with a specific firm and do not provide companies with data about the purchasing habits of their consumers from competitors. This means that companies have a rather limited picture of their consumers' actual shopping behaviors and will need to complement the information gathered by using other resources, such as industry-level purchase data.

Businesses can draw on a wide variety of loyalty programs, each with different advantages and disadvantages.[19]

- **Cash back** or **rebate programs** offer customers the option to earn money back from their purchases, normally in the form of a percentage of their total purchases during a certain period of time. From the consumers' perspective, this type of program is easy to understand, and consumers do not need to make any changes in their buying habits. From the company's perspective, this kind of plan can be expensive to implement. Cash back programs are very common among credit card companies.

- **Discount programs** offer consumers a fixed discount on the retail price of any given item. These programs are also very easy to understand, and they provide consumers with the instant gratification of the discount. However, from a business perspective, they may give customers the impression that the regular prices are too high. Sephora and Ulta both offer discounts to their loyal customers.

- **Frequency programs** are simple programs that reward consumers for a certain amount of purchases. For example, Biggby Coffee gives consumers a free cup of coffee for every 12 purchases of coffee. These programs use paper punch cards or, increasingly, the customer's cell phone to track the customer's visits.

- **Points programs** reward consumers with points, usually proportional to the amount they spent. These programs can be harder for consumers to follow. Many consumers simply forget

---

Share of wallet
the percentage of disposable income that customers spend with one business.

Cash back or **rebate programs**
offer customers the option to earn money back from their purchases, normally in the form of a percentage of their total purchases during a certain period of time.

Discount programs
offer consumers a fixed discount on the retail price of any given item.

Frequency programs
simple programs that reward consumers for a certain amount of purchases.

Points programs
reward consumers with points, usually proportional to the amount they spent.

about the points that they have accumulated and become inactive members of the loyalty program. Thus, companies need to remind consumers of their status and encourage them to continue their activity in the program. From a company perspective, these programs are easy to manage and control, and they also help avoid the tactic of discounts. Starbucks' loyalty rewards program gives consumers two stars (points) for every $1 spent and double bonus stars for more frequent customers.

- **Tiered programs** are more elaborate. These programs incentivize consumers to stay engaged on a consistent basis over time. The tiers are normally determined by the amount spent over a period of time. The more consumers spend, the higher the tier and rewards that are associated with it. For these programs to be effective, the rewards must be very attractive, especially in the higher tiers. The tiered system also provides consumers with a sense of superiority and accomplishment when they reach a higher level. However, demoting consumers from a high tier to a lower tier due to a decline in their spending can backfire and aggravate consumers. Managing tiered programs is more intensive than the other programs, and determining the cutoff of the tiers and the rewards given can be tricky. Airline loyalty programs typically are tiered.

Tiered programs programs that incentivize consumers to stay engaged on a consistent basis over time.

Delta Air Lines partners with American Express to offer prestigious tiered loyalty rewards program.

Measuring the Effectiveness of Loyalty Rewards Programs

The biggest challenge that companies face when managing loyalty rewards programs is to make sure that they are in fact effective in achieving their strategic goals. There are three common measures that help companies assess the effectiveness of their loyalty rewards programs.[20]

Participation level reflects the percentage of consumers from the total consumers of a business who enroll in the loyalty rewards program. A low enrollment might indicate that the program is not attractive enough to consumers – they don't see any value in it. It might also indicate that the business has not been able to secure its customers' loyalty, which is a much more serious problem.

Participation level the percentage of consumers from the total consumers of a business who enroll in the loyalty rewards program.

$$\text{Participation Level} = \frac{\text{Number of program members}}{\text{Total number of consumers}}$$

Of course, consumers' enrollment in a loyalty rewards program does not provide marketers with a full picture about the attractiveness of the program. Think about all the loyalty programs that you are enrolled in and never actively use. On average, an American family will be enrolled in 17 different loyalty rewards programs, but are active in less than 50% of them. For that reason, marketers also look at engagement rate.[21]

Engagement rate
the percentage of consumers who use the program out of the total number of consumers a business has.

1. **Engagement rate** reflects the percentage of consumers who use the program out of the total number of consumers a business has. Engaged consumers are those who redeem their rewards by cashing in their points, free offers, or rebates. Engagement rate gives marketers a better indication about the attractiveness of the program because the measure tells them how many consumers are redeeming the rewards.

$$\text{Engagement Rate} = \frac{\text{Number of consumers who engage}}{\text{Total number of consumers}}$$

Redemption rate
the percentage of rewards that were cashed in from all the rewards that were issued.

2. **Redemption rate** simply reflects the percentage of rewards that were cashed in from all the rewards that were issued. A high redemption rate suggests that the loyalty program is successful, and the consumers view it as providing real value to them. Ideally, the redemption rate should not be lower than 20%. This measure focuses on the number of rewards redeemed (not the number of consumers who redeemed their rewards – that's the engagement rate).

$$\text{Redemption Rate} = \frac{\text{Number of redeemed rewards}}{\text{Number of rewards issued}}$$

Word-of-Mouth Messages and Complaints

Word-of-mouth
an exchange of information between consumers about products, services, brands, experiences, promotions, deals, and anything that is consumption related.

Another expression of consumers' satisfaction is their inclination to talk about their purchases. Consumers love to talk about their purchases, regardless of whether they were good or bad. Take a look at your friends' Instagram posts. How many of them have posts about the recent movie that they streamed, the restaurant they dined at, or their latest purchase? **Word-of-mouth** is the provision and exchange of information between consumers about products, services, brands, experiences, promotions, deals, and anything that is consumption related.[22] Word-of-mouth messages can be oral or written, direct or indirect, online or offline. For many consumers, talking

Viral marketing
Leveraging social media networks to deliver and spread a company's message. Very similar to word-of-Mouth Marketing.

Buzz marketing
Using a specific marketing trigger (an event, activity, Commercial) that generates publicity, excitement, and conveys Information to the consumer, either online or Offline.

Referral marketing
A deliberate, systematic tactic that encourages current Consumers to recommend the product or brand to their Network, and thus helps grow the business' customer base.

Blog marketing
Promoting a product or service via a blog. It can be a Company blog, influencer blog or a brand ambassador blog. The blog content will be shared by its followers.

Social media marketing
Strategically utilizing variety of social media platforms to Connect with consumers to build a brand, promote a product, Increase awareness, facilitate sales, or drive website traffic.

Influencers and opinion leaders marketing
Leverage the expertise and influential abilities to gain Access to their followers and to communicate brand or Product messages to this targeted audience.

FIGURE 5.4 Terms Closely Related to Word-of-mouth Communication

about their purchases is part of their shopping experience. Figure 5.4 shows the terms that are closely related to word-of-mouth communication.

Research shows that consumers like to share positive word-of-mouth messages because doing so makes them look good, knowledgeable, and up to date. Nevertheless, negative word-of-mouth communication can be more influential with a stronger impact on consumers' behaviors. Think about a time that you searched for a product on Amazon. When you looked at all of the product's reviews, which reviews did you read first – the positive ones or the negative ones?

Overall, word-of-mouth is very influential. In fact, 92% of consumers report that they trust recommendations from friends and family more than advertising, and 88% of consumers trust online reviews as much as they trust recommendations from personal contacts. Furthermore, when making a purchasing decision, 74% of consumers reported that word-of-mouth recommendations from others played a major role in their choice.[23]

Some consumers who generate word-of-mouth can become very influential – they're often even called influencers, market mavens, or opinion leaders. Sometimes these consumers are experts, say, with a blog where they post their opinions about new products, such as when a car expert blogs about new models or a computer expert says something about new laptop models. Sometimes these people are influential due to their celebrity, whether it's related to the product or not, such as consumers following (or rejecting) certain celebrities' blogs about fashion.[24]

Sometimes companies can identify those influencers and make new product lines available for their consideration. The company is risking the possibility that the influencer might not like the new product, of course, but if the influencer can endorse the product, the company has just earned millions of positive exposures. According to the Word-of-Mouth Marketing Association (WOMMA), there are two types of word-of-mouth communication: organic and amplified.[25]

Organic word-of-mouth
unsolicited communication between individuals about a product or a service.

Amplified word-of-mouth or **word-of-mouth marketing (WOMM)**
consumption-related communication that is strategically solicited and promoted by companies as part of a planned marketing effort.

Organic word-of-mouth communication that is unsolicited communication between individuals about a product or a service.

Amplified word-of-mouth communication is a consumption-related communication that is strategically solicited and promoted by companies as part of a planned marketing effort. This type of word-of-mouth communication is also referred to as **word-of-mouth marketing (WOMM)**. In many cases, amplified word-of-mouth communication sparks organic word-of-mouth communication, if it is very successful.

Marketers can influence both forms of word-of-mouth communication. Organic word-of-mouth will reflect the company's effort to foster consumer satisfaction and relationships, and respond attentively to concerns and critiques. Amplified word-of-mouth will reflect marketers' efforts to create communities, provide tools and platforms for consumers to share their experiences, motivate influencers to promote their products and brands, create unique and interesting marketing triggers that will spark buzz or go viral, and actively track consumers' online conversations and sentiments. Reports indicate that WOMM is very effective, as it drives $6 trillion of annual consumer spending and is estimated to account for 13% of consumer sales.[26]

Word-of-mouth marketing offers other benefits to marketers than just extending their market reach and increasing sales. First, given that consumers often actively block marketing messages, such as commercials, ads, and marketing calls, using word-of-mouth marketing helps companies reach these consumers. Social networking and referral programs enable companies to expand their reach to broader target markets. Second, it's important to remember that consumers regard word-of-mouth communication as very trustworthy. Utilizing word-of-mouth marketing and influencers helps companies create trust with their prospective consumers and delivers their message in an authentic way. Third, word-of-mouth marketing enables small firms with limited resources and market reach to connect with potential consumers and build brand awareness in a relatively low-cost way.

Nevertheless, word-of-mouth marketing has some disadvantages as well. First, it is often slow to spread. Unless the content goes viral, it might take a long time for the marketing messages to reach consumers and have a real effect. Second, word-of-mouth marketing might be limited in its reach to consumers. This is especially true for small businesses with a small consumer base. Third, it is very hard for companies to track word-of-mouth marketing and assess its effectiveness. Finally, companies have very little control over word-of-mouth marketing. While the company might initiate a certain marketing message, it cannot control how consumers interpret it or transmit it to other consumers. The result could be negative feedback that the company can do little to change.

Complaints

Complaints
expressions of dissatisfaction with a product or a service made to the provider of that product or service.

What do consumers do if they are unhappy with their purchase? **Complaints** are expressions of dissatisfaction with a product or a service made to the provider of that product or service. Normally, when companies see very few complaints, they take it as a sign of consumer satisfaction. However, that may not be the case. Reports indicate that only one out of 26 consumers will actually complain. About 67% of consumers who have one bad experience with a company or a brand will simply abandon the company. And more than 90% of consumers will walk away from a company or a brand with whom they had two or three bad experiences. These consumers will not complain; they will just walk away. Surprisingly, consumers who take the time to complain are usually those who care about the company and are loyal to its brand.[27]

These statistics suggest that consumers' complaints can be an asset to a companies. They present an opportunity for companies to obtain valuable information about areas that need improvement. They are also an opportunity for companies to rectify the situation, address the source of dissatisfaction, and retain those customers. Consumers who have a satisfactory resolution of their complaint are likely to share their positive experience with others, more likely to repurchase, and less likely to switch to other brands than those who feel their complaint was handled badly, especially if they feel that the company did over and above to compensate them.

Companies should actively identify potential sources of complaints and address them immediately partly because today's consumers have more options than ever before. For example, consumers can express their dissatisfaction with regulatory agencies, the media, and other consumers. Consumers can even be motivated to take legal action if deemed necessary. Thus, managing consumers' complaints is a critical task for companies. They should also determine which consumers are more likely to complain and why.

Do the Right Thing!

Companies are often discouraged when their customers post negative reviews and complaints online. Sometimes the customer has a legitimate complaint, and the company can try to fix it. Sometimes the customer is just a whiner. Managers can then be tempted to edit or block such postings. Don't do it. First, those whiners can post elsewhere where you don't have control. Second, not being transparent reflects badly on the company, as if it has something to hide. Third, trust the rest of your customers and potential customers to spot a nonstop complainer. We've all read customer reviews of products that we (as customers, with no affiliation with the company) find ourselves thinking, "Wow, that customer is a whiner!"

Disposal of Products

This chapter is about the post-purchase phase of consumer buying, and mostly we've discussed themes about customer satisfaction or dissatisfaction. We close this chapter with a different consideration – after the purchase and consumption, what else does the consumer do?

What do you do with a product that you no longer need or want? Do you throw it away? Recycle it? Give it to someone else? Donate it? Resell it? **Disposal of products** reflects the process of getting rid of unwanted or used products, or any waste that is associated with them (e.g. their packaging). It is the last action consumers take in the decision-making process.[28]

Figure 5.5 shows different ways that consumers use to dispose of their unwanted products.[29] The decision to dispose of a certain product is a function of the consumers' attachment to that product. If we view our possessions as an extension of who we are, we can develop an emotional attachment to some of them. The stronger the attachment is, the harder it will be for us to dispose of these products. For example, we might dispose of clothing items that do not fit us anymore, are out of fashion, or are in bad condition. But most women will keep their wedding dress for years as a symbol of that meaningful event. Some will pass it along to their daughters as a wedding ritual.

Sometimes consumers will be motivated to discard their possessions due to external circumstances, such as moving or downsizing. And sometimes consumers just are not using products, but they have not decided whether or not to dispose of them. In such cases, they may decide to store them and postpone their decision. The average American normally uses his or her garage

Disposal of products reflects the process of getting rid of unwanted or used products, or any waste that is associated with them (e.g. their packaging).

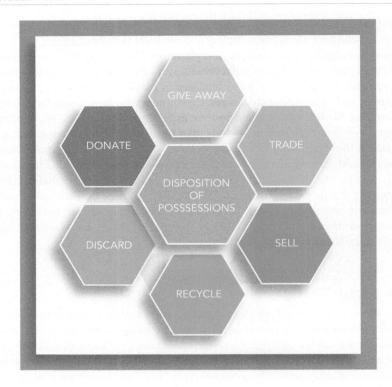

FIGURE 5.5   Forms of Disposition of Possessions

Hoarding disorder
the excessive
accumulation of
items, regardless of
their value or the
consumer's need for
them.

to store possessions that are not in use, either old or new. In extreme cases, for some consumers, the disposal of possessions is exceptionally hard. They become so attached to their possessions that they cannot bring themselves to get rid of them. This is known as a **hoarding disorder,**[30] which leads to the excessive accumulation of items, regardless of their value or the consumer's need for them.

In recent years, consumers have begun to place more importance on how they dispose of products. The harmful impact that our consumption culture has on the environment has motivated both consumers and companies to be more diligent in the disposal of products. Today, 72% of consumers prefer to buy from ethical and sustainable brands.[31] Companies are aware of these concerns. Many have taken measures to reduce the environmental impact of their business by making their products recyclable or by using recyclable materials in their products, as well as by finding ways to reduce the polluting effect of their production processes. We will discuss recycling in more detail in Chapter 15.

Another market trend that has developed as a result of consumers' concerns about the environment is the reuse of products. Today, many consumers would prefer to sell or donate their unwanted products as a way to minimize waste. Multiple platforms, such as Craigslist, Thredup, Poshmark, and Facebook Marketplace, have developed in recent years to offer consumers easy ways to do so, in addition to the traditional venues of garage sales and flea markets. The resale market is expected to reach $64 billion in the next five years. This is a growth rate that is 25 times faster than traditional retail over the past three years.[32] As such, some retailers have started to incorporate resale experiences into their businesses, enabling them to gain additional revenue from this trend. Finally, consumers can also donate their unwanted items. Over half of Americans reported that they donate clothing, food, or other personal items to charity.[33]

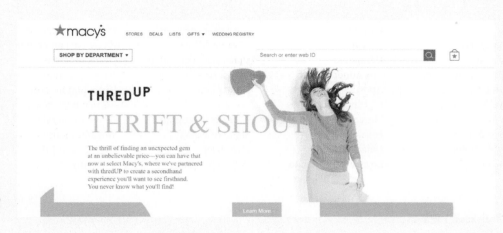

Macy's partnered with the Thredup to offer consumers a secondhand shopping experience in its stores.

SUMMARY

During the post-purchase behavior stage, consumers can experience emotions and attitudes such as satisfaction or dissatisfaction resulting from the experience with the product or service that they purchased or even with the shopping experience itself. This process is a subjective assessment that implicitly compares their initial expectations of the product and their perceptions about the actual performance of the product.

Two common measurement techniques of consumer satisfaction are the Customer Satisfaction Score and the Net Promoter Score. Measuring and monitoring satisfaction is critical because marketers can gain valuable insights into subsequent purchase behavior and make data-driven business decisions.

Consumer satisfaction and consumer loyalty are related terms, but they are distinct. Therefore, marketers need to measure consumer loyalty independently from satisfaction and not assume that a purchase indicates loyalty. One way of segmenting consumers based on loyalty is the Apostle model, which identifies four segments of consumers according to their satisfaction levels: loyalists, mercenaries, hostages, and defectors. Three common measurements of consumer loyalty are loyal customer rate, customer lifetime value, and churn rate.

One way for companies to encourage repeat purchases and loyal buying behavior is to develop consumers' loyalty rewards programs. These programs foster long-term relationships by incentivizing consumers with discounts, special offers, points, or free products. The downside is that these programs can be costly, and most companies fail to price and use them correctly, resulting in significant operation costs. Examples of loyalty programs businesses implement are cash back or rebate, discount, frequency, points, and tiered programs. Three common measurements used to assess the effectiveness of loyalty rewards programs are the redemption rate, engagement rate, and participation level.

Word-of-mouth marketing can take many forms, such as viral marketing, buzz marketing, referral marketing, blog marketing, and social media marketing. This type of marketing communication can be classified as organic, which is unsolicited, or amplified, which is promoted by companies. Consumers who are very good at word-of-mouth communication are called influencers, market mavens, or opinion leaders, and companies frequently want to find them and encourage their support of the brands.

Finally, the chapter considered how consumers dispose of products, which is partly a function of their attachment to a product. With consumers becoming more concerned with their ecological footprints, companies are shifting their strategies to incorporate environmentally friendly products and sustainable processes that minimize waste. Products may be reused by selling or donating them to benefit another consumer.

KEY TERMS

Post-purchase behavior
Satisfaction
Dissatisfaction
Cognitive dissonance
Regret
Buyer's remorse
Customer Satisfaction
   Score (CSAT)
Net Promoter
   Score (NPS)

Promoters
Passives
Detractors
Consumer loyalty
Apostle model
Loyalists or apostles
Mercenaries
Hostages
Defectors
Loyal customer rate

Customer lifetime
   value (CLV)
Customer acquisition
   cost (CAC)
Churn rate
Loyalty
   rewards programs
Share of wallet
Cash back
Rebate programs

Discount programs
Frequency programs
Points programs
Tiered programs
Participation level
Engagement rate
Redemption rate
Word-of-mouth
Organic word-of-
   mouth

Amplified
   word-of-mouth
Word-of-mouth
   marketing (WOMM)
Complaints
Disposal of products
Hoarding disorder

EXERCISES

1. Is there anything you buy where you are an extremely loyal supporter of the brand, even a brand zealot? What did the brand or company do to get you there – why do you like it so much? Conversely, have you ever had a purchase that was so bad, you promised yourself you'd never buy that again? What was it and why was your experience so bad?

2. Think about the last time you bought something that made you very satisfied as a customer. Did you post a positive comment online? If not, why not? Conversely, think of a recent bad experience. Did you post a negative comment online, and if not, why not?

3. Think of all the loyalty programs you're enrolled in – through your phone apps or cards. Which do you use frequently (and why) and how do you think the programs compare? For the loyalty programs you don't use a lot, what could the company do to entice you to buy more and engage with their loyalty program more?

4. Think about a recent purchase that you made, and you were not happy about. How can the company reduce your cognitive dissonance? Will you purchase from this company again?

5. On average, most companies report that 25% of their customers are unsatisfied. What can companies do make their consumers more satisfied? Think about the recourses that companies must invest in order to increase their consumers level of satisfaction. Under what conditions should companies stop trying to make their customers more satisfied?

6. "The customer is always right!" Do you agree with this statement? Explain your position on this statement.

ENDNOTES

1. https://www.cnn.com/travel/article/delayed-passengers-pizza/index.html.

2. M. C. Gilly and B. D. Gelb, "Post-purchase Consumer Processes and the Complaining Consumer," *Journal of Consumer Research* 9, no. 3 (1982): 323–8.

3. J. L. Giese and J. A. Cote, "Defining Consumer Satisfaction," *Academy of Marketing Science Review* 1, no. 1 (2000): 1–22.

4. J. Cooper, "Cognitive Dissonance: Where We've Been and Where We're Going," *International Review of Social Psychology* 32, no. 1 (2019): 7.

5. Harold Sigall, "Buyer's Remorse: The Consequences of Your Decisions," *Psychology Today*, August 17, 2017, https://www.psychologytoday.com/us/blog/wishful-thoughts/201708/buyer-s-remorse.

6. https://summitafricarecruitment.co.za/2020/08/17/causes-low-staff-turnover.

7. Qualtrics, "Customer Satisfaction (CSAT) Surveys: Examples, Definition and Template," https://www.qualtrics.com/experience-management/customer/satisfaction-surveys.

8. R. Owen, "Net Promoter Score and Its Successful Application," in *Marketing Wisdom*, ed. K. Kompella (New York: Springer, 2018), 17–29.

9. https://www.blueprnt.com/2018/09/17/net-promoter-score; F. F. Reichheld, "One Number You Need to Grow," *Harvard Business Review* 81, no. 12 (2004): 46–54.

10. https://www.genroe.com/blog/acceptable-survey-response-rate-2/11504.

11. R. L. Oliver, "Whence Consumer Loyalty?" *Journal of Marketing* 63, no. 4 (suppl 1) (1999): 33–44.

12. T. O. Jones and W. E. Sasser, "Why Satisfied Customers Defect," *Harvard Business Review* 73, no. 6 (1995): 88.

13. chrome-extension://oemmndcbldboiebfnladdacbdfmadadm/ https://media.bain.com/Images/BB_Prescription_cutting_costs. pdf.

14. Steve Smith, "How to Measure Customer Loyalty—12 Crucial Loyalty Metrics to Follow," *Loyaltylion*, May 21, 2019, https:// loyaltylion.com/blog/guest-post-how-to-measure-customer-loyalty-12-crucial-loyalty-metrics-tofollow#:~:text=Loyal%20 customer%20rate%20(LCR)&text=To%20measure%20your%20 loyal%20customer,customers%20in%20the%20same%20period.

15. https://blog.smile.io/repeat-customers-profitable.

16. P. Jasek, et al., "Comparative Analysis of Selected Probabilistic Customer Lifetime Value Models in Online Shopping," *Journal of Business Economics and Management* 20, no. 3 (2019): 398–423.

17. https://www.pymnts.com/news/loyalty-and-rewards-news/2017/ fis-svp-bob-legters-talks-retail-loyalty-in-the-age-of-ecommerce.

18. https://hbr.org/2011/10/customer-loyalty-isnt-enough-grow-your-share-of-wallet.

19. https://www.incremental.com.au/blog/different-loyalty-programs.

20. chrome-extension://oemmndcbldboiebfnladdacbdfmadadm/ https://www.loyalty360.org/Loyalty360/media/ResearchAnd ReportDocs/11-19-15_CrowdTwist_ROI_HowTo_WEB.pdf.

21. https://info.bondbrandloyalty.com/loyaltyreport-2021.

22. https://www.invespcro.com/blog/word-of-mouth-marketing.

23. https://www.nielsen.com/us/en/insights/article/2012/consumer-trust-in-online-social-and-mobile-advertising-grows.

24. https://www.superoffice.com/blog/customer-experience-statistics.

25. Word of Mouth Marketing Association, "Organic vs. Amplified Word of Mouth," 2004, retrieved March 30, 2011, http://womma. org/wom101/4.

26. https://www.invespcro.com/blog/word-of-mouth-marketing/#:~: text=Did%20you%20know%20word%20of,brand%20recommended %20by%20a%20friend.

27. M. C. Gilly, and B. D. Gelb, "Post-purchase Consumer Processes and the Complaining Consumer," *Journal of Consumer Research* 9, no. 3 (1982): 323–8.

28. J. L. Lastovicka and K. V. Fernandez, "Three Paths to Disposition: The Movement of Meaningful Possessions to Strangers," *Journal of Consumer Research* 31, no. 4 (2005): 813–23.

29. J. L. Lastovicka and K. V. Fernandez, "Three Paths to Disposition: The Movement of Meaningful Possessions to Strangers," *Journal of Consumer Research* 31, no. 4 (2005): 813–23.

30. D. Mataix-Cols et al., "Hoarding Disorder: A New Diagnosis for DSM-V?," *Depression and Anxiety* 27, no. 6 (2010): 556–72.

31. https://newsroom.accenture.com/news/more-than-half-of-consumers-would-pay-more-for-sustainable-products-designed-to-be-reused-or-recycled-accenture-survey-finds.htm.

32. https://www.cnbc.com/2020/06/23/thredup-resale-market-expected-to-be-valued-at-64-billion-in-5-years.html.

33. https://nonprofitssource.com/online-giving-statistics.

CREDITS

www.target.com

Jones, T. O., and W. E. Sasser, "Why Satisfied Customers Defect." *Harvard Business Review,* November–December 1995.

https://www.ndm.net/ecm/pdf/13926.digital_index_loyal_shoppers_ report.pdf

https://www.delta.com/us/en/skymiles/airline-credit-cards/american-express-personal-cards

https://www.macys.com/social/thredup

Figure 5.1: oatawa/Shutterstock

Figure 5.2: https://www.blueprnt.com/2018/09/17/net-promoter-score

Image p. 82: stas11/Shutterstock

Image p. 86: RSplaneta/Shutterstock

Image p. 89: Delta Air Lines, Inc.

Image p. 95: Macy's, Inc.

6

The Irrational Consumer: Biases and Situational Effects on Consumers' Decision-Making

LEARNING OBJECTIVES

After studying this chapter, you should be able to:

- Understand consumers' cognitive biases and irrational decision-making.

- Recognize how marketers can strategically leverage consumers' biases and effectively nudge them in the directions of their brands.

- Discern that numerous situational factors can affect consumers' choices.

- Identify consumer segments based on biases and differences in purchasing decisions.

Imagine you are at a movie theater, and you want to buy popcorn. The theater offers two sizes of popcorn buckets: a small bucket for $3 and a large size for $7. Considering these two options might lead you to the conclusion that the larger option is too expensive, as it is more than twice the price of the small one, and really, all you need is the smaller bucket for your own personal needs. Makes sense?

Let's assume that instead of two sizes of popcorn buckets, the theater offers three sizes: a small bucket for $3, a medium size for $6.50, and a large one for $7. When considering this new set of options, the large bucket of popcorn looks like a deal. In this case, most consumers are likely to choose the large bucket. As a marketing strategy, the medium-size option serves as a decoy intended to sway consumers' preference toward the large size.[1]

The Irrational Consumer

That example shows us that consumers do not always follow the rational decision-making steps presented in Chapter 4. The rational model posits that consumers identify a need or want, they create a consideration set of potential brands to buy, and they compare the brands by their attributes. The brand that is perceived to be better than the others on most of the attributes that the consumer cares about is the brand that is selected for purchase. The rational model of expected utility means that the selected brand is the one that consumers expect will give them the most utility, or value; in plain English, they'll like it the most.

THE DECOY EFFECT

DECOY

SMALL $3	LARGE $7

LARGE $7	MEDIUM $6.50	SMALL $3

Scenario A   *Scenario B*

The decoy effect.

In many situations, consumers use heuristics, or mental shortcuts, to guide them in their decision-making.[2] We will see that while doing so helps consumers make decisions more quickly, the problem is that the decision might not be very well "thought through" leading to what looks like irrational decision-making and unintended consequences.

Irrational does not mean that consumers are crazy; it only means they are not using the classic rational model. Furthermore, *irrational* does not mean that consumers cannot be predictable.[3] In fact, the notion that consumers are rather predictable in their irrationality and how they process certain kinds of information is what this chapter is about. There are numerous cognitive patterns that psychologists and behavioral economists have identified that induce predictable patterns of human behavior. This chapter covers decision dilemmas and related behaviors that marketers need to understand and can use strategically. It presents the concepts that are most useful to marketers, for marketers to watch out for in their own judgments and to consider in their customers' likely behaviors. In addition, there are several situational factors that marketers must understand that can prompt certain patterns in consumer thinking, so we'll discuss those as well. Let's start with understanding what heuristics and mental shortcuts are.

Heuristics and Cognitive Processing

A **heuristic** is a simplifying strategy that provides a shortcut in decision-making.[4] For example, for some product categories, consumers are brand loyal. They don't want to rethink whether their go-to brand is really the best for them. Instead, they've decided that their brand is sufficient, it does the job, maybe they even like it. Similarly, even for consumers who don't consider themselves "cheap" and who may have some money, for some product categories, the consumers are price sensitive. For example, if the purchase is in a product category they don't care much about, they may decide that they don't need to spend a lot. These cues – brand and price – are heuristics in that they provide a guiding principle to consumers in making purchasing decisions without having to rethink them every time.

Psychologists and behavioral economists talk about different cognitive systems that operate when consumers are doing rational decision-making versus using heuristics. Figure 6.1 shows

Heuristics simplifying strategies that provide shortcuts in decision-making.

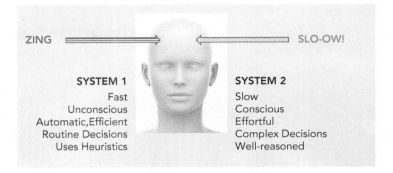

FIGURE 6.1 Thinking Systems 1 and 2

System 1
the information-
processing style
that operates when
consumers are using
heuristics.

the comparison of thinking system 1 and system 2. **System 1** is the information-processing style that operates when consumers are using heuristics – it is quick, not cognitively effortful, and probably little information search goes on. By comparison, **system 2** is the cognitive processing style of the decision-making model described in Chapter 4, the full-blown expected utility models, and in-depth thinking processes.[5] It's thorough, takes time and effort, and probably results in more precise evaluations.

A simple example for the differences between these systems relates to driving skills. Remember when you first started driving? You were consciously thinking about all the elements of driving (system 2), such as looking in the rearview mirror and using the turn signal. However, with time the elements of driving became almost automatic, unconscious (system 1). You don't have to consciously think about looking in the mirror. You simply do it with little thinking.

System 2
the cognitive rational
processing style of
decision-making.

These cognitive systems are also a bit fluid in the sense that consumers who are making decisions important to them, who perhaps should be using effortful system 2 thinking to formulate their choice, might revert to system 1 thinking, if, say, they're facing time pressure in making the purchase. Notice that if an effortful system 2 process should be used, and the quick system 1 is used instead, the consumer might come up with a result that seems suboptimal, at least compared to expected utility, going the route of system 2. It might nevertheless be optimal in the consumer's mind in the sense that it's the best decision the consumer could come up with under the time constraints involved. It is simply important to recognize that the heuristics might influence or even bias the consumer decision-making outcome.

Next, we discuss the factors that relate to the purchasing decision that might trigger the use of heuristics and mental shortcuts, the types of heuristics that consumers use that marketers should understand, and the situational factors that affect the use of these heuristics.

Importance and Difficulty in the Purchasing Decision

There is no doubt that the importance and the difficulty of the purchase will have a tremendous effect on the likelihood of consumers to take mental shortcuts. Tons of research indicates that the effort required of the rational expected utility decision-making model is typically expended when the decision is important to the consumer. Important can mean a lot of things, of course. An easy way that a consumer can make a brand choice is by simply buying the brand they bought last time. If the purchase is good again, they may keep buying that brand. If the purchase is unsatisfactory, the consumer will be unhappy, and that state of unhappiness with the brand might prompt consumers to think about switching brands. If so, consumers face making the decision about brand choice all over again, almost as if they hadn't been previously loyal to a brand. They have to start the decision-making process all over again.

Obviously, many factors can influence whether consumers perceive a particular brand choice as easy or difficult. For example, think about consumers making routine purchases versus new purchases where circumstances required something that is not typical. We discussed the differences between these two purchases in length in Chapter 4. For example, consider a typical trip to the grocery store. On the shopping list is toothpaste. This product is one that consumers buy regularly, it's not expensive, it's not that complicated, and the risk seems low. Consumers wouldn't be motivated to do extensive product comparison searches with every purchase, whether going online or studying the retailer's shelfing labels or the toothpaste package labels. Who has time for that – to reconsider a brand choice in every product category every time you shop for products you don't even care that much about? Instead, for such a routine purchase, consumers would put the brand of toothpaste that they usually buy into their shopping cart, an almost thoughtless exercise.

Customer Segment Differences in Purchasing Decisions

As we learned in Chapter 4, the importance of the purchasing decision will be reflected in consumers' level of involvement. Different consumers have different levels of involvement even when purchasing the same product (for example, some people might care more about their toothpaste choice than others). Because of this, marketers can leverage consumers' level of involvement, which is an internal factor that may result in irrational decision-making, as a segmentation tool.[6] Customers with low involvement basically don't care about purchases. Their decisions are often repetitive, straightforward, and have low risk; they are easier to make than high-involvement decisions. The more important a decision is to consumers, the higher is their involvement. The level of involvement is subjective and will change from one consumer to another – for example, some people purchasing a laptop may just hope that it's reliable, it enables the work they need to do, and it's not too expensive. In contrast, techies and gamers would be highly involved in such a purchase because their computers are a more integral part of their lives and identities.

Customer involvement is frequently correlated with other customer attributes. For example, techies just naturally spend more time learning about new tech products and features, and they'll consult blogs and experts for recommendations on products and brands. As a result, high-involvement customers tend to have greater expertise and more familiarity in the product category. Because highly involved consumers are more knowledgeable, they are also usually more confident in their buying decision. The differences between easy and difficult decision-making are summarized in Figure 6.2.

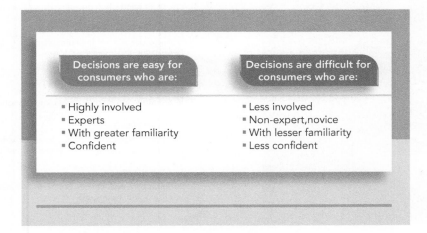

FIGURE 6.2   Ease of Decision for Different Customer Segments

So, the question is, do consumers engage in the extensive, effortful, rational decision-making process for easy and difficult purchase decisions, and for everything they purchase, whether it's high or low involvement? Of course, not. Unfortunately, the opposite of the word *rational* is *irrational*, but that's not actually accurate. Consumers aren't actually irrational or stupid (well, most aren't). Their decision-making may be perfectly rational, but if they don't care about the purchase that much (it's not important or it's low involvement), they may use a heuristic to help them make decisions instead of the complicated decision-making expected utility model.[7]

Heuristics and Potential Decision-Making Biases

Cognitive bias
a systematic error in the way we think and process information when making a decision.

There are numerous heuristics that decision makers use, any of which might result in some bias depending on the context. **Cognitive bias** is a systematic error in the way we think and process information when making a decision. The heuristics and biases that matter most to marketers follow. You can see additional biases in Figure 6.3.

The Compromise Effect

Decoy effect
a situation in which consumers are more likely to change their preference between two options when a third option is presented to them that makes one of the options more attractive.

The popcorn choice example given at the opening of this chapter demonstrates the notion of the **decoy effect**,[8] which refers to a situation in which consumers are more likely to change their preference between two options when a third option is presented to them that makes one of the options more attractive. In the case of the popcorn buckets, the large option asymmetrically dominated the medium option, leading consumers to choose the more expensive option. Marketers can also use the decoy effect to make consumers choose the middle option by utilizing the compromise effect.

Compromise effect
a situation in which consumers will be more likely to choose a middle option of a selection set and avoid choosing extreme options.

According to the **compromise effect**,[9] consumers will be more likely to choose a middle option of a selection set and avoid choosing extreme options.[10] This is an example of an environmental cue that may result an irrational decision-making. Let's see how it works. Imagine that

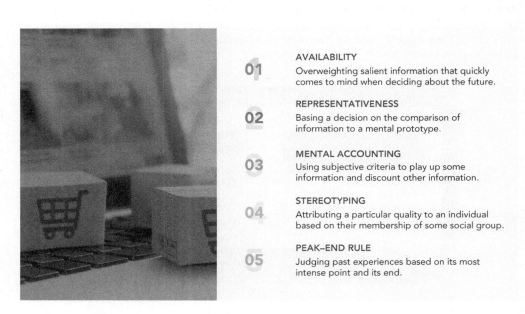

01 AVAILABILITY
Overweighting salient information that quickly comes to mind when deciding about the future.

02 REPRESENTATIVENESS
Basing a decision on the comparison of information to a mental prototype.

03 MENTAL ACCOUNTING
Using subjective criteria to play up some information and discount other information.

04 STEREOTYPING
Attributing a particular quality to an individual based on their membership of some social group.

05 PEAK–END RULE
Judging past experiences based on its most intense point and its end.

FIGURE 6.3 Additional Consumer Biases

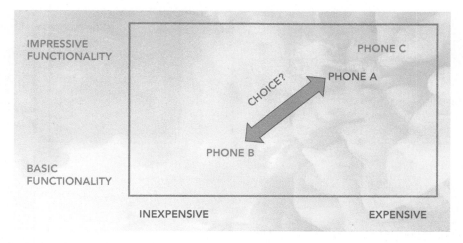

FIGURE 6.4 The Compromise Effect

you are looking to buy a new cell phone. The brand that you are considering has two versions of its newest model. Option A is more expensive and has better functionality, and option B is less expensive and with much less functionality. Which one would you choose? Well, if you care more about the phone's bells and whistles, you will choose option A. If you care more about the price, you will choose option B. But can marketers affect your decision?

Let's imagine that instead of two options, you had three, as presented in Figure 6.4. Option C is even more expensive and has more functionality than option A. When considering all options, option A seems like the best deal. When a consumer sees a wider array of phones, that new perspective makes option B seem less attractive since it has so little functionality. And option A seems relatively less expensive (less than C anyway). The company is happy if it sells option C, but it's mostly trying to nudge[11] consumers from the cheaper option B to the more expensive option A. (You can nudge a friend by bumping them shoulder-to-shoulder. In this context, the nudge is mental, a slight bump to encourage consumers to think of some features of a brand rather than others.)

In the compromise effect, the introduction of a more extreme product creates a contrast so that the middle option – the compromise – seems like the most rational choice and therefore the most desirable. In this case, the extreme option serves as a decoy. The effect is widespread, and you'll see it everywhere now that you know to look for it. Consumers reliably process information in this way, and companies reliably take advantage of that mindset.

Framing

Framing is probably the marketers' most frequently used cognitive positioning tool. **Framing** involves the interpretation of information, which depends in part on how it is presented; the context of the information helps shape the meaning and how the message is received.[12] For example, in the grocery store, ground beef is labeled "85% lean" because it makes you think, "Excellent! Mostly lean!", whereas a mathematically equivalent label of "only 15% fat" leaves the impression of that last, lingering word: *fat*. Mind you, in taste tests, beef marbled with greater fat is rated juicier and tastier (to nonvegans), or, as the marketer would say, "It offers a better taste experience." But who wants to introduce more fat into their diet?

Framing
the interpretation of information, which depends in part on how it is presented.

85% LEAN VS. 15% FAT

Framing is used across product categories. In sexual reproductive health care, various forms of birth control for men and women are said to be "99% effective." Health supplements are frequently touted with similar frames, such as "In testing, 90% of patients showed no major adverse symptoms," because it would be a downer to say, "In testing, 10% of test patients got rashes and migraines."

Anchor and adjust early information that consumers see helps to set the context against which new information is compared.

An effect that builds on framing is called **anchor and adjust**.[13] In this concept, marketers know that the early information that consumers see helps to set the context against which new information is compared. Then, as new information comes in, the consumers' attitudes might adjust more or less favorably. For example, suppose you go car shopping online or at a dealership. The first price you see on the car you want becomes the frame. Your perception of the car's price is now anchored at that value. As pop-up sales bots or salespeople offer deals, your price

shop me now

original price ~~99.50~~ *price now* **$49.50** ✓

Presenting the original price helps setting up the attractiveness of the new price.

valuation of the car starts shifting as you consider what deals might exist to help bring the price down as well as which add-ons you'd like and for which you'd be willing to pay more.

Anchoring and adjusting is a great marketing tool to encourage consumers to spend a bit more than they had anticipated. Think about media streaming plans, or cell phone minutes and data plans. There typically are inexpensive basic plans and many options of more expensive upgrades. Consumers aren't stupid; if they get talked into a more expensive package, they know they're paying more, but they can see clearly that they're getting more than what they would have gotten with a basic plan.

Reference Dependence or the Role of a Comparison

Part of how framing works is by getting consumers to think about their current status. The consumers' status quo becomes the comparison point from which marketers can suggest change.

For example, think of your various memberships, say, $59 a month for your health club access and $129 annually for Amazon Prime. Suppose you got an email in December announcing that next year's rate was going up 10%, but because you had been a member for more than a year, your rate would stay the same. You would feel good about the company (the gym or Amazon) because you dodged the rate increase. It might seem odd because in reality nothing has changed, but the company has induced your positive response because it reminded you of your current rate (your status quo or reference point), showed you an alternative reality that was undesirable (price increase), and then rescued you from that scenario. A year from now, when the company really does raise its rate, you'll think, "Well, at least I had a 'free' year without the price increase."

The notion of **reference dependence**[14] is simply that when consumers evaluate options or outcomes, it's hard to do so without comparing it to something.[15] That comparison value is the reference point. If the outcome looks better than the current reference level, it is called a **gain**; if the outcome is worse than the reference, it's called a **loss**.

Gains and Losses and Prospect Theory

Reference dependence is often described by comparing a positive or negative frame, that is, a gain or a loss relative to a consumer's status quo.[16] Here is a thought exercise to point out how perceived gains feel different from perceived losses.

Imagine that you found a $20 bill on the sidewalk as you were about to enter an office building. No one is around, the 20 bucks is yours, free and clear. On the 0 to 10 scale you see here, how would you rate that $20 find? Now, imagine that you're sipping a coffee at an outdoor cafe. You reach to pay the bill with cash (the cafe's phone app is down), and your $20 bill gets picked up by a breeze and floats quickly out into busy traffic. Bottom line, you're not going to see that $20 again. You reach back into your pocket because you still have to pay the bill. How would you rate that experience, on a scale from 0 to 10?

Typically, people report a +2 or +3 when finding the $20 and a −4 or −5 when losing the $20. The $20 is the same, but the loss feels worse than the gain feels good: the loss feels "really bad," whereas the gain feels only "pretty good." Figure 6.5 shows these perceptions in graph form. The theory is called **prospect theory** because it examines people's perceptions of their prospects or expected outcomes, and its most famous tagline is "Losses loom larger than gains."[17] In the figure, the perceived value (vertical axis) of the $20 gain is positive, but the perceived value of the $20 loss is far more negative (all relative to the 0−0 point, which is the reference).

Note that in the figure, a traditional economic prediction would be that the relationship would simply be the dashed line – that is, the $20 find would be as far up as the $20 loss would be down. But the relationship is not linear because that's not how people think. Also notice that even if the money found were a bit more than $20, the curve doesn't shoot up very fast – the curve shows **diminishing marginal utility**; that is, the increase in value or utility is rather small after the initial boost.

Reference dependence
using a reference point when evaluating options or outcomes.

Gain
when the outcome looks better than the current reference level.

Loss
when the outcome looks worse than the current reference level.

Prospect theory
examines people's perceptions of their prospects or expected outcomes.

Diminishing marginal utility
the increase in value or utility is rather small after the initial boost.

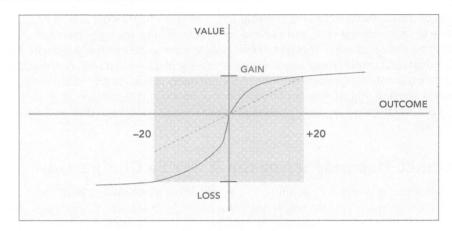

FIGURE 6.5   Prospect Theory: Losses Loom Larger Than Gains

Loss aversion
the idea that, relative
to the status quo
or reference point,
nobody wants to
suffer a loss.

Status quo bias
the notion that we'd
rather do nothing
than make a change
that could go bad.

Endowment effect
see more value in
things that we own.

This reliable finding – that losses feel worse than gains feel good – also relates to **loss aversion**, the idea being that, relative to the status quo or reference point, nobody wants to suffer a loss. Many people tend to be less oriented toward seeking gains than trying to avoid something bad. This fear can be paralyzing, sometimes resulting in **status quo bias**, the notion that we'd rather do nothing than make a change that could go bad. It is also related to the **endowment effect**,[18] that once we own something, we seem to value it more. Retailers take advantage of this idea when they offer a free return policy – few customers take them up on the returns because they've held the items in their hands; that is, they've owned, or have been endowed with, the items. Whatever we have now is preferable to the future unknown.

Another element of the endowment effect reflects the way we value products we own versus comparable products we do not own. Specifically, we will place higher value on products that we own compared to products that we do not own.

We tend to value things
more once we own them.

The status quo bias and endowment effect also seem to drive reactions by consumers who are asked to **opt in** or **opt out**[19] of various programs (they choose to be involved in the program or they don't). Marketers have looked at decisions in such diverse settings as financial investments and blood and organ donation choices. For example, let's say an employer offers health-care plan A as its default, and employees wishing to be covered under plan B must opt out of A and actively enroll in B. Few decide to switch out. It's easier to stay with the status quo; after all, it seems to have worked OK so far.

Opt in or **opt out** encourages consumers to enroll (or unenrolled) in various programs.

Opt in: Sign up here to subscribe!

A status quo mindset seems to be the concept underlying the **sunk cost fallacy**.[20] The sunk cost fallacy is our tendency to continue a behavior because we already invested time, effort, or money into it, regardless of whether or not the current costs outweigh the benefits. For example, suppose a company has been pouring money into a new product development project. Unfortunately, even with all the new product improvements, test markets are indicating that consumers are not warming to the idea. As a result, the company should probably end the project, but that's really hard to do. The reference point is that the company has been working on the project and has already "sunk" that much money into it. That commitment makes it difficult to walk away from all that sustained effort and resources. It's a fallacy because more money continues to be spent – throwing good money after bad.

Sunk cost fallacy the tendency to continue a behavior because we already invested time, effort, or money into it, regardless of whether or not the current costs outweigh the benefits.

One last twist on the experience of gains and losses is the role of **certainty and uncertainty**. Basically, when it comes to gains, certainty is preferred to uncertainty, whereas for losses, uncertainty is preferred. The comparisons usually take some form like this: As an example of certainty with gains, what would you prefer: $10 or flip a (fair) coin for a 50% chance at $20 (and a 50% chance at $0)? The economist's friend, expected utility, would say those expected values are the same.[21] However, most people would opt for the certain $10. For uncertainty with losses, which would you prefer: to have to pay $10 to get into an event or flip a (fair) coin for a 50% chance at having to pay $20 (or you get in for free)? For these loss or payout scenarios, people seem to want to take their chances; after all, it is not certain they will lose anything. Companies sometimes

Certainty and uncertainty being sure (or unsure) about an outcome.

experiment with uncertainty in loyalty programs, for example, when consumers buy five cups of coffee to get one free cup, versus buying five cups of coffee to get a free gift at the store, which may be a coffee or a tasty treat or a free lunch or a nice mug or a reusable shopping bag with the retailer's logo. The certainty lies in the fact that the consumer will receive something, but there is uncertainty regarding the particular gift, and that adds a little excitement.

Nonconscious Information Processing

Thus far we have focused on ideas involving marketers presenting explicit information in certain ways to consumers. Yet marketers can also activate more subtle, nonconscious triggers that can persuade consumers and influence their decisions and choices. Consider the following: You've been looking at prices online for a new pair of running shoes. You're trying to decide among Adidas, New Balance, and Nike, but the cookies on both your laptop and phone are sending you pop-up ads for Asics shoes. How annoying! Why do companies do that? That doesn't work, does it? Would it affect your purchase decision?

Here's what's operating with pop-up ads that you think you're barely paying attention to. The ads are making an impression at least nonconsciously, that is, below the radar. It's like the old idea of subliminal ads – running a millisecond ad in the middle of a movie to persuade you to go buy popcorn. Here, the pop-up ads (or ads in streaming content that you can't click through, or billboards you pass every day on your commute) are liminal – you can see them. The ads are getting into your brain through **mere exposure**.[22] As its name suggests, consumers are merely exposed to the ad. They aren't consciously engaged in thinking about the ad, but the ad appears again and again, and this repetition gives consumers a sense of familiarity. **Familiarity**,[23] through these multiple exposures, is helpful to marketers because familiarity breeds attraction – we like what we know, and something that is familiar seems like a less risky purchase proposition.

Mere exposure effect establishing familiarity via repetitive exposure.

Familiarity feelings of knowing something.

Heterogeneity level of individual differences.

Consumer Segments

For almost everything that marketers do, it is worth remembering that not all consumers are the same. Across the marketplace, consumers will exhibit **heterogeneity**, that is, individual differences, at least from segment to segment. In any given product category, some segments are brand loyal, and others are price sensitive. These features – brand quality and price – are in fact two of the most important heuristics marketers face. The marketers seeking to encourage consumers to switch and try their brands, or to spend more, must convince consumers that doing so will be to their benefit.

Some people simply like to shop. They like to learn a lot about brands and the comparative strengths and weaknesses of the options. Some people like to shop particularly for good deals; these aren't necessarily price-sensitive consumers – they might pay quite a bit for something, but they'll do so because they believe it's a good deal, it's worth it. Some people like to then share their opinions and expertise, in real life but more often through social media. They like being perceived as an influential consumer, a position they've earned through their extensive searches and thinking about how the brands line up. For such consumers, the rational decision-making model of Chapter 4 seems more relevant than the numerous heuristics discussed in this chapter. Of course, the opposite is true for consumers shopping in product categories they don't care much about: they'll rely even more extensively on heuristics, which they deem useful because, at the least, they'll save time and not have to think extensively about something they see as relatively unimportant in their lives.

Consumers also differ with respect to their attitudes about risk.[24] Many consumers are highly risk averse, whereas others may be risk seekers, being more adventurous in their decision-making and choices. For these consumers, the shape of the function in Figure 6.3 is slightly modified. For risk-averse consumers, the slope at the left is even steeper, because they really prefer safety, and losses freak them out. Conversely, for risk seekers, the slope at the right might be lifted, so that even a bit more incremental gain might make them a lot happier than other consumers.

> *"Everything in life has some risk. What you have to do is learn how to navigate it."*
> *Reid Hoffman, cofounder of LinkedIn*

Many of the cognitive mindsets began with the notion of reference dependence. Recall that a gain or loss was interpreted relative to something else. The usual comparison is the consumer's current state, but other referents can enter into the assessment as well. For example, consumers might look to their friends or coworkers for cues as to acceptable brands. We'll discuss the effects of social and cultural factors in Chapter 9. Alternatively, consumers might have in mind certain expectations that a particular purchase can help them achieve some personal goal, so those hopes become their reference point, and their happiness with the brand depends on those expectations. We discussed expectations and resulting experiences of customer satisfaction or dissatisfaction in Chapter 5.

Situational Factors

A consumer's purchase is an intricate combination of the consumer's own needs and wants, the marketer and the brand communications, and the situation in terms of a specific time and place that set the context of the decision-making. We've focused a lot in this chapter on how a consumer thinks; now let's focus more on understanding how the situation a consumer is in helps to explain the consumer's behavior. That is, if consumer decisions depend in part on situational factors, let's examine the most important ones. These include elements of time and seasonality, a consideration of who the purchase is for, ambient characteristics of retail settings, and, generally, the antecedents or precursors to the purchase.

Time: Time Crunch and Seasonality

One of the most important situational factors facing consumers as they navigate their shopping decisions is how much time they have to allocate to do so. For some purchases, there may be plenty of time to plan, but occasionally there may be a time crunch, which might arise for a variety of reasons. Consumers might be distracted by the busyness of their lives, for example, and not pay close attention to their Outlook calendars, then are surprised to see that a friend's birthday is coming up quickly. Even for consumers who plan ahead, a time crunch could arise when there is a problem with a retailer, for example, if an item is out of stock or the delivery options aren't fast enough.

Recall from Chapter 4 that sometimes consumers put a lot of thought into their decisions, for instance, when they are highly involved in the product category because they care a lot about the item they're about to purchase, or in the current context, because they have more time to plan and consider options. If so, consumers will engage in relatively detailed, more prolonged analysis, comparing brands feature by feature.

In contrast, when consumers don't want to exert as much cognitive effort, such as when a purchase is less important to them, or in this case, when consumers are experiencing a time crunch, they may make decisions and choices using heuristics. For example, consumers may decide to emphasize high-quality brands or value pricing when making a choice, without regard to other attributes. When heuristics kick in, the hope is that consumers can still make reasonably good (albeit not perfect) decisions. In addition, such consumers may be more susceptible to marketers'

BIASES ON SOCIAL MEDIA

In online shopping, think of how often you've seen a chart like this. A retailer offers its options online and puts a box around one option and labels it, "Our most popular plan." It's not quite peer pressure, but you start to think – well, how could all those other people be wrong? OK, I'll go with option 2!

efforts to nudge them toward a brand. The lack of time induces a situation that simulates the nudging scenario – in this case, it's not that the consumers don't care, it's that they don't have the time to put as much detailed processing into the decision, so they take a shortcut.

Convenience stores, such as 7-Eleven, and stores that are attached to gas stations provide all kinds of "must-have" products for people on the run. The snacks and foods are priced higher than in a grocery store because the attribute of the purchase that dominates is that consumers can get in and get out quickly, whether they're on the road or just running errands. Convenience stores arose to meet the need of perceived time crunches, and consumers are willing to pay the price premiums that in other circumstances they might not.

Similar to the appeal of convenience stores, think of all the goodies stocked within reach when checking out at a grocery store. Store managers know it is tempting to put a candy bar or a tabloid from the rack onto the belt for purchase. Such impulse purchasing is being hurt a bit by self-checkout. These lanes tend to not have the stacks of convenience items because the shopper is too consumed with the process of checking out. Thus, when consumers purchase more and line up for a checkout agent, they may purchase some of the last-minute impulse items, whereas when they purchase less and check themselves out, they are not exposed to the same opportunities, nor would they likely indulge.

Seasonality establishing familiarity via repetitive exposure.

A different kind of situational effect that also revolves around timing is **seasonality**.[25] Seasonality reflects a predictable trend in consumers' purchasing decisions and demand. It is well

FIGURE 6.6 Seasonal Patterns

known that the sales of toys pick up toward the end of the year in preparation for the holidays. But it turns out that many more purchases show peaks and ebbs throughout the year due to the relevance of the purchases for the particular season. For example, hot chocolate appeals more to consumers during the winter, and ice cream is more popular during the summer. It's not that consumer tastes change, it's that the situation has.

Figure 6.6 shows a variety of purchases and times that their sales peak. It's true that many toys are sold in November and December, but it turns out that a lot of jewelry is bought then as well. Chocolates and candies are purchased from October in preparation for Halloween through December, and sales pick up again right before Valentine's Day in February. Families wishing to visit theme parks must wait until the children are out of school, so the prolonged summer vacation months are the most popular (though, of course, theme parks see predictable attendance lifts during non-summer holidays as well). Soft drinks are sold in greater quantities throughout the heat of the summer. The end of summer and early fall see an uptick in sales of school and office supplies. There are also seasonal effects in services, such as the demand that accounting professionals experience prior to the April 15 tax-filing deadline.

Marketers know these seasonal effects just by looking at their own sales receipts. They can try to increase sales during traditionally off-season times, but such advertising and promotional efforts may not be worth their expenditure. Consumers simply need to be in the right frame of mind to be thinking about buying a snow shovel or lawn mower, for example.

Do the Right Thing!

Do companies have the right to charge more during seasons of greater demand? For example, should airlines, hotels, and theme parks be allowed to charge more during the summer and around holidays?

Who Is the Purchase For?

Consumer purchases aren't affected only by time. Another important factor is the intended recipient of the purchase. Consumers buying gifts for loved ones (close friends, family) often make great efforts to buy something extra special.[26] For these purchases, consumers will put in more thought and may do more brand comparisons. They are typically less price sensitive.

These effects are even more exaggerated when consumers are buying for their beloved children – nothing is too good for them. Yet not all gifts are special; for example, if token gifts are expected at the office, and some of those recipients are mere acquaintances, consumers will operate using motivations of satisficing (i.e. "Is it good enough?") and price sensitivity.

Consumers also obviously purchase a great deal of goods and services for themselves. Many of these purchases are recurrent needs, but other purchases may serve as a "self-gift." When consumers want to celebrate, say, to reward a recent accomplishment, they might indulge and buy something for themselves. Conversely, sometimes consumers engage in "retail therapy" to soothe their hurt feelings over a recent disappointment. Marketers can help guide consumers to satisfying choices in all these purchase-recipient situations. For example, there are numerous gift guides online that make suggestions for what might be a nice gift for a man or woman, a co-worker or boss, an IT friend, a gardening aunt, and others.

Search "Gift Guides" – one of the ways that consumers help each other online is to make suggestions for gifts for recipients who may be hard to shop for – a new partner, a boss, a picky friend, or your Mom!

Retail Ambience

Retail atmospherics refers to the store atmosphere that marketers create to attract customers.

Retail ambience or atmospherics refers to the store atmosphere that marketers create to attract customers. It includes all physical characteristics of a retail store, including looks, scent, music, and colors used. These characteristics often are used to form and support a unique brand image and differentiation. Marketers have tested and demonstrated known effects of various **retail atmospherics** factors.[27] For example, shoppers buy more and make quicker decisions when they're in retail outlets that have fast tempo music playing in the background, even if that ambient music is quiet and rather subtle. Somehow the sound gets under the consumers' skin and makes their credit cards want to dance. Conversely, in grocery stores, when slow music is playing, consumers seem to want to linger, and they buy more. Marketers have to decide what they want – slow music playing in restaurants also has the effect of slowing down turnover of the customers, but the customers who stay typically spend more (because of desserts and alcohol).

Scent is effective as well. There are olfactory cues greeting you as you enter The Body Shop stores, with the promise that a purchase will be pleasant and attractive. Think about the scent that wafts over as you try to walk by a Cinnabon store – oh wait, you can't walk by; the sugary smell pulls you in! These scents are part of their brands, and they serve as an advertisement for the stores.

What's that Smell?
scent atmospherics help in retail marketing

The environmental psychologist Paco Underhill discussed in his book *Why We Buy*[28] how a store layout affects consumers and encourages certain shopper traffic patterns. For example, he has suggested that department store retailers not put anything particularly important on display at the entrance of the store, because just inside the store, people are merely getting oriented to the layout, and they don't tend to pay a great detail of attention to what is right in front of them. Underhill refers to that space as a decompression zone. He also discovered that most people, upon entering a store, veer to the right (we point our feet in the direction we would point our cars), so retailers should put up eye-catching displays toward the right and welcome customers into the store.

There are numerous atmospheric factors that affect consumers and their willingness to buy. One factor is whether the store is crowded: Are there a lot of people in the aisles? Are the racks of merchandise set too close? Crowding and having a lot of people closely packed together may feel exciting in some situations, such as concerts, but generally it's off-putting in stores.

Other factors that impress consumers and affect their judgments are simply the neatness of the environment. For example, Figure 6.7 shows how much more inviting a store can look simply because its employees keep it neat – it's clear which store cares more about its consumers' perceptions. Even beyond retail, consumers care about appearances. For example, consumers want

FIGURE 6.7   Does this retailer's ambience make you want to shop there?

their dentist's office to be neat and clean, and when dealing with professionals such as real estate agents and lawyers, they want those offices to look professional and successful.

Marketers don't have as much control over such atmospheric factors when consumers are shopping online. If the consumer is browsing or shopping while distracted at home or at work or while commuting, there won't be the same level of engagement and investigation brought to the purchase decisions. However, a company's web page can be clear and easily navigable, with an appearance that is consistent with the brand image. These qualities serve to entice consumers just like an inviting real-life retail outlet.

Consumer Antecedents

A final set of situational factors that marketers must understand is that consumers bring their unique personalities to every purchase consideration. Some characteristics are stable traits, such as tending to be brand loyal across product categories or tending to shop for price deals. But other antecedent states are more temporary. For example, consumers are certainly affected by their physiology – are they hungry, thirsty, have to cut shopping short because they have to find a restroom? Consumers are people first, and these conditions affect their purchase decisions.

Beyond physiology, consumers may seek protection, such as installing security systems in their homes, but even on a short-term basis, they can feel psychological insecurities that may affect their purchasing – resisting, simplifying, or, the opposite, overextending their purchases to satiate their needs. As these life needs are met, consumers progress and make purchases based on other, more abstract criteria, such as buying something because consumers think "I'm worth it" (to borrow the tagline from L'Oréal).

The psychology of consumers is something marketers spend a great deal of time studying. The whole idea of retail atmospherics just discussed is to diffuse scent or ambient sound so as to induce pleasurable moods that might thereby encourage consumers to buy. A fun purchase or

	SITUATIONAL FACTORS	PHYSICAL FACTORS
PHYSICAL CONTEXT	• Physical surroundings • Retail ambience	• Scent, website layout • Music, store crowding
SOCIAL CONTEXT	• Usage situation • Social environment	• Purchase for selfor gift • Dinner with friends vs. in-laws
PURCHASE CONTEXT	• Time factors • Antecedent states • Rituals	• Time crunch, seasonality • Mood when shopping • Holiday shopping

FIGURE 6.8 Situational Factors That Affect Purchasing

a good deal can enhance a consumer's mood, which in turn can further perpetuate additional purchases.

There are clearly many kinds of situations that factor into consumer decision-making and purchasing. We've discussed time, social elements (e.g. a purchase for oneself or a gift), the ambience of the retail store, and antecedents such as the mood we're in when shopping. Figure 6.8 classifies these and other situational factors that may impact a consumer's choices into three categories – related to the physical setting, the social context, and the goal of the purchase itself.

SUMMARY

Understanding cognitive behavior is not about judging whether consumers' reactions are rational; it's simply important for marketers to be aware of how people process information. Through concepts derived from psychology and behavioral economics, marketing managers can get insights into how people – consumers but also themselves – interpret and process information. With a clearer knowledge of ways that people optimize decision-making and potential mindsets and biases that might enter in, marketers can be more effective at predicting consumers' likely subsequent behavior and even considering how to influence brand attitudes and choices.

Several of the cognitive mindsets revolve around how information is presented, and marketers need to understand the elements in these mindsets, as well as their interrelationships, For example, framing a message positively or negatively, that is, as a gain or a loss, is reliably effective in changing people's opinions. This knowledge helps marketers enhance their attempts at persuasion, knowing how information will be interpreted in certain predictable ways that can influence consumers' decisions.

Consumers don't make buying decisions in a vacuum. This chapter described several dimensions of situational factors that can affect consumer behavior. Time certainly affects consumers, whether they have enough of it (or experience a time crunch) and when consumers are making decisions during a product's seasonal life. The intended recipient of the purchase also affects what attributes a consumer might seek, such as spending more for a loved one or indulging oneself to celebrate a success. The ambience of the purchase location affects consumers, such as in-store neatness and crowding. Finally, consumers bring their own personal concerns to every purchase, and these factors serve as antecedents or precursors that also set the decision-making and purchase context.

KEY TERMS

Heuristics
System 1
System 2
Cognitive bias
Decoy effect
Compromise effect
Framing
Anchor and adjust
Reference dependence
Gain
Loss
Prospect theory
Diminishing marginal utility
Loss aversion
Status quo bias
Endowment effect
Opt in, opt out
Sunk cost fallacy
Certainty and uncertainty
Mere exposure effect
Familiarity
Heterogeneity
Seasonality
Retail atmospherics

EXERCISES

1. Write down a personal challenge you're experiencing, such as "I'm worried about an upcoming exam. I'm having a hard time with some of these concepts. I don't want to do poorly on the exam, but I'm freaked out enough that I find myself avoiding studying," or "I have an interview coming up for a company I care a lot about. I really want this job. It's easy to stay calm and be professional for interviews that I don't care as much about, but I'm worried I'm going to trip all over myself in this interview because it feels like the stakes are so high." Then exchange notes with the person seated next to you. Each of you write a way to help psych up your teammate by reframing the problem: "Don't think of it like that; think of it like this. . . . " If the challenge isn't too personal, share the problem and solution with the class.

2. Consumers typically aren't brand loyal across all purchase categories. Form two columns (on a piece of paper or in a document on your computer). On the left, list some of the brands you're really loyal to. On the right, list some products for which you don't care about the brand choice as much and would buy another brand, say, if it were on sale. Discuss your list with the person seated next to you. Are there any product categories where one of you is loyal to a brand, but the other person doesn't care? Discuss why and why not. Could the brand-loyal person persuade the other to try his or her favorite brand and stick with it? Discuss why and why not.

3. Discuss with a classmate the following scenario. Imagine you're both on a brand team at work. You're tasked with developing and possibly launching a new product. Your current brand sells well, and the new product is a variation intended to appeal to a different segment of consumers, the ones who seem to resist your current brand. The team has done some preliminary marketing research, and while the numbers are estimates, the company has been in this brand space a while, so the team feels that the numbers are likely in the right ballpark. Now imagine one of the following two scenarios, and remember, you're the decision maker, so you have to decide: Do you launch the new product or not?

- Scenario A: The report says the product should be moderately or very successful (the new product seems as if it will be well received by the new segment; that is, you've developed something they should like), and, therefore, the company should see a $10 million bump in sales. Do you recommend proceeding or not?

- Scenario B: The report says the product is likely to be moderately or very unsuccessful (sales would not be good, and you would have spent a lot of money on research and development, trade deals, etc.), resulting in a loss for your company of $10 million. Do you recommend proceeding or not?

Admittedly, in the real world, your answers would depend on other factors, such as the overall size of the company and brand (i.e. is $10 million a big number or not?), the company's culture in terms of its typical level of aversion to risk (i.e. does the company consider itself innovative and a go-getter, or is the leadership more conservative?), and so on. Nevertheless, discuss the two scenarios. Like the example in the chapter of finding or losing $20, discuss the cognitive mindsets affecting these comparisons. What do you suppose would happen in the real world?

4. Think about a product that you really like that is sold only during a certain season, such as a favorite candy right before Halloween. Why doesn't the company roll out that product to be available year-round? Do you appreciate the product more because its availability is scarce, so it is special, or do you think the company is forgoing profits by not making it available all the time?

5. We all do a lot of shopping online these days, but retail stores aren't gone yet. Which retail stores do you think have unique personalities – they give off a vibe when you're there, whether it's their music or their appearance, or other situational factors? Would the store be less appealing to you if it changed those factors? If the store manager wanted to appeal to a different target customer, how should those atmospheric factors change, or should they not change for brand consistency? (Assume the merchandise would still be relevant or would change to attract the new customer.)

ENDNOTES

1. J. Huber, J. W. Payne, and C. Puto, "Adding Asymmetrically Dominated Alternatives: Violations of Regularity and the Similarity Hypothesis," *Journal of Consumer Research* 9, no. 1 (1982): 90–98.

2. G. Gigerenzer and W. Gaissmaier, "Heuristic Decision Making," *Annual Review of Psychology* 62, 451–82.

3. D. Ariely, *Predictably Irrational: The Hidden Forces That Shape Our Decisions* (New York: Harper Perennial, 2010).

4. D. Kahneman, *Thinking, Fast and Slow* (New York: Farrar, Straus & Giroux, 2013).

5. Ibid.

6. G. Laurent and J. N. Kapferer, "Measuring Consumer Involvement Profiles," *Journal of Marketing Research* 22, no. 1 (1985): 41–53.

7. B. Shiv and A. Fedorikhin, "Heart and Mind in Conflict: The Interplay of Affect and Cognition in Consumer Decision Making," *Journal of Consumer Research* 26, no. 3 (1999): 278–92.

8. Huber et al., "Adding Asymmetrically Dominated Alternatives."

9. R. Kivetz, O. Netzer, and V. Srinivasan, "Alternative Models for Capturing the Compromise Effect," *Journal of Marketing Research* 41 (August 2004): 237–57.

10. A. Chernev, "Extremeness Aversion and Attribute-Balance Effects in Choice," *Journal of Consumer Research* 31, no. 2 (2004): 249–63.

11. R. H. Thaler and C. R. Sunstein, *Nudge: Improving Decisions about Health, Wealth, and Happiness* (New York: Penguin, 2009).

12. D. Kahneman and A. Tversky, "Prospect Theory: An Analysis of Decision under Risk," *Econometrika* 47, no. 2 (1979): 263–91.

13. B. Wansink, R. J. Kent, and S. J. Hoch, "An Anchoring and Adjustment Model of Purchase Quantity Decisions," *Journal of Marketing Research* 35, no. 1 (1998): 71–81.

14. B. G. Hardie, E. J. Johnson, and P. S. Fader, "Modeling Loss Aversion and Reference Dependence Effects on Brand Choice," *Marketing Science* 12, no. 4 (1993): 378–94.

15. Kahneman and Tversky, "Prospect Theory."

16. Ibid.

17. Ibid.

18. R. Weaver and S. Frederick, "A Reference Price Theory of the Endowment Effect," *Journal of Marketing Research* 49, no. 5 (2012): 696–707.

19. V. Kumar, X. Zhang, and A. Luo, "Modeling Customer Opt-in and Opt-out in a Permission-based Marketing Context," *Journal of Marketing Research* 51, no. 4 (2014): 403–19.

20. H. R. Arkes and C. Blumer, "The Psychology of Sunk Costs," *Organizational Behavior and Human Decision Processes* 35 (1985): 124–40.

21. P. Corr and A. Plagnol, *Behavioral Economics: The Basics* (New York: Routledge, 2018).

22. X. Fang, S. Singh, and R. Ahluwalia, "An Examination of Different Explanations for the Mere Exposure Effect," *Journal of Consumer Research* 34, no. 1 (2007): 97–103.

23. M. C. Campbell and K. L. Keller, "Brand Familiarity and Advertising Repetition Effects," *Journal of Consumer Research*, 30, no. 2 (2003): 292–304.

24. E. U. Weber and R. A. Milliman, "Perceived Risk Attitudes: Relating Risk Perception to Risky Choice," *Management Science* 43, no. 2 (1997): 123–44.

25. S. Radas and S. M. Shugan, "Seasonal Marketing and Timing New Product Introductions," *Journal of Marketing Research* 35, no. 3 (1998): 296–315.

26. J. F. Sherry Jr., "Gift Giving in Anthropological Perspective," *Journal of Consumer Research*, 10, no. 2 (1983): 157–68.

27. A. Sharma and T. F. Stafford, "The Effect of Retail Atmospherics on Customers' Perceptions of Salespeople and Customer Persuasion: An Empirical Investigation," *Journal of Business Research* 49, no. 2 (2000): 183–91.

28. P. Underhill, *Why We Buy: The Science of Shopping—Updated and Revised for the Internet, the Global Consumer, and Beyond* (New York: Simon & Schuster, 2009).

CREDITS

https://www.shutterstock.com/image-illustration/blank-white-female-head-side-front-575197756

https://www.shutterstock.com/image-photo/online-shopping-cardboard-box-cart-logo-1969055950

https://www.shutterstock.com/image-vector/vector-stamp-without-text-set-stamps-1194129391

https://www.shutterstock.com/image-vector/sale-design-price-tag-old-new-363180710

Kahneman, D., and A. Tversky "Prospect Theory: An Analysis of Decision under Risk." *Econometrica* 47 (1979): 263–91.

https://slidemodel.com/endowment-effect-and-businesses

https://www.shutterstock.com/image-vector/email-subscribe-online-newsletter-vector-template-1006985020

https://www.shutterstock.com/image-photo/portrait-young-girl-who-walks-outdoors-538273399

https://www.shutterstock.com/image-vector/valentines-day-design-realistic-red-gifts-1887556039

https://www.shutterstock.com/image-photo/man-holding-his-girlfriends-hand-making-535052770

https://www.shutterstock.com/image-photo/w9-tax-form-day-written-on-791780134

https://www.shutterstock.com/image-photo/sofia-bulgaria-may-27-2014-cocacola-202499044

https://www.shutterstock.com/image-photo/backpack-school-stationery-on-white-background-1157480194

https://www.shutterstock.com/image-photo/handmade-chocolates-square-box-428019718

www.etsy.com

https://www.google.com/search?as_st=y&tbm=isch&hl=en&as_q=cinnabon+store+in+mall&as_epq=&as_oq=&as_eq=&cr=&as_sitesearch=&safe=images&tbs=sur:fmc#imgrc=3cbZepjGO_KmiM

https://www.google.com/search?q=body+shop+store+in+mall+&tbm=isch&ved=2ahUKEwjyiLOUtu3nAhUJVFMKHYWxDe4Q2-cCegQIABAA&oq=body+shop+store+in+mall+&gs_l=img.3...43013.44833..45128...0.0..0.90.597.10......0....1..gws-wiz-img.EX29GmhMbpE&ei=j3NVXrKFEImozQKF47bwDg&safe=images&tbs=sur%3Afmc&hl=en#imgrc=2HZk46BEOIlUM

https://www.shutterstock.com/image-photo/interior-brand-new-fashion-clothes-store-134166194

https://www.shutterstock.com/image-photo/messy-clearance-section-clothing-store-colorful-1545976607

Unveiling the Black Box of the Consumer Buying Process

PART III

7

Consumer Motivation and Emotions

LEARNING OBJECTIVES

After studying this chapter, you should be able to:

- Be more aware of consumers' needs and the ways marketers can help address them.

- Learn about consumers' motivations and the ways marketers can help consumers translate their motivations into purchases.

- Understand that some motivations focus on consumers trying to maintain what is good in their lives or on striving to make their lives better.

- Realize that consumers experience emotions after striving to address their needs. If the motivation is thwarted, they will feel negative emotions such as frustration and the need to try to achieve the goal through another means. If the goal is achieved, consumers experience positive emotions.

- Appreciate that marketers can help consumers get rid of negative emotions and celebrate their positive emotions.

You're about to graduate and move to a different city. You need a car. You have a car, but it's not reliable; plus, you want to signal that you're on your way to being a successful business person. What kind of car do you buy? What are your motivations (need for transportation, social acceptance, and prestige)? How will you try to achieve those goals? How will you feel, depending on the kind of car you buy?

Motivation

Motivation
the driving force
behind our actions.

Motivation is defined as the driving force behind our actions.[1] We are motivated to achieve a certain goal, fulfill a need, or do something that upholds our values. Motivation is the underlying driver of any behavior. It involves investing effort and energy in achieving our desired results.

For consumers, motivation reflects the driving force to acquire a desired product, whether it is a material good, experience, or education, or any other form of product to satisfy our needs.

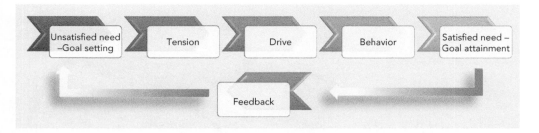

FIGURE 7.1 The Motivation Process

Figure 7.1 presents the basic motivation process. This process starts with our experience of an unsatisfied need. There are two types of needs:

- **Innate needs** (or primary needs) are physiological in nature and are required to sustain our body, for example, our need for food and a place to live.

- **Acquired needs** (or secondary needs) are psychological in nature. They are learned and developed throughout our lives in the context of our culture or social environment, for example, our need for love, esteem, and achievement.

When we have an unsatisfied need, we experience a discrepancy between our current state and an ideal or desired future state. At this point, we are motivated to form specific goals to satisfy the need. We make decisions with regards to what would be the best way to address our needs. The discrepancy between our current state and our desired state will create an inner tension that will lead to a motivation or drive us to alleviate the tension via the act of consumption. Once an action is taken, and the product has been purchased or consumed, the tension reduces. For example, if you are hungry, you experience a tension due to the gap between your current state and the desired end state in which you are not hungry. This tension will motivate you to satisfy your need for food. As such, your goal would be to get food.

The fundamental role of marketers is to identify consumers' needs and offer products and services that will satisfy these needs. While marketers cannot create needs, they can make needs salient to the consumer. Successful companies are those whose products and services clearly relate to consumers' needs. It is up to marketers to proactively make the connection between their products and the needs they satisfy and highlight that connection in their marketing communications to the consumer.

A good example of a company that leverages consumers' needs to offer them greater value is Blue Sky. Blue Sky is a leading planner brand in the United States that specializes in personalized and exclusive premium planners. The company understands that some consumers have high levels of **need for uniqueness**,[2] which is an acquired need to express their individuality and distinctiveness from others through their consumption and the products they use. As such, the company provides consumers with the option to personalize their planner. They can customize anything in the planner, including images, frame style, colors, fonts, and format. Consumers can truly make one-of-a-kind planners that reflect who they are. Offering personalization options increased Blue Sky's sales by 20%.[3]

Motivations and needs affect our emotions and our cognitions. Motivations affect how we process information and what we see in an ad, or whether we even notice an ad at all – motivations filter what we view as relevant and desirable. Motivations also affect our emotions and feelings – at first, the sense of tension is accompanied by negative emotions ("I'm crabby when I'm hungry!"),

Innate needs (or primary needs) – physiological in nature and required to sustain our body.

Acquired needs (or secondary needs) – psychological in nature.

Need for uniqueness an acquired need to express individuality and distinctiveness from others.

Blue Sky enables consumers to express their need for uniqueness by personalizing their planners.

while the reduction of tension will be associated with positive emotions ("Good pizza! Now, what did you want to talk about?").

Compulsive shopping behavior
an excessive preoccupation with shopping that has an adverse effect on their lives.

For some consumers, an emotional cycle develops if they suffer from **compulsive shopping behavior**.[4] These consumers have an excessive preoccupation with shopping that has an adverse effect on their lives. Research indicates that people who suffer from compulsive shopping behavior often experience depression, anxiety, and other negative emotions, which they try to alleviate, at least temporarily, by shopping. It is estimated that up to 8% of the adult population in the United States, 80% of whom are women, suffer from this disorder. Of course, sometimes consumers engage in retail therapy to lift their spirits when they're down, even if they don't have a compulsion problem.

Homeostasis
the motivation to maintain our current desirable state.

If we step back for a moment, in a broad sense, our behavior is directed by two kinds of motives. The first is **homeostasis**,[5] which is the motivation to maintain our current desirable state. Rooted in biology, this concept refers to the natural equilibrium the body strives to maintain. Our body is programmed to send us signals, such as hunger and thirst, to maintain that equilibrium. We follow these signals and act upon them. If we feel hungry, we will eat to bring our body back to a desirable equilibrium. Notice that, while hunger prompts the need to eat, what we want to eat is determined by our personal preferences and culture. The concept of homeostasis is very powerful, the notion of returning to a desired state; for example, if you are sad, you might watch a comedy to cheer you up.

Self-improvement
a wide range of behaviors aimed at changing our current state to a more desirable one.

The second type of motives refers to our **self-improvement** needs. Self-improvement involves a wide range of behaviors aimed at changing our current state to a more desirable one. It is the process of making various aspects of our lives better. As humans, we strive not just to maintain the natural equilibrium of our bodies, but also to go beyond that and add value to various facets of our lives. We can satisfy our self-improvement needs in many ways as well, depending on our personal preferences and our culture. You may want to improve your physical ability by exercising or improve your level knowledge by going to college. Our natural inclination for self-improvement provides marketers with the opportunity to offer us a wide range of products and services.

The Dynamic Nature of Motivation

Marketers have found two theories of motivation to be especially useful. The first is **Maslow's hierarchy of needs** and the second is **McClelland's needs theory**.

Maslow's hierarchy of needs
Maslow's theory of human motivation.

MOTIVATION ON SOCIAL MEDIA

WHAT IS YOUR MOTIVATION FOR USING SOCIAL MEDIA?

40% To stay up-to-date with news and events	**39%** To stay in touch with my friends	**38%** To find funny or entertaining content	**37%** To fill up spare time
33% General networking with other people	**33%** To share photos or videos with others	**31%** To research and find products to buy	**30%** Many of my friends are on social media

Maslow's Hierarchy of Needs

The psychologist Abraham Maslow introduced his theory of human motivation in 1943.[6] Since then, his theory has become one of the most influential motivational theories, with implications for disciplines other than psychology, including business and marketing. Maslow's theory is based on the following premises:

1. All human beings are motivated by the same sets of needs: physiological, safety, love and belonging, esteem, and self-actualization.

2. These needs are organized in a hierarchy.

3. Basic needs must be satisfied before higher-order needs can be addressed.

4. This order of needs may be changed as a result of external circumstances or individual differences.

5. Most behaviors are motivated simultaneously by more than one basic need.

As Figure 7.2 illustrates, Maslow's pyramid of needs is arranged in a hierarchy, from the basic physiological needs at the bottom to the top needs, what he calls self-actualization. In the figure, you'll also see examples of products that can help satisfy each need.

Physiological needs are the basic needs that are necessary for human survival, such as food and water. These needs must be satisfied before other needs can be addressed. For example, we know that our physical performance (e.g. speed while running) and mental abilities (e.g. sharpness on an exam or contributions to a business meeting) are better if we had a good night's sleep

Physiological needs
the basic needs that are necessary for human survival, such as food and water.

FIGURE 7.2   Maslow's Hierarchy of Needs

and we hadn't skipped breakfast. Typical products that can satisfied our physiological need are food items, water, medications, and toilet paper.

Safety needs reflect the fundamental needs for feeling safe and secure. There is physical safety (see the SimpliSafe home protection ad), emotional safety (e.g. feeling secure enough to speak up in a meeting or will my boss or a colleague make fun of me), and financial safety (many mutual funds and investments tout their expertise, even though that's not a guarantee of the stocks' performance). Products that normally are associated with safety are security system, insurance, antiviral vaccines, and investments.

Safety needs reflect the fundamental needs for feeling safe and secure.

SimpliSafe appeals to consumers safety needs.

Love and belonging consist of ties to family members and friends as well as romantic relationships. We have the need to belong to one or more social groups. What is critical for these needs to be fulfilled is the feeling of being loved by others as well as the feeling of love for others (or not quite love, then some affection). Health-care and psychological research continue to demonstrate that we need social networks – research shows that the lack of social connections and the feeling of isolation (i.e. an unmet need related to a sense of belonging) have negative effects on people's health and well-being. We can fulfill our need to belong by using social media, joining different clubs, enroll in dating sites, and giving items that reflect our relationships with others, such as a wedding ring.[7]

Esteem needs refer to our desire to feel good about who we are. We want to feel self-confident and valued by others. When esteem needs are fulfilled, people feel their achievements are valuable and important, and when these needs are not fulfilled, people can experience a sense of inferiority. L'Oréal Paris introduced its iconic tagline "Because you're worth it." Today L'Oréal leverages this tagline to recognize and honor women "who find beauty in giving back."[8] Many different products can fulfill our esteem needs, especially if they are luxury items, exclusive, or rare. Designer bag or watches, expensive cars and houses, and exclusive art items are all good examples.

Love and belonging consist of ties to family members and friends as well as romantic relationships.

Esteem needs our desire to feel good about who we are. We want to feel self-confident and valued by others.

L'Oréal honors women's' self-esteem.

Self-actualization needs reflect our motivation to live up to our potential, to be the best we can be, and to make the most of our abilities. Self-actualization takes different forms and varies from one individual to another. One can strive to be the best that one can be in sports, while someone else might aspire to be a savvy business person or an artist or a musician. According to Maslow, achieving self-actualization is rare, as we can always strive to do better. Self-actualization is reflected in Nike iconic slogan – "Just do it!" Products that help us fulfill our self-actualization needs are education, hobbies, travel, sports, theater.

Self-actualization needs our motivation to live up to our potential, to be the best we can be, and to make the most of our abilities.

Maslow's Elaborated Hierarchy of Needs

Maslow's elaborated hierarchy of needs includes three additional levels to the original hierarchy: cognitive needs, aesthetic needs, and transcendence needs.

Cognitive needs the desire to satisfy our curiosity by increasing our intelligence, knowledge, and understanding of the world around us.

Aesthetic needs the human need for beauty and aesthetically pleasing imagery, music, objects, and experiences.

Transcendence needs our desire to help others self-actualize.

Deficiency needs arise when needs in levels 1–4 are not fulfilled.

While Maslow's work was widely adopted, he continued working on his framework. He later refined his hierarchy to include three more levels: cognitive needs, aesthetic needs, and transcendence needs. The first two became to be levels 5–6, self-actualization placed at level 7. And the highest level was the transcendence needs (see Figure 7.3).

Cognitive needs (level 5) reflect the desire to satisfy our curiosity by increasing our intelligence, knowledge, and understanding of the world around us. It is a natural human tendency to explore, discover, and try to understand everything around us, everything we are involved in. When these needs are not fulfilled, people will experience a sense of confusion and even an identity crisis. Consumers with a high need for cognition tend to respond well to informative marketing messages.

Aesthetic needs (level 6) refer to the human need for beauty and aesthetically pleasing imagery, music, objects, and experiences. These needs may lead to feelings of intimacy with nature and everything beautiful. The restaurant ad addresses consumers' aesthetic needs by focusing on the presentation of food.

Transcendence needs (level 8) address our desire to help others self-actualize. In doing so, we move beyond ourselves to help others fulfill their needs. At this level, people are no longer motivated by factors that have personal consequences for them. They feel that their needs have been fulfilled, and now they can focus on helping others fulfill their needs.

Maslow classifies the lower 4 levels as deficiency needs and levels 5–8 as growth needs. **Deficiency needs** arise when needs in levels 1–4 are not fulfilled. This creates the tension we discussed that leads to a motivation to satisfy the need. This motivation will increase the longer the need is unfulfilled. Once the need has been fulfilled, the tension will be reduced, and the motivation will weaken. For example, when you are hungry, you are motivated to eat to fulfill this need. The longer you go without food, the hungrier you will become, to the point that you will find it hard

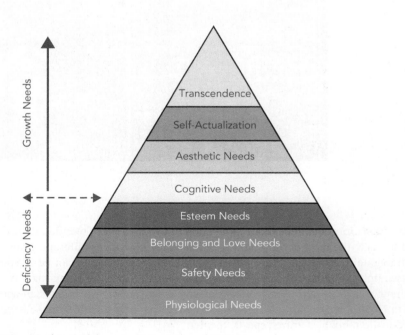

FIGURE 7.3   Maslow's Elaborated Hierarchy of Needs

Appealing to consumers' aesthetic needs is often used in ads for upscale offering.

to function and do anything else. Once you have eaten, you are no longer hungry, the urge to eat will vanish, and you will be able concentrate on other things again. While deficiency needs require fulfillment, they do not require 100% fulfillment for people to progress to the next level of needs.

Deficiency needs originate from a shortage, and the motivation for the need weakens when the shortage is replenished. This is a **push motivation**, an internal disposition that pushes an individual toward a desired end state. Once that state has been achieved, the motivation declines.

Growth needs arise when needs in levels 5–8 are not fulfilled. They do not occur due to a deficiency; rather, they stem from the desire to grow and develop (and growth needs are never 100% completely fulfilled). As people work toward fulfilling their growth needs, their motivation increases, and their desire to become even better increases as well. **Pull motivation** brings an individual toward a desired end state. For example, think about your first job. If you do it well, you expect to get promoted and get a better position. But you are probably not going to stop there, and you will work even harder toward your next promotion.

Marketers have found Maslow's hierarchy of needs very useful. The pyramid model provides marketers with a simple yet powerful tool to guide their strategic decision-making when designing and developing products and services to address consumers' needs and when communicating the value of their offerings to their customers. What makes this hierarchy so powerful is its versatility in application. Using this hierarchy, marketers can highlight different aspects of the value of their offerings to different segments of consumers based on their relevance and attractiveness. For example, a jeans manufacturer can highlight the durability of the jeans to hard-working consumers, and their style to consumers who care about fashion and appearance.

Maslow developed his theoretical framework as a reflection of Western culture. However, over the years, the hierarchy was revised to reflect needs that are characteristic to other cultures. For example, you can see how Maslow's hierarchy of needs was adapted to reflect Eastern cultures.

Push motivation an internal disposition that pushes an individual toward a desired end state.

Growth needs arise when needs in levels 5–8 are not fulfilled.

Pull motivation brings an individual toward a desired end state. For example, think about your first job.

THE GLOBAL MINDSET

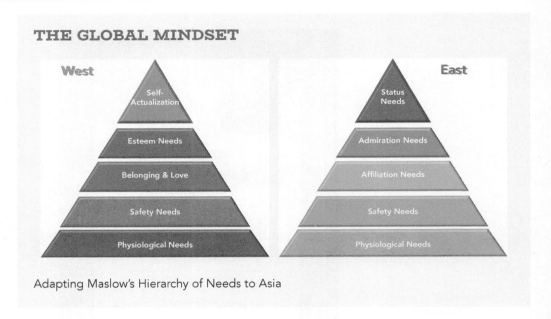

Adapting Maslow's Hierarchy of Needs to Asia

Maslow's hierarchy has been also applied to different contexts. For instance, in the internet figure, different qualities are characterized throughout the pyramid: technology and security are more basic, and social media platforms are more about addressing social belonging and esteem motivations.

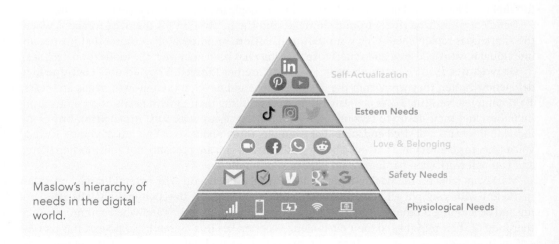

Maslow's hierarchy of needs in the digital world.

McClelland's Needs Theory

David McClelland built on Maslow's work and introduced his trio theory of needs in 1961.[9] McClelland identified three motivators that we all share: a need for achievement, a need for affiliation, and a need for power (see Figure 7.4). In his later work, McClelland added a fourth motivator: a need for avoidance.

Most of us are motivated by a combination of these needs, but typically one need is more dominant. Which of the needs will be more dominant depends on our life experiences and culture. For example, in Western cultures, the need for achievement is very prevalent as a motivator, whereas in Eastern cultures the need for affiliation is more prevalent.

The **need for achievement** reflects our motivation to excel. People with a high need for achievement usually seek feedback to monitor their progress. Such individuals are motivated to complete a task or achieve a goal out of intrinsic motivations that are not necessarily accompanied by material rewards. There is also a relationship with risk – people with a strong need for achievement avoid low- and high-risk situations – they believe that succeeding in low-risk situations is not a genuine achievement, while trying to succeed in high-risk situations is less certain.

The **need for power** reflects our desire to impact or influence the behavior of others. There are two main forms: personal and institutional. Exercising power at the personal level means influencing and controlling the actions or behaviors of others. This type of power is often regarded as undesirable (it's like a friend who is being bossy). At the institutional level, people with a high need for power will seek high-level positions in their companies. Such individuals will also be motivated to increase their personal status and prestige. Overall, people with strong power needs tend to be outgoing, outspoken, and proactive. They might be seen as bossy, forceful, or demanding if their need for power is excessive.

The **need for affiliation** refers to our desire to be loved and accepted by others. To do so, we actively seek social interactions. This need will motivate us to maintain harmonious relationships and avoid the pain of conflict or being rejected. People with a high need for affiliation prefer to work in teams and in positions that involve significant personal interaction, such as customer service or sales.

McClelland's Needs Theory a trio theory of needs that include a need for achievement, a need for affiliation, and a need for power.

Need for achievement our motivation to excel.

Need for power our desire to impact or influence the behavior of others.

Need for affiliation our desire to be loved and accepted by others. To do so, we actively seek social interactions.

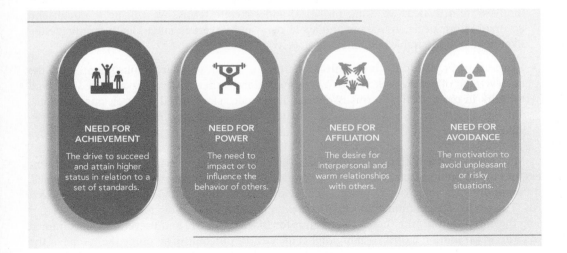

FIGURE 7.4 McClelland's Motivation Theory

Coca-Cola's campaign appeals to consumers' need for affiliation.

Share a **Coke** with a friend

Get in touch with a good friend, an old friend, or maybe even a new friend.
shareacoke.com.au

Need for avoidance
our desire and motivation to avoid unpleasant or risky situations, either consciously or unconsciously.

Push goals
goals that motivate you to avoid negative or undesirable consequences.

Pull goals
goals that motivate you to work toward desirable outcomes.

Regulatory focus theory
centers on the way people self-regulate their behaviors when attempting to achieve their goals.

Prevention-focused motives
our desire for safety and security, when we want to avoid negative outcomes and meet our responsibilities and duties.

Promotion-focused motives
our desire for growth, accomplishment, and the achievement of positive outcomes.

The **need for avoidance** was added by McClelland in his later work. It reflects our desire and motivation to avoid unpleasant or risky situations, either consciously or unconsciously. People with high-avoidance needs tend to experience more general anxiety, as well as fear of failure, fear of rejection, and even fear of success.

Regulatory Focus

Notice that Maslow's theory has the notion of deficiency goals as well as growth goals. **Push goals** are goals that motivate you to avoid negative or undesirable consequences. **Pull goals** are goals that motivate you to work toward desirable outcomes. McClelland also has the notion of going for something (achievement, power, affiliation) versus avoidance. A recent theory has encapsulated these approach-avoidance mindsets. According to **regulatory focus theory**, we regulate our behaviors either through a prevention focus or a promotion focus when we try to achieve our goals[10]:

- **Prevention-focused motives** refer to our desire for safety and security, when we want to avoid negative outcomes and meet our responsibilities and duties. When prevention-focus motives are activated, we think in logical and concrete terms. We will be thorough and accurate in our decision-making and avoid risky and uncertain situations to minimize the likelihood of undesirable outcomes.

- **Promotion-focused motives** reflect our desire for growth, accomplishment, and the achievement of positive outcomes. When promotion-focused motives are activated, we tend to think in more abstract terms. We tend to make decisions based more on our emotions, and we may be more willing to take risks to maximize the likelihood of achieving desirable outcomes.

Marketers can use both prevention- and promotion-oriented messages to motivate consumers and affect their search and purchase behavior. For example, during the COVID-19 crisis, different organizations tried to promote behaviors that would stop the spread of the coronavirus. The UNICEF ad is framed in terms of prevention motives—trying to avoid the risk of getting the virus. On the other hand, the Centers for Disease Control and Prevention ad is framed in terms of promotion motives – it highlights the desired outcome of stopping the spread of the virus. While both ads promote the same behaviors, they frame the motives for these behaviors differently.

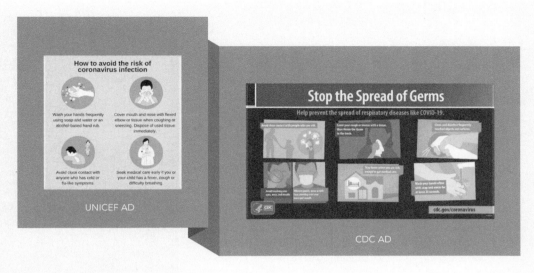

Prevention versus Promotion messages.

Consumers' Motivations

The theories we've seen so far are broad conceptualizations of human motivation. Motivations specific to consumers also look at the value that consumers obtain from their purchases.[11]

Utilitarian motivation[12] refers to our drive to acquire products or services that will help us solve a problem or accomplish a specific task. The value that we derive from a utilitarian purchase is functional, a means to an end, and the explanation for the purchase is rational. For example, if you are running low on gas, you will be motivated to go and buy gas so you can keep using your car. (In many cases, a utilitarian motivation is the motivation to maintain a desirable state, similar to the concept of homoeostasis.)

Hedonic motivation[13] reflects the drive to experience a sensory pleasure, meaning something that is emotionally gratifying and satisfying (hedonic means: feels good!). The value that we derive from a hedonic purchase is the actual experience involved in using or consuming the product. The experience is subjective by nature, and it is an end in itself. The more gratifying the product is, the greater the value it offers us.[14]

The Magnum ad is a good example of a product that provides hedonic value. You don't eat ice cream because you are hungry. You eat it because you want something tasty.

Some products offer both utilitarian and hedonic value to consumers. For example, buying a luxury car provides consumers with the utilitarian value of having transportation, but also with the hedonic value of the status it signals.

Utilitarian motivation
our drive to acquire products or services that will help us solve a problem or accomplish a specific task.

Hedonic motivation
the drive to experience a sensory pleasure, meaning something that is emotionally gratifying and satisfying.

General versus Consumer Goals

One way that marketers have organized all these kinds of goals is to classify consumer behavior as being motivated to achieve one of two kinds.[15]

1. **Generic goals:** These are desired outcomes that consumers pursue in order to satisfy physiological and psychological needs. For example, getting a good grade in your consumer behavior class is a generic goal.

Generic goals
desired outcomes that consumers pursue in order to satisfy physiological and psychological needs.

Nestlé is appealing to consumers' hedonic motivation.

Product-specific goals
desired outcomes that are associated with specific products and services.

2. **Product-specific goals:** These are desired outcomes that are associated with specific products and services. For example, buying Coca-Cola to drink is a product-specific goal.

For marketers, it is essential to relate their products to consumers' goals.[16] Even when the goals are generic, marketers can position their products as elements that can help consumers achieve their desired goals. If your generic goal is to become a better student, an ad that positions a computer as a learning aid will make it more appealing to you. If you have a specific product goal, say you're loyal to Coca-Cola, then you will not consider any other drink; you'll bypass a Pepsi vending machine, for example, unless you're desperate.

Notice that because generic goals sound broader, they provide marketers with a greater range of options to offer consumers ways to attain their goals. In contrast, product-specific goals typically make it harder for marketers to be relevant for their target market. In the beverage example, if you are looking for something to drink (a generic goal), and you don't care much about what it is, you will be open to different drink offerings. However, if you want that Coke (a product-specific goal), that's the only message that will appeal to you.

With all of these different goals, it's important for marketers to understand that achieving a goal can satisfy more than one need for consumers. For example, getting your degree helps you fulfill your self-actualization needs, and it also addresses your cognitive needs by learning new things, your need for esteem as a graduate with a degree, and your social belonging needs by making new friends in school.

Different consumers can be motivated by different needs yet aim to achieve the same goal. For example, you may be in school for cognitive needs more than a friend who is in school for social needs.

By contrast, consumers can be motivated by the same need but will aim to achieve different goals. For example, let's say that you are looking to buy a car that is safe and reliable, whereas your friend is looking to buy a car to signal status and accomplishment. You both may end up buying the same car, such as a Mercedes, that can satisfy your needs and your friend's needs. On the other hand, both you and your friend may be looking to buy a car that is safe and reliable. You might buy a Mercedes, and your friend might buy a Toyota.

Sometimes, instead of a purchase helping to satisfy multiple motivations, consumers can experience some inner conflict. For example, you might be leaning toward the Mercedes as being safe and reliable, but also, let's face it, it signals prestige and achievement. Yet at the same time, you probably consider yourself a smart shopper and know that they are expensive cars, and perhaps you're trying to save money for decent housing. Plus, really, you wonder, is it a better car than the Toyota your friend just bought?

How Does Motivation Work?

We've seen the different types of motivations, but what's next, and how does motivation work? As consumers, we don't buy products randomly. In fact, we are quite strategic when it comes to setting our goals. How do motivations get translated into more specific buying goals?

The goals we choose to pursue depend on our past experiences, physical abilities, personal preferences, ability to pay, and our culture, norms, and what we see as socially acceptable. To be motivated to achieve a goal, we must believe that the goal is attainable. If the goal seems unattainable, we might become discouraged and abandon that goal. For example, let's say you want to become better at playing basketball. If you set your goal as just playing better, your goal is attainable. But if you set your goal as playing as well as Lebron James, you might become discouraged along the way. Sometimes we will exchange one goal for another as our preferences change. One example is changing majors when you find out that another topic interests you more. These examples also mean that our needs, motives, behaviors, and goals are both independent and interconnected.

The Dynamic of Attaining Goals

You set a goal for yourself, and you achieved it. What will you do next? Remember that goals are the way we address our needs. Many of our needs are never fully satisfied. As we work toward satisfying current needs, future needs emerge. Even with simple physiological needs, when we fulfill them, it is only a temporary state that will change the next time we feel hungry or cold. For many of us, attaining our goals means setting new ones. For example, step one is completing your undergraduate degree, and step two is getting a great job or a graduate degree.

What happens when we fail to achieve our goals? We don't always achieve our goals because of a lack of resources, physical ability, or forces that are out of our control. When we feel that we cannot achieve our goals, or when we fail to do so, we often set up a substitute goal. Sometimes the substitute goal is a lesser version of the primary goal. For example, most students plan to finish their undergraduate studies within four years. However, for a variety of reasons, that's become increasingly difficult, so some graduate in five years. Sometimes the substitute goal provides the same benefits as the primary goal, just in a different form. For example, someone who was a serious runner but injured her knees has to pick a different form of exercise to achieve her personal goals of fitness.[17]

When we achieve (or do not achieve) our goals, positive (negative) emotions typically result. Let's see how.

Emotions

How do you feel when you accomplish your goal? Happy? Proud? And how do you feel when you fail to accomplish your goal? Sad? Achieving or failing to achieve your goal will evoke an emotional response. An **emotion** is an affective response to an external stimulus. It is relatively unconscious, spontaneous, and subjective and affects one's behavior.[18]

Emotions are closely related to motivation and goal attainment. If we consider consumers' decision-making as a motivational process, emotions play a critical role in this process. We know that consumer decision-making is not always rational. In fact, when it comes to shopping and consumption, the majority of the time we are motivated by our emotions rather than by our logic or needs. Purchasing a brand name product is an example of how emotions direct our consumption behavior. For example, for transportation, logically, one should buy a low-priced but reliable car rather than a Porsche.

There are many types of emotions that affect the way we interact with others, the way we live, and the way we shop. The psychologist Paul Ekman[19] identified six emotions that are considered basic or primary. **Basic emotions**[20] are those that we all experience. They include happiness, sadness, disgust, fear, surprise, and anger. This list was later expanded to include emotions such as pride, embarrassment, shame, and excitement. Regardless, all emotions share the same following characteristics:

- Every emotion is associated with instincts or a biological drive.
- Emotions are subjective and are based on people's experiences, personality, culture, and situation.
- Emotions are externally induced and reflect an affective reaction to an external stimulation.
- Emotions are very brief, and they can change rapidly.
- Emotions are action oriented and direct behavior.
- Emotions are never neutral. They are either positive (happiness, pride, excitement) or negative (sadness, anxiety, embarrassment).
- Every emotion is accompanied by a physiological or bodily reaction.

How do emotions affect us as consumers? And why do different people have different emotional reactions to the same situations?

According to the **cognitive appraisal theory**,[21] all emotions are generated from a cognitive evaluation process. The theory posits that emotions are the result of an appraisal (i.e. our cognitive evaluation, interpretation, and explanation of events). The emotional process starts with an event or a stimulus that triggers an evaluative response. We have an emotional reaction to this evaluation that, in turn, will determine our behavioral reaction.

This view proposes that different people can have different emotional and behavioral responses to the same event depending on their subjective evaluation (perception) and interpretation (cognitive) of the triggering event. For example, in the case of a friendship that comes to an end (the triggering event), one person might see the dissolution of the friendship as a negative event and experience emotions such as sadness, guilt, or even shame. These emotions will be manifested in behavioral reactions, such as crying or venting about the situation to other people. The other person, on the other hand, might view this event as a positive one and will experience emotions such as relief and happiness. For both people, their emotions, negative or positive, may lead to coping behaviors, such as going out with other friends.

The **PAD emotional state model**[22] offers a different way to understand emotional responses to objects, situations, and environments. This model asserts that all emotional responses have

Emotion
an affective response to an external stimulus.

Basic emotions
those that we all experience. They include happiness, sadness, disgust, fear, surprise, and anger.

Cognitive appraisal theory
posits that all emotions are generated from a cognitive evaluation process.

PAD emotional state model
asserts that all emotional responses have three dimensions: pleasure, arousal, or dominance.

three dimensions: pleasure, arousal, or dominance (PAD). The pleasure dimension reflects our perception of the environment as enjoyable or not. Happiness and joyfulness are examples of positive emotional responses related to the pleasure dimension, while unhappiness and boredom are examples of negative emotional responses. The arousal dimension refers to the intensity of our emotional reaction to the environment (whether positive or negative). The higher the intensity, the higher the arousal state that the environment stimulates. For example, anger is considered a high-arousal emotional response, while sadness is low arousal. Finally, dominance represents the extent to which we feel in control in our environment. Joyfulness is considered a high-dominance response, while happiness is a submissive response. Marketers used this model to research and understand consumers responses to advertisements, store atmosphere, aesthetics of website design, and different types of consumption experiences.

Negative Emotions Due to Not Achieving a Goal

It is worth understanding the various negative emotions that can arise if we do not achieve our goals. Naturally, failing to attain a goal is often accompanied by a feeling of frustration. We react differently to frustration and use different defense mechanisms to cope with it. The common defense mechanisms are as follows[23]:

1. *Rationalization:* When we use this defense mechanism, we try to figure out why we failed to attain the goal. The purpose of this defense mechanism is to avoid the true cause or reason for the failure that reflects badly on us. For example, failing to get a good grade on an exam might be excused by rationalizing that there was not enough time to study.

2. *Projection:* By using this defense mechanism, we attribute the reason for our failure to someone or something else, for example, a business owner of a failing business who blames consumers for his failure rather than the fact that the business sells overly expensive products or the salespeople are rude.

3. *Regression:* When confronted by the failure to achieve a goal, we sometimes revert to patterns of behavior we used earlier. In other words, we will react in a childish or immature way (e.g. "Fine! I didn't want that anyway!").

4. *Denial:* We often try to avoid feelings of frustration by ignoring the reality of failing to attain our goal. In other words, we shield ourselves from the awareness of our failure to maintain a positive image of ourselves. This is an undesirable defense mechanism that may have long-term negative psychological consequences, such as in the case of managers who refuse to acknowledge that their business strategy fails (e.g. coupling a high price point and luxury imagery with a Walmart distribution channel).

5. *Fantasy:* We use fantasies or daydreaming as a way to escape reality. We can also use fantasies to obtain imaginary fulfillment of our needs. The danger with this type of coping is that we can lose touch with reality and make ourselves incapable of taking more productive actions to improve our situation.

6. *Humor:* The use of humor as a defense mechanism is viewed as a mature and adaptive way of coping. Seeing the humorous and funny side of an adverse situation can help us minimize its negative effect.

7. *Passive aggression:* Aggression behavior is considered socially undesirable. We tend to avoid aggressive expressions of frustration. However, if the impulse to react aggressively

still persists, we express it in a passive and more socially acceptable way that may be related or unrelated to the primary goal. (You've probably already experienced people like this in your life – they're sneaky.)

8. ***Social comparison:*** A very common way to cope with the frustration of failing to achieve a goal is by comparing ourselves to someone else who performed even more poorly. Managers who see that their department is not doing well can compare it to a different department that performs even more poorly.

There are many other ways to cope with frustration. We choose our preferred defense mechanism based on the situation, the importance of the goal, and our own style. For marketers, frustration offers an opportunity to offer products and services that will ease the negative feelings associated with it. Marketers should actively communicate this benefit of their offerings to consumers when it's relevant.

Do the Right Thing!

Is it fair when marketers use emotional appeals? Is it acceptable to make people feel that their teeth must be very shiny and white, otherwise no one will find them attractive or hire them? Laundry detergents try to shame us that we don't want to have "ring around the collar" (staining on shirts from the day's sweat and dirt). Protein World recently advertised a slender model in a bikini and asked, "Are you beach body ready?" to encourage purchasing its supplements for weight reduction. The company was quickly accused of body shaming. Yet excess weight induces health risks, so was the ad appeal wrong?

Marketers and Consumers' Emotions

Research shows that emotions – positive or negative – can be a powerful strategic tool for marketers. Motista conducted a two-year study about the impact of consumers' emotional connection to brands on their behavior.[24] The study included more than 100,000 consumers of more than one hundred brands. The results indicated that consumers who are emotionally connected to a brand are significantly more valuable to these brands than consumers who were just satisfied with a brand. How?

Compared to satisfied consumers, emotionally connected consumers spent almost twice as much money, had three times greater lifetime value, were loyal to the brand for a longer time, and recommended the brand significantly more often. This study demonstrated that an emotional connection to a brand is a strong motivator of consumers' behavior. It underscores the need for marketers to leverage these emotional connections as an effective, long-term strategy to promote their business. But how can marketers create such emotional connections between their brand and consumers?

Evoking Emotions as a Marketing Strategy

Since consumers react to emotional stimuli instinctively and unconsciously, emotions provide marketers with the opportunity to influence the consumption behavior of their target market and connect with consumers on a meaningful level.[25] They can accomplish these goals in two ways: emotional branding and emotional advertising. Both strategies are designed to evoke consumers' feelings in a way that will influence their buying behaviors.

"People don't buy for logical reasons. They buy for emotional reasons."

Zig Ziglar, personal development trainer

Emotional branding[26] is a marketing practice of forming meaningful connections between brands and consumers by arousing their emotions. When we have an emotional connection to a brand, we view it as an extension of our self-identity. We care about the brand. We see it as a brand that reflects not just what we buy, but also who we are. By crafting emotional relationships with consumers, brands can establish a strong differentiation from other brands and strengthen their position in the marketplace.

In addition, an emotional connection to a brand will result in a heuristic or shortcut in consumers' decision-making. In other words, consumers will not go through a rational decision-making process when deciding which products or brands will fulfill their needs. Instead, consumers will automatically choose the brand that they feel emotionally related to. Examples of brands that form successful emotional connections with consumers are Harley-Davidson, Apple, and Coca-Cola.

Emotional advertising[27] refers to the purposeful use of images and slogans in marketing messages to evoke consumers' emotions in a way that will make them notice, remember, share, and buy the products or services. Normally, emotional advertising triggers a single emotion, such as happiness or anger, to influence consumers' responses and buying behavior.

Marketers can trigger positive or negative emotions via their marketing messages based on their strategic goals. Emotional advertising is directly related to emotional branding. Such emotional ads support the authenticity of the brand by strengthening and reminding consumers about its emotional facets.

Emotional branding
a marketing practice of forming meaningful connections between brands and consumers by arousing their emotions.

Emotional advertising
a purposeful use of images and slogans in marketing messages to evoke consumers' emotions in a way that will make them notice, remember, share, and buy the products or services.

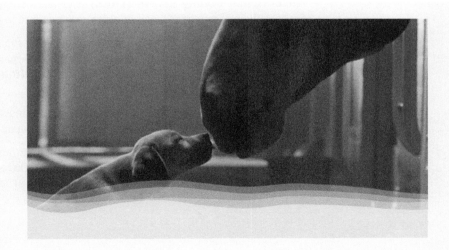

Budweiser uses emotional advertising in their commercials.

When Budweiser runs an ad, what are company's marketing team going to say, "Hey, we're a beer"? We've all heard of the brand and probably have tried it, and many consumers don't even have a particularly beer-discerning palate. So, Budweiser runs Super Bowl ads showing the friendship of a dog and a Bud horse that are cute and amusing and make viewers happy and at least subtly encourage consumers to support the brand.[28]

Studies have established that emotional advertising is very effective. A neuromarketing study of 1400 advertising campaigns showed that those with emotional content generated a 31% increase in sales, whereas ads that relied simply on facts generated only a 16% increase.[29]

The driver of this superior performance of emotional ads is the fact that they are much more memorable. Emotional ads are about three times more likely to be remembered by consumers compared to ads with weak or no emotional connections.[30] While consumers might not always remember what an ad communicated to them, they will remember the emotions it evoked. These emotions will be aroused again at the point of purchase.

Another benefit of emotional advertising relates to the increase in the word-of-mouth communication it evokes. Emotional ads that arouse strong positive emotions are more likely to go viral. Consumers are more sensitive to excessive negativity and will avoid emotional ads that evoke extreme negative emotions. Moderate emotional negativity will be more effective in driving consumers' behavior. (A good deal of political advertising is intended to raise negative emotions.)

Measuring Emotional Marketing

The effectiveness of emotions in directing consumers' buying behaviors makes it imperative for marketers to be able to measure and monitor them. Two aspects of emotions need to be measured: the intensity of the emotion (arousal) and the valence of the emotion (positive or negative).[31] Today technology offers marketers a variety of ways to measure our emotional reactions to marketing messages:

- *Self-report measures* use surveys to ask consumers directly to indicate their emotions about the marketing stimuli of interest on traditional surveys.

- *Facial Action Coding System* (**FACS**) uses technology to capture facial expressions and encodes the movement of facial muscles as a response to marketing stimuli.

- *Neurophysiology* measures the area of the brain that is in charge of emotions and its physiological activity. This is done by using brain scanning (e.g. electroencephalography [EEG] and functional magnetic resonance imaging [fMRI]) and biometrics (e.g. heart rate, galvanic skin response).

- *Implicit association* uses various tests, such as fast reaction times, to measure unconscious, uncontrollable emotions that people may be unwilling or unable to report.

- *Sentiment analysis* uses text analysis techniques to analyze and interpret the content of unstructured text. This kind of measure enables marketers to identify consumers' sentiment toward an ad, the product, or the brand in the context of social media posts or product reviews.

SUMMARY

Intent to purchase is great, but without action (a behavior like purchasing) and the driving force of effort and energy behind it, there is no business transaction. Motivation is important because communicating clearly and effectively how the brand's products and services best fulfill a need or add value to a consumer's life is crucial for the success of the business. Competing brands will try to communicate the same message, but the winners in each category do it best by showing exceedingly more value throughout the entire process of doing business with their brand.

Maslow's hierarchy of needs gives marketers a solid foundation to build from with its eight different levels. This framework is useful in guiding strategic decision-making when designing and developing products and services for consumer needs because it can highlight different aspects of value. Marketers can then segment their consumers based on the relevance and attractiveness of the needs their offerings fulfill. McClelland's motivation theory adds to Maslow's work by identifying four motivating forces behind our needs: achievement, power, affiliation, and avoidance.

Goals are a way for consumers to meet their needs. They are intentional and guide their behaviors according to their desired outcomes. Motivation and goals are connected because one must be motivated to achieve a goal but must believe that the goal is attainable. Even though motivation and goals are connected, they are still independent by nature and can work together or nearly in opposition.

Marketers tap into consumer goals and motivations by running advertising campaigns showing how their products or services help individuals achieve their goals. A second way marketers use consumer goals to their advantage is by communicating the benefits of their products or services in a way that eases the negative feelings (e.g. frustration) associated with not achieving a desired outcome goal. Ensuring that their product is a part of the solution, and not the problem, is key.

Since most of the time consumers are motivated by their emotions, a marketing strategy that emphasizes forming meaningful connections between consumers and the brand is best. Brands that do this successfully build a strong relationship with consumers that reaps benefits, such as more money being spent on the brand's products and/or services, greater lifetime value, strong brand loyalty, and motivation to recommend the brand.

KEY TERMS

Motivation
Innate needs
Acquired needs
Need for uniqueness
Compulsive shopping
 behavior
Homeostasis
Self-improvement
Maslow's hierarchy
 of needs

Physiological needs
Safety needs
Love and belonging
Esteem needs
Self-actualization needs
Maslow's elaborated
 hierarchy of needs
Cognitive needs
Aesthetic needs
Transcendence needs

Deficiency needs
Push motivation
Growth needs
Pull motivation
McClelland's Needs
 Theory
Need for achievement
Need for power
Need for affiliation
Need for avoidance

Push goals
Pull goals
Regulatory focus theory
Prevention-focused
 motives
Promotion-focused
 motives
Utilitarian motivation
Hedonic motivation
Generic goals

Product-specific goals
Emotion
Basic emotions
Cognitive appraisal
 theory
PAD emotional
 state model
Emotional branding
Emotional advertising

EXERCISES

1. In small groups, talk about an item you have on you right now, something you're wearing or something in your backpack. Discuss the various needs it meets. What are different ways to communicate these needs? What are other products that could have satisfied those needs?

2. The chapter mentioned Harley-Davidson, Apple, and Coca-Cola as brands that some consumers have emotional connections to. What brands do you have an emotional connection to? Why? Are there other brands that could serve as alternatives, or would they not be equivalent?

3. Consider the need for affiliation. Think of some brands that seem to help people try to achieve greater social interactions and identification with others.

4. Find two advertisements of similar products. What are the needs and motivations that are used in the ads to target consumers? Can you think about additional needs or motivations that can be used to promote this product?

5. In pairs or in teams, pick a product and come up with three different slogans representing three different needs based on Maslow's conceptualization.

ENDNOTES

1. D. McClelland, *Human Motivation* (New York: Cambridge University Press, 1988).

2. K. T. Tian, W. O. Bearden, and G. L. Hunter, "Consumers' Need for Uniqueness: Scale Development and Validation," *Journal of Consumer Research* 28, no. 1 (2001): 50–66.

3. https://www.dckap.com/casestudy/bluesky.

4. M. M. P. Sarghie, "Using Social Marketing to Tackle Compulsive Buying," *Social Marketing Quarterly* 27, no. 1 (2021): 3–12.

5. P. M. Parker and N. T. Tavassoli, "Homeostasis and Consumer Behavior across Cultures," *International Journal of Research in Marketing* 17, no. 1 (2000): 33–53.

6. A. H. Maslow, *Motivation and Personality* (New York: Harper & Row, 1970).

7. M. Rosenberg, *Society and the Adolescent Self-image* (Princeton, NJ: Princeton University Press, 1965).

8. https://www.lorealparisusa.com/women-of-worth/honorees.aspx.

9. D. McClelland, *Human Motivation* (New York: Cambridge University Press, 1988).

10. E. W. Wan, J. Hong, and B. Sternthal, "The Effect of Regulatory Orientation and Decision Strategy on Brand Judgments," *Journal of Consumer Research* 35, no. 6 (2009): 1026–38.

11. R. Dhar and K. Wertenbroch, "Consumer Choice between Hedonic and Utilitarian Goods," *Journal of Marketing Research* 37, no. 1 (2000): 60–71.

12. P. L. To, C. Liao, and T. H. Lin, "Shopping Motivations on the Internet: A Study Based on Utilitarian and Hedonic Value," *Technovation* 27, no. 12 (2007): 774–87.

13. E. C. Hirschman and M. B. Holbrook, "Hedonic Consumption: Emerging Concepts, Methods and Propositions," *Journal of Marketing* 46, no. 3 (1982): 92–101.

14. K. C. Karnes, "What Is Emotional Branding and How to Use It Effectively?," https://clevertap.com/blog/emotional-branding/#:~:text=Emotional%20Branding%20vs.&text=Emotion%20can%20be%20applied%20more,structural%20integrity%20of%20the%20brand.

15. J. R. Bettman, M. F. Luce, and J. W. Payne, "Consumer Decision Making: A Choice Goals Approach," in *Handbook of Consumer Psychology*, eds. C. P. Haugtvedt, P. M. Herr, and F. R. Kardes (New York: Routledge, 2008), 589–610.

16. R. P. Bagozzi and U. Dholakia, "Goal Setting and Goal Striving in Consumer Behavior," *Journal of Marketing* 63, no. 4 (1999): 19–32.

17. C. E. Kopetz et al., "The Dynamics of Consumer Behavior: A Goal Systemic Perspective," *Journal of Consumer Psychology* 22, no. 2 (2012): 208–23.

18. Y. Bruce Lee, "Here Are the 27 Different Human Emotions, According to a Study," *Forbes*, September 9, 2017, https://www.forbes.com/sites/brucelee/2017/09/09/here-are-the-27-different-human-emotions-according-to-a-study/?sh=6ae049bd1335.

19. https://www.paulekman.com/about/paul-ekman.

20. F. J. Laros and J. B. E. Steenkamp, "Emotions in Consumer Behavior: A Hierarchical Approach," *Journal of Business Research* 58, no. 10 (2005): 1437–45.

21. R. S. Lazarus and S. Folkman, *Stress, Appraisal, and Coping* (New York: Springer, 1984).

22. A. Mehrabian and J. A. Russell, *An Approach to Environmental Psychology* (Cambridge, MA: MIT Press, 1974).

23. S. Yi and H. Baumgartner, "Coping with Negative Emotions in Purchase-related Situations," *Journal of Consumer Psychology* 14, no. 3 (2004): 303–17.

24. Alan Zorfas, "*Leveraging the Value of Emotional Connection for Retailers*," 2019, https://www.motista.com/blog/leveraging-value-emotional-connection-retailers. https://www.motista.com/resource/leveraging-value-emotional-connection-retailers01#:~:text=Motista%20conducted%20a%20two%20year,across%20more%20than%20100%20brands.&text=Implications%20of%20activating%20emotional%20connection,those%20who%20really%20need%20to.

25. R. P. Bagozzi, M. Gopinath, and P. U. Nyer, "The Role of Emotions in Marketing," *Journal of the Academy of Marketing Science* 27, no. 2 (1999): 184–206.

26. C. J. Thompson, A. Rindfleisch, and Z. Arsel, "Emotional Branding and the Strategic Value of the Doppelgänger Brand Image," *Journal of Marketing* 70, no. 1 (2006): 50–64.

27. D. J. Moore and W. D. Harris, "Affect Intensity and the Consumer's Attitude toward High Impact Emotional Advertising Appeals," *Journal of Advertising* 25, no. 2 (1996): 37–50.

28. https://www.cnbc.com/2019/02/01/budweiser-spends-big-on-super-bowl-targets-small-markets-.html.

29. H. Pringle, *Brand Immortality: How Brands Can Live Long and Prosper* (London: Kogan Page Publishers, 2008).

30. https://www.psychologytoday.com/us/blog/inside-the-consumer-mind/201302/how-emotions-influence-what-we-buy.

31. K. A. Machleit and S. Eroglu, "Describing and Measuring Emotional Response to Shopping Experience," *Journal of Business Research* 49, no. 2 (2000): 101–11.

CREDITS

https://www.shutterstock.com/image-vector/shield-check-mark-tick-symbol-secured-1831454515

https://www.shutterstock.com/image-photo/kiev-ukraine-january-12-2021-google-1904792044

https://www.shutterstock.com/image-photo/kiev-ukraine-february-26-2016-collection-387461323

https://www.shutterstock.com/image-photo/kiev-ukraine-april-23-2015-google-272871035

https://www.shutterstock.com/image-photo/kiev-ukraine-may-30-2016-collection-428643526

https://www.shutterstock.com/image-vector/zoom-cloud-meetings-logoremote-working-applicationzoom-1741198607

https://hipwallpaper.com/chinese-backgrounds/

https://www.marketingmag.com.au/hubs-c/share-a-coke-campaign-post-analysis/

https://twitter.com/fly2midway/status/1249442293209280513

https://twitter.com/unicefphils/status/1236252801912668163

https://www.effie.org/case_database/case/EU_2016_1027

https://www.youtube.com/watch?v=dlNO2trC-mk

Image p. 122: Blue Sky the Color of Imagination, LLC.

Image p. 124: SimpliSafe, Inc.

Image p. 125: L'Oréal Paris

Image p. 127: alex989/Whitegrass

Image p. 128: solomon7/Shutterstock, Creative Instinct/Shutterstock, rvlsoft/Shutterstock, solomon7/Shutterstock, solomon7/Shutterstock, rvlsoft/Shutterstock, cve iv/Shutterstock, rvlsoft/Shutterstock, tanuha2001/Shutterstock, rvlsoft/Shutterstock, pluie_r/Shutterstock

Image p. 130: The Coca-Cola Company

Image p. 132: Unilever

Image p. 137: Budweiser Brasil

8

Consumer Personality and Self-Concept

LEARNING OBJECTIVES

After studying this chapter, you should be able to:

- Use concepts of personality and self-concepts to know how to talk to consumers.

- See how the psychology of the big five personality traits transfer to consumer traits.

- Translate personality ideas to the notion of a brand's personality.

- Use the idea of a consumer's self-concept – the actual or ideal self-concept and the self-concept about the consumer's self or social interactions for good marketing.

- Understand that the brands consumers buy, use, and display say something about their identity, and marketers can help make those connections.

Time to get a new pair of running shoes! You go to a store selling a brand that you like, but you see another brand on sale. Do you buy the first brand because "it's you," or do you buy the second brand because of its big discount?

To answer that question for consumers, we need to know more about them as people. This chapter talks about three big ideas: consumers' personalities, consumers' self-concepts, and consumers' attitudes. For each of these three important concepts, we'll describe the main idea and show how marketers can use them.

Personality

How does your personality affect what you like and what you buy, and how can marketers strategically leverage their consumers' personality? This chapter is about consumers' personalities and how different personality traits affect consumption behavior.

Personality the individual's unique characteristics and distinct patterns of thoughts, feelings, and behaviors.

Personality refers to an individual's unique characteristics and distinct patterns of thoughts, feelings, and behaviors.[1] Such distinctiveness stems from a combination of inherent genetic dispositions and environmental factors and experiences. Environmental factors include family of origin and culture, as well as age, race, gender, and sexual orientation. While personalities can change over the course of time, most people's personalities remain fairly consistent throughout their life. What's key for marketers is that aspects of consumers' personalities help predict what they will buy. Personality affects more than purchases; social media gurus have described different kinds of social media personalities.

PERSONALITY ON SOCIAL MEDIA

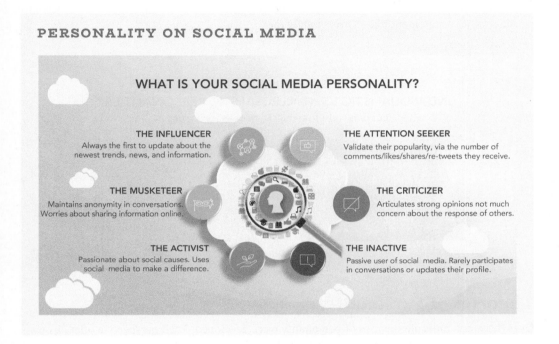

WHAT IS YOUR SOCIAL MEDIA PERSONALITY?

THE INFLUENCER
Always the first to update about the newest trends, news, and information.

THE ATTENTION SEEKER
Validate their popularity, via the number of comments/likes/shares/re-tweets they receive.

THE MUSKETEER
Maintains anonymity in conversations. Worries about sharing information online.

THE CRITICIZER
Articulates strong opinions not much concern about the response of others.

THE ACTIVIST
Passionate about social causes. Uses social media to make a difference.

THE INACTIVE
Passive user of social media. Rarely participates in conversations or updates their profile.

Consumer psychologists talk about personality in the following ways[2]:

- *Consistent and stable:* People tend to behave in a similar way in different situations and over time. In other words, there is some order and patterns to people's behaviors.

- *Psychological and physiological:* Obviously, a personality is part of a consumer's psychology, but aspects of personalities also derive from biological processes and needs.

- *Predicts behaviors:* Personality helps explain and predict how people act in a variety of situations and over time.

- *Multiple expressions:* Personality is expressed via our thoughts, feelings, relationships, and other social interactions. It is also reflected in our consumption behavior and buying decision-making.

These characteristics of personality make it highly valuable to marketers. The consistency and stability of personality and the fact that it predicts a variety of behaviors help marketers leverage their consumers' personality in a reliable way. In other words, marketers can expect that targeting a certain personality will generate the same behavioral response most of the time. Such **personality-based marketing**, the use of consumers' underlying psychological profiles as drivers of marketing strategies, can be a highly powerful tool for segmentation (see Chapter 2), brand positioning, marketing communication and promotion, product personalization and customization, and even product development. Personality insights, gathered by extensive market research (see Chapter 3), present marketers with the opportunity to better understand and connect with consumers. Nevertheless, marketers always need to be aware of personality differences

personality-based marketing
the use of consumers' underlying psychological profiles as drivers of marketing strategies.

across cultures as well. The image below shows a classification that contrasts people who are relatively independent (individualistic) versus those who appreciate their group interconnections (collectivist).

Personality-based marketing works for the benefit of consumers as well. We love products that express or match our personality or our self-concept. Remember how many times you reacted to a product with a statement like "This is totally me!"

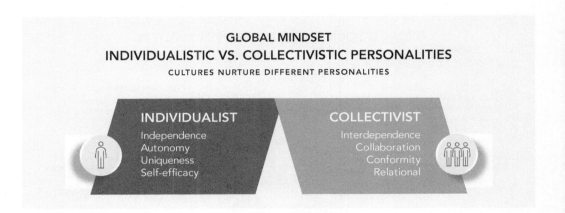

Theories of Personality

Over the years, multiple theories of personality were developed. Each perspective offers its own unique perspective of personality. But they all share the assertion that personality is the basis of individual differences and that it is a driver of behavior. Personality theories fall into one of three major perspectives:

- The psychoanalytic perspective

- The humanistic perspective

- The trait perspective

The Psychoanalytic Perspective

Psychoanalytic perspective highlights the important role of early childhood experiences and the influence of the unconscious mind and sexual instincts in the formation of personality.

Id the primitive, unconscious component of personality.

Ego governs personality in a more rational way.

The **psychoanalytic perspective** is mostly focused on how personality develops. It highlights the important role of early childhood experiences and the influence of the unconscious mind and sexual instincts in the formation of personality. Psychiatrist Sigmund Freud introduced the psychosexual theory of development, in which he described a personality as composed of the id, the ego, and the superego.[3]

- The **id** is the primitive, unconscious component of personality. It is responsible for impulses, needs, and drives, such as sexual and biological drives. It is pleasure driven and selfishly oriented. The id is in control when you eat junk food rather than a salad.

- The **ego** is more consciously controlled. It governs personality in a more rational way than the id.

The DKNY ad says "be tempted," appealing to your ID!

- The **superego** regulates a person's ideals and morals, which are shaped by family and society. It reflects the person's understanding of what is right and wrong and will result in a sense of guilt when misbehaving. (If the id gets you to eat junk food, the superego will make you feel guilty.)

Neo-Freudian theorists, such as Erik Erikson, Carl Jung, and Alfred Adler, endorsed the importance of the unconscious, but they didn't believe as much in other aspects of Freud's theory. These theorists emphasized the critical role of social interactions in shaping one's personality. Jung, for example, introduced the notion of archetypes, which marketers use when they try to portray idealized people in their ads, such as a heroic athlete.

Marketing professor Gerald Zaltman implemented a consumer insights technique based on these notions of the subconscious. He invented ZMET (Zaltman metaphor elicitation technique) where marketers show consumers photos (or have them bring their own pictures) and ask them about the pictures, the consumers' lives, and eventually moving toward questions about brands.[4] The idea is that, because the subconscious seems to drive buying and brand choices, direct survey questions may be too conscious or rational, whereas images can help tap consumers' desires. See more marketing implication of the id, ego, and superego in Figure 8.1.

The Humanistic Perspective

Humanistic psychology developed in the 1960s somewhat in reaction to Freud. In particular, humanists didn't like that psychodynamics characterized human behavior as determined by factors beyond one's control. The humanistic perspective emphasizes that individuals have free will

Superego regulates a person's ideals and morals, which are shaped by family and society.

Humanistic perspective emphasizes that individuals have free will and that people are basically good and have a need to live to their full potential.

ID

Reflected in ads that tap into consumers unconscious and signal that their products will provide them with pleasurable experiences and desirable outcomes. Relevantproducts: clothing, makeup, cars, jewelry, chocolate.

EGO

Reflected in messages that are rational or call for delay in gratification. These messages aim to control current impulsive behaviors for future benefits. Relevant products: savings, programs, diet products, insurance.

SUPEREGO

Reflected in ads directed to consumers conscience and indicates the right course of action. What is the best thing to do, or should avoid doing? Often highlights social conventions. For example, healthy eating, don't drink and drive, charitable and environmental causes.

FIGURE 8.1 Marketing Implications of the Id, Ego, and Superego

and that people are basically good and have a need to live to their full potential. It also maintains that conscious experiences are more influential than the unconscious.

Humanistic theories (developed by Abraham Maslow, Carl Rogers, and others) take a holistic view of the individual and regard personal growth and self-actualization as the key motivators of behavior. For example, you go to college because you are motivated by the desire to improve yourself and your future options. (Abraham Maslow's hierarchy of needs theory is covered in Chapter 7.)

The Trait Perspective

These days, the most popular approach to understanding consumer personalities is to look at consumer traits. For example, if you like going to social events, meeting new people, and socializing, then you are an extrovert. If you have a friend who does not like going to social events and prefers spending time alone watching TV, your friend is an introvert. The difference between you and your friend is easily observed, and it will have implications for preferences and purchase behaviors. The trait perspective is not concerned with conscious or unconscious processes or stages throughout life. Rather, it centers on individual aspects of personalities or traits in order to gain a deeper insight into personality and personality differences.

Big five theory focuses on five personality traits which under different combinations they create the individual's unique personality.

The predominant trait theory of personality, known as the "big five theory," developed as follows. First, Hans Eysenck identified three dimensions of personality: extraversion-introversion, emotional stability-neuroticism, and psychoticism. Then Robert McCrae and Paul Costa extended Eysenck's work to describe five traits[5]: openness, conscientiousness, extroversion, agreeableness, and neuroticism. This **big five theory** is also known by the acronym OCEAN. See Figure 8.2 for a detailed explanation of each trait. These theories assert that combinations of the trait dimensions create the individual's unique personality.

So how does all of this help marketers? If marketers understand personality traits, they're in a better position to be able to do market segmentation (on the basis of personalities, not just simpler demographics), then find an ideal target segment for their brand. For example, presumably people who score high on the openness to experiences trait would be ideal for companies to target

Openness to Experiences

This trait is characterized by intellectual curiosity, creativity, and favor novelty. Consumers who score high on openness are more likely to prefer variety, new and unique products, and new experiences.

Conscientiousness

This trait reflects good impulse control, goal-directed behavior, and high levels of achievement. Conscientious consumers like routine and are predictable in their buying behavior. They are mindful about their environment and will care about sustainable products and brands.

Extraversion

This trait refers to being outgoing, very social, expressive, excitable, and energetic. Extraverted consumers will seek interact with brands and companies. They are also more likely to engage in word-of-mouth communication, and some even become influencers.

Agreeableness

This trait includes characteristics such as altruism, trust, kindness, affection, and other prosocial behaviors. Consumers who score high in agreeableness tend to value altruistic and socially responsible brands and will be involved in charitable and prosocial activities.

Neuroticism

This trait involves unpleasant emotions such as sadness, anxiety, and moodiness. Consumers who score high on neuroticism tend to be unpredictable in their responses to marketing messages and will need time to become comfortable with brands and products.

FIGURE 8.2 The Big 5 Personality Traits—the O.C.E.A.N. Model

for introducing new products with innovative features. Similarly, consumers who score high on extraversion can be targeted by marketers as social media influencers. Some personality traits are more consumer related and can be more beneficial for marketers. Figure 8.3 presents examples of consumers' related personality traits.[6]

Do Brands Have Personalities?

One of the fun ways that marketers have used the idea about personalities is to think about brands as having personalities. When you think about it, it seems plausible to talk about a brand as having a distinctive personality, much as people do.

For example, think about Coca-Cola. If Coca-Cola were a person, how would you describe its personality? **Brand personality**[7] is a set of human characteristics and traits that are associated

Brand personality a set of human characteristics and traits that are associated with a specific brand.

Materialism

The importance a person places on acquiring and owning material possessions. Materialistic consumers will favor objects over personal relationships.

Impulsiveness

The degree to which an individual acts without forethought and takes unnecessary risks with little consideration of the consequences. These consumers will make unplanned purchases motivated by emotions.

Innovativeness

Reflects the degree of novelty individuals seek in their products and personal experiences. Often it is domain specific. Consumers who are very innovative will be receptive to new product offerings.

Need for Uniqueness

The degree to which individuals seek to create personal and social identities that are distinct from others through the products and brands they acquire and use. Such consumers will prefer unique and unusual products.

Need for Cognition

Reflects the individual's inclination to engage in and enjoy complex, inquisitive, analytical thoughts and activities. Consumers with a strong need for cognition will seek out more information about products and brands.

FIGURE 8.3   Consumers' Related Personality Traits

with a specific brand. Marketers often intentionally attribute human characteristics to their brand name in order to create a desirable brand personality in the minds of their target audience. By creating a brand personality, marketers seek to evoke an emotional response in consumers, which will affect their consumption behavior.[8]

A strong brand personality offers several advantages. First, it creates a clear and differentiated brand image. Second, it increases the brand's equity and helps the company secure a competitive advantage. Third, it enables consumers to connect with the brand on a deeper emotional level and provides the company an opportunity to form strong relationships with consumers. Finally, a clear brand personality directs the firm's communication and marketing messages in terms of voice, tone, and style.

> *"Personality is critical to success – for brands as well as people. Don't leave it to chance!"*
>
> *Sir Richard Branson, founder of the Virgin Group*

This ad appeals to consumers' need for cognition by providing detailed information about the product.

Jennifer Aaker identified five brand personalities (see Figure 8.4) to guide brand positioning[9]:

- **Excitement:** These brands are trendy, daring, imaginative, carefree, spirited. Examples: Tesla, Red Bull, Coca-Cola, Nike.

- **Sincerity:** Sincere brands are down-to-earth, authentic, honest, kind, thoughtful. Examples: Disney, Hallmark, Amazon, Patagonia.

- **Ruggedness:** Rough, tough, outdoorsy, masculine. Examples: Jeep, Harley-Davidson, Timberland, Cabela's.

- **Competence:** Reliable, successful, hardworking, accomplished. Examples: Volvo, Google, Intel, Microsoft.

- **Sophistication:** Glamorous, upper class, elegant, prestigious. Examples: Tiffany, Rolex, Gucci, Apple.

Marketers can choose to focus on one dimension or to combine dimensions for a unique brand personality. Apple focuses on one key dimension: competence. It is a leader in its category, offering products that are innovative, very reliable, and easy to use. Coca-Cola is associated with the "excitement" and "sincerity" dimensions. The brand represents youthfulness and fun, and it is also honest and down-to-earth.

An alternative approach to focusing on a single personality trait is developing a more holistic personification of a brand in the form of personality archetypes. Figure 8.5 presents 12 different brand personality archetypes. A **brand personality archetype** connects the brand value proposition to consumers' basic desires, motivations, and needs.[10] It gives the brand a more human feel that makes it easier for consumers to connect with it. Because brand archetypes convey the brand value, it remains consistent over time. Disney, for example, can be characterized as a magician

Brand personality archetype connects the brand value proposition to consumers' basic desires, motivations, and needs.

FIGURE 8.4   Brand Personality Framework

Brand personality framework
includes five brand personalities: excitement, sincerity, ruggedness, competence, and sophistication.

brand archetype, a visionary brand that makes our dreams come true. Harley-Davidson, on the other hand, is the outlaw, a rebellious brand that defies the status quo. To which brand archetype do you connect the most?

Self-Concept

The second big idea in this chapter is the notion of consumers' self-concepts. We'll consider such questions as How do you see yourself as a consumer? Do you think you are a rational consumer? An impulsive one? The way you view yourself as a consumer reflects your consumer self-concept.[11]

Self-concept
the way people view themselves.

Self-concept, or self-identity, is the way you view yourself in different roles in your life. It's a mental picture of who you are, what makes you similar to or different from other people, and your strengths and weaknesses. Such an image includes your behavior, attitudes, abilities, opinions, preferences, beliefs, and other defining characteristics. For example, you might view yourself as a good student or a smart shopper as part of your overall self-concept, and you will take actions to support these views of your self-concept.

While a consumer's personality is considered to be stable throughout life, a consumer's self-concept is more malleable and can change as a result of people's experiences and interactions with others. It is shaped mainly during childhood and adolescence as people form their own identity as independent adults. Throughout this process, people's self-concept crystallizes and becomes much more organized, defining their perceptions about who they are and what is important to them.[12]

For marketers, the notion of self-concept is very important. They can offer and position products in a way that helps consumers formulate and reinforce their self-concepts as well as signaling to others in the brand choices they make.

The Innocent

Happy, optimistic, and honest. These brands aim to make us feel hopeful, warm, and fuzzy. Examples: Nestlé, Coca-Cola, Dove, Aveeno.

The Sage

Wise, intelligent, and curious. These brands encourage learning and want to help the world gain insight and understanding. Examples: Google, Wikipedia, CNN.

The Explorer

Adventurous, loves a challenge. These brands inspire us to push our limits and experience our environment. Examples: REI, Jeep, Patagonia.

The Outlaw

Rebellious, non-conforming, and bold. These brands challenge us to defy the status quo and break the rules. Examples: Harley-Davidson, Virgin, Diesel.

The Magician

Imaginative, a dreamer, visionary. These brands that make our dreams come true, they see our future and make it a reality. Examples: Disney, Tesla, Absolute.

The Hero

Brave, selfless, saves the day. These brands encourage us to become better so we can achieve our goals and improve the world. Examples: Nike, Michelin, Goodwill.

The Lover

Affectionate, emphatic, enjoys the good things in life. These brands foster relationships and intimacy. Examples: Cadillac, Victoria's Secret, Godiva, Gucci.

The Jester

Funny, playful, optimistic, joyful. These brands want to bring us joy and enable us to have a good time. Examples: Ben & Jerry's, M&M, Budweiser.

The Every man

Down-to-earth, reliable, friendly. Brands that create welcoming and inclusive communities. Examples: Target, Ikea, WWF, Levi's.

The Care giver

Nurturing, caring, trustworthy. Brands that want to look after us and protect us. Examples: ADT, Campbell Soup, Norton, UNICEF, Johnson & Johnson.

The Ruler

Polished, assertive, articulate, in control. These are typically luxury brands and aim to create wealth and success. Examples: Rolex, Louis Vuitton, Cartier, Hermès.

The Creator

Artistic, unique, creative. Brands that enable us to express our individuality, that create value. Examples: Lego, Xbox, Crayola.

FIGURE 8.5 Brand Personality Archetypes

This Nike ad expresses the athlete's self-concept view of herself.

There are three characteristics about self-concepts to note:

1. **Self-concept is organized.** It is a coherent structure of all of our feelings and ideas about ourselves. In order to maintain a harmonious view of who we are, we organize all of our experiences, feelings, opinions, and other elements that define us in a way that "fits" our perception of ourselves. For example, the woman in the Nike ad defines her self-concept as an athlete and rejects the somewhat stigmatizing self-concept of a female athlete. Consumers buy products that align with their self-concept and avoid purchasing products that are not consistent.

2. **Self-concept is learned.** Our self-concept develops and forms as we grow. It is shaped by our experiences and interactions with others, and by learning what is right and what is wrong, what is desirable, and what is not. Notice that our self-concept can differ from the way others view us.

   Marketers play an important role in "teaching" consumers what is socially desirable or not. Ads, commercials, and other marketing messages often portray desirable images that motivate consumers to purchase products and services that will help emulate such ideals. A notable example is the communication of what is regarded as the desirable image of a woman. Often such an image will depict a young, thin, often submissive individual rather than a leader. Recently, this image has been strongly criticized. As a result, many companies have started to use "real" or "realistic" models for their products. Even Victoria's Secret has adjusted the image of its "angels" by using models who are not extremely thin as their typical models.[13]

3. **Self-concept is dynamic.** Since our self-concept is actively shaped by our experience, it can change. We might have an experience that challenges our self-concept if our behavior

Victoria's Secret embraces different appearances for their angels.

does not match our belief about what is the right way to react, so we might change our self-concept to match our behavior. For example, we might have a self-concept as being a good consumer. However, if we learn that we overpaid for a product we purchased, we might change our perception. On the other hand, we might disregard this incident to maintain our original positive self-concept as a good consumer. A conflict between our self-concept and our behavior will make us experience cognitive dissonance, as discussed in Chapter 5. Challenges to our self-concept can have positive results as well. Let's say that we have a self-concept of being a poor consumer. An incident in which we scored a great deal might drive us to change our self-concept to being a good consumer. Thus, our self-concept continually develops as we disregard experiences that do not match our self-concept and embrace those experiences that we see as supportive in forming a favorable perception of ourselves.

The Structure of Self-Concept

The self-concept is important to psychologists and marketers. As a result, there is a lot of research in this area. Some psychologists have suggested that the self-concept consists of three self-representations[14]:

1. The **individual self**, which refers to the personality traits that make us unique.

2. The **relational self**, which corresponds to our relationships with others, such as friends and family. The relational self highlights elements that we have in common with others.

3. The **collective self**, the part of our self-concept that reflects our membership in various social groups, such as a political party, university, or sports team. It is formed based on the level of identification and shared attributes with these groups (the in-group). It also differentiates us from members of other groups to which we do not belong (the out-group). It can affect our brand choices as we try to fit in with certain groups.

Individual self
the personality traits that make us unique.

Relational self
highlights elements that we have in common with others.

Collective self
the part of our self-concept that reflects our membership in various social groups.

This ad appeals to the donor's individual self.

PAHO website appeals to donor's collective self.

Marketers can leverage these self-representations to better target consumers. Compare the two blood donation ads with regard to how marketers can address different self-representations to achieve the same goal. One ad appeals to the potential donor's individual self, and the other ad appeals to the collective self.

Carl Rogers, one of the founders of humanistic psychology, discussed self-concepts as being composed of self-image, self-esteem, and the ideal self:

1. **Self-image** reflects the way we see ourselves. It includes a mixture of attributes, such as our physical characteristics (e.g. height, weight, eye color), social roles (e.g. mother, husband, manager, student), and personality traits (e.g. introverted, generous, impulsive). Our self-image does not always overlap with reality. We sometimes have an inflated perception, think we're better (or worse) at something, and our self-image might not match the way others view us. An overly negative self-image will lead to low self-esteem and insecurity, and an overly positive self-image might be perceived as overconfident and arrogant. Marketers can appeal to our self-image, positive or negative, in order to affect our behavior. Tapping into our negative self-image will motivate us to move away from our current state or change our attitude, while tapping into our positive self-image will motivate us to maintain it.[15]

   Self-image
   the way we see ourselves.

2. **Self-esteem** refers to how much we value ourselves. Our self-esteem derives from our evaluation of our value compared to others as well as the way others respond to us.[16] A positive response from others about our behavior will boost our self-esteem. Similarly, when we compare ourselves to others and find that we are better than them in a certain domain, our self-esteem increases. Note that we can have high self-esteem in one domain of our life (I'm a good student) and low self-esteem in another (I'm a lousy cook) at the same time. Consumption can be very instrumental in boosting and influencing our self-esteem. Figure 8.6 indicates the factors that influence our self-esteem and the role of consumption[17] in doing so.

   Self-esteem
   how much we value ourselves.

3. The **ideal self**[18] is what we aspire to become in the future. Usually, it is an improved mental image of our current self-image. There is often a gap between our current and our ideal self-image. This incongruity can hurt our self-esteem, but it can be motivating. If the

   Ideal self
   what we aspire to become in the future.

REACTIONS OF OTHERS

01

Self-esteem is affected by the reaction we get from other people. For example, if people compliment us, think highly of us, or value our opinion, we experience high self-esteem. Complimenting our purchases and even mimicking them will also have a positive effect on our self-esteem.

COMPARISON WITH OTHERS

02

Self-esteem is a result of the comparison we make between ourselves and significant others. Feeling more successful or better than others will boost our self-esteem. Scoring a great deal might increase our self-esteem as well, because it will make us feel that we are a better shopper than others.

SOCIAL ROLES

03

Self-esteem depends on the status of our social role. Prestigious roles such as being a manager or the best worker of the week have a positive effect on our self-esteem. Purchasing prestigious brands will have a similar effect on our self-esteem

IDENTIFICATION

04

Self-esteem depends on the status of the people, social groups, organizations, and other important elements in our lives that we identify with. For example, identifying with a successful basketball team will have a positive effect on our self-esteem.

FIGURE 8.6   What Influences Our Self-esteem?

incongruity between who we are and who we want to be is small, it usually motivates us to improve ourselves (see more about motivation and self-actualization in Chapter 7). But when the incongruity between our current self-image and our ideal self is larger, it can be discouraging. The Nike ad strikes a nice balance, demonstrating how marketers can target our ideal self to motivate our behavior.

Obviously, psychologists have spent a great deal of time trying to understand personality and self-concepts – that's their job. Marketers use this information to have empathy; they're trying to see how consumers think about themselves. If consumers see themselves in a certain way, marketers can connect better to them if they include imagery (words and visuals) to help consumers relate to the brand.

Types of Self-Concepts

These ideas come together in Figure 8.7, "Types of Self-Concepts." The idea here is that our self-concept is multidimensional in nature.[19] One dimension refers to the visibility of our self-concept: the personal level versus the social level (this is like the individual or collective perspective). The second dimension refers to the state of our self-concept: actual versus ideal. These dimensions create four types of self-concepts:

Actual personal self the benchmark by which we assess what we have achieved so far.

1. **Actual personal self:** How do you see yourself in different domains of your life? What are your current attributes, traits, abilities, qualities, virtues, and vices? The actual personal self is the benchmark by which we assess what we have achieved so far. How do you see yourself as a student, a son or daughter, an employee? Consumers tend to buy products and brands that support or enhance their current self-concept and avoid products that they regard as not aligning in order to maintain self-consistency and self-integrity.

Ideal personal self a driver for self-improvement.

2. **Ideal personal self**: Who would you like to become? How do you see yourself in the future? What are the qualities and attributes that you aspire to have? The ideal self is constantly evolving and changing as you achieve your personal goals. It is a driver for self-improvement.

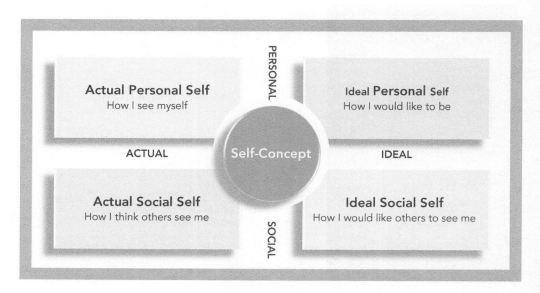

FIGURE 8.7   Types of Self-Concepts

3. **Actual social self:** This is sometimes referred to as the "looking-glass" self. It reflects how we think others perceive us. We use social interactions as a mirror that reflects how others view us. This reflection influences our perceptions about our self-worth, values, and behavior. As consumers, we purchase products and brands that will enhance our public image in the eyes of others. For example, students like wearing T-shirts with their college colors, names, and mascots to show their affiliation with their schools.

> **Actual social self**
> how we think others perceive us.

4. **Ideal social self:** Regardless of who we are or who we want to become, this element of our self-concept is how we would like other people to view us. It stems from our need for social approval. We behave in a way that we believe will make others think highly of us. Not surprisingly, the ideal social self will drive us to buy products that we think others will approve of, or we avoid buying brands and products (even if we like them) to avoid the disapproval of others.

> **Ideal social self**
> how we would like other people to view us.

The interplay between the private and public aspects of our self-concept as well as the interplay between the actual and ideal aspects of our self-concept will affect our well-being and self-esteem. We will strive to maintain **self-congruence** and consistency between our actual and ideal self-concepts both on the personal and the public levels.[20] Any discrepancy or incongruence between our actual and ideal selves will lead to adverse feelings, such as lower self-esteem, anxiety, and depression. In a similar manner, a discrepancy between the private and public aspects of our self-concept will lead to heightened feelings of self-doubt and psychological pain.[21] Marketers often find that consumers purchase mundane, practical products guided by their current self, whereas conspicuous consumption and purchases of status products are driven by a consumer's ideal self and social factors.

> **Self-congruence**
> consistency between our actual and ideal selves.

As you can see, consumers are complicated – that's what makes them interesting in life and challenging for marketers. If we step back and put these concepts together, we are talking about "social cognitive theory." The main idea is that consumers' personalities reflect an interconnection among person, behavior, and environment. Specifically, the person is the consumer's personality, his or her characteristics and cognitive processes. The behavior is what marketers are most interested in: the individual's purchasing frequency, intensity, and valence of attitudes. Environment is anything in the consumer's context, including social influences, such as friends and family and social media, but also physical environmental factors, such as a retail setting.

Do the right thing!

What do you think of when you see these self-concept ideas as ways to describe consumers and ways for marketers to appeal to consumers? Is it wrong to get inside consumers' heads like that? It seems so personal. . . . Are there ways to do it well? The long-running ad for the Army that says "Be all you can be" is trying to encourage people to strive to be their best. Most marketing communications are positive framed, along the lines of "This is how you'll be better if you buy our brand." Is that acceptable? If not, what would be better?

Possessions as an Extension of the Self

Just as marketers have considered brand personalities, they have thought about what we own and what we buy in relation to our self-concepts. What do your possessions say about you? According to the **extended self** theory introduced by Russell Belk, our possessions are a direct extension of our self-identity.[22] We purchase products not just for their utilitarian value but also for their symbolic value. They help us construct, maintain, and project a desired self-image. Our possessions

> **Extended self**
> our possessions are a direct extension of our self-identity.

help define who we are, as much as who we are defines what we buy, use, give away, or dispose of. The extended self is not restricted to material objects. People, places, pets, and other items can be used for self-extension purposes. The extended self is not restricted to physical items or to the physical world. We express who we are online via avatars, our posts, likes, shares, and other online activities.[23] Building on the notion of congruency, we will seek congruency between our self-concept and the products and brands we purchase.

Naturally, not all of our possessions become part of our extended self. It depends on how important the product is to our identity. For example, we may fully appreciate that our toothpaste seems to give us good dental visits, and its taste is refreshing. But that doesn't mean we go around saying, "I'm a Crest (or Colgate) person!"

The marketers' role is to try to get consumers to think about how the brand helps with their personal identities. They can try to influence the decision-making process prior to purchase. They also can strengthen these connections in post-purchase follow-ups and social media.

Pets can be part of our extended self.

Consumer Values

These ideas about a consumer's personality and self-concept relate to their values, not in the economic sense (value being a trade-off of quality and price), but in terms of defining who the consumer is, so the marketer can communicate in a way that appeals to their values. The most central things consumers care about are referred to as their **core values**. Core values are the principal beliefs of a person or organization, such as desiring a sense of security or the pursuit of happiness. Consumers' values are important to marketers because they reflect their priorities and preferences; they guide decision-making and are derivers of behavior. Indeed, 83% of millennials stress the importance of alignment between their values and the values of the brands they purchase.[24] Young consumers begin to understand and adopt values (without necessarily

Core values
the most central things consumers care about.

knowing it), and that's referred to as **enculturation**. When people live (even temporarily) in another country, they observe and sometimes begin to adapt the local values, and that's called **acculturation**.[25] For example, individuals who move from a more collectivistic culture to the United States may choose to acculturate and adopt its individualist cultural value.

In the United States, values include individualism, freedom, efficiency, hard work, youthfulness, patriotism, some level of fitness, and a good level of material comfort. These values affect marketers. Many brands highlight their core values in a way that appeals to consumers. For example, Coca-Cola is associated with youthfulness, Airbnb promotes hospitality, Apple's value is creativity, and Zillow highlights the value of ownership.

Enculturation
understanding and adoption of values.

Acculturation
adoption of the values of a different culture.

The website of Ram Commercial highlights the value of hard work.

So How Does This Affect Marketers?

We've discussed numerous marketing actions that can be taken to communicate and persuade consumers based on personality and self-concept. Some of the concepts seem easier to translate to marketing than others, but with some creative conversations among the brand team, a lot of it is useful and applicable.

For example, in the big five personality traits, it's easy to imagine marketers of outdoor gear appealing to the segment of consumers who are open to new experiences. What a great fit! By comparison, at first glance, it might seem that the trait of neuroticism is one that consumers wouldn't want to acknowledge in themselves, but, again, let's think it through. Everybody buys a laptop, but there are different kinds of laptops, and different brands and companies; some are nerdy, and others emphasize nice design (e.g. Apple). Neurotic consumers may not be as interested in Apple ads that emphasize sleek designs and instead may prefer those by Dell that are heavy on features and attributes. The listing of features appeals to their neurotic self.

The five consumer traits also obviously provide marketers with ideas about how to appeal to different consumer segments. For example, for materialistic consumers, it's easy to play up elements of conspicuous consumption, say, or being "one-up" compared to a friend who doesn't wear the latest fashion. Other consumers would reject materialism and embrace a simpler lifestyle (one that is not as materialistic), so the messaging needs to be very careful. A "look at me in my new jacket" ad would play well with the materialists and not so much with the nonmaterialistic consumers.

SUMMARY

This chapter explains the importance for marketers of consumers' personalities, their self-concepts, and their attitudes.

An individual's personality is made up of unique characteristics and distinct patterns of thoughts, feelings, and behaviors. There are three major perspectives on personalities: psychoanalytic, humanistic, and traits. The psychoanalytic perspective explores how personality develops and highlights the importance of childhood experiences, as well as the influence of the unconscious mind in the formation of personality and its three components of id, ego, and superego. The humanistic perspective highlights how individuals have free will, are basically good, and have a need to live to their full potential. The trait perspective looks at how a person's traits help explain the person's personality. Personality traits that are particularly relevant to consumer behavior include materialism, impulsiveness, innovativeness, need for uniqueness,

and need for cognition. Marketers also imbue their brands with personality to evoke a positive consumer response and enhance potential buying.

Consumers' self-concept is the way they view themselves in different roles in their lives. The nature of self-concept is that it is organized, learned, and dynamic. Self-concept is an umbrella concept that also includes self-image and self-esteem. These concepts explain how consumers see themselves and value themselves. Four influences of self-esteem are reactions of others, comparison with others, social roles, and identification. Self-concept is multidimensional and can be broken into two main levels: personal versus social and actual versus ideal. The interplay between the private and public aspects of our self-concept as well as the interplay between the actual and ideal aspects will affect our well-being and our self-esteem.

KEY TERMS

Personality-based marketing	Superego	Brand personality archetype	Self-esteem	Extended self
Personality	Humanistic perspective	Self-concept	Ideal self	Core values
Psychoanalytic perspective	Big five theory	Individual self	Actual personal self	Enculturation
Id	Brand personality	Relational self	Ideal personal self	Acculturation
Ego	Brand personality framework	Collective self	Actual social self	
		Self-image	Ideal social self	
			Self-congruence	

EXERCISES

1. Freudian psychoanalytic theory is often the focus of jokes (it sounds outdated or not cool), yet it sustains because there seems to be some sense to its core – that we often have multiple motivations and they may be in conflict with one another. With a classmate, go online and Google images for ads, and find an ad for a brand that seems to speak to a consumer's:

   Id

   Ego

   Superego

   In a small team of classmates, see if someone can come up with an example of a brand they like and buy, in part because it offers a favorable self-presentation (e.g. a brand of clothing that is fashionable, a brand of phone that says they're rich or techy). See if someone else will offer an example of a brand that they love but are embarrassed to admit it!

2. With a classmate, look over the list of five brand personalities. How would you describe your university or business school?

Could a university be "exciting" or "sincere"? Could a program within the business school be "rugged" or "sophisticated"?

3. Look at your social media profile. What would you say is your social media personality? If you were a brand, what would be your personality? Ask one of your friends to look at your social media profile and tell you what would be your brand personality? Did you both reach out to the same conclusion? If not, why do you think is the reason or reasons for that?

4. Pick five items that you consider an extension of your self-identity. Show these items to one of your friends. Ask them to describe a person who own these items. How accurately did they describe you? Are there any discrepancies in their description? If yes, why do you think is the reason or reasons for that?

5. Think about your self-concept. What are the notable differences between your actual personal self and your actual social self? What are the differences between your actual personal self and ideal personal self? How do you think marketers can leverage such differences in targeting consumers?

ENDNOTES

1. https://www.apa.org/topics/personality.

2. A. E. Kazdin, *Encyclopedia of Psychology,* vol. 2 (Washington, DC: American Psychological Association, 2000), 10517–106.

3. S. Freud, "The Ego and the Id," in *The Standard Edition of the Complete Psychological Works of Sigmund Freud*, vol. 19 (London: Hogarth House, 1923–1925), 1–66.

4. R. H. Coulter and G. Zaltman, "Using the Zaltman Metaphor Elicitation Technique to Understand Brand Images," in *Advances in Consumer Research,* vol. 21, eds. C. T. Allen and D. R. John (Provo, UT: Association for Consumer Research, 1994), 501–7.

5. R. R. McCrae and P. T. Costa Jr., "The Five-Factor Theory of Personality," in *Handbook of Personality: Theory and Research*, eds. O. P. John, R. W. Robines, and L. A. Pervin (New York: Guilford Press, 2008), 159–81.

6. M. L. Richins and S. Dawson, "A Consumer Values Orientation for Materialism and Its Measurement: Scale Development and Validation," *Journal of Consumer Research* 19, no. 3 (1992): 303–16; K. C. Manning, W. O. Bearden, and T. J. Madden, "Consumer Innovativeness and the Adoption Process," *Journal of Consumer Psychology* 4, no. 4 (1995): 329–45; K. T. Tian, W. O. Bearden, and G. L. Hunter, "Consumers' Need for Uniqueness: Scale Development and Validation," *Journal of Consumer Research* 28, no. 1 (2001): 50–66.

7. J. L. Aaker, "Dimensions of Brand Personality," *Journal of Marketing Research* 34, no. 3 (1997): 347–56.

8. L. Malär, H. Krohmer, W. D. Hoyer, and B. Nyffenegger, "Emotional Brand Attachment and Brand Personality: The Relative Importance of the Actual and the Ideal Self," *Journal of Marketing* 75, no. 4 (2011): 35–52.

9. Aaker, "Dimensions of Brand Personality.

10. M. Mark and C. S. Pearson, *The Hero and the Outlaw: Building Extraordinary Brands through the Power of Archetypes* (New York: McGraw Hill Professional, 2001).

11. D. Oyserman, "Self-Concept and Identity," in *Perspectives on Social Psychology. Self and Social Identity,* eds. M. B. Brewer and M. Hewstone (Hoboken, NJ: Blackwell Publishing, 2004), 5–24.

12. B. W. Roberts and W. F. DelVecchio, "The Rank-Order Consistency of Personality Traits from Childhood to Old Age: A Quantitative Review of Longitudinal Studies," *Psychological Bulletin* 126, no. 1 (2000): 3.

13. https://www.allure.com/story/victorias-secret-plus-size-model.

14. M. B. Brewer and W. Gardner, "Who Is This 'We'? Levels of Collective Identity and Self Representations," *Journal of Personality and Social Psychology* 71, no. 1 (1996): 83–93.

15. S. Hosany and D. Martin, "Self-Image Congruence in Consumer Behavior," *Journal of Business Research* 65, no. 5 (2012): 685–91.

16. R. W. Tafarodi and W. B. Swann Jr., "Self-Liking and Self-Competence as Dimensions of Global Self-Esteem: Initial Validation of a Measure," *Journal of Personality Assessment* 65, no. 1 (1995): 322–42.

17. A. Stuppy, N. L. Mead, and S. Van Osselaer, "I Am, Therefore I Buy: Low Self-Esteem and the Pursuit of Self-Verifying Consumption," *Journal of Consumer Research* 46, no. 5 (2020): 956–73.

18. Malär et al., "Emotional Brand Attachment and Brand Personality."

19. C. Isackson and M. Bok, *Destination Images as Reflections of Consumers' Self-concept – A Qualitative Study.* (2015)

20. Hosany and Martin, "Self-Image Congruence in Consumer Behavior."

21. Malär et al., "Emotional Brand Attachment and Brand Personality."

22. R. W. Belk, "Possessions and the Extended Self," *Journal of Consumer Research* 15, no. 2 (1988): 139–68.

23. R. W. Belk, "Extended Self in a Digital World," *Journal of Consumer Research* 40, no. 3 (2013): 477–500.

24. https://smallbiztrends.com/2020/02/brand-values-alignment.html.

25. L. N. Penaloza, "Immigrant Consumer Acculturation," in *ACR North American Advances*, vol. 16, ed. Thomas K. Srull (Provo, UT: ACR, 1989), 110–18.

CREDITS

https://topdogsocialmedia.com/10-types-of-social-media-users

https://www.designcrowd.com/design/11979071

https://www.shutterstock.com/image-photo/colorful-textured-background-276379487

https://popsop.com/2013/09/burger-king-reducing-fat-content-by-40-in-the-new-satisfries-in-the-u-s/

Aaker, J. L. "Dimensions of Brand Personality." *Journal of Marketing Research*, 34, no. 3 (1997): 347–56.

https://www.adsoftheworld.com/media/print/mcdonalds_einstein

https://www.adweek.com/creativity/lane-bryant-bashes-victorias-secret-im-no-angel-campaign-163944/

https://in.pinterest.com/pin/569775790349159413/

https://www.paho.org/en/wbdd2021

https://iconicfox.com.au/brand-archetypes

https://pixabay.com/illustrations/search/tux/

https://www.shutterstock.com/image-photo/attractive-woman-enjoying-on-beach-1343352860

Isackson, C., and M. Bok, *Destination Images as Reflections of Consumers' Self-concept – A Qualitative Study* (2015).

https://www.growthrabbit.com/spy-competitors-facebook-ads-research/barkbox-facebook-ads-landing-page

https://www.ramtrucks.com/ram-heavy-duty/commercial.html

Figure 8.1: Africa Studio/Shutterstock

Figure 8.6: Kitja Kitja/Shutterstock

Image p. 145: The Donna Karan Company Store LLC

Image p. 149: Burger King

Image p. 152: Nike Inc.

Image p. 153: Lane Bryant

Image p. 154: Pan American Health Organization (PAHO)

Image p. 158: BarkBox

Image p. 159: FCA US LLC.

Learning and Memory

9

LEARNING OBJECTIVES

After studying this chapter, you should be able to:

- Appreciate how consumer learning is essential for consumer behavior.
- Consumers learn about brands from experience and from what marketing tells them.
- When choosing brands, consumers draw from their memories about the brands.
- Understand that marketers should provide consumers with information that will direct their choices and encourage them to buy.

To get a consumer's attention, some ads feature celebrities who endorse a brand. As consumers we know that these people are paid, but we still learn something from the ads. We learn that Nike supports Colin Kaepernick, and that might make us feel good to buy Nike. Katy Perry puts bags of Popchips in front of her and says, "Nothing fake about 'em" – okay, a little silly, but it hits home that the chips may be healthier for us. Daniel Craig endorses an Omega watch, and we might think, "Maybe to celebrate my next promotion, I can wear James Bond's watch as well." What's going on when we make these connections? Marketers are tuning in to how consumers learn, and they are trying to shift consumers' attitudes.

Consumer Learning

How do you learn about new products, or even what products *not* to buy? Consumers have many sources of information – brands make certain claims in ads, but consumers are frequently skeptical of a company's communications. In addition to advertisements, consumers can see products online or in person at stores and judge for themselves about whether they're interested in buying. These days, one of the most frequent sources of information is online – in searches or social media.

What is the goal of this proliferation of information, whether the information comes from the company or is sought out by the consumer? It's learning – learning about what brands are good, or at least good for what the consumer needs, and what brands wouldn't cut it.

Learning
the gain of
information.

More precisely, what is learning? The most common definition of **learning** is when consumers gain information, whether from their direct experience or from word-of-mouth, as well as marketing efforts such as advertising, or just by observing other consumers.[1] When learning "sticks," it becomes part of our memory (discussed later in this chapter). Marketers try to get consumers to learn about their brands and products and remember the brand positioning or the products' features and benefits to enhance consumers' positive attitudes (which are discussed in the next chapter). As Figure 9.1 shows, there are several elements of learning.[2] Three of them are of significant importance:

1. Learning is an ongoing, lifelong, dynamic process.

2. The driver of the change is the learner's experience, such as the individual's own direct experience with a product or even an ad, or indirectly through word-of-mouth by seeing what others say about the brand (friends and coworkers and also strangers online).

3. Learning can lead to changes that may be gradual and subtle or quick and dramatic, and they may be long-lasting.

Marketers care about learning because it is a fundamental element in consumers' decision-making (as you may recall from Chapter 4). Every aspect of consumer behavior is affected by knowledge and experience. Marketing gurus would even go so far as to say that learning is the foundation of consumer behavior. We seek more information when we are unfamiliar with specific brands and products. We stop buying products that we have had a bad experience with. We share pleasant shopping experiences with others. Sometimes we like to explore new products. For example, the Facebook ad of Fabletics[3] encourages consumers to learn more about why other consumers love the brand.

Our ongoing process of learning as consumers presents a valuable opportunity for companies to direct our learning process and influence it. Learning is part of the consumer's journey. Thus, by mapping our learning process as consumers, companies can affect our resulting

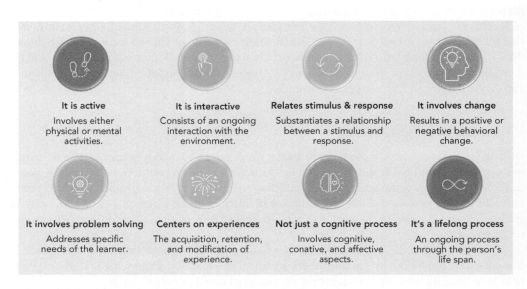

FIGURE 9.1 The Key Characteristics of the Learning Process

USING A TEASER ON SOCIAL MEDIA

Fabletics is offering a teaser, and now women want to know more!

consumption behavior. Companies use many different tactics to help us learn about their brands and products. One of the most effective strategies is to provide us with the opportunity to experience the products firsthand via free samples or trial periods – from little munchies at Costco to a test drive for a car. Experiencing the product directly enables us to form attitudes about it, such as Disney+ encourages consumers to try the channel for free.

Two perspectives of learning theories can help marketers understand consumers' learning process better and provide guidance as to how to influence it in a way that brings about the desired purchasing behavior. The first is the behavioral perspective of learning, and the second is the cognitive perspective of learning.[4] Behavioral learning theories posit that learning is a response to external stimuli and focus on observed behavior – the consumer does something different, for example, trying and buying a different brand. Cognitive learning theories regard learning as a function of an internal mental process – the consumer might think more favorably or more knowledgably about a brand. Let's look at each.

Behavioral Learning Theories

Behavioral learning theories see learning as a behavioral response to external events or cues. These theories focus on the relationship between a stimulus and a response. They give less importance to the internal and unobservable process of learning. The focal interest is the stimulus and the change in the behavior, and that's what indicates learning.[5]

Behavioral learning theories see learning as a behavioral response to external events or cues.

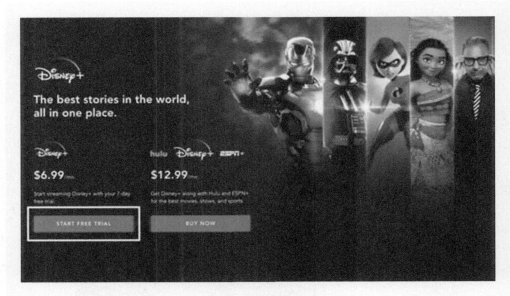

Disney+ encourages consumers to try the channel for free.

Classical conditioning
paring two independent stimuli to each other to generate a new learned response.

Neutral stimulus
a stimulus that initially does not result in any particular behavior.

Unconditioned stimulus
a stimulus that leads to an automatic response.

Unconditioned behavioral response
a natural reaction to an unconditioned stimulus.

Conditioned stimulus
a previously neutral stimulus that produces the same behavior as unconditioned stimulus, after repeated association with it.

Classical Conditioning

The Russian physiologist Ivan Pavlov introduced the notion of classical or Pavlovian conditioning. It is considered one of the fundamental ways we learn about the world around us. According to this theory, two independent stimuli are paired with each other to result in a new learned response.[6] The process of learning occurs when a **neutral stimulus** that initially does not result in any particular behavior is associated with an **unconditioned stimulus** (a stimulus that leads to an automatic response) that reliably results in an **unconditioned behavioral response** (a natural reaction to an unconditioned stimulus). When the two stimuli are paired, the neutral stimulus becomes a **conditioned stimulus**[7] (a previously neutral stimulus that produces the same behavior as unconditioned stimulus, after repeated association with it). Over time, it will produce the same behavioral response as the unconditioned stimulus independently.

In his famous experiment with dogs (Figure 9.2), Pavlov gave the animals food (an unconditioned stimulus). In response, the dogs salivated (an unconditioned response). At the same time, he rang a bell near them (a neutral stimulus), which resulted in no behavioral response. But with time, as Pavlov paired the food with the ringing of the bell, soon enough, the dogs associated the sound of the bell with the food and would salivate (a conditioned response), even when they just heard the bell (a conditioned stimulus) without being given food. Pavlov concluded that the dogs learned that the sound of the bell was a reliable predictor of food. He was able to evoke an automatic, reflexive response to a previously neutral stimulus.

How does this experiment relate to marketing? Classical conditioning has long been and still is an effective and impactful tool for marketing messages and brand building. The notion of sponsorship is built on the premise of this theory.

For example, a few years ago, PepsiCo took over the sponsorship rights for the National Basketball Association from Coca-Cola,[8] which had been the league's official sponsor for 28 years. If we think about classical conditioning in this context, the NBA games are the unconditioned stimulus

FIGURE 9.2 Classical Conditioning

that elicits pleasurable and joyful feelings for its fans (an unconditioned response). When pairing the NBA games with the PepsiCo brand (which is neutral in the NBA setting), marketers hope to make the brand a conditioned stimulus that will evoke a conditioned response of pleasurable and joyful feelings, even when presented in other contexts. The positive feelings can transfer back and forth as well – people attending the games who like Pepsi might feel good about its connection to the NBA.

PepsiCo is now sponsoring the National Basketball Association games.

	SLOGAN	USED SINCE
MAXWELL HOUSE	Good to the last drop	1917
WHEATIES	Breakfast of Champions	1927
DEBEERS	A diamond is forever	1948
KFC	Finger lickin' good	1952
KIT KAT	Have a break… Have a Kit Kat.	1957
NIKE	Just do it.	1988

FIGURE 9.3   Repetition in Marketing

Repetition
a recurrent exposure
to the same stimulus.

To this day, marketers rely heavily on classical conditioning. All of these concepts come from classical conditioning theory: repetition, stimulus generalization, and stimulus discrimination.

Repetition refers to recurrent exposure to the same stimulus. The more we are exposed to the same stimulus, the easier it is for us to remember it, and the more likely that it will result in a change in our behavior. There's something about repeated exposure that gives us a comfortable feeling of familiarity, and we begin to like the brand.[9]

As you can see from Figure 9.3, some messages have been used for decades and are still effective.[10] Repetition makes messages sound more familiar to consumers, and that familiarity increases their trust in the message.

For that reason, marketers repeat their marketing messages over and over, utilizing different media outlets. Studies show that marketing messages are more effective when repeated. The notion of **effective frequency** reflects the number of times a message needs to be repeated in order to generate the desired behavior from consumers.[11] There is no exact magic number. Long ago a marketer working at General Electric claimed that the magic number was 3. That is, when you see an ad for the first time, you think, "Oh, that's interesting; I hadn't known that." When you see the ad for the second time, you think, "Oh, yeah, that brand," and maybe the ad provides a little bit more knowledge. When you see the ad for the third time, you think, "Uh, not that again; I get it already!" and you stop listening.[12]

Effective frequency
the number of times
a message needs to
be repeated in order
to generate the desired
behavior from
consumers.

**Advertising
wearout**
a decline in the
effectiveness of the
message due to repetition overload.

These days marketers think the magic number is closer to 7 or 10. It's worth testing with marketing research as the ads are airing. Marketers need to use repetition carefully and avoid **advertising wearout,** in which the effectiveness of the message declines due to repetition overload.[13] Like a song you've heard too many times, when it comes on the radio, you have Siri change the station to tune it out. Or think of the ads that employ repetition, like the "Hey, we're at 1-800-555-1212, that's 1-800-555-1212; one more time, that's 1-800-555-1212!" Who likes that? Yet the tradition continues because, after that commercial, you'll remember that if you want to call the company, it's 1-800-555-you know the rest.

Whether wearout occurs at three or seven ad exposures also depends on the complexity of the message: if the ad is for a new beer, there's not much to explain, but if the ad is for a "new-to-the-world" kind of product, it may require more ad exposures before consumers understand the value proposition. At the point of wearout, the advertising is becoming ineffective; it isn't helping consumers learn, and it isn't persuading them to buy. If the ad is becoming less effective, that also means the return on investment for that ad spending is dropping.

Stimulus generalization occurs when a new stimulus that is similar to a previously associated stimulus evokes the same response as the previously associated prompt. Think about all the "wanna-be" brands – the little brands want to be associated with the big brands in the minds of consumers; some small brands even strive for confusing consumers. Within the company, stimulus generalization is the basis of product line and brand extension strategies.[14]

Product line extension includes incorporating a product that is a slight variation of a well-established product line.[15] An example is when Starbucks introduces a new flavored coffee. This strategy leverages the reputation of the brand and the familiarity of consumers.[16] It is estimated that more than 50% of all new products introduced to the market each year are line extensions.[17]

Brand extension is similar to line extension in that it also leverages the familiarity and reputation of an existing brand when incorporating a new product. The difference is that a line extension normally refers to the introduction of a new product in the same product category, whereas a brand extension refers to the introduction of a new product in a different product category.[18]

An example is when Starbucks introduced Doubleshot Energy.[19] For this strategy to be successful, the new product needs to be significantly different from the brand's original product category, yet related to it in a way that will ensure that it will not confuse consumers. For example, Arm & Hammer introduced an underarm deodorant spray, but it didn't do well because consumers didn't think it was aligned well with the brand's original category of cleaning products.

Stimulus generalization occurs when a new stimulus that is similar to a previously associated stimulus evokes the same response as the previously associated prompt.

Product line extension introducing a product that is a slight variation of a well-established product line.

Brand extension leveraging the familiarity and reputation of an existing brand when incorporating a new product.

Starbucks' line extensions.

Stimulus discrimination occurs when only the original stimulus elicits a response, and it is not transferable to other stimuli.

Stimulus discrimination is the opposite of stimulus generalization. It occurs when only the original stimulus elicits a response, and it is not transferable to other stimuli.[20] Stimulus discrimination characterizes brands that have a very distinct and differentiated image. Companies such as Procter & Gamble and L'Oréal use this strategy – they build a unique and differentiated brand image for each of their brands. Doing so enables these companies to address the needs of a wide range of consumers in an effective and authentic way.[21]

L'Oréal uses stimulus discrimination strategy with its multiple brands across the world.

Another use of classical conditioning is in introducing, updating, or creating company and brand logos. A company may even hope that its logo will be confused with that of the market leader. As Figure 9.4 shows, some logos are straightforward in what they convey: consumers understand immediately what brand is being featured. Target has a target logo, and with time, even if the store name were to be dropped, consumers would recognize this symbol as Target. IBM's logo says, "IBM"! YouTube's logo says "YouTube," and on it goes.

Figure 9.4 also reminds us of how neutral many logos begin. These are all car brand logos, and have very little inherent meaning until the consumer is exposed to them repeatedly. Yes, the Lexus logo looks somewhat like an "L," and the Acura like an "A," and a "Hyundai" like an "H," but how do we know that "H" is for Hyundai and not Honda, for example? Consumers learn to associate the brand name with the logo through multiple exposures of marketing communications.

Finally, the figure also provides two pairs of examples where the logos might create some confusion among consumers. Sometimes marketers do this purposely, but whether Gucci (with its intertwined Gs) and Chanel (ditto its Cs) unfolded as similar strategically, who knows. The PayPal and pandora logos look similar (Google them!), and presumably this is just coincidence, given that they are not competitors. The bottom line is that classical conditioning can help marketers teach consumers about a lot of things, logos included.

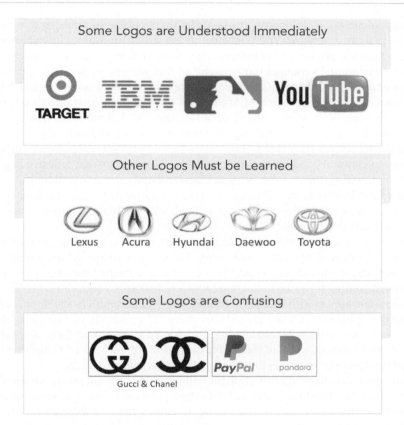

FIGURE 9.4 Learning About Logos

Do the Right Thing!

Is it unethical when one brand makes its logo look so similar to the market leader's brand that consumers get confused? This is known as logo infringement, and many lawsuits have been filed (for and against Starbucks, McDonald's, Adidas, etc.). How similar is similar? What percentage of consumers have to be confused before it is said to be infringement? Isn't it said that "Imitation is the best form of flattery"? Although is that what you want your brand to be – a copy? Wouldn't it be more exciting to create an original brand and show consumers why you're better than the brand you were thinking of copying?

Operant Conditioning

Operant conditioning, also known as instrumental conditioning, is another learning theory based on building associations. This theory, attributed to B. F. Skinner, focuses on the association between a particular behavior and a consequence. However, the order of the stimulus and the behavior differ from that in classical conditioning. In classical conditioning, the stimuli precede the behavioral response. Operant conditioning posits that first we exhibit a behavior, then we alter it based on the rewards or punishments we receive as a result.[22]

Operant conditioning alteration of a behavior based on the rewards or punishments.

Reinforcement
a procedure, negative
or positive, that alters
a response to a
stimulus.

According to operant conditioning, the behavior precedes the stimulus, and learning occurs through trial and error. Rewards and punishments are strong motivators for behavioral change. According to Skinner, this form of **reinforcement** (a procedure, negative or positive, that alters a response to a stimulus[23]) changes our behavior so that we will try to obtain a desired reward or avoid an undesired punishment. Therefore, rewards promote a behavior, and punishments reduce or even eliminate a behavior. Marketers use the notion of rewards and punishments to promote positive behaviors, such as in the ad of Healthworks that promotes healthy eating, or to eliminate bad behaviors, such as smoking, drinking and driving, and bullying.

Another difference between classical conditioning and operant conditioning is the nature of the response. In classical conditioning, the response is involuntary and reflexive (e.g. drooling). In operant conditioning, the response in most cases is voluntary and intentional.

**Schedule of
reinforcement**
setting up a rule
indicating on which
instances a behavior
will be reinforced.

The role of the learner is also different. Classical conditioning views the learner as passive, while operant conditioning views the learner as an active participant. Figure 9.5 summarizes the differences between the theories.[24]

Marketers often use operant conditioning. Coupons, rebates, cashback, and loyalty rewards programs are all forms of operant conditioning. Loyalty rewards programs reward consumers for their purchases, so the consumers purchase even more. Loyalty programs use a **schedule of reinforcement** (setting up a rule indicating on which instances a behavior will be reinforced),[25] which provides consumers with rewards at **fixed ratios** (reinforcing a behavior only after a specified number of responses), such as a reward after every "X" number of purchases or "$X" amount of money spent. Such reward mechanisms are so powerful that some form of loyalty rewards programs are now offered by 90% of the businesses in the United States.[26] Consumers have been conditioned to expect such rewards for their loyalty and repeat purchases.

Fixed ratio
reinforcing a behavior
only after a specified
number of responses.

There are other schedules of reinforcement within operant conditioning, but marketers don't use them as often. The fixed ratio approach used by loyalty cards basically says, "After every 5th or 10th purchase, the consumer gets something of value, such as a freebie or a discount." The **variable ratio** schedule (reinforcing a behavior after an unknown or random number of responses[27]) says that, *on average*, after every fifth purchase, the consumer gets a discount. This process is not popular with marketers or consumers because it introduces uncertainty. The consumer having just bought five coffees and is now buying a sixth might be hoping to get it for free, but the "average" means that they may not get a free coffee until number 7, or number 10, for that matter.

Variable ratio
reinforcing a behavior
after an unknown or
random number of
responses.

Fixed interval
reinforcing a behavior
after specific (predict-
able) amount of time.

There are also schedules based on time intervals. A **fixed interval** schedule of operant conditioning reinforcement says, "Every five days (five days is the interval), we will send you an email

	CLASSICAL CONDITIONING	OPERANT CONDITIONING
Role of the learner	Passive	Active
Timing of stimulus	Before the response	After the response
Timing of the response	After the stimulus	Before the stimulus
Nature of response	Involuntary	Voluntary in most cases, but can be involuntary as well

FIGURE 9.5 Classical Versus Operant Conditioning

with product news or discounts linked to our website." Finally, a variable interval process says, "On average, every five days, we will send you an email"; thus, the email might be sent on day 4 or day 8, for example.

Of these operant conditioning schedules of reinforcement, the one that most marketers use, and the one that most consumers expect, is the fixed ratio rule. The others are not as attractive because the variable (ratio or interval) schedules introduce uncertainty, and the fixed interval rewards consumers as a function of time, rather than anything they do to engage with the company.

Cognitive Learning Theories

Cognitive learning theories focus on internal mental processes as a central part of learning.[28] The focus is less on what you do as a result of learning and more on the fact that your thinking has changed – your attitude toward a brand may become more (or less) favorable, or you gain expertise, and you have a clearer understanding of why you want to buy one brand or another.

Cognitive learning theories focus on internal mental processes as a central part of learning.

Cognitive learning theories seek to understand how the human mind works while we learn and how we process information mentally. They view individuals as active learners who seek to solve problems and learn by processing information, storing it, retaining it, and retrieving it when needed.

For example, think about receiving an email or text message about a promotion or a sale on a product you like. You may not buy it immediately, but when you consider purchasing it, you will likely remember that promotion and use it.

The origin of the cognitive perspective of learning is credited to Jean Piaget, who was an educational psychologist. Piaget believed that in order to understand a behavior, one must understand the mental processes that lead to it.

The cognitive perspective of learning was further developed by Albert Bandura as the **social cognitive theory**, which reminds us that learning happens in a social context and is reflected in the interaction between a person, the environment, and behavior. While there are internal factors at play, such as our attitudes and beliefs, there are also external forces, such as social norms and the influence of others (see Figure 9.6).[29]

Social cognitive theory posits that learning happens in a social context and is reflected in the interaction between a person, the environment, and behavior.

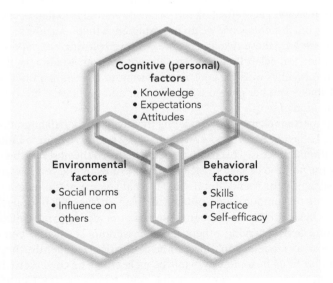

FIGURE 9.6 Social Cognitive Theory of Learning

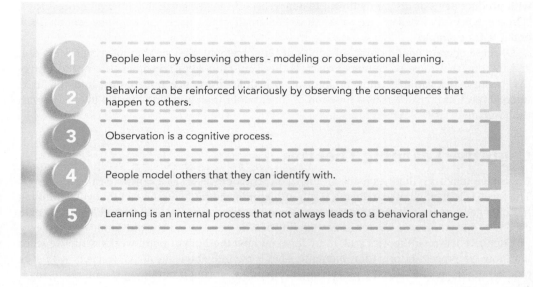

1 People learn by observing others - modeling or observational learning.

2 Behavior can be reinforced vicariously by observing the consequences that happen to others.

3 Observation is a cognitive process.

4 People model others that they can identify with.

5 Learning is an internal process that not always leads to a behavioral change.

FIGURE 9.7   Characteristics of Social Cognitive Learning

Observational learning
(or vicarious learning) – learning by watching others, then change our own attitudes or behaviors accordingly.

Modeling
the process of mimicking and imitating the behavior of others.

Vicarious reinforcement
or **punishment** – reinforcing a behavior by observing another's being reinforced or punished.

Social models
the people we choose as models. They don't have to be celebrities.

For marketers, two aspects of social cognitive learning are especially relevant (see other characteristics of social cognitive learning in Figure 9.7).[30] The first is **observational learning** (or vicarious learning); that is, we learn by watching others, then change our own attitudes or behaviors accordingly. For learning to occur, we need to store our observations and use them at a later point to guide our behavior. Unlike classical or operant conditioning, our behavioral response can lag in time. It may not occur at the same time as the stimulus.

Another aspect of cognitive learning is **modeling**, the process of mimicking and imitating the behavior of others. This is vicarious learning because we learn by watching others. It's like being influenced by other people's opinions on social media. In contrast to classical or operant conditioning, here our responses do not occur as a result of a direct experience. The positive or negative consequences of the observed or modeled behavior is called **vicarious reinforcement** or **vicarious punishment**. Their effect on our behavior is similar to that of the direct reinforcement of rewards or punishments, only we do not experience them ourselves.

It is not hard to see why these two aspects of cognitive learning are important to marketers. Why does TAG Heuer use celebrity endorsers? Because if Tom Brady and Brad Pitt wear one of their watches, the watches must be cool, and we want to be cool like Brady and Pitt. When a model for L'Oréal shakes out her gorgeous head of hair and declares, "I'm worth it," consumers might think, "Well, aren't I worth it too?"

There are two important elements of modeling that need further elaboration. First, modeling is not an automatic behavior. We process every behavior we observe prior to imitating it. Bandura called this a mediational process. This process occurs between the observed behavior (the stimulus) and imitating (or not) the behavior (the response). For example, you may notice and admire the unique dress style of your friend. But if you feel that you cannot imitate it successfully, or if you feel that imitating this unique style would result in an unfavorable response from others, you will not imitate this behavior. The mediational process of modeling is presented in Figure 9.8.

Second, modeling and observing others are not random behaviors. Our **social models**, the people we choose as models, don't have to be celebrities. Frequently, they are people who are relevant or similar to us in some way – maybe a classmate or coworker who we admire for something and want to emulate. These are people with whom we can identify. In most cases, these individuals have higher status, more expertise, or greater authority. Examples include parents, teachers, supervisors, and celebrities.

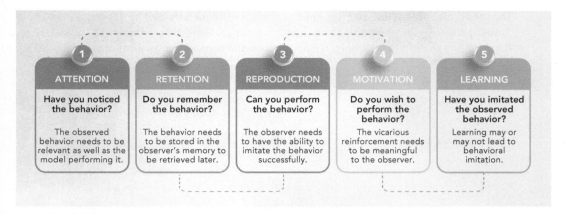

FIGURE 9.8 The Mediational Process of Modeling

One study found that mothers mimic their teenage daughters' consumption behavior if they regard them as having more knowledge and information about the latest trends in fashion (the mother assumes the daughter is more informed about what's currently in style). This phenomenon has also been termed the **consumer doppelganger**.[31]

Consumer doppelganger mimicking a person's consumption behavior if we regard him/her as expert in this domain.

Mothers mimic their teenage daughters' consumption behavior if they view them as fashion experts.

By observing these social models, we learn the correct, socially acceptable way to behave and act. Many factors can influence the likelihood that we will model or mimic others. For example, the more similar the models are to us, the more likely we are to copy their behavior. We are also more likely to mimic simple behaviors than complex ones. We are more likely to mimic a behavior that results in a reward than a behavior that does not.

The use of celebrity endorsements is based on the notion of social modeling. It's not as if we know celebrities personally, but we know about them. Consumers also follow complete strangers online, such as bloggers we turn to frequently. Their opinions and behaviors are a form of social modeling.

Celebrity endorsements are based on the notion of social modeling.

Getting many followers catapults some online personalities into the role of influencers, which carries some prestige, so providing word-of-mouth information becomes social for the influencers as well as for the consumers being influenced. Figure 9.9 presents some of the effects that influencers have on consumer decision-making and purchasing behavior.

Product recommendations

49%

Of consumers rely on influencers for product recommendations.

Trust in business

72%

Of consumers trust a business more if it was recommended by influencers

Purchasing considerations

44%

Of consumers indicated they considered purchasing a product based on influences posts.

Purchasing decisions

94%

Of consumers trust influencers more than friends or family when making purchasing decisions.

Trust in word of mouth

92%

Of consumers trust i influencers' reviews more than ads or celebrity endorsements.

Social media platform

89%

Indicated that Instagram is the most important social media channels for influencers.

FIGURE 9.9   Social Media Influencers and Their Effect On Consumers

Involvement Theory and Its Effect on Consumer Learning

One important factor that affects our willingness and motivation to learn is the degree of involvement we have in the subject of the learning. How important or how relevant is the subject matter to us – is that a brand or product category we care a lot about, or not really? That importance, or our involvement, will determine our motivation and level of effort that we will invest in the learning process.

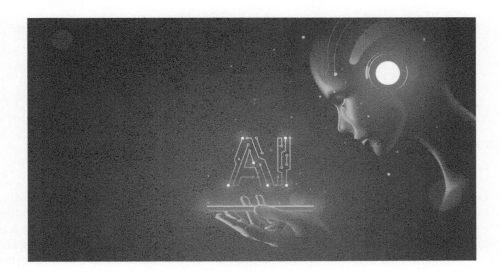

Involvement depends on how we like to spend our time. For example, think about your least favorite course. You probably invest less time and effort studying the materials for this course than you invest in studying the materials for your favorite course. **Involvement theory** posits that we will engage in less information processing in low-involvement situations and extensive information processing in high-involvement situations – we spend more time thinking about things we enjoy.[32] Similarly, a product that is important to us, such as one that is very risky, expensive, or visible to others, is more likely to result in an extensive learning process.

Part of consumer learning is a function of how consumers notice and interpret the information around them. That's all a part of consumer perception, and we talk about this topic next.

Involvement theory posits that we will engage in less information processing in low-involvement situations and extensive information processing in high-involvement situations.

Memory

Marketers work hard on getting consumers to learn about the features and benefits of their brands. The hope is that what consumers learn will affect their attitudes (something we discuss in the next chapter) and, of course, their purchases. Still, the learning doesn't work unless the learning "sticks," and by that we mean that consumers remember what they've learned about the brand. So let's discuss memory – what it is, how it works, and how marketers can plant ideas in consumers' heads that will be remembered.

Attention, Encoding, Storage, and Retrieval

Psychologists talk about memory as a cumulation of four processes: attention, encoding, storage, and retrieval (see Figure 9.10).[33] **Attention** reflects the process by which we choose which information we will devote resources to process it and which information we will screen out. We

Attention the process by which we choose which information we will devote resources to process it and which information we will screen out.

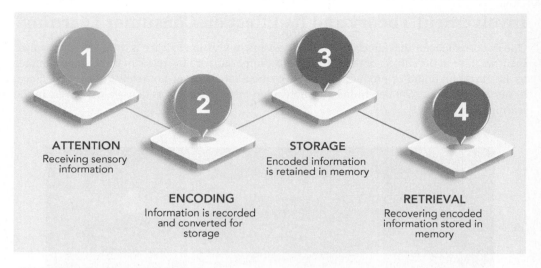

FIGURE 9.10 . The Stages of Memory

Encoding
involves how consumers receive the information, start thinking about it, and possibly storing it in memory.

Memory storage
putting the coded information into memory.

Memory retrieval
the cognitive process that involves accessing information that we've stored in memory.

are exposed to endless information we receive via our senses. However, we do not process all of it. Our attention focuses on only a small fraction of the information we are exposed to. **Encoding** involves how consumers receive the information, start thinking about it, and possibly store it in memory. Information can be received visually (e.g. an ad or brand packaging), through sound (e.g. brand jingles in ads), or semantically; that is, consumers hear an ad or read a product review and may try to remember the meaning of what they've just seen.

Memory storage is putting the coded information into memory. There is short-term memory, for example, when you see an ad and you repeat the brand name to yourself many times, rehearsing it, to remember it so you can look it up online. Short-term memory is indeed very short, around 30 seconds or so, and it's not very big. People can store about seven items, plus or minus two, before they get overwhelmed and start making errors. By comparison, long-term memory can last weeks, years, or a lifetime. Think about a favorite song that you first heard as a kid – you could probably sing it and nail the lyrics, without even thinking about it, because the song is in your long-term memory.

Memory retrieval is the cognitive process that involves accessing information that we've stored in memory. Sometimes we have such information readily available. Perhaps you remember detailed. Think of friends who know the statistics of their favorite sports team. That information seems to be quickly accessible. Sometimes, though, you may have probably had the experience where we thought we knew something, "It's on the tip of my tongue!" and yet can't seem to pull it up to memory.[34]

Marketers understand these three parts of the memory process because each must be activated for the brand benefits to be learned by a consumer and to have a later impact on that consumer's purchasing. If the consumer doesn't see the message, the memory can't be encoded or stored. That's why marketers have to spend a lot of the ad budget to make sure the message gets out widely so many consumers will see it. If the consumer understands and encodes the message, the marketer hopes it will get stored in long-term memory. This storage is more likely accessed if the consumer sees the message multiple times. That's why there is repetition in advertising. How often do you need to see that green talking gecko for Geico? And marketers have to be sure

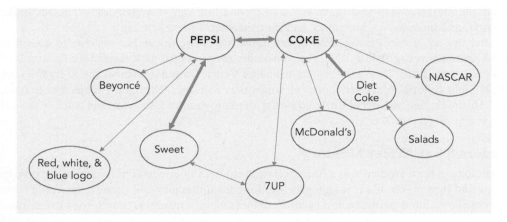

FIGURE 9.11   Brand Association Network

that their message will be retrievable. A gecko sounds like the word *Geico*, which helps, because a little talking lizard might not normally make you think of auto insurance.

Brand Association Networks

A helpful way to think about learning and memory is to visualize it. Figure 9.11 shows a brand association network that depicts brands and brand attributes as if they were like neurons in a consumer's brain.[35] Any two nodes (a brand or an attribute) are linked to represent when consumers think they are connected.

For example, this consumer (or consumer segment) links Pepsi and Coke. The two competitor brands are closely interconnected (note the strong, bold link between the brands). Other strong connections are that people think that Pepsi is sweet and that there's a link between Coke and Diet Coke. Strong links mean that when the consumer thinks of one of these things, say, Coke, then the first things that pop into their head as associated with Coke would be Pepsi and Diet Coke. When the consumer hears "Pepsi," their strongest connections make them think of Pepsi being sweet and, of course, Coke as well. Other links in the figure depict connections that are not as strong, even some that are weak (the Coke to 7UP link). If a brand and an attribute are not linked in the network, it means that the consumer doesn't think of them as connected. For example, if a consumer were asked, "Tell me about Coke," he or she wouldn't respond with anything having to do with Beyoncé.

Marketers gather these brand associations and map them into networks like this diagram. Then the brand team can look to see whether they like the attributes that consumers link to their brand or should try to get consumers to think differently about the brand.

Measuring Memory

When marketers want to assess whether they've gotten into the heads of consumers, they run marketing research tests on consumers' memory. Memory tests are about recall or recognition.[36] **Memory recall** functions when consumers are asked, for example, in phone interviews on the day following the Super Bowl, "What ads do you remember seeing?" The consumers list all the ads they remember. That's recall. It is unprompted. If a brand or ad is remembered by

Memory recall the retrieval of information from the past.

recall, the marketer feels that the advertising expenditure was very successful. The ad "broke through" and spoke to the consumers, and the consumers remembered it.

After the consumers list the ads they recall, the marketing researcher switches to questions about **memory recognition**. Here, the consumers are prompted with reminders, for example, when they are asked, "Do you remember the ad for Geico? Do you remember the ad for the Ford truck?", and so forth. Marketers hope the consumers will say, "Oh, right, I remember that ad, too." The marketing researcher can follow up with more questions, such as "Did you like the ad? Will you go buy a Ford?"

Factors That Affect Memory

Psychologists have studied numerous factors that affect how consumers remember certain things and how much of a message gets into long-term memory and then is accessible later. One consideration is **primacy** and **recency effects** when consumers are exposed to information.[37] The idea here is that information that is encountered first or last will be remembered better than all the information in the middle. For example, suppose you're thinking about celebrating your graduation or promotion by buying a new high-end television screen. You research brands online, and you encounter some nice comparisons, such as those in *Consumer Reports*, or you just read posted reviews at Amazon. You read and read and read; after all, this is a fairly expensive purchase. The TVs you read about first will make an impression, and the TVs you read about last will make an impression, and all the TVs you read about in between will be a blur.

The context in which consumers learn the information also matters. Here, think about meeting someone at work; you learn their name, but then several days later, you see them at Starbucks and are at a loss. The work context serves as a clue, but that's gone when you see the person at the coffee shop. Even a consumer's mood can create this effect of **context dependence**. For example, if a pop-up ad plays a fun jingle, and it makes the consumer a little happy, then the consumer may remember the brand better while shopping (in stores or online) if they're in a good mood. Context can be the environment. For example, you might have seen a hair-styling product while you were in Target, you didn't buy it at the time, but then when you were shopping in your grocery store, you looked for that hair product, but the brand and package and color just weren't jogging your memory because the retail shelves look so different, with different assortments of products.

Another factor that affects memory is called the **categorization theory**.[38] This idea refers to how consumers encode information. Say Honda comes out with a new car that is winning all kinds of major races. It begins a rollout to consumers, and it might face resistance because consumers think of "practical, reliable, not super expensive" when they think of Honda. Consumers don't tend to think of Hondas as superfast race cars that compete with Ferrari. The theory suggests that consumers have categories of cars – we think of small and inexpensive cars, or bigger, family cars, or exotic and expensive race cars, and we tend to put Honda in that first category. So the marketer would have a challenge getting people to think about Hondas in other car categories.

One place that marketers can push on categorization theory is with brand extensions. For example, Ziploc, the company that makes those handy plastic resealable bags, began creating food containers, plastic boxes with lids. That new product does not seem to be a big stretch for Ziploc – it takes something the company is good at (storage) and brings that benefit over to a new product line.

Memory recognition
the ability to identify a stimulus that has been previously encountered as a familiar one.

Primacy effect
information that is encountered first will be remembered better or the best.

Recency effect
information that is encountered last will be remembered better or the best.

Context dependence
context in which learning occurs.

Categorization theory
storing information in the memory by categorizing it.

Ziploc storage containers are an example of categorization and brand extension.

SUMMARY

If marketers want consumers to buy their brands, they need to understand how consumers think and learn. Marketers who understand the consumer learning process will be more effective in communicating with consumers and providing them with useful guidance to influence the desired purchasing behavior.

The behavioral learning theory focuses on consumers' responses to external cues, while the cognitive learning theory focuses on the internal mental processes as a central part of learning. Both of these perspectives help marketers think about developing marketing messages and brand building or promotions, such as coupons and loyalty rewards programs.

Many times marketers provide consumers with external cues to trigger the learning process. Consumers also seek out information to guide their decision-making process. They do this is through observational learning and modeling, both of which are part of the social cognitive theory. Using celebrity endorsements is one way that marketers influence the learning process of consumers. Consumers often seek out social models who are relevant or similar to themselves, or models to whom they aspire.

Marketers will often conduct marketing research to see whether consumers have learned what the advertisements had intended to communicate. They might measure aspects of consumers' memory, including recall and recognition. They might measure aspects of consumers' attitudes to see if the marketing campaign has successfully added positive attributes in the consumer brand association network.

KEY TERMS

Learning

Behavioral learning theories

Classical conditioning

Neutral stimulus

Unconditioned stimulus

Unconditioned behavioral response

Conditioned stimulus

Repetition

Effective frequency

Advertising wearout

Stimulus generalization

Product line extension

Brand extension

Stimulus discrimination

Operant conditioning

Reinforcement

Schedule of reinforcement

Fixed ratio

Variable ratio

Fixed interval

Cognitive learning

Social cognitive theory

Observational learning

Modeling

Vicarious reinforcement

Social models

Consumer doppelganger

Involvement theory

Attention

Encoding

Memory storage

Memory retrieval

Memory recall

Memory recognition

Primacy effect

Recency effect

Context dependence

Categorization theory

EXERCISES

1. With a friend from class, share the names of influencers (celebrity or not) whose endorsements (ads or blogs) have influenced your purchasing or the way you think about a certain brand or category of purchasing. Do you think there are some products for which you're more open to their recommendations? If so, what are they? Are there some products for which you would be less inclined to consider recommendations of others? If so, what are they?

2. We may think that classical conditioning is just for dogs or that we're too smart for operant conditioning, but for the latter, consider how many loyalty programs you have on your phone. Would you switch brands, or do the rewards of the loyalty program make you stick with it, in terms of both your behavior (buying) and your attitudes (you like the brand more)?

3. Think about two or three jingles that you like. How did you learn them? How many times would you guess you've heard them? What does the jingle actually tell you about the brand?

Have any of the jingles worn you out yet – you've heard them so many times that you actually think more negatively about the brand?

4. On average there are over 50 commercials aired during the Super Bowl. How many of them do you remember? The average cost of a 30-second commercial during the Super Bowl is over $5.6 million. Yet, as you just experienced, consumers tend to forget most of them. Why do you think marketers invest so much money on Super Bowl commercials? Is it worth to them? If you were to make recommendations to a company as to how to increase the recall of their commercial, what do you think would be the most effective time to air a commercial during the Super Bowl? Explain your recommendation.

5. Find two ads that use stimulus generalization and two ads that use stimulus discrimination. How effective do you think they are? Would you recommend a different strategy for these products? Explain your recommendation.

ENDNOTES

1. S. J. Hoch and Y. W. Ha, "Consumer Learning: Advertising and the Ambiguity of Product Experience," *Journal of Consumer Research* 13, no. 2 (1986): 221–33.

2. J. E. Ormrod and B. D. Jones, *Essentials of Educational Psychology: Big Ideas to Guide Effective Teaching* (Boston, MA: Pearson, 2018).

3. https://growrevenue.io/effective-facebook-ad-examples.

4. D. G. Myers and N. C. DeWall, *Psychology,* 13th ed. (New York: Macmillan Learning, 2021).

5. D. H. Schunk, *Learning Theories* (Englewood, *NJ: Prentice Hall,* 1996), 53.

6. C. T. Allen and T. J. Madden, "A Closer Look at Classical Conditioning," *Journal of Consumer Research* 12, no. 3 (1985): 301–15.

7. https://dictionary.apa.org/conditioned-stimulus.

8. https://www.reuters.com/article/us-pepsico-nba/pepsi-takes-over-nba-sponsorship-rights-from-coke-idUSKBN0N41HI20 150413.

9. M. C. Campbell and K. L. Keller, "Brand Familiarity and Advertising Repetition Effects," *Journal of Consumer Research* 30, no. 2 (2003): 292–304.

10. https://www.businessinsider.com/the-greatest-slogans-and-taglines-in-advertising-history-2019-7.

11. J. R. Rossiter and S. Bellman, *Marketing Communications* (Upper Saddle River, NJ: Pearson/Prentice Hall, 2005).

12. H. E. Krugman, "The Impact of Television Advertising: Learning without Involvement," *Public Opinion Quarterly* 29 (1965): 349–56. Krugman was a marketer working at General Electric.

13. D. W. Stewart, "Advertising Wearout: What and How You Measure Matters," *Journal of Advertising Research* 39, no. 5 (1999): 39–43.

14. B. D. Till and R. L. Priluck, "Stimulus Generalization in Classical Conditioning: An Initial Investigation and Extension," *Psychology and Marketing* 17, no. 1 (2000): 55–72.

15. B. G. Hardle, et al., "The Logic of Product-Line Extensions," *Harvard Business Review* 72, no. 6 (1994): 53.

16. L. O. Wilson and J. A. Norton, "Optimal Entry Timing for a Product Line Extension," *Marketing Science* 8, no. 1 (1989): 1–17.

17. https://yourbusiness.azcentral.com/revitalizing-brand-4213.html.

18. S. M. Broniarczyk and J. W. Alba, "The Importance of the Brand in Brand Extension," *Journal of Marketing Research* 31, no. 2 (1994): 214–28.

19. https://stories.starbucks.com/stories/2009/starbucks-doubleshot-energycoffee-stakes-its-claim-in-the-ready-to-drink-en.

20. J. Hoegg and J. W. Alba, "Taste Perception: More Than Meets the Tongue," *Journal of Consumer Research* 33, no. 4 (2007): 490–8.

21. R. M. Henderson and R. Johnson, "L'Oréal: Global Brand, Local Knowledge," *Harvard Business School Strategy Unit Case* (2011): 311–8.

22. J. P. Peter and W. R. Nord, "A Clarification and Extension of Operant Conditioning Principles in Marketing," *Journal of Marketing* 46, no. 3 (1982): 102–7.

23. https://dictionary.apa.org/reinforcement.

24. https://www.explorepsychology.com/classical-vs-operant-conditioning.

25. G. R. Foxall, "The Behavioral Perspective Model of Purchase and Consumption: From Consumer Theory to Marketing Practice," *Journal of the Academy of Marketing Science* 20, no. 2 (1992): 189–98.

26. https://www.forbes.com/sites/blakemorgan/2020/05/07/50-stats-that-show-the-importance-of-good-loyalty-programs-even-during-a-crisis.

27. https://www.simplypsychology.org/schedules-of-reinforcement.html.

28. Schunk, *Learning Theories*, 53.

29. A. Bandura, "The Self System in Reciprocal Determinism," *American Psychologist* 33, no. 3 (1978): 334–58.

30. https://www.simplypsychology.org/behaviorism.html.

31. A. Ruvio, Y. Gavish, and A. Shoham, "Consumer's Doppelganger: A Role Model Perspective on Intentional Consumer Mimicry," *Journal of Consumer Behaviour* 12, no. 1 (2013): 60–69.

32. S. E. Beatty, P. Homer, and L. R. Kahle, "The Involvement–Commitment Model: Theory and Implications," *Journal of Business Research* 16, no. 2 (1988): 149–67.

33. https://courses.lumenlearning.com/boundless-psychology/chapter/introduction-to-memory.

34. M. Morrin, "The Impact of Brand Extensions on Parent Brand Memory Structures and Retrieval Processes," *Journal of Marketing Research* 36, no. 4 (1999): 517–25.

35. D. R. John, B. Loken, K. Kim, and A. B. Monga, "Brand Concept Maps: A Methodology for Identifying Brand Association Networks," *Journal of Marketing Research* 43, no. 4 (2006): 549–63.

36. R. P. Bagozzi and A. J. Silk, "Recall, Recognition, and the Measurement of Memory for Print Advertisements," *Marketing Science* 2, no. 2 (1983): 95–134.

37. R. G. Peters and T. H. Bijmolt, "Consumer Memory for Television Advertising: A Field Study of Duration, Serial Position, and Competition Effects," *Journal of Consumer Research* 23, no. 4 (1997): 362–72.

38. B. Loken, L. W. Barsalou, and C. Joiner, "Categorization Theory and Research in Consumer Psychology: Category Representation and Category-based Inference," in *Handbook of Consumer Psychology*, eds. C. P. Haugtvedt, P. M. Herr, and F. R. Kardes (Mahwah, NJ: Taylor & Francis/Erlbaum, 2008), 133–63.

CREDITS

Ormrod, J. E., and B. D. Jones. *Essentials of Educational Psychology: Big Ideas to Guide Effective Teaching.* Boston, MA: Pearson, 2018.

https://www.designcrowd.com/design/11979071

https://www.disneyplus.com/brand/disney

https://drinksfeed.com/pepsi-replaces-coke-as-nba-sponsor-ending-28-year-partnership/

https://www.businessinsider.com/the-greatest-slogans-and-taglines-in-advertising-history-2019-7

https://www.shutterstock.com/image-photo/alameda-ca-oct-26-2021-grocery-2068266326

https://www.shutterstock.com/image-photo/penang-malaysia-29-jan-2020-l-1640723050

https://www.explorepsychology.com/classical-vs-operant-conditioning/

Bandura, A. "The Self-System in Reciprocal Determinism." *American Psychologist* 33, no. 3 (1978): 334–58.

https://www.simplypsychology.org/behaviorism.html

https://ivypanda.com/essays/the-nivea-skin-care-product-ad-discussion

https://www.invespcro.com/blog/social-media-influencers

https://www.shutterstock.com/image-vector/cyborg-woman-look-logo-ai-hanging-1684712782

https://courses.lumenlearning.com/boundless-psychology/chapter/introduction-to-memory

https://www.amazon.com/Ziploc-Containers-Variety-Pack-Count/dp/B01IH2TRI8

https://www.shutterstock.com/image-photo/tiffany-trump-marla-maples-hottie-nottie-182557235

Image p. 165: Techstyle Fashion Group
Image p. 166: STAR
Image p. 167: John Raoux/AP Images
Image p. 169: Sheila Fitzgerald/Shutterstock
Image p. 170: TY Lim/Shutterstock
Image p. 175: Everett Collection/Shutterstock
Image p. 176: Beiersdorf, Inc.
Image p. 177: Andrey Suslov/Shutterstock
Image p. 181: S.C. Johnson & Son, Inc.

10 Consumer Attitude Formation and Change

LEARNING OBJECTIVES

After studying this chapter, you should be able to:

- Understand how consumers form and change their attitudes.

- Learn about different kinds of attitudes.

- See the connection between consumers' attitudes about a brand or a product and their likelihood to purchase it and tell others about it.

- Understand that marketers can (and should!) influence consumers' attitudes toward their products and brands, as well as consumers' attitudes toward their competitors' offerings.

Imagine the next time you're in the grocery store. You're there to pick up three things. First, you are running low on cereal. You usually get Honey Nut Cheerios, and sure enough, there it is, and it's on sale as well. Nice! Second, in the frozen foods aisle, you want to pick up a DiGiorno stuffed pizza, but they're out. Ack! You're upset! Stupid store. You'll have to go somewhere else to pick up your favorite 'za. Third, you need to pick up peanut butter. Usually, you get Jif, but Skippy is on sale, so, whatever, Skippy it is.

Why did you react so differently to these three purchases? You're very happy about the Cheerios, rather annoyed about the pizza situation, and somewhat indifferent about the peanut butter. The different reactions reflect your different brand attitudes.

Attitudes

This chapter is about consumers' attitudes: how attitudes are formed, how they change, how they affect brand preferences. We also discuss what marketers are doing to affect consumers' attitudes and change them. Think about a brand you like. Why do you like it? What would make you dislike it? Now think about a brand you do not like. Why don't you like it? What could the brand do to make you like it?

Attitudes
overall evaluations, positive or negative, of a given object, such as a brand, or another person.

Attitudes refer to our overall evaluations, positive or negative, of a given object, such as a brand, or another person.[1] Simply put, attitudes reflect how much we like or dislike something or someone. Our attitudes are important because they guide the way we view the world, how we express our beliefs and values, and, consequently, how we behave. Our attitudes can change, so our behaviors can change as well. If you like a product, it is likely that you will buy it. However, if you stop liking it, it is safe to assume that you will stop buying it as well.

The role of attitudes as guiding our thoughts, feelings, and behaviors and the fact that they can change are very important to marketers (see Figure 10.1), because it gives marketers the opportunity to influence consumers' attitudes toward their products and brands, as well as toward their competitors' offerings.[2] Most marketing messages and promotional tactics are designed around this goal – to provide consumers with information or experiences needed to change their attitudes, based on the assumption that such changes in attitude will lead to a change in consumption behavior.

While consumers form attitudes about all kinds of things that interest marketers, including brands, products, shopping venues, ads, how to shop, and with whom to shop, all attitudes share the same basic characteristics. Figure 10.2 presents the common characteristics of attitudes.[3]

Attitudes have an object. When we form an attitude, it is normally about something specific, which is the object of the attitude. This object can be a brand, a product, a cause, a price, people, a place, a way of behavior, a piece of information, and so on.[4]

Attitudes are learned. We form our attitudes based on our experience with the object, or information we gathered from various sources, such as family and friends, the Internet and online reviews, the media, and direct marketing. Our attitude can change if we have a new experience or if we get new information about the object. While attitudes can lead to behaviors, the connection is not always that simple. For example, we might like vanilla ice cream. We had it once and found out that we like it. But that does not mean that we will have it every time we eat ice cream. We might choose to try different flavors as well.

Attitudes have structure. Our attitudes are organized and tend to be generalizable, which means that an attitude about an object will be generalized to a class of objects.[5] This helps consumers to simplify their purchasing decision-making. For example, we may be happy about the many automobile manufacturers that are producing electric vehicles or hybrids. When we are in the market for a new car (or even a new used car), the fact that the car is electric or hybrid might matter more to us than the brand of the car. Later in the chapter, we discuss the structure of attitude in more depth.

Attitudes have direction, degree, and intensity. When we form an attitude toward an object, it has a direction or valence.[6] Valence means the attitude is either favorable or unfavorable.

FIGURE 10.1 The Importance of Attitudes

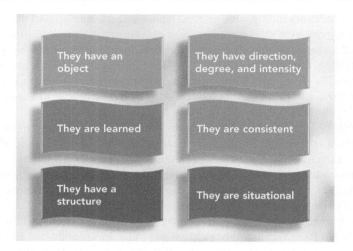

FIGURE 10.2   Characteristics of Attitudes

The degree of an attitude is the extent to which we like or dislike the object – we may like or dislike an ad or a political candidate, but how much? Do we like the ad or person a little or a lot? Do we dislike the ad or person a little or a lot? The intensity of an attitude reflects how strongly we are confident about our attitudes. For example, if you are an IT expert, and you like or dislike a new laptop, your attitude is probably rather confident because you are knowledgeable. If you are dining out at a restaurant that serves a cuisine you don't know much about, you may like or dislike the food, but you may not dismiss the whole cuisine or restaurant on the basis of that one dish – you just aren't confident that you know enough.

Marketers know these elements of attitudes. They know that the greater the intensity and degree of a consumer's attitude, the harder it will be for marketers to change it. Think about your favorite brand; what would make you dislike it? Think about your least favorite brand; what would make you like it? It would be a marketing challenge.

Attitudes are consistent with behavior. While our attitudes do not always lead to immediate behavior, they do tend to be consistent with the behavior they reflect.[7] Since our attitudes can change, the change is most likely to, in turn, change our behavior to maintain consistency. For example, if you care about sustainability, you most likely will purchase sustainable products and consume them in a sustainable way.

Attitudes are situational. Our attitudes form within and are affected by a specific situation. The situation reflects the event or circumstances at a specific time that had influenced the consistency between the attitude and its related behavior.[8] Instead of an attitude leading to an apparently consistent behavior, this may instead lead us to behave in a way that is inconsistent with our attitude. This is especially important when measuring attitudes, because under different circumstances we may get different responses.

Explicit and implicit attitudes
the way internal drives and motivations interact with external stimuli to form attitudes.

Types of Attitudes

As you can see, people's attitudes can be highly complex. In fact, we normally hold several different types of attitudes.[9]

Explicit and implicit attitudes – These types of attitudes refer to the way our internal drives and motivations interact with external stimuli (e.g. ads and social media endorsements of brands) to form our attitudes.[10] Explicit attitudes are those that we are aware of. They form in a conscious and deliberate way, which makes them easy to self-report. Implicit attitudes are unconscious and automatic. They form in an involuntary way, and we are not aware of their formation. It's not uncommon for an explicit attitude and an implicit attitude to contradict each other. For example, one of the tricky potential contradictions that people have to struggle with is that explicitly no one would embrace being biased against other kinds of people. Yet implicitly, it may be the case that some people are more comfortable with some kinds of other people and less comfortable with others. How can we strengthen our implicit attitudes to be better and more supportive toward all others? It's difficult in part because the attitudes are implicit.

Extraversion and introversion attitudes – While we learned in Chapter 7 that extraversion and introversion are personality traits, they also form different types of attitudes.[11] Since some consumers are highly social and outgoing, and others are quiet and reserved, they will form different attitudes about objects and situations. For example, an extrovert would love to go to a music concert of a favorite band, in part to enjoy the music and experience it with others, whereas an introvert would prefer to simply stream the band's music for their own personal enjoyment.

Rational and irrational attitudes – We like to think that we are rational people, but as Chapter 6 indicated, we do have very predictable biases. Many of these biases are rooted in the way we form our attitudes. Rational attitudes are those that are formed based on objective values, normally established through practical experience. These types of attitudes are easy to measure and explain. For example, you may not like spicy food, because when you tried it once, it burned your mouth and didn't taste good to you. By contrast, irrational attitudes are those attitudes that we form without any grounded reason, and they are more intuitive in nature. These are attitudes that we hold "just because." For example, you may not like the color red. Why? You may not know exactly. These types of attitudes are hard to measure, because people will come up with an explanation for an irrational attitude to be perceived as rational (i.e. they'll rationalize their preference).

Extraversion attitudes
attitudes are predominantly motivated by external factors.

Introversion attitudes
attitudes are predominantly motivated by internal factors.

Rational attitudes
formed based on objective values, normally established through practical experience.

Irrational attitudes
formed without any grounded reason, and they are more intuitive in nature.

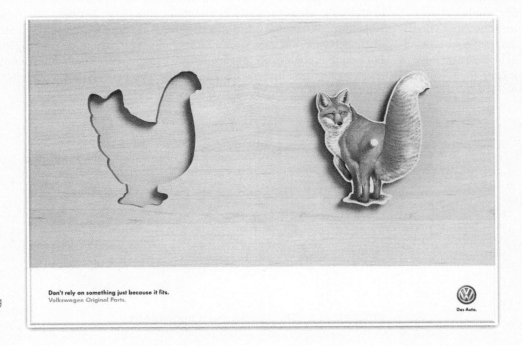

Don't rely on something just because it fits.
Volkswagen Original Parts.

Das Auto.

Volkswagen is using a rational attitude message.

The Components of Attitudes

Attitudes have three components, the ABC: affective, behavioral, and cognitive (Figure 10.3).[12]

Affective component – This component of attitudes reflects feelings, emotions, and sentiments toward a product or a brand. The relationship between attitudes and emotions is bidirectional. That is, attitudes can influence emotions about a product or brand, and a consumer's emotional state may heighten and intensify the current experience with the product or the brand positively or negatively. For example, let's say that you and your friends go out to a new restaurant to celebrate the end of the school year. Your good mood will probably encourage you to stay longer in the restaurant, spend more money there, and maybe even post about it favorably on social media.

Behavioral component – This component of attitudes refers to behaviors toward an object. The behaviors that marketers care about the most are consumers' purchases or intentions to purchase a specific product or brand. In fact, marketers know that a behavioral intention (saying you intend to buy the brand) is a better predictor of behavior (the actual buying) than attitudes toward the object (liking the brand). In other words, liking a brand or product is less likely to predict that you will purchase it, but your intention to buy a brand or product is a better predictor of whether you will buy it or not.

Cognitive component – This component of attitudes refers to thoughts and beliefs about a product or brand based on information (including ads) or direct experience. Note that cognitions or beliefs are not necessarily facts. **Beliefs** are convictions that we form based on our previous experiences and may not necessarily be based on logic or fact.[13] For instance, you might believe that Intel processors are superior to AMD processors. Even if you encounter information that suggests that this may not be the case, you might disregard it and continue to hold your original belief.

Note that attitudes and the ABC components can be explicit or implicit. Both affect our behaviors. However, in the case of explicit attitudes, we are consciously aware of their effect on our beliefs and behaviors, while in the case of implicit attitudes, such an effect is unconscious. While consciously we might strive to maintain consistency between our attitudes and our behaviors, sometimes the cognitive and affective components of attitude do not always align with our subsequent behavior. Then we know that something more implicit is strong and affecting the behavior. For example, cognitively and explicitly we might wish to buy groceries that are healthy, but when snack foods sneak into our bags and make it home with us, it's obvious that some implicit, affective factor had asserted itself in the decision-making.

Affective component of attitude reflects feelings, emotions, and sentiments toward an object.

Behavioral component of attitude refers to behaviors toward an object.

Cognitive component of attitude refers to thoughts and beliefs about an object based on information or direct experience.

Beliefs convictions that are form based on previous experiences and may not necessarily be based on logic or fact.

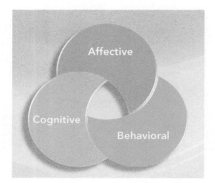

FIGURE 10.3 The Tricomponent Attitude Model

"Facts are irrelevant. What matters is what the consumer believes."

Seth Godin, American Author

How Do Attitudes Form? Where Do They Come From?

We form our attitudes over the years through our interactions with others, and they become part of our cognitive system. Yet there are some common factors that affect the formation of our attitudes.

Personal experiences – Most of our attitudes are formed based on our direct experiences with people and situations. Socialization and social norms play a big role in the way we form our attitudes. Our personal experience will have a strong effect on our attitude formation, and attitudes that are formed based on personal experience are difficult to change. For example, when we are pressed for time between classes, we might run over to pick up lunch, and we have a choice of Panera or Wendy's. We might like Panera because we feel virtuous about buying a salad there, and maybe we've seen that the service is typically pretty quick, and the workers are polite. In contrast, maybe our experiences at the campus Wendy's have been less impressive, maybe the place didn't look as clean or neat, maybe there were a couple of times when the staff was rude, and so on. Other Wendy's locations might be better (or other Panera locations might be worse), so someday in the future, such as when we move for a job, out attitudes might be revised, but for now, our attitudes have been shaped by these series of campus experiences.

Observation of others' attitudes – Our social environment has a tremendous effect on the formation of our attitudes.[14] Parents, teachers, peer groups, aspiration groups, coworkers, supervisors, neighbors – all can potentially affect our attitudes. Since our early years, we observe other people's attitudes and shape our own accordingly. As young children we model our family and friends and often shape our attitudes in a way that aligns with theirs. As we grow older, we start modeling others, such as our teachers, coworkers, and supervisors. Unlike personal experience, this form of attitude formation is indirect in nature. By observing others and modeling our attitudes accordingly, we minimize our social risks and maximize our potential rewards. For example, if your mother bought Crest toothpaste when you were growing up, you probably buy Crest rather than Colgate. Or if the popular kids in your middle school always wore Nikes, you might still carry a lingering attitude that Nikes are cool.

Association – We often come across a new attitude object that we can associate with a familiar old attitude object. In cases like that, we may project our attitude about the familiar object onto the new one. Marketers often build on this type of attitude formation when developing brand and product extensions. They are assuming that if consumers had a positive attitude toward one of their products or their brand in general, there is a higher chance that they will project this positive attitude onto the new offering.

Personality – As we learned in Chapter 8, personalities involve traits and characteristics that make us unique and different from others. This also means that our responses to stimuli like brands and ads are different and that they will lead to variation in attitudes across individuals. Our own personal biases will also have an effect on the formation of our attitudes. For example, as students from all over converge on your campus, everyone brings their own food preferences, and others may wonder, "Why do you like everything to be deep-fried?" "Why do you like rice, or rice and beans, with everything?" It's all part of who we are.

Mass communication and direct marketing – In this age of extensive communication and media accessibility, it is not surprising that we form our attitudes based on information we obtain from different mass sources.[15] We read other consumers' reviews on products we are interested in to decide whether or not to purchase them. We are exposed to advertising that aim to alter our attitudes toward certain products or services. We may even look for independent studies comparing different brands and products to figure out which one is the best for us. Furthermore, today's direct marketers are using sophisticated methods to personalize marketing messages that target smaller consumer segments in a personalized way. This increases the ability and likelihood of such messages to effectively change consumers' attitudes. These and many other sources of mass communication will affect the way we form our attitudes on a wide range of objects.[16]

Attitudes and Consumer Behavior

Theory of planned behavior predict an persons' intention to engage in a specific behavior.

If marketers are interested in attitudes mostly to be able to predict consumer behavior, what is the relationship between these concepts? According to the **theory of planned behavior**, three key factors will affect the relationship between attitudes and behavior[17]:

1. The attitude toward the behavior – a stronger attitude toward the behavior is more likely to result in a consistent behavior. For example, a person with strong conservative or liberal political beliefs is more likely to vote for a candidate who shares those beliefs, whereas it is more difficult to predict the votes of people whose political beliefs are more centric. A person who really likes peanut M&M's will probably buy them rather than plain M&M's or Reese's peanut butter cups.

2. Subjective norms reflect our beliefs about how others, such as our parents and friends, view this behavior, and whether we believe others will approve or disapprove of this behavior.

3. Perceived behavioral control refers to our assessment of our ability to actually engage in the behavior successfully.

Tricomponent attitude model predict intentions of engaging in the behavior, which in turn will lead to our actual behavior.

Taken together, these factors will predict our intentions of engaging in the behavior, which in turn will lead to our actual behavior. The theory of planned behavior, also known as the **tricomponent attitude model,** is depicted in Figure 10.4.

Predicting consumer behaviors is very challenging for marketers under three conditions: (1) when the consumers' attitude toward the brand or purchasing the brand is weak (if the con-

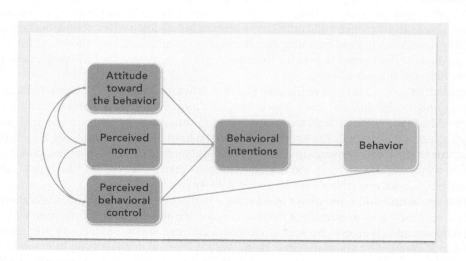

FIGURE 10.4   Relationship between Attitudes and Behaviors

sumers don't care, how can the marketer hope to predict their likelihood of buying or not with any degree of accuracy?), (2) when consumers anticipate that others will not approve of their behavior (if consumers anticipate disapproval, they might not even say aloud what they like because they don't want others to make fun of them or criticize them), and (3) when consumers do not have the ability or the resources to pursue a specific behavior (a consumer may like a Ferrari but just can't afford one). In these cases, attitudes and behaviors will be somewhat inconsistent; that is, knowing the attitude won't help predict the behavior.

Notice too that such cases (weak attitudes, expecting disapproval, or not being able to achieve the desired behavior) induce feelings of psychological discomfort. In order to resolve it, consumers might adjust their attitudes to match their behavior, or they might change their behaviors to match their attitudes.

Measuring the various aspects of the planned behavior model is not easy. Consumers are often unaware of their attitudes, perceived norms, or perceived behavioral control. This makes their responses unreliable and will affect the predictive ability of the model.

Marketing researchers spend a good deal of time trying to measure all the elements that contribute to consumers' attitudes to try to predict the likelihood that consumers will behave in certain ways – usually whether they will buy/try the brand or not. Surveys can ask, "How much do you like [the brand, features of the brand, its price, its convenience in the consumer's lifestyle, etc.]?" At the end of the day, what the marketing team wants to know is "Will you buy?" and also, given the whole notion of social modeling and influence that we've been discussing, "Will you recommend our brand to others?"

Variants of Attitude Models

The fact that attitudes can direct consumers' behavior is so important to marketers that there are actually several useful theories that were developed to understand the link between attitudes and behaviors. For example, there is a **theory of reasoned action,** which looks like the tricomponent attitude model depicted in Figure 10.4 except it doesn't have the perceived behavioral control factor.[18] The theory suggests that what determines that people's intention to perform a behavior is what that drives their behavior. The intention to engage in a behavior is a function of a person's attitude toward the behavior. What does that mean for marketers? In product categories where consumer control is important, keep the tricomponent attitude model. If control doesn't seem, the theory of reasoned action uses attitudes, norms, behavioral intentions, and behaviors (i.e. all the other pieces of the tricomponent attitudes model).

The psychologist Martin Fishbein quantified attitudes in the **multi-attribute theory.**[19] This theory recognizes that there are many features of a brand, and consumers might like some of those attributes more than others. For example, a Prius is great for the environment, inexpensive to run because it uses so little gas, is small, and is easy to park, all great attributes. But any product has downsides. Maybe the Prius isn't the sexiest car out there, maybe it's not big enough for your dogs, and maybe it doesn't go from 0 to 60 very quickly. Besides assessing how much the consumer likes each attribute, the multi-attribute theory also assesses how important each attribute is. Then the data are combined in the following equation:

$$A_{ijk} = \sum(B_{ijk} \times I_{ik})$$

Here's what that equation says. The attitude for attribute i (e.g. good gas mileage) for brand j (e.g. a Prius, Honda, or Tesla) as perceived by consumer k is calculated as the sum (sigma, $\sum$) of the product of two components: B_{ijk}, which are the beliefs (B) that consumer k holds of whether

Theory of reasoned action suggests that what determine that people's intention to perform a behavior is what's drives their behavior, which is a function of a person's attitude toward the behavior.

Multi-attribute theory recognizes that there are many features of a brand, and consumers might like some of those attributes more than others.

brand j is good in terms of attribute i or not, and multiplied by I_{ik}, which is how important (I) consumer k thinks that attribute i is for all brands. We describe several more theories later in the chapter that relate specifically to attitude change. For now, we turn back to the question "What does all this mean for marketers?"

Do the Right Thing!

The multi-attribute theory makes it seem as if marketers can get consumers to have more positive attitudes about their brand and less positive attitudes about competitors' brands in either (or both) of two ways: they can change the consumer belief perception, and/or they can change whether consumers think that a belief is important or not. Marketers want to brag about how great a particular feature is (to get a high score on the belief part of the equation) and emphasize how important that feature is (to get a high score on the importance part). Are both of those strategies acceptable to you? What about in trying to get consumers to think less favorably about competitors – do we go after the beliefs about the attributes, or the importance of the attributes, or does it matter?

Attitudes and Type of Purchases

The three components of attitudes are related to each other. However, we do not experience them in a specific or fixed order. An interesting fact for marketers is that the types of purchases we make typically result in a different sequence of the attitude components.

High-involvement purchases
those that are infrequent, costly, very important to consumers, and regarded as risky.

Low-involvement purchases
small, mundane, routine purchases, inexpensive, relatively unimportant to consumers, those are made automatically without really thinking about them and those that carry very low risk.

- **High-involvement purchases** refer to purchases we care deeply about. While these are often expensive, high-risk, or large purchases, we sometimes care about things that are inexpensive. For example, many dog owners care deeply about the food their dogs are eating. They will invest much time and effort to learn about the benefits of different products before choosing the right one for their beloved dog. Engaging in rational decision-making by doing more research, gathering more information, and evaluating more alternatives based on the products' features is indicative of this type of purchase. For example, for most people, buying a car or house is a high-involvement purchase. We will evaluate multiple options and choose the one we believe is the best for us and the one we like the most. The role of marketers in this type of purchase is to provide information and ways to reduce the risk involved in these major purchases. For these high-involvement purchases, cognition plays a strong role in consumer attitudes.[20]

- **Low-involvement purchases** are small, mundane, routine purchases, those that we make automatically without really thinking about them and those that carry very low risk. When making such purchases, we often do so because we recognize the need for a product (cognition) and we buy it (behavior) almost immediately. We might reflect on our feelings (emotions) about the purchase later. For example, you may notice that you are running out of gas, which leads you to stop at the first gas station, fill up your tank, and drive on without thinking much about this purchase. In low-involvement purchases, marketers seeking to attract new customers should provide promotions at the point of sale to induce buying or brand-switching behavior.

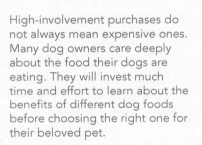

High-involvement purchases do not always mean expensive ones. Many dog owners care deeply about the food their dogs are eating. They will invest much time and effort to learn about the benefits of different dog foods before choosing the right one for their beloved pet.

- **Experiential purchases,** such as a trip to Disney World or another amusement park, are hedonically motivated – they operate heavily on emotions. We often rationalize them cognitively after we have made the purchase. For example, donations to nonprofits are frequently motivated by emotions. We feel sorry about the little puppy or the poor boy in the commercial, and we donate money to the cause. We rationalize this behavior by thinking that this is the right thing to do. Another form of experiential purchase is an impulse purchase. We often purchase things spontaneously simply because they can make us feel better (e.g. ice cream).[21]

- **Behavioral influence purchases:** In some instances, our consumption behavior occurs with little thought or feeling. We may not even be aware of the fact that our behavior is being influenced by others or by environmental cues. For example, retail marketers often use scents or music to impact our behavior. A scent might make us feel hungry, and the music can make us stay in the store longer, which increases the likelihood of purchasing products.

The great news for marketers is that attitudes allow for flexible ways of engaging consumers. Attitudes are formed in different ways, and they are related to the types of products we purchase, so marketers have a wide range of options and opportunities to influence our consumption behavior. Of course, marketers should be smart and choose the right tactics and strategies. For example, given that we buy ice cream for hedonic reasons, providing us with information about its nutritional value would not be the right approach.

Experiential purchases are hedonically motivated; they operate heavily on emotions.

Behavioral influence purchases purchases that are influenced by others or by environmental cues.

What Functions Do Attitudes Serve?

Functional theory of attitudes posits that attitudes and beliefs are significant to various psychological functions.

Utilitarian function of attitudes reflects subjective assessment of the benefit an object can provide.

Knowledge function of attitudes forming an attitude based on knowledge and information.

Value-expressive function of attitude enables consumers to convey their core values, self-concept, and beliefs to others.

Understanding the functions of consumers' attitude can help marketers to influence their consumption behavior more effectively. According to the **functional theory of attitudes,**[22] attitudes and beliefs are significant to various psychological functions. It identifies four basic functions of attitudes (see Figure 10.5).

Utilitarian function. As we learned in the previous chapter, as consumers we try to maximize rewards and minimize punishment. As such, we develop attitudes based on our evaluation about the level of pleasure or pain a specific object will provide us with. In other words, we will purchase products because they are beneficial to us, because we like them, or because they are valued by our social environment. At the same time, we will avoid purchasing products that have no use to us, we don't like, or they might result in a negative social response.[23] For example, if your generic computer mouse stopped working soon after you bought it, you are probably not going to buy the same brand again because you have experienced the "pain" of using this product. You may consider buying a Logitech mouse because you believe it's a good and reliable brand with reliable products. Using that company's product will not generate the same pain you have experienced with the generic brand. Utilitarian function – basing your attitudes on the evaluation of the product's ability to get the job done.

Knowledge function. This function helps consumers to simplify their decision-making process. We normally make purchasing decisions based on what we know (or do not know) about a product or a brand. This knowledge-based attitude helps us to avoid making purchasing mistakes and make better purchasing decisions. In other words, consumer attitudes help to avoid undesirable situations and approach more desirable situations.

Insurance companies can benefit from understanding the concept of the knowledge function of attitudes. For example, Farmers Insurance launched the "More You Know" campaign, which provides consumers with knowledge about different situations that will require good insurance coverage. Farmers Insurance understands that most consumers lack the knowledge to assess the coverage of their insurance policies and provided them with useful information.

Value-expressive function. This function enables consumers to convey their core values, self-concept, and beliefs to others. This is a positive expression of the values consumers hold and care about, and it's reflected in consumers' lifestyles.[24] For example, if you value the protection of the environment, you may purchase products that convey this value, such as

 **UTILITARIAN FUNCTION**
- Consumers are looking to maximize rewards and minimize punishment.
- The benefits of the product are important in appealing to this function.

 KNOWLEDGE FUNCTION
- Based on what consumers know about the product or brand.
- Helps consumers to simplify their decision-making process.
- Information about the product is important in appealing to this function.

 VALUE-EXPRESSIVE FUNCTION
- Enables consumers to convey their core values, self-concept, and beliefs to others.
- Reflected in consumers' lifestyle.
- Highlighting positive expressions of the product or brand is important in appealing to this function.

 EGO-DEFENSIVE FUNCTION
- Helps consumers to protect themselves from threatening information, feelings of low self-esteem, or insecurity.
- Focusing on the ways the product boosts consumers self-esteem and confidence is important in appealing to this function.

FIGURE 10.5 The Functions of Attitudes

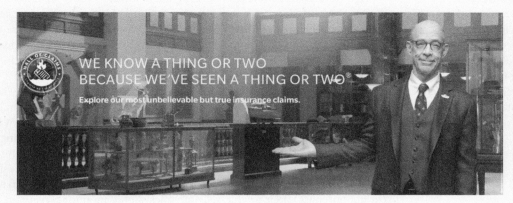

Insurance companies often leverage the concept of the knowledge function of attitudes in their messages.

recycled and eco-friendly products or an electric car, such as a model from Tesla. Indeed, Tesla leverages consumers' value-expressive function of attitudes in different ways. Consumers today are concerned about carbon footprint and air pollution and other environmental issues. Tesla offers multiple innovative and exciting solutions to these concerns in the form of cars, solar panels, and other products. By driving a Tesla car or purchasing the company's solar panels, consumers express their social responsibility values while elevating their social status by using these upscale and stylish products. Addressing consumers' value-expressive function of attitudes helps Tesla to establish its position as a leader in these categories.

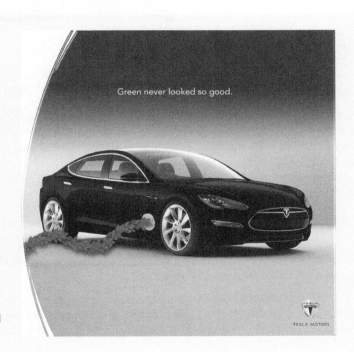

Value-expressive function: Ads are great at conveying to consumers the values and benefits they will experience if they purchase the featured product.

Ego-defensive function of attitude helps consumers protect themselves from feeling threatened, or from experiencing feelings of low self-esteem or insecurity.

Ego-defensive function. This function of attitude helps consumers protect themselves from feeling threatened, or from experiencing feelings of low self-esteem or insecurity. Ego-defense is a defense mechanism for consumers to boost their self-esteem. We use this function every time we do something that we know is wrong, such as when we eat unhealthy food, skip exercising, or watch TV instead of working or studying. We justify these actions by thinking that tomorrow we will start eating healthier foods or exercise or work harder or longer.

Companies use the ego-defensive function of attitude extensively. They market products in a way that aims to boost consumers' self-esteem and confidence. They "help" us find the reasoning that will make us form a positive attitude toward their brand or products. The commercial for Beats by Dre headphones featuring LeBron James, for example, is telling us that we "deserve the best"; that is, we deserve these headphones.

You now understand the important role that attitudes play in purchasing decisions and behaviors and how critical it is for firms to learn about the attitudes that drive consumers to purchase (or not purchase) their products. Companies should monitor consumers' attitudes constantly via marketing research. The information and knowledge about consumers' attitudes are especially important if a company is trying to change them, as we see in the next section.

Ego-defensive function: Making consumers feel good about themselves.

Can Marketers Change Consumers' Attitudes?

One of the biggest challenges that companies face is creating favorable consumer attitudes toward their brands and changing negative ones.[25] We all have attitudes toward brands and companies formed over the years through our own experiences or the shared experiences of others, stories from friends, or postings on social media.

All companies, regardless of their size or prominence in the marketplace, must create, control, and often proactively change what we think about them.

- Successful companies that are market leaders in their category still invest time, resources, and effort to sustain and reinforce consumers' positive attitudes.

- Companies that are not market leaders try to enhance consumers' attitudes to attract more customers and increase their market share.

- Companies in bad situations, such as those experiencing a drop in sales, an increase in consumer complaints, more competition, or a scandal that affects their reputation, would need to engage in a strategic effort to change consumers' attitudes.

The reason for the need to change consumers' attitudes will determine the strategy a company adopts for doing so as well as the message and subsequent actions. Companies often conduct ongoing marketing research to monitor consumers' attitudes to be in a position to change attitudes if necessary.

Nevertheless, changing attitudes can be very challenging. In particular, for companies seeking to change consumers' attitudes, it can be even harder, because consumers today have very little trust in marketing messages that come from companies. Building on the ABC model (affect, behavior, and cognition), marketers can attempt to change consumers' attitudes by changing one or more of its components.[26]

- *Changing the affect component:* Emotions are a powerful motivator. Companies can try to change how consumers feel about their brands by linking them to a favorable stimulus.[27] This strategy is the basis of the corporate social responsibility and charitable initiatives many companies are involved in. There must be a strategic fit between the brand and the favorable stimulus in order to induce the desired change in attitude; otherwise, consumers will not see the link as authentic to the brand. An excellent example of this connection is the Whirlpool Care Counts initiative.[28] Whirlpool created this program to increase the school attendance rate of students at risk by providing them with access to clean clothes. The company installed washers and dryers in 82 schools in 18 cities across the United States, providing access to clean clothes for more than 38,000 students. The result? More than 50% of the students who participated in the program were no longer at risk for chronic absenteeism by the end of the school year, and about 95% of them demonstrated increased motivation in class and were more likely to participate in extracurricular activities. Now, what is your attitude toward Whirlpool?

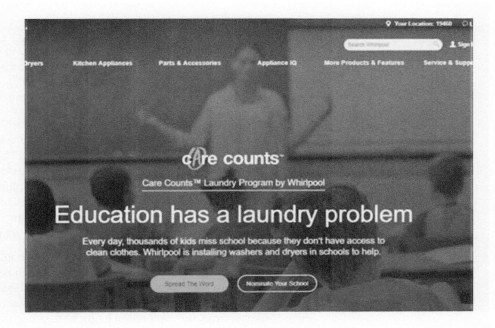

Care Counts and Whirlpool remind us that children in school have many needs, not just good teachers and textbooks, but basics like clean clothes.

- *Changing the behavioral component:* We would like to believe that we are rational consumers who make rational decisions when it comes to buying products. Accordingly, companies providing consumers with a rational reason to consider a new product or a new brand might have an effect on their attitudes. Such a reason should be directly related to the value of the brand or product value. Examples include having unique and desirable features that other products do not have, such as convenience, price or price discounts, or a warranty. For example, Waterpik introduced an innovative toothbrush to the market that uses water to floss your teeth as you brush them.[29] If you are concerned about your dental hygiene, this unique feature might prompt you to switch from your current brand to Waterpik.

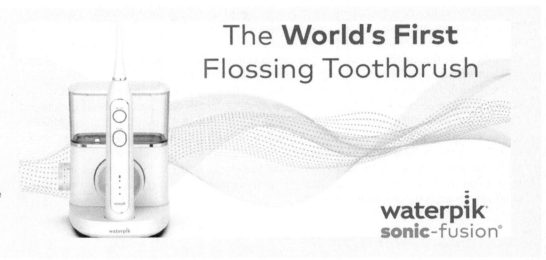

Changing the behavioral component of attitude.

- *Changing the cognitive component:* Marketers can also try to change consumers' beliefs. Of course, this is very hard to do because consumers tend to be suspicious of marketing messages that attempt to influence their attitudes.[30] More specifically, marketers can take one of the following approaches to change the cognitive part of consumers' attitudes:

    1. *Changing consumers' current beliefs.* Changing the beliefs that people hold is extremely difficult, even if these beliefs are erroneous. Marketers need to reiterate their message to overcome consumers' persistence in their attitudes. The "Got Milk" campaign is an excellent example of a message that seeks to change the attitude of consumers toward milk and increase its consumption. The campaign has been running for over two decades, with more than 70 commercials and 350 milk mustache ads. The campaign has featured celebrities such as Bill Clinton, Whoopi Goldberg, and the Simpsons. It is estimated that on any given day about 80% of US consumers are exposed to the simple question Got Milk?

       Sometimes marketers try to change consumers' beliefs about competitors' brands. They do so by making a direct or indirect comparison with the competitors' products or brands and demonstrating their superiority. However, this strategy is extremely risky. First, by making such a comparison, marketers are providing competitors with free advertising and visibility. Second, in some cases, the comparison might be regarded as an acknowledgment that the other brand is superior. Third, there is a good chance that competitors will retaliate. That was the case with the ad comparing Samsung to Apple's iPhone. Apple responded with their own comparison ad. The battle on consumers' attitude is a serious one.

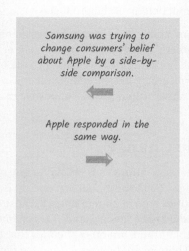

Samsung was trying to change consumers' belief about Apple by a side-by-side comparison.

Apple responded in the same way.

2. *Changing the importance of a belief.* If a consumer belief is sticky, marketers can instead try to change the importance or significance of the belief (remember the "I" term in the multi-attribute model described previously?). For example, today many consumers are concerned about the effect they have on the environment. All else being equal, many consumers prefer to purchase products from cruelty-free and environmentally friendly brands. Marketers can make this belief stronger and more salient to the purchasing decision-making process. Marketers of online retail companies changed our belief that we must go to the store to buy the products we need. Even cars are being sold online and without visiting the dealership.

3. *Adding a belief about a brand or a product.* If a marketer has trouble changing a belief, then a new belief can be added – as long as it does not conflict with currently held beliefs. In some cases, this can be done by adding an attribute to an existing product through innovation and enhancing its value. Cell phone manufacturers today highlight the quality

Carvana attempts to change the importance of a belief when shopping for a car.

of the camera in the device as a selling point. While the camera quality is not related to the quality of the cell phone as a communication device, marketers have associated the two as a signal of the overall quality of the product.

As you can see, consumers' brand attitudes are not permanent. Marketers can change them by providing consumers with new information, changing their beliefs, and providing consumers with opportunities to experience the brand. At the same time, marketers with brands that consumers like shouldn't rest and do nothing; they should constantly reinforce those positive attitudes with supportive marketing messages.

Theories of Attitude Change

Needless to say, changing consumers' attitudes is crucial to any company. That's why there are many models for attitude change. Don't think that one theory is always the best. The fact that there are several competing theories is good for marketers because they can use whichever theory seems most relevant for the brand challenges at hand. This chapter has focused on the primary theories that you need to know, but there are other theories that focus on certain elements that can be very important as well. Those main theories follow (see Figure 10.6).

According to the **elaboration likelihood model**, there are two main ways that consumers cognitively process incoming information, such as seeing an ad or reading product reviews online.[31] The so-called central route means that the consumer is very carefully and thoughtfully considering the ideas and the content of the message. The peripheral route means that consumers are paying attention to other things – not the main content of the message, but cues such as whether the brand is being shown by an attractive model or celebrity. (Peripheral and central processing are a bit like type I and type II processing that we've seen when we discussed behavioral economics and nudges.)

Recall the concept of **cognitive dissonance**[32] discussed in Chapter 5. According to this theory, most of us want to hold beliefs that are consistent and not contradictory. So, if for some reason a consumer is considering two attitudes that are at odds, something has to change. The fact that the two different beliefs aren't consistent means the consumer experiences dissonance, and that's uncomfortable. That dissonance then motivates the consumer to change one of the attitudes. For example, suppose a consumer is a huge fan of brand X, and that consumer cares about sustainability. But then suppose the consumer sees the CEO of the company make some statements about how the company cares about the quality of its products but can't worry about the environmental impact of its packaging. The consumer is going to experience dissonance: how can the consumer

Elaboration likelihood model proposes two approaches to persuade people or change their attitude, the central route and the peripheral route.

Cognitive dissonance a situation in which consumers question whether their buying decision was the right one.

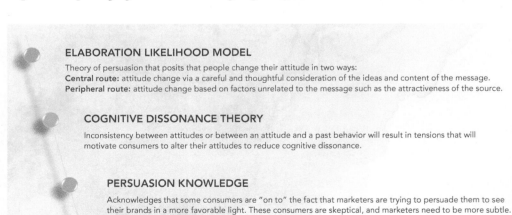

ELABORATION LIKELIHOOD MODEL
Theory of persuasion that posits that people change their attitude in two ways:
Central route: attitude change via a careful and thoughtful consideration of the ideas and content of the message.
Peripheral route: attitude change based on factors unrelated to the message such as the attractiveness of the source.

COGNITIVE DISSONANCE THEORY
Inconsistency between attitudes or between an attitude and a past behavior will result in tensions that will motivate consumers to alter their attitudes to reduce cognitive dissonance.

PERSUASION KNOWLEDGE
Acknowledges that some consumers are "on to" the fact that marketers are trying to persuade them to see their brands in a more favorable light. These consumers are skeptical, and marketers need to be more subtle.

FIGURE 10.6 Theories of Attitudes Change

continue to like the brand when the consumer hears the CEO say something that does not support something else the consumer cares about? The consumer can stop liking the brand – boycotts are made of such conflicts. Or the consumer can think, "Well, I'm sure they're doing the best they can about packaging, and anyway, that company isn't the biggest problem out there in terms of harming the environment." That is, the consumer starts to downplay the sustainability issue.

The **persuasion knowledge model** is important to marketers because it acknowledges that many consumers know that advertising is intended to persuade them to like a product and subsequently buy it.[33] These consumers are said to be skeptical of marketing communications. They are savvy enough to know what marketers are trying to do, so they try to resist the marketing efforts of persuasion. To reach these consumers, marketers have to be more subtle and try to show how a product can benefit these consumers, whether or not the consumers wish to resist the efforts in changing their attitudes.

Persuasion knowledge model acknowledges that people use their persuasion knowledge to deal with persuasion attempts.

Measuring Success in Changing Attitudes

Natural questions for marketers and marketing researchers to ask are "If we've made efforts to change consumers' attitudes, were we successful?" and "We spent a boatload of money on some advertising; did we get a decent return on investment?"

Marketers typically measure two things: attitude toward the ad (A_{ad}) and attitude toward the brand (A_{brand}). Marketing survey questions addressing these attitudes are usually very straightforward. Using a 10-point scale, where 1 is "I didn't like that ad and 10 is "I liked that ad very much," survey participants would be asked, "How much did you like that ad?" (A_{ad}). Similarly, the A_{brand} survey question would ask participants about the brand being studied – a brand the survey participants typically buy or something the interviewer has just shown them. The participants then assess the brand to say whether they like it or not.

Obviously, the survey can drill down for more details, such as "What about the ad did you like or not like?" or "What brands do you like better?" or so forth. These simple measures give a snapshot as to whether the marketing efforts have been helpful in making consumers' attitudes more favorable to the brand and ad.

USING SOCIAL MEDIA TO AFFECT CONSUMERS' ATTITUDES

Attitude of US Adults Toward Influencers, by Generation, July 2021

% of respondents in each group

	Gen Z (18-24)	Millennials (25-39)	Gen X (40-54)	Baby boomers (55+)
Expose me to new products or services	58%	53%	42%	23%
Make me more likely to purchase new products or services	38%	40%	29%	9%
Influence my perception of a product or service	33%	31%	30%	17%
Do not engage with influencers	9%	14%	24%	46%
Other	1%	0%	0%	2%
None	9%	6%	13%	17%

Source: R.R. Donnelley & Sons Company, "The (Un)Expected Report," Oct 5, 2021

270028　　　　　　　　　　　　　　　eMarketer | InsiderIntelligence.com

SUMMARY

Marketers need to understand consumer attitudes. Attitudes are comprised of multiple elements, in particular, the ABC of affect or emotion, behaviors and intentions, and cognition or beliefs. Attitudes can change, and marketers can change them. The changeability gives marketers the opportunity to make consumers think that their brand is better than the competition's. Any company benefits from reinforcing consumers' positive attitudes about its brands, from successful companies that do not want to lose business, to companies that want to compete better and get consumers to see them in a more positive way.

Attitudes are more complex than we first think. However, that is good news for marketers because it means there are several angles to use in communicating with consumers and trying to change their perceptions of brands. Attitudes are formed about an object such as a brand or company. They are usually learned and not innate; thus marketers can influence in teaching consumers about the positive benefits of their brands. Attitudes can be positive or negative and strong or weak. Consumers with strong, negative feelings about a brand may be challenging to persuade, but consumers with weaker or more moderate attitudes may be more changeable, and consumers with positive feelings about a brand may already be brand-fans.

Attitudes can serve many functions. They can be utilitarian, when consumers ask themselves prior to a purchase, "Will this product serve my needs?" Attitudes can contribute to consumers' knowledge bases so they are better informed when they make decisions. Attitudes express who people are, which often motivate them to buy things that are social signals, telling others "This is me." Attitudes can have an ego-defensive function, which protects consumers and keeps them feeling safe and good, which marketers can leverage by suggesting consumers buy nice things because they deserve those nice things.

Attitudes and learning are very important to marketers because they help predict consumer behavior. We see more about these relationships throughout the book, including Chapter 12, which discusses how a consumer's country and culture can affect his or her preferences and choices.

KEY TERMS

Attitudes	Behavioral component of attitude	Theory of reasoned action	Behavioral influence purchases	Value-expressive function of attitude
Explicit and implicit attitudes	Cognitive component of attitude	Multi-attribute theory	Functional theory of attitudes	Ego-defensive function of attitude
Extraversion attitudes	Beliefs	High-involvement purchases	Utilitarian function of attitudes	Elaboration likelihood model
Introversion attitudes	Theory of planned behavior	Low-involvement purchases	Knowledge function of attitudes	Cognitive dissonance
Rational attitudes	Tricomponent attitude model	Experiential purchases		Persuasion knowledge model
Irrational attitudes				
Affective component of attitude				

EXERCISES

1. Think about your favorite brand. What could the company do that would change your attitude toward the brand and not like it? Now think about your least favorite brand. What could the company do that would change your attitude and like it? Based on your answers, what strategies can companies implement to make consumers like their products and brands?

2. Sometimes a company can get us to think about their brand more positively, but we nevertheless keep buying a different brand. Why do we do that? The reasons are important to remember when you're on a brand team – that there are obstacles and challenges for marketers, some about changing attitudes and consumer learning, other issues that require attention (e.g. pricing? availability? acceptance by friends?).

3. With a friend from class, each of you rate the following brands on a scale from 1 to 5, with 1 being you don't like it at all and 5 being you think it's terrific:

   a. Coke

   b. Pepsi

   c. Microsoft

   d. Apple

   e. Disney

   f. Netflix

   g. Coors

   h. Budweiser

Look at the brands where you disagree. For example, if you like Coke a lot, and your friend likes Pepsi, try to have a conversation to persuade the other to like your brand more. How will you do this? How can you appeal to your friend to change their attitude?

4. Marketers emphasize measuring attitude toward the ad and attitude toward the brand. Think of an example of an ad that

you liked for a brand that you don't. Think of an example of an ad that you hated even though you liked the brand. What did the first ad do right, and what did the second ad do wrong? What advice would you give that brand team?

5. In pairs or in small teams, pick a product or a brand and compose slogans that reflect each of the four different functions of attitudes.

ENDNOTES

1. D. G. Myers and N. C. DeWall, *Psychology,* 13th ed. (New York: Macmillan Learning, 2021).

2. M. Hogg and G. Vaughan, *Social Psychology,* 5th ed. (London: Prentice Hall, 2017).

3. Ibid.

4. R. H. Fazio, "Attitudes as Object-Evaluation Associations: Determinants, Consequences, and Correlates of Attitude Accessibility," in *Attitude Strength: Antecedents and Consequences,* eds. R. E. Petty and J. A. Krosnick (Hillsdale, NJ: Lawrence Erlbaum, 1995): 247–82.

5. L. R. Fabrigar, T. K. MacDonald, and D. T. Wegener, "The Structure of Attitudes," in *The Handbook of Attitudes.* Eds. D. Albarracín, B. T. Johnson, and M. P. Zanna (Hillsdale, NJ: Lawrence Erlbaum Associates Publishers, 2005), 79–125.

6. H. Cantril, "The Intensity of an Attitude," *Journal of Abnormal and Social Psychology* 41, no. 2 (1946): 129.

7. G. R. Goethals and R. F. Reckman, "The Perception of Consistency in Attitudes," *Journal of Experimental Social Psychology* 9, no. 6 (1973): 491–501.

8. G. R. Foxall and M. M. Yani-de-Soriano, "Situational Influences on Consumers' Attitudes and Behavior," *Journal of Business Research* 58, no. 4 (2005): 518–25.

9. M. Perugini, "Predictive Models of Implicit and Explicit Attitudes," *British Journal of Social Psychology* 44, no. 1 (2010): 29–45.

10. M. Grumm, S. Nestler, and G. Von Collani, "Changing Explicit and Implicit Attitudes: The Case of Self-Esteem," *Journal of Experimental Social Psychology* 45, no. 2 (2009): 327–35.

11. Jung, C. G. and H. Godwyn Baynes, *Psychologische Typen* (Zurich: Rascher, 1921).

12. S. A. McLeod, "Attitudes and Behavior," *Simply Psychology,* May 21, 2018, https://www.simplypsychology.org/attitudes.html.

13. C. P. Duncan and R. W. Olshavsky, "External Search: The Role of Consumer Beliefs," *Journal of Marketing Research* 19, no. 1 (1982): 32–43.

14. L. N. Chaplin and D. R. John, "Interpersonal Influences on Adolescent Materialism: A New Look at the Role of Parents and Peers," *Journal of Consumer Psychology* 20, no. 2 (2010): 176–84.

15. I. Ajzen, *Attitudes, Personality, and Behavior* (London: McGraw Hill Education, 2005).

16. G. A. Churchill Jr. and G. P. Moschis, "Television and Interpersonal Influences on Adolescent Consumer Learning," *Journal of Consumer Research* 6, no. 1 (1979): 23–35.

17. I. Ajzen, "The Theory of Planned Behavior," *Organizational Behavior and Human Decision Processes* 50, no. 2 (1991): 179–211; S. Taylor and P. Todd, "Decomposition and Crossover Effects in the Theory of Planned Behavior: A Study of Consumer Adoption Intentions," *International Journal of Research in Marketing* 12, no. 2 (1995): 137–55.

18. M. Fishbein, "A Theory of Reasoned Action: Some Applications and Implications," *Nebraska Symposium on Motivation* 27 (1979): 65–116.

19. M. Fishbein and S. Middlestadt, "Noncognitive Effects on Attitude Formation and Change: Fact or Artifact?," *Journal of Consumer Psychology* 4, no. 2 (1995): 181–202; J. R. Bettman, N. Capon, and R. J. Lutz, "Multiattribute Measurement Models and Multiattribute Attitude Theory: A Test of Construct Validity," *Journal of Consumer Research* 1, no. 4 (1975): 1–15.

20. P. G. Patterson, "Expectations and Product Performance as Determinants of Satisfaction for a High-Involvement Purchase," *Psychology and Marketing* 10, no. 5 (1993): 449–65.

21. L. Van Boven and T. Gilovich, "To Do or to Have? That Is the Question," *Journal of Personality and Social Psychology* 85, no. 6 (2003): 1193.

22. D. Katz, "The Functional Approach to the Study of Attitudes," *Public Opinion Quarterly* 24, no. 2 (1960): 163–204.

23. K. E. Voss, E. R. Spangenberg, and B. Grohmann, "Measuring the Hedonic and Utilitarian Dimensions of Consumer Attitude," *Journal of Marketing Research* 40, no. 3 (2003): 310–20.

24. K. G. DeBono, "Investigating the Social-Adjustive and Value-Expressive Functions of Attitudes: Implications for Persuasion Processes," *Journal of Personality and Social Psychology* 52, no. 2 (1987): 279.

25. https://www.mckinsey.com/business-functions/marketing-and-sales/our-insights/understanding-and-shaping-consumer-behavior-in-the-next-normal#.

26. R. E. Petty, D. T. Wegener, and L. R. Fabrigar, "Attitudes and Attitude Change," *Annual Review of Psychology* 48 (1997): 609–47; R. E. Petty and P. Brinol, "Attitude Change," in *Advanced Social*

Psychology: The State of the Science, eds. R. F. Baumeister and E. J. Finkel (New York: Oxford University Press, 2010), 217–59.

27. C., Yoo, J. Park, and D. J. MacInnis, "Effects of Store Characteristics and In-store Emotional Experiences on Store Attitude," *Journal of Business Research* 42, no. 3 (1998): 253–63.

28. https://www.whirlpool.com/care-counts.html.

29. https://www.waterpik.com.

30. A. Drolet and J. Aaker, "Off-target? Changing Cognitive-based Attitudes," *Journal of Consumer Psychology* 12, no. 1 (2002): 59–68.

31. R. E. Petty and J. T. Cacioppo, "The Elaboration Likelihood Model of Persuasion," in *Communication and Persuasion*, Springer Series in Social Psychology (New York: Springer, 1986).

32. E. Harmon-Jones and C. Harmon-Jones, "Cognitive Dissonance Theory after 50 Years of Development," *Zeitschrift für Sozialpsychologie* 38, no. 1 (2007): 7–16.

33. M. Friestad and P. Wright, "The Persuasion Knowledge Model: How People Cope with Persuasion Attempts," *Journal of Consumer Research* 21, no. 1 (1994): 1–31.

CREDITS

Hogg, M., and Vaughan, G. *Social Psychology,* 5th ed. (London: Prentice Hall, 2017).

https://www.reddit.com/r/AdPorn/comments/1o7dun/almapbbdo_ad_for_volkswagen_dont_rely_on

McLeod, S. A. "Attitudes and Behavior." *Simply Psychology* (May 21, 2018), https://www.simplypsychology.org/attitudes.html

http://ec2-52-72-69-122.compute-1.amazonaws.com/how-balto-the-sled-dog-paved-the-way-for-modern-working-dogs

https://www.stealingshare.com/farmers-insurance-commercial-actually-tells-you-who-the-ad-promotes

https://ericalynnbell.wordpress.com/category/advertising/#jp-carousel-132

https://www.google.com/url?sa=i&url=https%3A%2F%2Ftwitter.com%2Fslamonline%2Fstatus%2F605398414935719936&psig=AOvVaw1bnz3IYB4sVRGKuQFoXTsd&ust=1622242920005000&source=images&cd=vfe&ved=0CAIQjRxqFwoTCLDj5LL96vACFQAAAAAdAAAAABAD

https://www.thedrum.com/news/2018/09/20/carvana-s-new-york-market-launch-holds-true-its-unconventional-car-buying-methods

https://www.canadianbusiness.com/companies-and-industries/r-i-p-got-milk-marketing-campaign-ends-after-20-years-and-plummeting-milk-sales

https://grin.co/blog/influencer-marketing-statistics

Consumers' Perception

It is not unusual for brands to revise their logo every once in a while. Companies are motivated to do so by the need to freshen up their look and maintain relevancy in the eyes of consumers.

The problem? Sometimes such a change can backfire, as Gap learned when attempting to change its logo. The new logo featured Gap's name in a clean font, with a small blue square overlapping the *P*. The results? Overwhelmingly caustic criticism from angry consumers describing it as cheapy, tacky, and ordinary. Not exactly the words that brands would like to be associated with. So what happened? A neuro study showed that our brain is hardwired to react negatively to sharp edges. Furthermore, consumers did not perceive the Gap logo as new or cool. When it comes to logos and visual ad campaigns, colors, shapes, and fonts have a tremendous effect on how we perceive things. After only six days, Gap retracted its new logo and reinstated its old one.[1]

How Consumers View the World

Perception is the process through which we make sense of the world around us.[2] It's how we embed meaning in everything we see, do, and experience. The process of perception (see Figure 11.1) encompasses the way we select, organize, and interpret the sensory information we receive from our environment within the context of our existing knowledge. Our perceptions will drive our attitudes and behaviors.

Perception
the process through which we make sense of the world around us.

Marketers who try to understand consumer perception will be the best equipped at getting consumers to think and act in ways they want. Let's start with the five senses and see how they can affect the way we view a brand, product, ads, price, and value – everything that consumers and marketers care about.

Look at the car in the picture below. What do you see? Do you see an old car? Or do you see a collectible? The answer depends on your interest in cars and your previous knowledge about them. While some people may simply see an old car, others may recognize what is considered the most expensive car ever sold, for the price of $70 million. What makes this car worth that? It is an extremely rare Ferrari and a Tour de France winner. But is it really worth so much? Apparently, David MacNeil, the founder and CEO of WeatherTech, who purchased the car, thought so. His perceptions about the value of the car led him to pay the unprecedented price.[3] In the next section, we discuss the perceptual process in detail.

1963 Ferrari 250 GTO

The Perceptual Process

The process in which we interpret the world is described in Figure 11.1. There is actually a pre-perception phase, and that is when the consumer is dealing with the sensory input (e.g. tasting a product, watching an ad). Then perceptual process has three stages: selection, organization, and interpretation. On the basis of how consumers select, organize, and interpret information, there will be an impact on their attitudes, behaviors, and emotions, which is called the output in Figure 11.1. In this chapter, we discuss sensory input and the three stages of the perceptual process. The output stage contains topics that are discussed in other chapters.

Perceptual Input

We experience the world through our senses – sight, smell, taste, sound, and touch. They are the physiological bases of perception. We are exposed to many stimuli at any given moment. Exposure reflects our encounter with stimuli either intentionally or accidentally.[4] However, we are

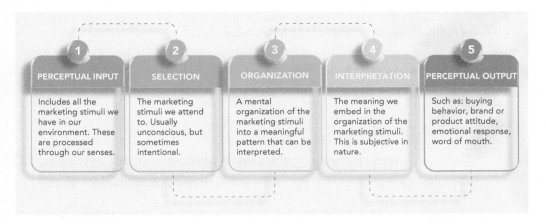

FIGURE 11.1 The Perceptual Process and Consumer Behavior

incapable of processing all of the stimuli we are exposed to and screen out the majority of them. Yet some stimuli will grab our attention.

Sensation is input that our sensory receptors obtain from the physical world.[5] It is the response of our sensory organs to a specific stimulus through the use of our sensory functions – hearing, seeing, smelling, tasting, and feeling (see Figure 11.2). Marketers activate our sensory functions in many ways, including through the use of their products, colors of their brands, smell of their products and stores, music in the stores, packages, advertisements, and commercials.

Marketers are smart and use the five senses to highlight their brands. Here are some examples:

1. *Sight:* Colors are a marketer's best friend – think of Pepsi's red, white, and blue logo or Google's multi-colors, or UPS's "What can brown do for you?" slogan. Note that colors are perceived differently in different cultures, as the figure below shows.

2. *Smell:* Think of walking by a Cinnabon or a Body Shop store or a coffee shop in the mall. Or consider the perfume spritzer people in the big department stores.

3. *Taste:* Think of sampling foods at Costco or trying different flavors of ice cream at Baskin-Robbins.

Sensation
input that our sensory receptors obtain from the physical world.

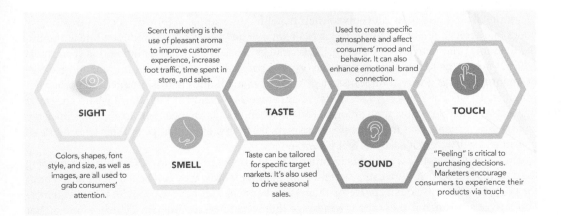

FIGURE 11.2 The Five Senses and Marketing

4. *Sound:* Harley-Davidson and Ferrari spend a lot of time and money to get their vroom-vrooms just right. Think of jingles in advertisements.

5. *Touch:* Haptic marketing is the use of touch. Apple knows its importance in the design of its computers, tablets, and phones. They're sleek and elegant.

The Global Mindset

	WESTERN AMERICA	ASIA	MIDDLE EAST	LATIN AMERICA
YELLOW	Happiness, warmth, caution	Scared, royalty, courage	Happiness, strength mourning	Death, sorrow, mourning
GREEN	Nature, luck, greed	Nature, youth, infidelity	Strength, luck, fertility	Nature, death, danger
RED	Danger, love, passion	Happiness, joy, celebration	Danger, caution, evil	Fire, religion, passion
BLUE	Trust, authority, masculinity	Immortality, strength, femininity	Safety, immortality, masculinity	Trust, religion, serenity
PURPLE	Wealth, royalty, fame	Wealth, nobility, mourning	Wealth, virtue, omen	Death, sorrow, mourning

Adapted from Colors Across Cultures: A Color Psychology Guide For Brands.

Absolute threshold the lowest level of stimulus intensity required from us to experience a sensation.

Differential threshold or just noticeable difference (JND) the minimum level of difference between two stimuli that consumers can detect at least half of the time.

Shrinkflation offering smaller size packages or smaller quantities of the product while maintaining the same price or even increasing it.

Subliminal message a message that consumers are not consciously aware of, but it still might affect their behavior.

Sensation depends in part on the intensity of the input. The lowest level of stimulus intensity required from us to experience a sensation is referred to as the **absolute threshold**. It is the point at which we differentiate between "no stimulus" and "stimulus." For example, how strong must a smell be for us to notice it?

We also may have trouble differentiating between two stimuli with a similar intensity. This phenomenon is referred to as the **differential threshold** or the **just noticeable difference (JND)**,[6] the minimum level of difference between two stimuli that consumers can detect at least half of the time. For example, how different must two shades of color be for you to notice the difference between them?

Marketers can use both concepts to their benefit. An example is the **shrinkflation** strategy, when marketers offer smaller size packages or smaller quantities of the product while maintaining the same price or even increasing it.[7] This strategy is based on the assumption that consumers will not notice the difference between the original package or quantity and the smaller package or quantity. This is a very common strategy used by many brands across product categories. For example, a Twix bar has lost 13.8% of its weight since 2014, and Kit Kat Chunky bars are 16.7% lighter.[8] Another common application of JND is when brands change their logo. Sometimes the change is noticeable. But in most cases marketers try to make the change in their logo subtle so consumers will accept it easily as being familiar.[9]

Do we need to notice a stimulus in order for it to affect our behavior? Not always, according to some researchers. Stimuli can be subliminal. In other words, they can be too weak or too brief for people to be consciously aware of them, yet they will still have a behavioral consequence. Similarly, a **subliminal message** is a message that consumers are not consciously aware of, but it still might affect their behavior.[10] Amazon's logo contains a subliminal message indicating that you can find all you need, from A to Z, on the company's website.[11] Do you agree?

Shrinkflation strategy –
The bags look similar, but are they? One is skinnier 180 g versus 200g!

Amazon's subliminal messages are smart – getting packages from point A to point Z, and a smile thrown in as well!

Marketers know that consumers are bombarded with many marketing messages every day. To cope, consumers consciously and subconsciously block this **perceptual overload** of exposure to stimuli.[12] Selecting the stimuli that we actually interpret is the next step in the perceptual process.

There is also the notion of "mere exposure," where consumers begin to gain a sense of familiarity with something that they see again and again even if they haven't put any cognitive effort into it.[13] For example, most consumers would say that they pay no attention to billboards posted along roads of their commute or posted in subway trains. Yet such ads always yield good memory tests, even if people can't remember where they've seen the ad before. Even better, consumers think they must know something about the brand: maybe they've tried it before, maybe a friend told them about it, somehow they know the brand, and as a result have more positive attitudes about the brand.

Perceptual overload
receiving too many stimuli to be able to process.

Perceptual Selection

While we are exposed to an infinite number of stimuli every day, our brains cannot process each and every one of them. We normally filter out irrelevant or less significant information. Both internal (personality, motivation) and external (contrast, repetition) factors will have an effect on the type of information that will be received or filtered out.[14]

When it comes to marketing-related stimuli, we are even more selective. In reality, we process only a small fraction of all of the marketing messages we receive. In fact, it is estimated that we

Perceptual selection
occurs when we filter out irrelevant or less significant information.

Perception and Social Media

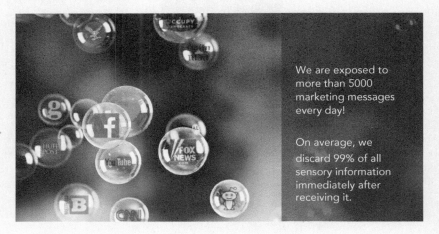

We are exposed to more than 5000 marketing messages every day!

On average, we discard 99% of all sensory information immediately after receiving it.

are exposed to over 5000 marketing messages every day. Think of how few of those marketing messages get your attention!

Attention
the process by which we choose which information we will devote resources to process it and which information we will screen out.

Attention is the allocation of mental resources to process a specific stimulus.[15] Attention has a range of intensities and can be either planned and goal directed, or incidental and spontaneous. For example, you might intentionally search for a YouTube video about a specific topic and watch it, which reflects intentional attention. On the other hand, you might watch a YouTube video you just come across that looks interesting to you, which reflects incidental attention. Our attention creates a sensation.

What affects our selection of stimuli and our attention?

1. *The stimulus – the thing we may notice and think about (or not):* Marketing-related stimuli have a wide range of elements that affect consumers' perceptions. Examples include the brand name, the type of product, its physical features (color, size, functions), the packaging, the placement in the store, the price, any associated promotion, the ad itself, the medium of the ad, and the value offered to the consumer. Any element that we do not like or is not relevant to us will cause us to ignore the stimulus. We ignore brands and colors we don't like, and we pay closer attention to those we do like.

2. *Our frame of reference and relative situation:* Our previous knowledge and experiences affect what we expect to see. We tend to disregard stimuli that are not aligned with what we expect or with our previous knowledge. Surprising stimuli might grab our attention. For example, placing beer and snacks close together in a store would probably prompt consumers to buy both products because they are normally eaten together.

3. *The consumers as individuals:* Consumers have motives. They tend to be more open to considering stimuli that are related to what they need, want, or are trying to achieve. The stronger the motive, the greater the likelihood that they will be attuned to stimuli that are related to the motive and dismissive of stimuli that are unrelated to it. For example, if you are looking to buy a new cell phone, you will be more receptive to marketing messages about new phones or deals. However, you will dismiss such messages once you purchase a new phone.

Without even knowing it, consumers use perceptual selection as a filtration system to sort through which of the environmental stimuli we are exposed to will reach our consciousness.[16] Put differently, we all have biases when it comes to receiving and processing stimuli that are the result of the interaction between the nature of the stimulus, our expectations, and our motives.

What are our potential biases?

- **Selective exposure:** We actively expose ourselves to marketing messages that are pleasant and enjoyable, and we avoid those that we find upsetting.[17] We also actively seek out marketing messages that support and confirm our consumption choices.

- **Selective attention:** We are selective in the attention we give to the marketing messages we are exposed to. We pay more attention to those marketing messages that are relevant to us, meet our needs, or match our interests.[18] We also disregard messages that are irrelevant to us or that do not align with our needs and interests.

- **Perceptual defense:** When we are exposed to stimuli that we view as conflicting, threatening, or unacceptable, we shield ourselves from them to minimize their effect.

- **Perceptual blocking:** We actively protect ourselves from the influx of stimuli.[19] We install ad blockers on our computers, subscribe to TV or radio services without commercials, and set all marketing messages to automatically move to our spam box. These actions are a major concern for marketers who are trying to connect with consumers via traditional marketing channels that are now actively blocked.

Selectivity is a big challenge for marketers. Advertisers often ask, "How can we break through the clutter?" They know consumers see many ads (television, in-store, pop-ups, etc.), and consumers have trained themselves to ignore most of it. So the ad has to be a little different to catch their attention.

Perceptual Organization

Once we have selected the stimulus we are paying attention to, we create a mental representation of the stimulus to see it as a coherent whole. According to the **gestalt principles of organization,** the whole of a stimulus is different than the sum of its parts. There are several principles that guide our perceptual organization, all frequently used as marketing tactics.[20]

Figure-ground relationship. According to this principle, we separate stimuli into either figure elements or ground elements. The focus of attention is the figure element, while the ground elements create an undifferentiated background.[21] The Plants for the Planet organization uses this principle in its ad. The leaf is the figure, and the missing parts create the industrial pollution in the background.

Perceptual proximity. This principle refers to our brain's tendency to group together stimuli that are in close proximity to each other and recognize them as part of the same object.[22] Even if the individual stimuli are not connected, our brain will still process them as one meaningful picture and will group them into a single unit or pattern. This principle helps us avoid processing multiple stimuli and enables us to process information faster and more efficiently. Unilever uses this principle to create an eye-catching logo. All of the little icons are grouped together to form the letter *U*.

Perceptual closure. This principle posits that our brain tends to perceive a stimulus as a whole even in the absence of one or more of its parts, which might be hidden or totally absent. We consciously or unconsciously complete the missing pieces in our brain. The logo of the Ontario Soccer Association uses this principle to create an interesting and engaging logo. Our brain automatically completes the parts of the logo to form a coherent image of a soccer ball.

Selective exposure active exposure to marketing messages that are pleasant and enjoyable, and avoidance of upsetting messages.

Selective attention being selective in the attention given to the marketing messages we are exposed to.

Perceptual blocking actively blocking out stimuli.

Perceptual defense ignoring or distorting stimuli that view as conflicting, threatening, or unacceptable.

Gestalt principles of organization posits that the whole of a stimulus is different than the sum of its parts.

Figure-ground relationship separating stimuli into either figure elements or ground elements.

Perceptual proximity the brain's tendency to group together stimuli that are in close proximity to each other and recognize them as part of the same object.

Perceptual closure the tendency of the brain to perceive a stimulus as a whole even in the absence of one or more of its parts, which might be hidden or totally absent.

Figure and ground in Plant for the Planet ad.

Perceptual proximity – Grouping all icons together to form the letter U.

Perceptual similarity perceiving objects that are visually similar as a single group rather than individual items.

Perceptual anomaly breaking a similarity pattern can highlight the dissimilar object or objects.

Note that in order to achieve successful closure, we must have prior knowledge about the complete stimulus.

Perceptual similarity. This principle holds that our brains perceive objects that are visually similar as a single group rather than individual items. Similarity can be based on shape, color, size, texture, or any other visual element. In other words, similarity does not imply what the object is, rather what it looks like.

The opposite of similarity can also be used to attract consumers' attention. Thus, breaking a similarity pattern can highlight the dissimilar object or objects. This is called **perceptual anomaly.**[23]

Perceptual closure –
We see these discon-
nected ovals as a full
soccer ball.

BASF uses perpetual anomaly
to attract attention.

Perceptual Interpretation

Perceptual interpretation
the meaning embedded in a stimuli.

Schemata
mental models used to organize information in a way that allows our brain to interpret it more efficiently.

Perceptual distortions
mistakes that made when interpreting stimuli.

You have been exposed to a stimulus and organized its information in a coherent way. Now you need to give it meaning. **Perceptual interpretation** is the meaning we embed in everything we see. Our interpretation is subjective and more deliberate than previous stages of perception. As we noted earlier, it depends on our previous knowledge, expectations, and motives. We assign meaning to the stimuli we are exposed to using schemata. **Schemata** are mental models used to organize information in a way that allows our brain to interpret it more efficiently.[24] When we activate our schemata, we use these mental models as shortcuts to make assumptions about something we are observing.

Our interpretation also depends on the clarity of the stimulus. Many stimuli are ambiguous. The more ambiguous they are, the more open they are to interpretation. As a result, in many cases we will project ourselves onto the stimulus and interpret it in a way that reflects our views, attitudes, needs, and motives. In other words, the more ambiguous the stimulus is, the more subjective our interpretation will be.

For example, you might buy a perfume whose scent reminds you of a person or a place from your childhood. But for others, this scent is meaningless and unrelated to their childhood. This means that we often misinterpret the stimuli we are exposed to.

Perceptual distortions are mistakes that we make when we interpret the stimuli we encounter.[25] Figure 11.3 outlines some of the most common biases in our perceptions. The question is, are these biases and misinterpretations good or bad for marketers? It depends. There is no doubt that such misinterpretations can work against marketers. If our first impression of a brand or product is an unfavorable one, it will be very hard to correct that impression. However, marketers can also leverage these misinterpretations. For example, the effect of physical appearance is used widely in advertisements and commercials. This is such an effective strategy that it has been criticized as creating unrealistic expectations in consumers.

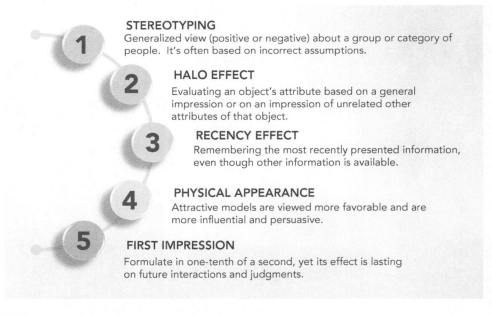

1 STEREOTYPING
Generalized view (positive or negative) about a group or category of people. It's often based on incorrect assumptions.

2 HALO EFFECT
Evaluating an object's attribute based on a general impression or on an impression of unrelated other attributes of that object.

3 RECENCY EFFECT
Remembering the most recently presented information, even though other information is available.

4 PHYSICAL APPEARANCE
Attractive models are viewed more favorable and are more influential and persuasive.

5 FIRST IMPRESSION
Formulate in one-tenth of a second, yet its effect is lasting on future interactions and judgments.

FIGURE 11.3 Types of Perceptual Distortions

How Do Marketers Use Information on Consumer Perception?

As we noted at the beginning of this section, perception is one of the most powerful strategies for marketers.[26] A favorite tool of marketers is the perceptual map. While a geographic map has directions of North–South and East–West, a perceptual map presents a brand with its competitor brands in two dimensions to represent different product attributes. For example, for soft drinks, North–South might be "diet" or "non-diet" drinks, and East–West might be "colas" versus "uncolas."

> *"A brand is just a perception, and perception will match reality over time."*
>
> *Elon Musk*

Positioning

Brand or product **positioning** reflects the utilization of the marketing mix to influence consumer perceptions regarding a brand or product relative to competitors.[27] The purpose of a positioning strategy is to shape a distinct image or identity of the brand or product in the consumer's mind. Marketers seek to create such an image by highlighting the unique benefits of their brand or product that are significantly different from their competitors'.

As we noted in Chapter 2, every element of the marketing mix must support the positioning of the brand and the product. In its essence, positioning is all about shaping consumers' perceptions, impressions, ideas, and feelings about the brand or product.

When crafting a positioning strategy, marketers often use a **perceptual map**, a visual representation of customers' perceptions about the specific attributes of the brand or product.[28] Perceptual maps are useful tools for indicating to marketers the perceptions of their consumers in relation to competing brands regarding specific attributes that are important to the consumer, whether functional or symbolic. They can also help marketers identify untapped market opportunities or a competitive advantage relative to other brands. In addition, marketers can monitor the movement of their brand or other brands on the map over time, which shows the development of the market and indicates any changes in consumers' perceptions.

Figure 11.4 shows a perceptual map that illustrates how consumers think about several brands of athletic shoes. The horizontal axis displays the perceptions by consumers of how reliable the

Positioning
the utilization of the marketing mix to influence consumer perceptions regarding a brand or product relative to competitors.

Perceptual map
a visual representation of customers' perceptions about the specific attributes of the brand or product.

FIGURE 11.4 Perceptual Map of Athletic Shoes

quality of the shoe brands are. Will the pair of shoes last six months? A year? Asics are thought to be reasonably good quality, and Keds are thought to be just OK (which is consistent with Keds' positioning). Along the vertical axis, we see two of the brands are rather expensive (Golden Goose and Moncler), Keds are inexpensive, and Nike, New Balance, and Asics are in between. Perceptual maps are a great visual to depict consumers' perceptions, as well as marketing managers' hopes as to how to position or tweak and reposition their brands. If you're the New Balance brand manager, you have to worry about Nike and Asics, but not really Moncler, Golden Goose, or Keds. Do you have aspirations to charge as much as Moncler or Golden Goose? Could you do it? Would consumers think you're worth it? Perceptual maps help brand teams think about these discussions.

Did you know that when you go shopping in a typical supermarket, you pass about 600 items per minute? With so many competing messages, how can marketers make you notice their product? How can they stand out in the crowd? Packaging plays a significant role in brand positioning and sales. It is not surprising that marketers invest a great deal of time and effort in researching the most effective packaging for their product and brand.

Colors, images, shapes, fonts, texture, size, and other packaging elements are all considered in relation to consumers' needs, competitors' offerings, and product value and positioning. While packaging was originally considered part of the product elements in the marketing mix, its role in brand positioning is much more prominent.

Effective packaging should convey the positioning of the brand in a manner that is consistent with other brand messages. It should also signal core brand values, communicate specific product characteristics, such as sustainability and ease of use, and convey information about the content and quality of the product, as well as its intended use.

Perceptions About Price, Quality, and Value

Marketers have many tools they can use to influence consumers' perceptions and their brand's position in the marketplace, from branding to advertising, and we talk about these topics throughout the book. Here we play up the importance of two more tools. First is the price point of the brand: is the brand perceived by consumers as high-end quality, thus deserving of a high price? Or is it a cheap brand, so the price should be low? Or is it "OK" quality with "OK" price netting out to reasonable value? Second is the level of risk: some purchases are seen as being riskier than others. We'll see what that means and how marketers can manage those perceptions.

Price is one of the elements of the marketing mix (see Chapter 2). While price is regarded as a functional element of a product, consumers' perceptions play an important role in the pricing strategy. Price is the most influential factor in decisions about purchasing. When you find a product you like, one of the first things you do is to check the price, right? Based on this information, you decide if the product is "worth" it. This is a subjective evaluation of whether you are willing to pay that price. What you are really assessing is your perceptions about the benefits you receive in exchange for the price you have to pay. Value is typically defined as "quality of what I bought"/"how much I paid." As Figure 11.5 illustrates, this assessment will result in a decision to buy or not to buy the product.

Can marketers change our perceptions about the relationship between price and value in a way that will sway us to purchase their product? Yes, they can. There are two main strategies marketers can follow: increase the perceived value of the product or change consumers' perceptions about the price to match the perceived value.

Increasing the Value of the Product

1. Highlight the benefits that the product offers, especially the unique benefits that are not offered by competitors. Examples include the product's special design, exceptional service, or delivery time. Sellers try to highlight key features of their product, to show consumers it would be a smart purchase.

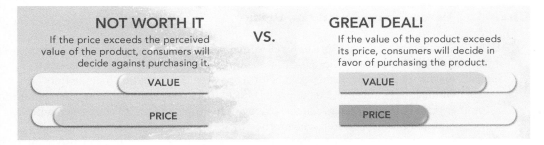

NOT WORTH IT
If the price exceeds the perceived value of the product, consumers will decide against purchasing it.

VALUE

PRICE

VS.

GREAT DEAL!
If the value of the product exceeds its price, consumers will decide in favor of purchasing the product.

VALUE

PRICE

FIGURE 11.5 Price Versus Value Assessment

2. Add benefits to the product, ideally, unique benefits that are not offered by competitors. For example, with Amazon's prime membership, consumers are eligible for free one-day shipping and free returns. These added benefits enhance the attractiveness of the product.

3. Improve the quality of the product. Doing so includes creating packaging that signals quality and placing the products in stores and environments that signal quality. Consumers will pay more for quality products. Sellers of high-end products will emphasize that their products are made from the "highest-grade materials."

4. Create a sense of urgency. Consumers will pay more for products that are scarce or are being offered for a limited time. Amazon often offers Lightning Deals, and these create a sense of urgency. Amazon strengthens the appeal by showing the percentage of the deal that has already been claimed (e.g. 9%).

5. Make it personal. Make the benefits of using the product, whether utilitarian or for pleasure, salient to the consumer. For example, the Power Bank featured below could have framed its message to say something like "Never run out of power." This would make it a more personal appeal and increase its attractiveness.

6. Develop a strong brand. Consumers will pay more for well-established and well-known brands.

Increasing the value of the product on Amazon.

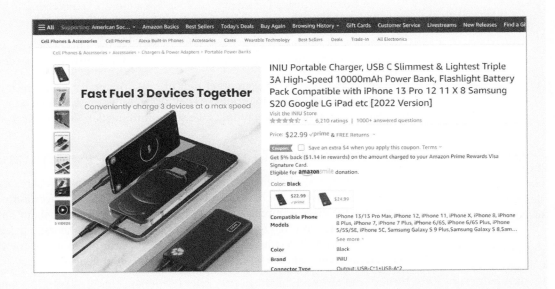

Changing Perceptions About the Price

Reference price
the price consumers think is a reasonable and fair price for a product.

Price anchoring
providing consumers with a price point that they can refer to when setting their reference point.

1. Help consumers set a reference price. A **reference price** is the price consumers think a reasonable and fair price for a product.[29] Consumers set their reference price based on internal information (the price they paid before) or external information (competitors' prices, manufacturer's suggested retail price [MSRP], the price of other options) in relation to another price point. Marketers can use **price anchoring** and provide consumers with a price point that they can refer to when setting their reference point.[30] It's not unusual for Amazon to show an "anchor" or typical price of a product (say, $16.99) and also point out to consumers how much they are saving in dollars ($2.55) and as a percentage (15%). This strategy is especially important today when consumers can easily search for price information and compare products.

2. Provide different tiers or price options if possible. By doing so, marketers can actually steer consumers toward the option they prefer consumers buy. Let's say that you are considering purchasing a data plan. Your provider offers you three options: 3 GB for $35 a month, 5 GB for $50 a month, or 10 GB for $65. Obviously, the last option is the most attractive one, and it is likely that most people will choose it. However, if the last option were $95, it is more likely that most people would choose the second option because the last option does not seem as attractive anymore.

3. Offer promotions, bundles, and sales. In addition to Lightning Deals, Amazon might offer coupons for additional savings. Buying something that is on sale is much more attractive to consumers.

4. Give something for free. Free is a powerful word. We all love free things. Consumers prefer to buy products that are shipped for free, such as the Power Bank, to similar products that charge shipping fees, even if the "free" shipping product is a bit more expensive.

5. Use the magical number 9. Ending prices with the number 9 is an old trick but is still effective. The original price of the Power Bank was $16.99.

6. Reframe the price. For subscriptions or donations, presenting the overall annual or monthly price in smaller amounts will increase consumers' willingness to engage in them. For example, instead of saying, "Donate $18 a month," marketers can say, "For little more than 50 cents a day, you can help a child in need."

7. Offer a loyalty rewards program. Who doesn't like free gifts? Knowing that they are being rewarded for purchasing things they need is very attractive to consumers.

As you can see from the example of the Power Bank, companies often employ multiple tactics when it comes to their pricing strategy. They also alter their price based on market developments (e.g. more competitors), the product's life stage (introduction vs. maturity), and demand.

Perceived risk
the sense of uncertainty that we experience every time we make a purchase.

Marketers Must Manage Consumers' Perceptions About Risk

One of the biggest challenges that marketers face is consumers' perceptions about the risk involved in making a purchase. **Perceived risk** is the sense of uncertainty that we experience every time we make a purchase.[31] Every time we make a decision about purchasing a product, we factor in the risks that are involved in such a purchase. If the risk outweighs the benefits of the product, we will decide against the purchase. Figure 11.6 outlines the factors affecting our perceptions about risk, the types of risks, and their consequences.[32]

Functional risks
concerns about product failure or underperformance.

Functional risks – Functional risks refer to our concerns about product failure or underperformance. For example, after nearly 100 incidents with Samsung Galaxy Note 7 phones overheating

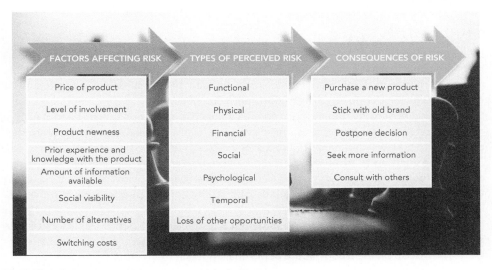

FIGURE 11.6 Perceived Risk and Consumer Behavior

and sometimes injuring the owners, the US Department of Transportation banned these devices from all airline flights.[33]

Physical risks – Some products are more hazardous than others. For example, guns are regarded as a riskier purchase due to potential injuries and even loss of life if used improperly. Similarly, as discussed in the previous example, product malfunctions can inflict physical injuries on users.

Financial risks – The relationship between costs and benefits is the number one concern when it comes to making a purchasing decision. The greater the financial risk, the greater the likelihood that it will outweigh the benefits associated with the product. Financial risks do not encompass only those that are involved at the time of purchase. They also include future losses. For example, when you buy a car, you don't just consider if you can afford it right now. You also consider the cost of maintenance, miles per gallon, and resale value, all of which pose financial risks.

Social risks – Our social status affects us more than we are willing to admit. What others think about our purchases sometimes outweighs what we think about them. Our purchases not only indicate who we are, but they also signal our social status and social relationships. We avoid purchasing a product that we believe will not be socially accepted, and we purchase products that are socially accepted and that signal our desired social affiliation.

Psychological risks – Consumers today are more conscious than ever about the values their brands stand for and the image their brands convey. We will avoid brands that we feel do not reflect our values and beliefs.

Temporal risks – We often invest a great deal of time and effort searching for the best product for us. This time investment is valuable, and we want to avoid going through it again if we make the wrong choice. We also do not want to waste time repairing the product if it malfunctions.

Loss of other opportunities – With most products we have multiple options to choose from. Sometimes we are even overwhelmed by the number of options we have. The last thing we want to do is make the wrong decision, especially if we find out that other options are no longer available.

Physical risks concerns about the outcomes of product failure.

Financial risks the relationship between costs and benefits.

Social risks concerns about what others think about us.

Psychological risks concerns about the values brands stand for and the image their brands convey.

Temporal risks concerns about the time invested in searching for a product, repairing it, or replacing it.

Loss of other opportunities concerns about losing an option to buy a product.

Do the Right Thing!

Is it wrong for marketers to make claims to consumers about their brands? Of course, not – not if they don't overdo it, no more than you try to position yourself as positively as possible when you're talking to job recruiters (or potential new partners). Here are some current developments relating to ethics and consumer perception:

As marijuana becomes legalized in more US states, the industry is thinking about ethical marketing standards in advertising. The discussions revolve around such things as emphasizing health and wellness benefits and not being too "juvenile" in the imagery used in ads.

As some companies strive toward more sustainable practices (e.g. in their packaging), others are being criticized for "greenwashing," that is, making claims about caring about the environment when in fact they are doing nothing constructive to achieve more sustainable goals.

Ethics are entering into the world of data and artificial intelligence (AI). It's not just a concern for privacy and security of consumers' data (though that's still big and not completely resolved). Online platforms are being challenged in many ways. For example, places to post opinions (Twitter, Facebook) are trying to sort what postings are so vile that they should be censored and withdrawn. E-retailers are often using data to make recommendations of more (and more and more) stuff a consumer should buy, and sometimes the suggestions are hard to resist. Do these suggestions make a consumer materialistic? Or should the consumer simply figure out a way to resist?

How Can Marketers Address These Perceptions About Risk?

Offer free trials. By enabling consumers to interact with the brand and product, marketers can ease concerns about how well the product works.

Offer a warranty. Providing a warranty signals to the consumer that the company is confident about the quality of its product. Offering a long-term warranty promotes consumers' trust in the brand. This element also affects concerns about physical and functional risks.

Offer a money-back guarantee. Knowing that you can get your money back without cost will help minimize consumers' concerns about financial risks.

Offer promotions. Promotional offerings such as 50% off or buy one, get one (BOGO) can increase the perceived value of the product and reduce perceived risk.

Provide testimonials or other forms of social approval. It is critical to marketers to provide consumers with evidence of social acceptance. Using testimonials, influencers, and endorsers will help minimize the social risks associated with the product.

Reassure consumers. Consumers want to feel that they made the right choice regarding their purchase. Marketers should follow up with their consumers and reassure them about the choice they made.

Offer exceptional service. Consumers want to know that if they have problems with the product, the company will be there to help as soon as possible. Think about how frustrating it is to call customer service and be put on hold for a long time. Exceptional service eases concerns about wasting time on a product.

Build a strong brand. Strong brands enjoy high levels of consumers' trust. Consumers feel more secure and reassured when they purchase products from well-established brands with good, reliable reputations. Think about Apple, Amazon, Harley-Davidson, Nike, and Disney: all enjoy high levels of consumers' trust that help mitigate multiple risks.

SUMMARY

Consumers' perceptions are so important! Marketers try to shape and influence how consumers think about their brands, but in the end, consumers' perceptions are most important. Marketers must understand what goes into those perceptions and how consumers come to think about a brand and competitors' brands the way they do.

Perceptions begin with sensations, and one goal of marketing is to provide external cues to trigger a desired behavior. Doing that can prove challenging. Consumers are bombarded with many marketing messages each day – how do marketers even begin to capture their attention? Brands incorporate a variety of elements, such as colors, images, and fonts, in advertisements and packaging to align their offerings and values with consumers' needs to break past that initial barrier. Doing so helps to position a brand favorably in the consumers' eyes.

There are multiple risks associated with a purchase that consumers take into consideration when determining whether to purchase a product or service, including functional, physical, social, and psychological, but financial risk is frequently the most influential factor for consumers in numerous product categories. Thus, a top priority for marketers is to help mitigate the financial risk associated with a purchase. This can be done in a number of ways, such as by offering free trials and money-back guarantees, which signal confidence in the product.

By putting the consumers' needs before the sale, marketers can provide a positive experience for consumers, from beginning to end. Hopefully, that leads to a desired purchasing behavior and, better yet, brand loyalty.

KEY TERMS

Perception
Sensation
Absolute threshold
Differential threshold or just noticeable difference (JND)
Shrinkflation
Subliminal message
Perceptual overload

Perceptual selection
Attention
Selective exposure
Selective attention
Perceptual defense
Perceptual blocking
Gestalt principles or organization

Figure-ground relationship
Perceptual proximity
Perceptual closure
Perceptual similarity
Perceptual anomaly
Perceptual interpretation
Schemata

Perceptual distortions
Positioning
Perceptual map
Reference price
Price anchoring
Perceived risk
Functional risks
Physical risks
Financial risks

Social risks
Psychological risks
Temporal risks
Loss of other opportunities

EXERCISES

1. Think of the five senses. Marketers often appeal to the visual in packaging and advertising, but think of a few brands that appeal to your other senses. For example, for smell, think of the scent of the Cinnabon's store in a mall; for sound, think of catchy jingles; for taste, think of samples at Costco; for touch, think of how online retailers are offering you the chance to try on clothing and return the merchandise if you don't like it when you have it in your hands and try it on.

2. Lots of people are brand loyal to Coke or Pepsi and say that they can tell the difference between them, but it turns out that few really can. With a partner, set up a blind taste test. In one room, have liters of Coke, Pepsi, Diet Coke, Coke Zero, Diet Pepsi, and a store brand cola. Pour small amounts of each soda into serving cups, take them into another room, and have your test subjects drink each and try to identify them. See how far the accuracy is below 100%.

3. Pick a product category you know a lot about. List five to seven competitor brands. Draw a perceptual map placing the brands on the map. What do the East–West and North–South dimensions represent? Why were those attributes the ones that mattered to you most?

4. For each of the types of perceptual distortions, find an ad or commercial that leverages these distortions to promote a product.

5. Find an ad or commercial that uses one of the perceptual elements discussed in the chapter. Share it with your classmates.

ENDNOTES

1. https://www.bbc.com/news/magazine-11517129.

2. Bennett L. Schwartz and John H. Krantz, *Sensation and Perception*, 2nd ed. (Los Angeles, CA: Sage, 2018).

3. https://journal.classiccars.com/2019/07/25/mcneil-soars-in-collector-ratings-after-buying-ferrari-250-gto.

4. S. Shapiro, "When an Ad's Influence Is Beyond Our Conscious Control: Perceptual and Conceptual Fluency Effects Caused by Incidental Ad Exposure," *Journal of Consumer Research* 26, no. 1 (1999): 16–36.

5. Dennis Proffitt and Drake Baer, *Perception: How Our Bodies Shape Our Minds* (New York: St. Martin's, 2020).

6. S. H. Britt and V. M. Nelson, "The Marketing Importance of the 'Just Noticeable Difference,'" *Business Horizons* 19, no. 4 (1976): 38–40.

7. https://www.cbsnews.com/news/grocery-prices-rise-supermarkets.

8. https://www.bbc.com/worklife/article/20180510-the-food-you-buy-really-is-shrinking.

9. https://www.businessinsider.com/brands-that-announced-plans-to-change-review-racist-mascots-logos-2020-6.

10. C. Trappey, "A Meta-analysis of Consumer Choice and Subliminal Advertising," *Psychology and Marketing* 13, no. 5 (1996): 517–30.

11. https://www.businessinsider.com/subliminal-messages-in-12-popular-logos-2016-5.

12. N. K. Malhotra, "Information and Sensory Overload. Information and Sensory Overload in Psychology and Marketing," *Psychology and Marketing* 1, no. 3–4 (1984): 9–21.

13. R. B. Zajonc, "Mere Exposure: A Gateway to the Subliminal," *Current Directions in Psychological Science* 10, no. 6 (2001): 224–28.

14. C. W. Park and V. P. Lessig, "Familiarity and Its Impact on Consumer Decision Biases and Heuristics," *Journal of consumer research* 8, no. 2 (1981): 223–30.

15. S. Yantis and R. A. Abrams, *Sensation and Perception*, 2nd ed. (New York: Worth, 2016).

16. E. Bruce Goldstein and J. Brockmole, *Sensation and Perception*, 10th ed. (Boston, MA: Cengage, 2016).

17. S. Iyengar, et al., "Selective Exposure to Campaign Communication: The Role of Anticipated Agreement and Issue Public Membership," *Journal of Politics* 70, no. 1 (2008): 186–200.

18. S. Ratneshwar, et al., "Benefit Salience and Consumers' Selective Attention to Product Features," *International Journal of Research in Marketing* 14, no. 3 (1997): 245–59.

19. M. B. Holbrook and J. Huber, "Separating Perceptual Dimensions from Affective Overtones: An Application to Consumer Aesthetics," *Journal of Consumer Research* 5, no. 4 (1979): 272–83.

20. J. Wagemans, et al., "A Century of Gestalt Psychology in Visual Perception: 1. Perceptual Group and Figure-Ground Organization," *Psychological Bulletin* 138, no. 6 (2012): 1172–217.

21. J. Wagemans, et al., "A Century of Gestalt Psychology in Visual Perception: I. Perceptual Grouping and Figure–Ground Organization," *Psychological Bulletin* 138, no. 6 (2012): 1172.

22. Y. Jia, et al., "Physical Proximity Increases Persuasive Effectiveness Through Visual Imagery," *Journal of Consumer Psychology* 27, no. 4 (2017): 435–47.

23. M. B. Shapiro, "Experimental Studies of a Perceptual Anomaly: 1. Initial Experiments," *Journal of Mental Science* 97, no. 406 (2018): 90–110.

24. D. E. Rumelhart, "Schemata and the Cognitive System," in *Handbook of Social Cognition,* vol. 1. Eds. R. S. Wyer Jr. and T. K. Srull (Hillsdale, NJ: Lawrence Erlbaum, 1984), 161–88.

25. M. B. Holbrook, "Using a Structural Model of Halo Effect to Assess Perceptual Distortion Due to Affective Overtones," *Journal of Consumer Research* 10, no. 2 (1983): 247–52.

26. Lorna Keane, *"Customer Perceptions: Knowing and Measuring How Your Consumers Think,"* 2020, https://blog.globalwebindex.com/marketing/customer-perceptions.

27. W. Dou, et al., "Brand Positioning Strategy Using Search Engine Marketing," *MIS Quarterly* 34, no. 2 (2010): 261–79.

28. A. J. T. Lee, et al., "Mining Perceptual Maps from Consumer Reviews," *Decision Support Systems* 82 (February 2016): 12–25.

29. T. Mazumdar, S. P. Raj, and I. Sinha, "Reference Price Research: Review and Propositions," *Journal of Marketing* 69, no. 4 (2005): 84–102.

30. P. K. Kopalle, A. G. Rao, and J. L. Assuncao, "Asymmetric Reference Price Effects and Dynamic Pricing Policies," *Marketing Science* 15, no. 1 (1996): 60–85.

31. V. W. Mitchell, "Consumer Perceived Risk: Conceptualisations and Models," *European Journal of Marketing* (1999).

32. Utpal M. Dholakia, "An Investigation of the Relationship between Perceived Risk and Product Involvement," in *Advances in Consumer Research,* vol. 24. Eds. M. Brucks and D. J. MacInnis (Provo, UT: Association for Consumer Research, 1997), 159–67.

33. https://www.faa.gov/news/updates/?newsId=86685#:~:text=Individuals%20who%20own%20or%20possess,be%20shipped%20as%20air%20cargo.

CREDITS

https://www.shutterstock.com/image-photo/imola-classic-26-october-2018-ferrari-1698890560

https://summalinguae.com/language-culture/colours-across-cultures

https://sco.wikipedia.org/wiki/File:Unilever.svg

https://www.rnbdesign.com/ads--video-campaign.html

https://en.wikipedia.org/wiki/Ontario_Soccer_Association

https://www.amazon.com/ref=nav_logo

https://smile.amazon.com/INIU-High-Speed-Flashlight-Powerbank-Compatible/dp/B07CZDXDG8/ref=sr_1_3?crid=2FVX3JD2PXWE7&dchild=1&keywords=iniu+power+bank+10000mah&qid=1629056703&sprefix=iniu+power%2Caps%2C172&sr=8-3

https://lt298.wordpress.com/2017/05/07/doritos-and-just-noticeable-difference

Figure 11.4: Stadium Enterprises LLC, Moncler S.P.A., NIKE, INC., Keds, New Balance, ASICS Corporation

Figure 11.6: Adapted from Utpal M. Dholakia (1997)

Image p. 206: Mau47/Shutterstock

Image p. 209: Frito-Lay North America, Inc.; Amazon.com, Inc.

Image p. 210: Alberto Brea

Image p. 212: Plant-for-the-Planet Foundation; Unilever

Image p. 213: SportsEngine, Inc.; BASF SE

Image p. 217: Amazon.com, Inc.

12 Consumers' Social and Cultural Context

LEARNING OBJECTIVES

After studying this chapter, you should be able to:

- Envision the many ways that consumers define themselves, in part by their sociocultural groups including gender, ethnicity, age, and shared values.

- Understand that these reference groups facilitate consumer comparisons and consumption decisions.

- Understand the different bases by which reference groups may be formed, such as age, gender, race, and ethnicity.

- Understand that marketers can leverage group influence to position brands and target groups of consumers and influence consumption decisions.

Your brand team meets every Wednesday, from 8:00 to 9:00 a.m. sharp, in a boardroom in which there is coffee and tea available. There are always biodegradable and recyclable paper cups available to drink from, but you noticed last week that your boss poured coffee into a Tervis mug, drank from it during the meeting, and took it back to the office when the meeting was done. You were obviously not the only person to notice, because this week, a colleague you don't like (call this person Mr. Suckup) has a Tervis mug of his own. Peer pressure? Do you go and buy a Tervis mug? Or do you show individuality and buy a stainless steel YETI mug? (After all, Tervis mugs are plastic, and the world has a plastic problem, so there!) What will your choice say about you?

Do consumers care that much about what others will think about purchases? Certainly not all the time, but very often, especially if these are purchases of products that are visible to others. Consumers know that the brands that they choose can reflect on them: will the brand reflect well of them, signaling that they are innovative, smart, cool, elegant, environmentally sensitive, and so forth? Or will the brand reflect poorly on them, signaling that they are behind the times, or cheap, or not really in touch?

Consumers make choices based mostly on their needs and desires. Yet another big influence on their choices can be the people around them – their family and friends, people in their online social networks, and, as the Tervis versus YETI example indicated, their coworkers. If we step back to view the perspective of the consumer a little more broadly, we'll see that most of us identify with certain groups, such as by age or ethnicity or gender. Let's look at some examples to see how it works.

Reference Groups

A **reference group** is a person or group of people that consumers think about and make comparisons to; these comparisons can influence their attitudes, perceptions, values, opinions, and consumption behavior.[1] There are multiple types of reference groups, but three are especially influential:

Membership groups are the groups that consumers currently belong to or are associated with. A membership group can be primary or secondary, formal or informal.[2] **Primary membership groups** are those groups that consumers interact with frequently and regularly, such as your family or your classmates. **Secondary membership groups** include groups that consumers have infrequent and irregular interaction with (e.g. professional organizations, country club). That can be a sports club or online interest groups. **Formal groups** are groups that have formal structure and roles, whereas **informal groups** are those that are formed around joint interests of their members, such as brand communities.

Dissociative groups are groups with whom consumers do not share similar opinions, values, or attitudes. Because of this, consumers would be motivated to distance themselves from these groups.[3] If a brand has a celebrity endorser who is known to be liberal, then conservatives might shun the brand. Or if the brand is one your parents like, you might feel the need to break out and show your own identity by finding a different brand.

Aspirational groups are groups that consumers identify with and would like to be associated with. Normally, these groups will have a higher status than that currently held by the individual. For example, you might have aspirations to belong to the exclusive club of Fortune 500 CEOs.

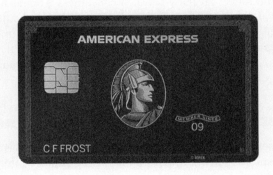

Aspirational Group – American Express Centurion Credit Card: By invitation only. You will need an average of $16.3 million in assets to be invited.

One of the first times consumers experience reference groups is in middle school or high school. Think of the cliques from when you were younger – the nerds, the jocks, the cool kids, the druggies, the loners, and so on. Suppose that one of your classmates from that time, Mia, plays on the school's field hockey team and is kind of a jock.

- Her membership reference group would be other jocks. That group would be influential when she was buying her next athletic shoes or sweat-wicking workout clothing.

- She might not aspire to be a nerd – they'd be a dissociative group for her, but she might look to them when she chooses her next laptop.

- The cool kids are often an aspiration group (who doesn't want to be liked?), and here, if there was some trend-setting fashion, Mia might consciously or subconsciously begin to copy their clothing choices.

Reference group
a person or group of people that consumers think about and make comparisons to.

Membership groups
groups that consumers currently belong to or are associated with.

Primary membership groups
groups that consumers interact with frequently and regularly.

Secondary membership groups
groups that consumers have infrequent and irregular interaction with.

Formal groups
groups that have formal structure and roles.

Informal groups
groups that are formed around joint interests of their members.

Dissociative groups
groups with whom consumers do not share similar opinions, values, or attitudes.

Aspirational groups
groups that consumers identify with and would like to be associated with.

FIGURE 12.1   Consumers' Reference Groups

A different way to categorize reference groups is by their closeness to the individual consumer (see Figure 12.1). Some reference groups are based on the characteristics of the individual consumer and reflect diversity between consumers. The next level that is closest to the individual is family, followed by friends, social status groups, subcultures, and culture, which is the most distanced from the individual (we will discuss culture in Chapter 13). However, note that the closeness of a reference group is not necessarily reflective of its influence on an individual's consumption behavior. For example, you may find that your friends have more influence on your consumption behavior than your parents.

Different Bases of Reference Groups

It is sometimes helpful to distinguish reference groups as we've just done, such as dissociative versus aspirational, but in putting marketing strategy into practice, it helps to be more specific. Marketers will look at data on their customers – who buys their brand, what's their profile, in terms of age, gender, ethnicity, and so on. Marketers can also attempt to appeal to a different target segment by repositioning the brand. Let's see what consumer characteristics marketers pay the most attention to.

Individual Diversity

There are many ways that consumers differ from each other, and increasingly our societies are trying to mature to be respectful of these differences. Some of the demographics that marketers use frequently in targeting and messaging include: age, gender, race, and ethnicity.

Age and Generational Cohorts

For marketers, a consumer's age tells them a lot about that individual.[4] It is natural for people to form more friendships with others around their own age, beginning with having been in school together or around the same time. They grew up with the same musical influences, and they've lived through the same high-visibility events, from the same nut-job reality TV stars to the same politicians and talking heads to the same economic cycles. If you're thinking about buying a new car or tablet or finding a new restaurant, you read reviews online and talk to your network – many people in any consumer's network are of the same generation.

Figure 12.2 presents the labels you're familiar with, along with the dates that identify each category. The Gen Alpha are the youngest named group. The Millennials might be their parents, and Gen Z (or iGens) are older brothers and sisters. The Gen Xs are the Millennials' bosses, and the Millennials are Gen Z's bosses in turn; the Boomers are the old lot. (Well, there are people who are older – the "Silent Generation" are people born between 1928 and 1946, and their consumption patterns involve health care and the transfer of wealth to younger generations.)

You know your generation best, but some highlights describing the generation differences are provided in Figure 12.2. Notice first their relative sizes – the reason that you heard (ad nauseam) about Boomers and Millennials is because there are so many of them; they also have the most money and the greatest purchasing power. These are huge waves of consumers, and more consumers means more demand for whatever products they're seeking. Gen X and Gen Z can sometimes enjoy economic surpluses, such as better prices as brands and companies compete for their attention. At risk of some overgeneralizations, Gen Z has been described as pretty easygoing, that is, relatively tolerant of others. Millennials have been described as not materialistic, valuing experiences over things. But marketers should not underestimate Gen Alpha. They don't have money of their own, but they have great influence on their parents' (Millennials) buying behaviors. They are very expressive when it comes to the products and brands they prefer – it's called "pester power" (pester Mom and Dad until they get what they want).

The figure highlights some qualities that marketers can use. If Gen Z are socially driven, brands and companies need to emphasize that. And, of course, Gen Z is seriously online. Millennials care about causes or social marketing, which isn't to say other generations do not, but rather these consumers would appreciate hearing about a company's CSR (corporate social responsibility) efforts. Gen Alpha are visual learners and prefer interactive and engaging marketing messages.

	BABY BOOMERS 1947–1964	GENERATION X 1965–1979	MILLENNIALS 1980–1996	GEN Z 1997–2015	GEN ALPHA 2016–2024
AKA	Boomers	Latch-key kids	Generation Y	iGen	?
US population	81.3m	61.2m	92.7m	65.2m	35m
Descriptors	• Believe in the "American Dream" • Less influenced by peer pressure • Financially stable • Loyal to brands	• Value flexible work arrangements • "Big picture" perspective • Skeptical • Independent • Tech-savvy	• Favor experiences • Innovative • Work smarter vs. harder • Social-cause driven • Multitaskers • Tech-savvy	• Tolerant of others • Entrepreneurial • Tech-dependent • High ethnic diversity • Skeptical • Social-cause driven	• Virtual learners • Flexible family structure experience • Diversity oriented • Influence their parents' buying behavior
Marketing	Maintain trust, deliver on promises Email marketing and direct mail	Coupons, loyalty programs, provide quality service	Relate products to experiences, Align brand with a social cause	Embrace multiculturalism Use digital video in ads	Aim to be inspiring, engaging, want to be involved and co-create
Iconic technologies	Radio, Black & White TV	VCR, PC, Walkman	Internet, email, cell phones, SMS, DVD	Tablets, apps, Facebook, Wii, PS3	Smart speakers, TikTok, iPods, AI technology
Favorite brands	Home Depot, USPS, Tide, Lowe's, FedEx, Amazon, Hershey, AAA	Google, Amazon, Netflix, UPS, Home Depot, Cheerios	Google, Netflix, Target, YouTube, Amazon, Samsung, Dollar Tree	Google, Netflix, Oreo, Apple, Doritos, Amazon, YouTube, Walmart	Amazon, Tesla, Zoom, Disney, Netflix, Hulu, Alexa, Siri

FIGURE 12.2 Generations of Consumers

Differences between generations can be subtle. For example, consumers who are born at the end of one generation and at the start of another will be influenced by both. Sometimes differences between generations are less subtle; for example, the "OK Boomer" backlash is understandable. When older consumers criticize younger people about why they don't seem loyal to a job or aren't buying homes, and so on, it's an unfair criticism because the Millennials in particular graduated during rather rough economic times – jobs were fewer, so they and Gen Zs creatively began the "temp economy." These younger consumers couldn't afford houses right away and were fine with sharing vehicles and housing. In contrast, the economy was booming when the Boomers boomed.

As one last characterization of generational differences, Figure 12.2 shows some of the most favored brands per group. Amazon makes everyone's list, to some degree, but otherwise there is great variety. Marketers often use strategies such as co-branding or nostalgia marketing, and knowing a generation's favorite brands is very useful in planning what would be attractive in marketing campaigns.

It is particularly important to be reminded that the marketing team is likely to be diverse in the ages of the team members, and it is unlikely that the whole team represents the generation that is the brand's target segment. Understanding differences in generations of consumers helps marketers design products and ad campaigns properly suited to the customers the team is hoping to engage.

Gender

It is no surprise that gender or sexual orientation or sexual identity affect many consumer preferences and purchases.[5] Figure 12.3 shows some brands that are stereotypically more appealing to men, other brands that appeal more to women, and some brands that are attractive across the board.

It may seem to be a good goal to try to position a brand to appeal across boundaries, but the truth is, it's difficult to do so. For one thing, the landscape regarding gender and sex has gotten more complicated. Consider the acronym LGBTQQIP2SAA (lesbian, gay, bisexual, transgender, questioning, queer, intersex, pansexual, two-spirit, androgynous, and asexual)[6] – each of these groups of people shares some commonalities, and they experience many differences. It is challenging for a brand to be all things to all people. Instead, marketers talk about targeting, to focus

MALE APPEAL	NEUTRAL APPEAL	FEMALE APPEAL
Gillette	Apple	Dove
Sony	Mini Cooper	Jimmy Choo
Microsoft	Burger King	Givenchy
Heineken	Kroger	Christian Louboutin
Mustang	Facebook	Ulta
Playboy	Toyota	Chanel
Old Spice	Amazon	TikTok
Tesla	Nike	Kellogg's
Duluth	Panera Bread	Always

FIGURE 12.3 Brands and Gender

and try to please one group (or a few groups), then perhaps branch out with a brand extension to include another group (or groups).

In general, men and women tend to look for different cues before they buy.[7] For example:

- Women want to hear about a product's benefits, whereas men want a more linear presentation of a product's features. Men also like analytical comparisons, such as when ads compare two brands, attribute by attribute (e.g. car A costs more than car B, but it also gets better gas mileage, but car B looks cooler).

- The shopping process is different: women see shopping as an event that is fun, and it can be a challenge to be a smart shopper, whereas men, in general, view shopping more as a necessary task – just get it done.

- In stores or online, women ask for help because they think that's efficient, whereas men don't really want to ask for help because it feels like a sign of weakness.

- When men and women search for information online, women like to see stories about satisfied customers, whereas men want to stick more to the facts.

We'll discuss family and household purchasing dynamics shortly, but it is important to remember that women drive the majority of purchasing; some 70–80% of household buying is done by women.[8] They control over $32 trillion in worldwide spending.[9] (For the purposes of your own career advancement, and that of your brand, don't ignore this consumer segment.)

In some product categories, women seem to be paying more than what men would pay. See the "Do the Right Thing: Gender and Pricing" box for examples. It's rare to find products that charge men more than women – but, for example, bars sometimes offer drink deals for women and almost never for men. The manufacturers and service providers claim there is a reason (usually to cover greater incurred costs), but decide for yourself.

Do the Right Thing!

Is it unethical to charge women more than men for products or services? Industries aren't stupid (or they don't want to get sued or have bad PR), so they usually defend their "price discrimination" with a reason:

Industry	Why? (or so they say!)
Dry cleaning	Women's more delicate fabrics
Hair salons $5+ more	Longer hair, more complicated
Razors 50% more	Cover more surface area
Health insurance	Greater usage
Mortgages	Claim men search for better rates
Car prices $300 more	Claim men haggle longer
Shampoo 50% more	Added perfume

The Family and Stages in the Household Life Cycle

Figure 12.4 paints a slightly different picture. This information doesn't replace the generations; it complements it. The idea is simple: as people go through life, their wants and needs change,

NEW COUPLES
First homes
Nicer car
Durables (e.g. more
furniture)

PARENTS OF OLDER KIDS
Computer
Family vacations
Orthodontist
Kids' hobbies
(sports, music)

OLD DUDES
Health care
Downsize
(housing)

YOUNG AND SINGLE
Clothing
Basic furniture
Basic kitchen apps
Cologne

PARENTS WITH YOUNG KIDS
Kids' clothing
Toys
Minivan
Life insurance

EMPTY NESTERS
Kids' education
Vacations
Hobbies
Investments
Wills

FIGURE 12.4   Household Purchasing Progression

and the kinds of products that appeal to the consumers in each stage of life also change.[10] These phases hold true for any generation.

Young adults tend to start out single. They might be educated, they might make decent salaries, and they need to establish their own households (assuming they aren't living in their parents' basement). Single people spend considerable amounts on clothing and their appearance to attract significant others, and they spend money on basic housing needs, travel, and entertainment.[11]

In the next stage, young couples who are living together, married or not, can be a really attractive group for marketers. The couple has a combined income, and without needing to spend money on kids yet, they might have a substantial amount of discretionary income to spend on whatever they wish. They might buy housing, rather than renting an apartment. They might trade in their less expensive cars for something nicer. They might buy nice furniture rather than continue to use the pieces they had while in the dorms. If both members are establishing their careers, their incomes will be growing steadily. If one member seeks further education, they might curtail their spending a bit and live a somewhat more moderate lifestyle for a short while, knowing they're investing to an even brighter future. A couple is the beginning of a family unit, and some purchase decisions will involve both parties.

What happens next? Surprise! When a kid arrives, things get more complicated for the family but are rather predictable for marketers – that young family will need diapers, kids' clothing, toys, and lots of other things. The adults might also plan ahead, perhaps buying life insurance to be sure the kids are taken care of, should anything happen to one or both of the parental units.

The parenthood stage of couples with at least one child living at home is the longest stage of the family life cycle. Parenthood (also known as the "full-nest" stage) usually extends over more than 20 years. Because of its long duration, this stage can be divided into shorter phases: the preschool phase, the elementary school phase, the high school phase, and the college phase. Throughout these parenthood phases, the interrelationships of family members and the structure of the family gradually change. The financial resources of the family also change, as one or both parents progress in a career and as child rearing and educational responsibilities gradually increase and eventually decrease as children become self-supporting. Throughout these phases, purchases are predictable. Parents begin spending on services such as child-care workers and tutors. Even young kids expect to have smartphones, and their parents begin learning how to do things such as block certain websites on their home computers.

Next is the "empty nest" stage. Post-parenthood refers to older married couples who no longer have children living at home. Because parenthood extends over many years, the start of this stage can be somewhat traumatic for parents as well as possibly liberating in other ways. For many parents, this stage represents the opportunity to do all the things they could not do or afford while their children lived at home or went to college. During this stage, most married couples are more financially secure – they may have savings and investments, and they have fewer expenses (no mortgage or college tuition bills). They're also likely to have more leisure time. As a result, empty nesters are an important market for luxury goods, new automobiles, expensive furniture, and vacations to faraway places.

At the end of the household cycle, one spouse might die, and the other spouse might need to simplify and establish a more economical lifestyle. The surviving spouse may wish to divest some belongings by giving away household goods to nonprofits. That person is also likely to incur more medical bills.

What else happens throughout the household life cycle? Marketers see very reliable trends. One such trend that develops and changes is who a very young child uses as a reference group. Early on, naturally the kids look to their parents and older brothers and sisters. The family is how kids become to be socialized – and everything plays a role. The family unit affects a young person's morals and religious principles, the kid's interpersonal skills, manners, and speech, their aspirations for education and career goals, everything. With time, kids turn more to their classmates and peers to determine what will make them popular at school, and if the parents disapprove, that's even better. Friends influence style and fashion, fads that are "in," and, in general, what is accepted and approved of in terms of consumer behavior.

It is also the case that marketers know that kids as young as two or three years old begin seeing connections between advertising and items in stores, and they make shopping requests by pointing (or screaming).[12] Some items in the household are joint family purchase decisions (see Figure 12.5), and other decisions are dominated by the husband or the wife or the male or the female depending on the product category.

At this point, you've got the hang of it. The age and generation differences and the family life cycle phases are two dimensions of consumer reference groups that affect whose opinions consumers seek, and their resulting brand choices. Let's see a few more dimensions of consumer reference groups.

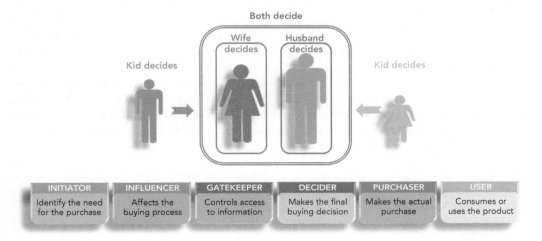

FIGURE 12.5 Decision-Making in the Family

When a consumer is in a group, such as a family, and is buying for the group, purchase decisions get more complicated. Kids may have input on some items and not on others. Adults often negotiate and come to agreements: person A selects some items, while person B selects others. Usually, this division of labor is based on the fact that one person has more expertise in that product category or is simply more involved, that is, cares more about that product category. Then that person makes those product purchase decisions, and the other person gives in because he or she doesn't care or doesn't know or because of the underlying implicit agreement in the relationship.

Marketers distinguish between what they call joint and autonomic decision-making. In joint decision-making, more than one person is consulted, often only the adults in the household, and typically for the bigger ticket items (housing, cars, trips). The question is, "What should we buy?" In autonomic decision-making, one person makes the decision, for which the other ceded responsibility and cooperated by accepting the decision maker's choice. Here the question is, "What do I think is best for the family?"

Social Class and Socioeconomic Status

Other ways that consumers differ are the social class to which they belong and their socioeconomic status. These concepts are related but not identical. Let's see how they can affect marketers.

Social Class

Social class
a group of people who share the same socioeconomic status.

Marketers often speak of social class.[13] **Social class** refers to a group of people who share the same socioeconomic status. This is a concept that is thought to be grounded in one's childhood. Through early and continued life experiences, consumers come to have certain preferences and expectations about what they can buy and can't buy, what they want to buy and don't want to buy, and so forth, so social class affects many life choices, including brand choices. Social class is thought to be a rather "sticky" concept in that if someone grows up in a somewhat impoverished environment but then comes to make a large salary later in life, the person often still thinks as he or she did in those early formative years. That mindset might result in individuals' being careful in spending money even if they have plenty of it.

Socioeconomic Status

Socioeconomic status
reflects a combined measure of a person's social status and economic standing.

Even if marketers refer to social class, they typically mean the consumers' current socioeconomic status (SES).[14] **Socioeconomic status** is certainly mostly about a person's income (or the household's income), but it is usually also measured as a function of education level, occupation, type of residence (own a house or rent an apartment), and so forth. Those things are often positively correlated.

For consumers and marketers, reference groups based on SES are easy to understand: Is your budget tight, or do you have large piles of cash? There are so many ways that income affects brand choices, from constraining consumers who cannot afford items they desire to spurring consumers who want to buy the brands and products that signal their belonging in the right echelons of society.

Figure 12.6 shows an example of price points for different cars. Two varieties of brands are presented to remind us that all consumers, no matter what they can afford, still have plenty of choices. And consumers in higher socioeconomic classes could always purchase "down," that is, buy a car that is less expensive than they could afford, whereas the reverse is not true: a consumer in the lower middle-income group cannot typically afford a car targeted for upper middle-class consumers.

Sometimes consumers engage in "conspicuous consumption," in which they buy items that they can barely afford to impress others.[15] But, in general, consumers purchase within their

FIGURE 12.6 Automobiles Targeted to Different Socioeconomic Status

economic means. Income is a very real constraint; it determines consumers' selection of housing, and housing often determines the nearest, most affordable grocery store – Walmart or Whole Foods. Even for the individual consumer, retail prices matter – for a "regular" haircut, someone might go to an inexpensive Supercuts, but that same person might pay a little more right before a big interview, figuring that the extra expense is a good investment.

A consumer's occupation is another objective indicator of socioeconomic status. Occupation can be a proxy for income, and it may also carry some prestige, such as if the consumer is a doctor, firefighter, scientist, or engineer. While socioeconomic status is directly tied to indicators such as income, social class can be somewhat subjective. That is, what is the economic level the consumer identifies with, based on their life experiences?

A consumer's economic base is so important that marketers have come up with descriptions:

- *Upper–upper class:* They've often inherited wealth and expect great privilege.

- *Nouveau riche:* They think that "money is king" – they've made it, they've earned it, they'll spend it.

- *Upper–middle class:* They're often high-achievement consumers and professionals, often a desirable target for marketers.

- *Middle class:* They aspire to be even better off, and they'll often follow the trends set by the upper–middle class (they may have less to spend than upper–middle-class consumers, but there are more of them).

- *Lower class or the working poor:* Recall Maslow's hierarchy of needs; these consumers care about covering the basics and hope that they can meet at least modest economic needs. Not surprisingly, these consumers can feel quite insecure and uncertain about their futures.

- *Underclass:* Consumers at rock bottom who are unlikely to be a marketer's target segment but may be a focus for an organization's CSR efforts.

Obviously, a consumer's wealth affects purchases. Most consumers make choices within their means, but most also are influenced by advertisements that show options to which they might aspire. These socioeconomic status characterizations show that not only do consumers vary in what they can buy, their attitudes and the way they go through life differ, and these affect their purchasing and consumption decisions as well.

How Subcultures Work

Everyone knows that there are broad cultural differences from country to country (see Chapter 13), but even within a country there are subcultures.

A **subculture** is a group of people who share some traits or preferences.[16] Some of the strongest subculture and reference group identities are age or the generation into which an individual was born; where the consumer is in the household life cycle; the consumer's gender, ethnicity, and socioeconomic status; and where the consumer lives. All of these factors help define consumers and affect their brand and purchase preferences.

Subculture
a group of people who share some traits or preferences.

The Who sang, "Whooo are You? Who, who, who, who?" (a.k.a. theme song for CSI!)

The Owl hoots, "Who! Who?" and the TV show *CSI* leverages the fact that the Who's song is popular. We all grow up with favorite songs, and later they become a touchstone of nostalgia. Marketers are smart about this; they think about the target audience of their brand, and the television commercial might then feature a song that was popular for that subculture, such as the age of the consumers. Popular songs used in commercials include Marvin Gaye's "I Heard It Through the Grapevine" for California Raisins, Rare Earth's "I Just Want to Celebrate" for Gatorade, ELO's "Do Ya" for Monster.com, and the Spinners' "Rubberband Man" for OfficeMax.

Given these aspects of subculture, it is worth understanding how and why there are differences from one subculture to another – why is it that there even are subcultures? The dynamics at play include consumers wishing to be like others, while other consumers, or the same consumers but in different situations, wish to express their individuality. For some product categories, consumer choices signal their identities to others, but sometimes, the purchase of a particular product is a signal to the consumer themselves, a self-signal.

Desire for Conformity and Desire for Uniqueness

Desire for conformity
a motivation for consumers to fit in with others.

The **desire for conformity** is a motivation for consumers to fit in with others.[17] They desire other people's approval, so they observe the group norms and try to comply. As they conform, consumers will experience a greater feeling of belonging to that group, which enhances affection to the group and group members as well as to the individual consumer's identity as having achieved a sense of belonging to that desired group. A popular group phenomenon these days is the **brand community**.[18] We will learn more about the term in Chapter 14 on social media, but basically brand communities are collections of like-minded consumers, such as consumers who all like a brand and perhaps share tips and photos of their use of the brand in their lives. A brand community or a group of friends and some work groups are examples of groups where the members all have roughly equal status. The motivation for conformity is a consumer's desire to be like all or most of them. Alternatively, sometimes there are more distinctive **opinion leaders**,[19] such as people within brand communities who are thought to be experts within an industry. Their views are highly trusted and have the power to influence other consumers' decision-making.

Brand community
a communities that is formed based on the emotional attachment to a brand.

Perhaps they're blog writers, or in groups of friends, there can be leaders, such as the "coolest" of the friends, or in work groups, the opinion leader is typically someone with authority, such as the boss (e.g. the Tervis mug example at the beginning of the chapter).[20] In this case, the motivation for conformity is more about a consumer getting the approval of that leader or boss, and the other group members behave similarly.

Opinion leaders
experts in a specific consumption domain. They are highly trusted and have the power to influence other consumers' decision making.

Sometimes consumers seek to model their behavior after others who have some source credibility, such as when a model advertises for cosmetics, or when an athlete supports an athletic shoe or equipment. Conforming to what an expert endorses seems sensible to many consumers. Sometimes the opinion leader is more local, such as dressing for one's partner, or making food choices for one's family.

Motives for conformity would move that person to start behaving like the others. On the other hand, sometimes consumers wish to stand out, to show their individuality. That is, different consumers, or the same consumers in different situations, may feel a **desire for uniqueness**, which is a motivation for consumers to stand out as special, and not just one in the crowd.[21] One example of this is research that shows that when consumers dine out with friends, they typically order dishes that are different from everyone else at the table. The table as a whole shows variety in the orders because consumers in such social settings don't want to be seen as copying the others. Sometimes the presence of others can affect the norms that consumers are sensitive to, in this case driving them to behaviors that are the opposite of conformity.

Desire for uniqueness
the motivation to stand out as special, and not just one in the crowd.

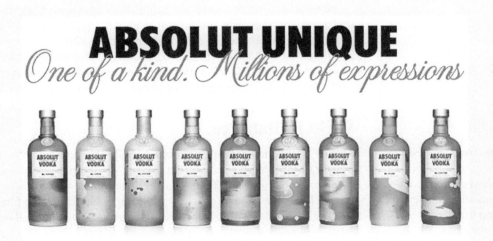

Absolut is appealing to consumers' desire for uniqueness.

These different desires vary with age. For example, think about young kids mimicking others' behavior to be closer to those friends, then seeking more uniqueness in adolescence as they try to forge their own identities, somewhat in rebellion to their familial norms. Conformity might be desired again when a young adult is hired – this new hire will probably be observant, watching others and learning their norms to try to figure out how to behave, how to be liked, how to get promoted, and so forth. Later, as consumers mature, there may be a comfort and more self-security in one's own choices. Part of learning a group's norms is to gain knowledge about when one needs to stick to certain norms versus when a person can let loose. For example, even in an informal company setting, it still might be frowned upon to wear shorts on casual Friday.

To complicate things further, sometimes these motives are held privately, and sometimes we display them more publicly. For example, sometimes men and women dress to impress others. We want others to notice us. We might select a nice suit or accessories to make a statement – "I am successful, and I like nice things. I deserve nice things."

Sometimes we dress to signal to ourselves – hey, lookin' good, nice clothing, nice hair, etc., with no concern yet as to what others think. In such situations, consumers contemplate, "Who am I?" and "Who do I want others to think I am?" In doing that, consumers are **self-monitoring**, or getting a sense of how they may be perceived in subsequent social settings.[22] Public versus private signaling can also vary when one's actual self has not yet caught up with one's ideal self, such as striving to be seen as a very successful young corporate employee but feeling inexperienced and nervous. Brands help consumers wear it well and overcome and send stronger signals.

Consumers use some products for conspicuous consumption; that is, the products are "worn" publicly to make a statement. Other products contribute more to the consumers' defining and expressing themselves to themselves. Consumers are complex, in that the signaling, public or private, may be about consumption and success, but they can just as readily be announcing that they embrace voluntary simplicity, eschewing leather, or jewelry, or when successful CEOs and entrepreneurs wear jeans and hoodies. Consumers may not wear status symbols modeled after an aspirational group because they already feel as if they have achieved and are successful.

All of these dynamics are true: consumers seek to belong to some groups, and they seek to stand out as being different from other groups. But it's funny – the effect that others have on us may be greater than is warranted because it's been shown that others don't actually notice us or care about our appearance as much as we think they do. (This helps explain why people are such poor witnesses generally, also, because they're paying less attention to others than they are to themselves.)

These social norm dynamics can bring about unintended negative effects. For example, these same normative pressures are thought to underlie problems with body image. When consumers are trying to look like their friends or aspire to be as attractive as models, it creates a dysmorphia, a negative way of thinking about their bodies as being undesirable. These issues affect men and women, and may manifest in eating disorders or steroid use, for example. Marketers could do the world a favor and get consumers to embrace their diverse individuality: you be you!

World in Balance

Balance theory is another important concept that underlies the subculture effects discussed throughout this chapter.[23] Basically, balance theory looks at connections between a consumer and other consumers and brands to see if the links are consistent. Consider the connections depicted in Figure 12.7a. A consumer likes his or her friend, the friend likes (maybe even recommends) a particular brand, so the consumer is positively inclined toward the brand and perhaps tries it. Multiply the signs on the sides of the triangle: $(+1) \times (+1) \times (+1) = (+1)$. The result is positive, and it indicates that the relationships are in balance.

But suppose the consumer's friend likes a brand that is manufactured by a company known to mistreat its workers (see Figure 12.7b). The consumer is less persuaded by the friend, and the

---

Self-monitoring
the ability to regulate and monitor self-presentations, attitudes, emotions, and behaviors.

Balance theory
looks at connections between a consumer and other consumers and brands to see if the links are consistent.

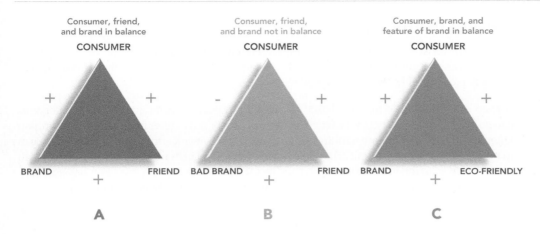

FIGURE 12.7   Balance Theory

consumer–brand link may be negative. The product $(+1) \times (+1) \times (-1)$ is negative; thus, the relationships are out of balance. The psychological state of imbalance is uncomfortable (I like my friend but I can't believe that they support that company), and the consumer is motivated to make some change. Either the consumer will think up some allowances that the brand can't be that bad (to restore a positive consumer–brand link), or there is a falling out with the friend, so that the consumer–friend link also becomes negative. Then the relationships are balanced once again because $(-1) \times (+1) \times (-1) = (+1)$. (Maybe friends don't fall out over brands very often, but think of friends discussing political candidates.)

Marketers use balance theory in various ways. Typically, one point in the triangle is a consumer and another point is the brand in question. But as Figure 12.7c indicates, there can be other entities involved. Instead of the third point being another person, it could be a brand feature, such as whether the detergent that a consumer uses is eco-friendly. If the consumer cares about environmental brands, and the brand is not environmentally damaging, then the triangle would be in balance. If not, the consumer will probably seek another brand. Balance theory can help predict whether a consumer will be loyal to a brand or switch to alternative brands. Many contextual factors help determine a consumer's liking for brands, such as their country of origin and culture.

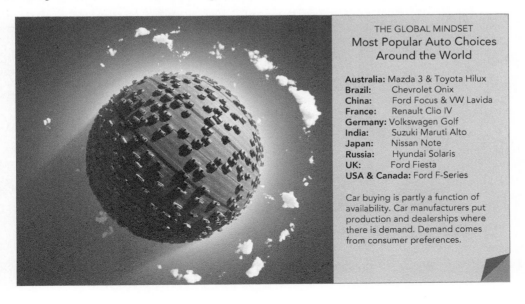

THE GLOBAL MINDSET
Most Popular Auto Choices Around the World

Australia: Mazda 3 & Toyota Hilux
Brazil: Chevrolet Onix
China: Ford Focus & VW Lavida
France: Renault Clio IV
Germany: Volkswagen Golf
India: Suzuki Maruti Alto
Japan: Nissan Note
Russia: Hyundai Solaris
UK: Ford Fiesta
USA & Canada: Ford F-Series

Car buying is partly a function of availability. Car manufacturers put production and dealerships where there is demand. Demand comes from consumer preferences.

Race and Ethnicity

Another characteristic of a consumer that affects reference groups is the subcultures of race and ethnicity.[24] These are important concepts, so let's begin with definitions. Let's draw from the official, widely recognized source of Wikipedia:

Race
a grouping of humans based on shared physical or social qualities into categories generally viewed as distinct by society.

Ethnic group
a grouping of people who identify with each other on the basis of shared attributes that distinguish them from other groups.

Affirmative action
a set of policies and practices within a government or organization seeking to increase the representation of particular groups based on their gender, race, sexuality, creed, or nationality in areas in which they are underrepresented, such as education and employment.

- A **race** is a grouping of humans based on shared physical or social qualities into categories generally viewed as distinct by society. The term was first used to refer to speakers of a common language and then to denote national affiliations. By the seventeenth century, the term began to refer to physical (phenotypical) traits. Modern science regards race as a social construct, an identity that is assigned based on rules made by society. While partially based on physical similarities within groups, race does not have an inherent physical or biological meaning.

- An **ethnic group** or ethnicity is a grouping of people who identify with each other on the basis of shared attributes that distinguish them from other groups, such as a common set of traditions, ancestry, language, history, society, culture, nation, religion, or social treatment within their residing area. Ethnicity is sometimes used interchangeably with the term nation, particularly in cases of ethnic nationalism, and is separate from but related to the concept of races.[25]

- **Affirmative action** applies to both of these distinctions and more: it refers to a set of policies and practices within a government or organization seeking to increase the representation of particular groups based on their gender, race, sexuality, creed, or nationality in areas where they are underrepresented, such as education and employment.

With respect to race and ethnicity, some products and services are targeted to certain groups, and variants on those products and services are targeted to other groups. Sometimes, as with other consumer subcultures, even when a brand is targeted to one group, another group might embrace the brand more enthusiastically. If the brand team is smart, the marketers pursue how to please the new group of consumers. The marketers will go with the flow (of money).

Figure 12.8 shows some race and ethnicity differences. The broad generalizations in these data seem to indicate that Asian Americans and then Hispanic Americans do a better job than others of eating fresh fruits and vegetables. That will pay off in healthier, longer lives, no doubt.

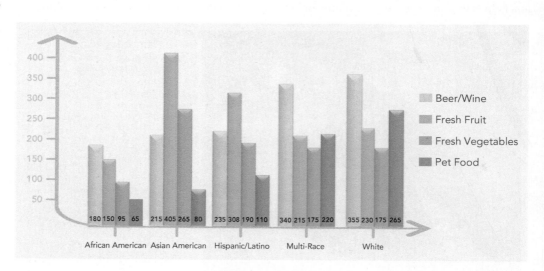

FIGURE 12.8 Annual Spending on Select Food Items by Race and Ethnicity

The chart also indicates that Whites drink more alcohol and spend more on their pets than other groups.

These findings are not stereotypes because they are based on data; however, they are data aggregated to a high group level, which means that not all people in any one of the categories necessarily behave in the way that the chart suggests is indicative of that group. These differences seem rather benign, but sometimes differences can begin to bubble up into potential conflict. For example, when one group brings in or tries to "appropriate" something that is targeted at or popular with another group, the results can feel jarring. It can feel a bit insulting to the first group that the second group is trying to emulate the brand choice.

There are many ways to consider diversity in race and ethnicity. Marketers hoping to design a product for any subculture would be wise to do marketing research even within the group. For example, how do Hispanic American families compare with each other, as well as how do they compare with Chinese American families? In addition, just as we saw that kids first emulate their family in brand choices but later turn to peers, marketers know that families new to a country like the United States first stick to what they know, naturally, but the kids in the family, being thrown into school with others, begin to acculturate and adopt brand preferences of their classmates and friends, bringing those influences back home with them. For any person new to another country, it can be challenging to figure out how to fit in. This can be especially tough on young people who are trying to please Mom and Dad at home but friends at school. They may be bilingual, which marketers refer to as code switching – speaking one language at home and another in school. And brands that the family are loyal to aren't the ones that friends think are cool.

Race and ethnicity are consumer characteristics that marketers care a lot about. First, they're trying to be sensitive, but also they're trying to figure out how to increase sales by offering products that different groups might prefer.

Toyota "Más Que Auto" ("More Than a Car") campaign targeted Hispanic Americans.

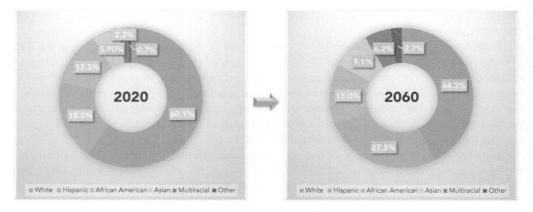

FIGURE 12.9 Racial and Ethnic Profile of US Population in 2020 and 2060. Adapted from Tara Bahrampour and Ted Mellnik 2021

Many countries have multiracial and multiethnic populations. In the United States, Whites are currently about 58% of the population, Hispanics 18.7%, African Americans 12.1% , Asians 6.1%, and people who identify as multiracial or other 2.2% and 0.7%, respectively.[26] As Figure 12.9 depicts, when experts use demographic trajectories to predict changes, the White percentage is expected to shrink, and other groups are expected to grow, particularly the Hispanic population percentage.

Some brands strive to be popular with certain groups (that's targeting), and others just seem to find that various groups consider their brands appealing. For example:

- Jeep is popular among conservatives, Chevrolet with Hispanics, Lexus with Asian Americans, Land Rover with African Americans, Jaguar with liberals, Nissan with grad students, Tesla with rich people.

- BrandZ found that the most valued brands in the United States are Amazon, Apple, and Google.[27] For Latin America, it's Bradesco (financial services), Itaú (also banking), and Corona (beer). For India, it's HDFC Bank, LIC (life insurance), and Tata Consultancy (IT). For China, it's Alibaba (e-commerce), Tencent (entertainment, AI), and Moutai (liquor).

Area of Country

Consumers differ across the globe, as we'll see in detail in Chapter 13, but there are also consumer differences within regions of countries. For example, the map below shows the results of a marketing study in *Food & Wine* magazine regarding which beers would be on various restaurant menus, depending on the region of the country.

There are many ways to divide regions within countries. Sometimes marketers focus on geographic territories (as in the figure). Do consumers in the South appreciate different brands compared to consumers in the North? Manufacturers of salsa know that consumers in the Southwest, for example, like hot, spicy foods, but such salsas are too spicy for consumers in the Northeast.

A different way of classifying consumers according to regional differences is simply whether the consumer lives in an urban or rural setting. Obviously, housing and transportation differences abound, and these in turn affect other choices. A small apartment downtown typically cannot accommodate a great deal of furniture, nor larger families or a menagerie of pets.

There are all kinds of subcultures. Marketers think about these subcultures – age, household life cycle, gender, race and ethnicity, socioeconomic status, and where one lives – when considering segments of consumers. Yet other subcultures also exist. For example, think of a corporate

Food & Wine magazine surveyed which beers are being sold in different regions of the country.

culture such as an entrepreneurial firm, even large ones like Google, which may allow informal clothing and offer a flexible work environment and desk spaces, all of which is different from more traditional companies. Even within companies, there are typically differences; for example, the "creatives" (e.g. the marketing/advertising people) will be a subculture that is different from the finance department.

Social Media and Sociocultural Marketing: Brand Fans!

- Are you a nut for LEGOs? There's an app for that! At ideas.lego.com, consumers can submit product ideas and enter contests to show off their awesome creations!→Check out Kermit made of LEGOs!

- Are you a Harley aficionado? Their online brand community is famous – owners and riders post photos of themselves ("Here's me and my ride!"), groups they ride in, place they've been!

- At Sephora.com/community, consumers can talk to other brand fans, ask for and provide advice, post pix of themselves and their friends, watch tutorials.

SUMMARY

Consumers buy products and services for all kinds of reason. They might need or desire something, but then the brand choice is a decision that lets them send a signal to others (social) or to themselves about who they are and what they value.

Reference groups are a useful way to think about how consumers are similar to each other and yet different, group to group. The consumers who share elements of their identity, such as age, gender, race or ethnicity, are not all the same, and they will not all buy the same things. But there is sometimes a great deal of similarity that helps marketers target some consumers with certain products that they know are popular with other consumers who are similar.

People also have personal motivations, such as to conform to their reference group(s) or to express individuality and stand out from their group(s). Balance theory helps explain the dynamics underlying group differences along the numerous dimensions of subcultures discussed in this chapter. Consumers want to belong to certain groups and, at the same time, signal that they are not a member of other groups. These reference groups are usually a function of age, household cycle, gender, race and ethnicity, socioeconomic status, and where the consumer lives.

KEY TERMS

Reference group
Membership groups
Primary membership groups
Secondary membership groups

Formal groups
Informal groups
Dissociative groups
Aspirational groups

Social class
Socioeconomic status
Subculture
Desire for conformity
Brand community

Opinion leaders
Desire for uniqueness
Self-monitoring
Balance theory
Race

Ethnic group
Affirmative action

EXERCISES

1. Select a brand from Figure 12.3 that appeals to men (or women) and discuss how a brand extension might be launched that could cross over and appeal more to women (or men).

2. It is very likely that on your next job, you'll be on a brand team that is targeted to some group of consumers who are unlike you – they might be much older, have less education or wealth, or be of a different ethnicity. Discuss what you can do to relate to consumers so that you'll have good instincts when you're developing products and advertising to reach them.

3. Create a list of five things that you buy (e.g. grocery item, school supply, clothing, laptop, phone). For each, discuss who you'd go to for advice: Who would be your opinion leaders, and where would you seek out word-of-mouth advice? Who serves as your membership reference group, your aspiration reference group,

and who would you never go to for such advice (your dissociative reference group)?

4. List three social media influences that you follow in different product categories. What makes them influences? What is their main value proposition? What benefits do you get by following them? Compare your answers with those of your classmates. What are the communalities and differences between your observations?

5. In pairs or small groups, pick a product and a brand and think about the best way to target different generational cohorts. What are your recommendations? Why?

6. In pairs or small groups, pick a product and a brand and think about the best way to promote it using a female appeal, a male appeal, and a neutral appeal. Which appeal works best for this product or brand? Why?

ENDNOTES

1. R. K. Merton and A. S. Rossi, "Contributions to the Theory of Reference Group Behavior," in *Social Theory and Social Structure*. Ed. R. K. Merton (New York: Free Press, 1968), 279–334.

2. K. White and D. Dahl, "Are All Out-Groups Created Equal? Consumer Identity and Dissociative Influence," *Journal of Consumer Research* 34, no. 4 (2007): 525–36.

3. K. White and D. W. Dahl, "To Be or Not to Be? The Influence of Dissociative Reference Groups on Consumer Preferences," *Journal of Consumer Psychology* 16, no. 4 (2006): 404–14.

4. D. J. Brosdahl and J. M. Carpenter, "Shopping Orientations of US Males: A Generational Cohort Comparison," *Journal of Retailing and Consumer Services* 18, no. 6 (2011): 548–54.

5. E. Koc, "The Impact of Gender in Marketing Communications: The Role of Cognitive and Affective Cues," *Journal of Marketing Communications* 8, no. 4 (2002): 257–75.

6. https://www.bbc.com/news/uk-england-tees-46418045#:~:text= LGBTQQIP2SAA%20stands%20for%20lesbian%2C%20gay,Local% 20Democracy%20Reporting%20Service%20said.

7. J. McKay-Nesbitt, N. Bhatnagar, and M. C. Smith, "Regulatory Fit Effects of Gender and Marketing Message Content," *Journal of Business Research* 66, no. 11 (2013): 2245–51.

8. https://www.forbes.com/sites/forbescontentmarketing/2019/ 05/13/20-facts-and-figures-to-know-when-marketing-to-women.

9. https://www.catalyst.org/research/buying-power.

10. P. Vyncke, "Lifestyle Segmentation from Attitudes, Interests and Opinions, to Values, Aesthetic Styles, Life Visions and Media Preferences," *European Journal of Communication* 17, no. 4 (2002): 445–63.

11. R. E. Wilkes, "Household Life-Cycle Stages, Transitions, and Product Expenditures," *Journal of Consumer Research* 22, no. 1 (1995): 27–42.

12. D. R. John, "Consumer Socialization of Children: A Retrospective Look at Twenty-five Years of Research," *Journal of Consumer Research* 26, no. 3 (1999): 183–213.

13. R. P. Coleman, "The Continuing Significance of Social Class to Marketing," *Journal of Consumer Research* 10, no. 3 (1983): 265–80; S. Dawson and M. Wallendorf, "Associational Involvement: An Intervening Concept Between Social Class and Patronage Behavior," in *Advances in Consumer Research,* vol. 12. Eds. E. C. Hirschman and M. B. Holbrook (Provo, UT: Association for Consumer Research, 1985), 586–91.

14. M. E. Slama and A. Tashchian, "Selected Socioeconomic and Demographic Characteristics Associated with Purchasing Involvement," *Journal of Marketing* 49, no. 1 (1985): 72–82.

15. A. O'Cass and H. McEwen, "Exploring Consumer Status and Conspicuous Consumption," *Journal of Consumer Behaviour: An International Research Review* 4, no. 1 (2004): 25–39.

16. J. W. Schouten and J. H. McAlexander, "Subcultures of Consumption: An Ethnography of the New Bikers," *Journal of Consumer Research* 22, no. 1 (1995): 43–61.

17. D. N. Lascu and G. Zinkhan, "Consumer Conformity: Review and Applications for Marketing Theory and Practice," *Journal of Marketing Theory and Practice* 7, no. 3 (2015): 1–12.

18. A. M. Muniz and T. C. O'Guinn, "Brand Community," *Journal of Consumer Research* 27, no. 4 (2001): 412–32.

19. L. R. Flynn, R. E. Goldsmith, and J. K. Eastman "Opinion Leaders and Opinion Seekers: Two New Measurement Scales," *Journal of the Academy of Marketing Science* 24 no. 2 (1996): 137–47.

20. Ibid.

21. R. E. Goldsmith, R. A. Clark, and E. B. Goldsmith, "The Desire for Unique Consumer Products, Innovativeness, and Conformity," in *Proceedings of the 2007 Academy of Marketing Science (AMS) Annual Conference.* Eds. D. Sharma and S. Borna (Cham, Germany: Springer International, 2007), 206–10.

22. S. W. Gangestad and M. Snyder, "Self-Monitoring: Appraisal and Reappraisal," *Psychological Bulletin* 126, no. 4 (2000): 530.

23. F. Heider, *The Psychology of Interpersonal Relations* (New York: John Wiley & Sons, 1958).

24. D. Burton, "Ethnicity, Identity and Marketing: A Critical Review," *Journal of Marketing Management* 16, no. 8 (2010): 853–77.

25. J. Holland and J. W. Gentry, "Ethnic Consumer Reaction to Targeted Marketing: A Theory of Intercultural Accommodation," *Journal of Advertising* 28, no. 1 (1999): 65–77.

26. https://www.census.gov/quickfacts/fact/table/US/PST045219.

27. https://www.reuters.com/technology/amazon-apple-most-valuable-brands-chinas-rising-kantar-survey-2021-06-21.

CREDITS

https://www.forbes.com/advisor/credit-cards/reviews/centurion-from-american-express

https://www.shutterstock.com/image-photo/smart-phone-tik-tok-logo-which-1622314633

https://www.shutterstock.com/image-vector/cute-owl-cartoon-holding-blank-sign-162983006

https://www.facebook.com/absolut.unique.vodka

https://www.autoinsurancecenter.com/the-average-fan-of-car-brands.htm

https://www.shutterstock.com/image-illustration/planet-car-100677619

https://www.effie.org/case_database/case/NA_2016_441056 "lego creations" https://www.google.com/search?as_st=y&tbm=isch& hl=en&as_q=lego+creations&as_epq=&as_oq=&as_eq=& cr=&as_sitesearch=&safe=images&tbs=sur:fmc#imgrc=tTybO XhMDn9ZNM

Figure 12.6: Mike B/Pexels; Shadman Samee/Flickr; Mikes-Photography/Pixabay; Peulle/Wikimedia Commons/ CC BY-SA 4.0; General Motors Company; Mercedes-Benz AG; FCA US LLC

Image p. 225: American Express Company

Image p. 234: Teguh Mujiono/Shutterstock

Image p. 235: Absolut Unique Vodka

Image p. 237: Photobank.kiev.ua/Shutterstock

Image p. 239: Toyota Motor Corporation

Image p. 241: Andrey Belenko/Flickr

DIVERSE PERSPECTIVES THAT COMPRISE US ALL

PART IV

13 The Global Consumer

LEARNING OBJECTIVES

After studying this chapter, you should be able to:

- See how consumers around the world are becoming more and more attractive to companies that want to grow.

- Understand the considerations and challenges involved in global expansion to encourage consumer reception in new markets.

- Appreciate that successful expansion into the global market requires marketers to overcome gaps in how consumers behave in the home country versus the new country.

- Understand what is needed to create a successful global brand – how can marketers get consumers everywhere to like their brand?

When Avon, one of the largest manufacturers of cosmetics, considered entering Japan, it sounded like a good idea. Japanese women were well known for their beauty culture.[1] Using its door-to-door selling strategy, Avon attempted to move into the Japanese market. However, for the first four years, it failed to make a profit. Why? There were several factors that led to Avon's failure in Japan. First, Avon found it difficult to recruit saleswomen, because Japanese women did not feel comfortable selling products to people they are not familiar with – they were leery of strangers because they were concerned that either they or the stranger would be embarrassed. Furthermore, in Japan, the home is considered a safe haven, a private sanctuary, so to welcome a stranger such as an Avon saleswoman into the home would be very unusual. Avon's story highlights the importance of understanding consumers. It is critical when operating domestically, and it's even more critical when targeting consumers in another culture.

Avon's solution was simple. Each of their representatives was assigned to their neighborhoods, where they already knew their potential customers.

Going Global?

Our world is become increasingly small. Put your finger just about anywhere on a map of the world, and consumers can buy products from that place. Technology, instant communication, transportation, and accessible information all create new marketing opportunities and challenges for brands. All organizations, domestic or global, are experiencing the pressures of **globalization**,

Globalization
the proliferation of products, technology, information, and business opportunities across national borders and cultures.

246

with its proliferation of products, technology, information, and business opportunities across national borders and cultures.[2] For many companies, going global is very tempting. As their own markets become increasingly competitive, going global seems like the best option for growth. But is it? The "world" is bigger than one's own country, but consumers "out there" are different. Who is to say those consumers will like the brand as much as consumers in the home country?

Global marketing refers to a company's commitment of resources to strategically develop and deliver sustainable value across multiple foreign markets by addressing consumers' needs, wants, and demands to generate revenue and gain a competitive advantage.[3] Figure 13.1 presents the decision process of companies when they consider expanding to global markets.

The first decision a company must make is whether or not it *should* go global. This is not a trivial decision. There are multiple reasons why firms go global. They are motivated by either proactive or reactive goals. Proactive goals are goals that are initiated within the company, such as taking advantage of economies of scale or having a global vision. Reactive goals are goals that are triggered by external forces, such as competitive pressures or avoiding the loss of opportunities in growing markets.

An organization's goal in going global will determine its **global marketing strategy** – the adaptation of the marketing strategy to foreign markets.[4] This strategy will include the STP (segmentation, targeting, and positioning) process of a foreign market, the mode of entry, and the level of adaptation of the marketing mix.

Just as consumers are key to any company's success, they are also key to its success in global markets. And as we learned from Avon's story, no company should go global before it can be certain that it can provide true value to its target market. The value a brand or company offers to consumers in its home country can be (and is in many cases) very different in a different country. That is not necessarily a bad thing:

- Jeep, which is not considered a prestigious brand for a car in the United States, is considered a prestigious brand in other markets, such as India and Israel.[5]

- Pizza Hut is an upscale fine dining restaurant in China. It's a restaurant that you take your boss to if you want to impress him or her. And you better call and make reservations to ensure that you will be seated.[6]

Global marketing
the company's commitment of resources to strategically develop and deliver sustainable value across multiple foreign markets by addressing consumers' needs, wants and demands to generate revenue and gain a competitive advantage.

Global marketing strategy
the adaptation of the marketing strategy to foreign markets.

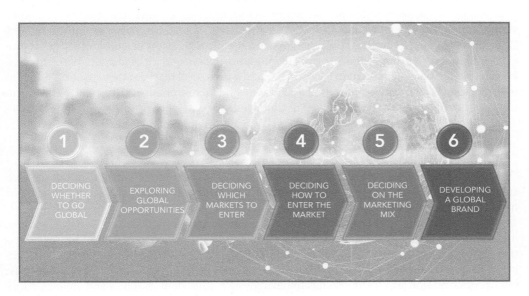

FIGURE 13.1 Strategic Decisions in Global Marketing

The most well-known brands in the world.

Global segmentation
the process of identifying specific segments of consumers – on a country, regional, or consumer – that will have similar needs or attributes and will response similarly to the same marketing mix.

Pluralization of consumption
the pursuit of similar segments with the same needs across multiple national markets.

Demographic segmentation (global)
dividing the market based on the demographic characteristics of the consumers in different countries.

Exploring Global Options

If it looks as if consumers in other countries might like the brand, a company makes a decision to go global. the next step is to explore the options as to how to do so and where.[7] The brand team should begin by considering segmentation, targeting, and positioning (recall Chapter 2). We know that segmentation helps to identify the markets that offer the greatest potential. **Global segmentation** is the process of identifying specific segments of consumers – on a country, regional, or consumer level – that will have similar needs or attributes and will respond similarly to the same marketing mix.[8]

It is possible that consumers in different countries may have the same needs or attributes and thus belong to the same segment that ranges across multiple national markets. For example, young students need reliable laptops, whether they are in the United States or Taiwan or New Zealand. Theodore Levitt called this phenomenon the **pluralization of consumption**.[9] It provides brands with the opportunity to pursue multiple segments on a global scale. While marketers can use the same segmentation bases that describe their local markets, they require a different interpretation because they can be used on a macro level (across countries), not just on the micro level (within countries), as we discussed in Chapter 2.

Demographic Segmentation

On a macro level, demographic segmentation is based on measurable characteristics of the consumers in the countries being considered for brand expansion: income, population size, age distribution, gender, education, and occupation.

National income – The World Bank has segmented global markets into low, low-middle, middle-high, and high-income countries based on gross national income (GNI). This segmentation basis is very valuable to marketers as it determines the purchasing power of the target market. This is particularly important for big ticket and relatively expensive products such as cars, electronics, and fine jewelry. It also has implications for other demographics and characteristics of these segments, which provide marketers with additional information.

	Low-Income Countries	Lower–Middle-Income Countries	Upper–Middle-Income Countries	Upper-Income Countries
GNI per capita*	<$1,025	$1,026-$3,995	$3,996-$12,375	>$12,375
GDP (in trillions)	$0.6 (0.7%)	$6.7 (7.8%)	$24.4 (28.4%)	$54.1 (63.1%)
Population size (thousands)	668,454.96	2,913,363.3	2,855,862.79	1,235,852.83
Population growth	2.6%	1.4%	0.7%	0.5%
Median age	18.4	25.4	33.7	39.9
Birth rates (per 1K people)	35	20	14	10
Literacy (adults over 15)	63%	77%	95%	--
Industrialization	Limited (farming)	Labor-intensive industries	Rapidly industrializing	High
Other	Political instability	Cheap labor	Growing middle class, rising wages	High cost of labor

* * Gross national income, World Bank Data

FIGURE 13.2   Income-based World Segmentation

Figure 13.2 shows that low-income countries have high birth rates, rapid population growth, high levels of illiteracy, and often experience political instability. Upper-income countries have low birth rates, slow population growth, high levels of literacy, and a high level of industrialization, but also high labor costs. The organization's goal for going global should direct the choice of segment or segments to target. For example, a company might choose a low-middle-income country for production but an upper-income country for selling its end product.

Population size versus economic growth – Two other popular global bases of segmentation are the country's population size and its level of economic growth, because they represent the best promise for market expansion. Figure 13.3 shows estimates that large emerging economies, such as the BRICS (Brazil, Russia, India, China, and South Africa) will experience the most growth in the next 20 years.[10]

1	China	58,499
2	India	44,128
3	US	34,102
4	Indonesia	10,502
5	Brazil	7,5369
6	Russia	7,131
7	Mexico	6,863
8	Japan	6,779
9	Germany	6,138
10	UK	5,369

*Projected ranking of economies based on gross domestic product purchasing power parity ($ billion)

FIGURE 13.3   Dominate Economies in 2050*. Adapted from pwc 2022.

For low-cost items such as soft drinks and candy, population is often a more valuable segmentation variable than income because sales are based on volume. However, these data should be evaluated cautiously, because the largest market – low-income and low-middle-income countries – account for about 46.7% of the world's population, but only for 8.5% of the world's gross domestic product (GDP).[11] In other words, the biggest markets are not always the most profitable.

For a country to be considered a big emerging market (BEM), it needs to meet the following criteria:

1. Have strong rates of growth or the potential for growth

2. Be physically large

3. Have significant populations

4. Have considerable markets for a wide range of products

5. Have undertaken economic reform

6. Be of major political importance in its region

7. Be a regional economic driver

8. Support growth in neighboring markets

PESTEL model
a strategic framework used to gain a macro picture of an industry environment.

Marketers today who are searching the globe for business opportunities have ample sources of statistics about potential markets they are considering. The **PESTEL model** is a very useful tool for gathering insights into such markets.[12] However, remember that on their own, raw statistics are nearly meaningless. Marketers need to understand the strategic implications of these statistics and the extent to which they would need to adjust their marketing strategies in order to operate successful in global markets. For example, because India's big consumers are younger than those in Japan, Japanese manufacturers may not have great luck introducing their high-end luxury cars in India. In addition, in the same way that marketers must monitor changes in local markets, they need to do so in global markets. Such changes can create opportunities for companies, but they can also create threats.

It's important to remember that consumers are not totally homogeneous. There are typically micro-level segments within a country, based on where the consumers live, their income, and other factors.

THE PESTEL MODEL

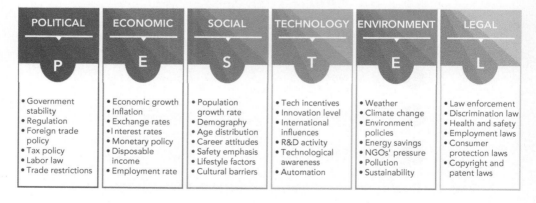

Selecting a Global Market to Enter

After scanning the global market and identifying potential opportunities, the next decision is about which of these opportunities should be the target.[13] Companies consider a variety of factors. We unpack these factors in the discussion that follows. These factors should address the questions presented in Figure 13.4. The figure makes clear that just as when marketing their brands in their own country, firms need to consider both internal and external factors when deciding which specific foreign market to target.

Internal Factors

Whether a brand will succeed with consumers in a new market depends on the company and those new consumers. The company factors are the "internal factors" for marketers:

1. The company's assessment of the consumers' needs, wants, and demands. When going global, one thought exercise is to consider the extent to which the consumers in the new country differ from the consumers the company already serves.

2. The company's ability to provide them with real sustainable value. Here, too, the brand team cannot simply assume that something their consumers value will translate to consumers in another culture.

3. The company's ability to derive revenue and gain a competitive advantage in this market.

Figure 13.5 provides a checklist of questions for a **global marketing targeting** that are internal to the company that it can apply to any new country it is considering entering. For example, say a software company has a great portfolio of apps that it wants to make available beyond England. Two large markets, of course, are India and China. India has the benefit of English fluency (so the English app brand managers don't have to worry about translation) but has the downside in that there are plenty of IT-savvy engineers in India who don't really need to import apps when they can create their own, and probably do so better, given that they can adapt local versions. Thus, in terms of value, a launch might be faster and more successful in India, but it might not be a sustainable competitive advantage as local competition would develop rapidly.

Global marketing targeting
choosing which markets to enter across the globe.

OFFERING FAMILIARITY
Is the company targeting a market where consumers are familiar with its product(s)?

BRAND RECOGNITION
Is the company targeting a market where consumers have some level of recognition of the brand?

DIFFERENTIATED VALUE
Is the company targeting a market where it can offer differentiated value that addresses the consumers' needs?

FOCUSED RESOURCES
Is the company targeting a market where its invested resources will generate the highest return?

FOCUSED SEGMENTS
Is the company focusing on segments where it can be effective with its marketing tactics?

COMPETITIVE ADVANTAGE
Is the company targeting a market where it can establish a strong and lasting competitive advantage?

FIGURE 13.4 Guidance Questions for Choosing a Global Market

INTERNAL DECISION FACTORS

CONSUMERS' NEEDS → VAUE → PROFIT →

- Do I have consumers (now, in the future)?
- What are their needs?
- Do they know my brand, product, country?
- Can I understand them?
- Do they use similar products?
- Does my product fit this market?

- Is my value sustainable?
- Does it give me a competitive advantage?
- Can I stay true to my value?
- Is it desirable?
- Is it deliverable?

- Is the benefit greater than the cost?
- Do I have enough resources to enter this market?
- Do I have ways to minimize costs?
- Do I have the experience needed?

FIGURE 13.5   The Global Targeting Process

External Factors

Even very capable brand teams must also face the "external factors" about the new country's consumers. These factors reflect the "global gap" between the brand's home country and the foreign target market, as presented in Figure 13.6. The main external factors that matter include the cultural, economic, political, and demographic "distance" (i.e. cultural differences) between the two markets – home and new target. The gap between the brand's home market and its foreign target market will determine not only the potential of the target market but also the risks that are involved.

Cultural Distance

Culture
a set of values, belief, and traditions that are held by a specific social group and handed down from generation to generation.

Culture is a set of values, beliefs, and traditions that are held by a specific social group and handed down from generation to generation. Culture is a major factor in how consumers are similar and different. It has a visible and invisible side to it. A country's culture is a key environmental

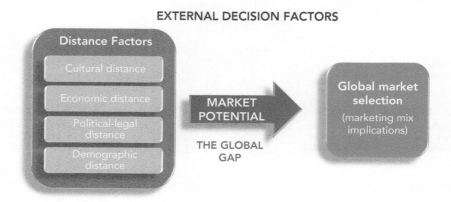

FIGURE 13.6   The Global Targeting Process

characteristic that underlies any behavior, including consumers' behavior. Preferences, perceptions, values, lifestyle, and beliefs are all affected by one's culture.[14]

Cultural distance is the gap or the extent of differences in values and communication styles between cultures. Cultural distance is the number one cause of business failures abroad. When you cross the cultural borders, your understanding of the market is inherently distorted by your own preferences, perceptions, values, lifestyle, and beliefs.[15]

A good example of a product failure due to a cultural bias is the attempt that Pampers made to enter Japan. The company's packaging had a picture of a stork delivering a baby. In Western cultures, the stork is associated with a common folk tale about where babies come from. However, in Japan, it is a giant peach that floats on the river that delivers the baby. Needless to say, Japanese parents did not understand the symbol of the stork, which drastically affected the sale of the product. After pulling the product off the market and repackaging it, Pampers was able to enter the Japanese market successfully.

A very common and powerful tool to diagnose cultural distance is **Hofstede's six cultural dimensions** (see Figure 13.7). Here are the definitions (we will see examples in a moment)[16]:

- **Power distance** reflects the extent to which people accept the notion that some people are more in power (e.g. bosses) compared with being egalitarian (e.g. teams at work).

- **Uncertainty avoidance** is high in cultures where people like to know precisely what is going on, and they are uncomfortable with a lot of ambiguity.

- In **individualistic** cultures, people are a bit more out for themselves, whereas in **collectivistic** cultures, people are more supportive of one another in their groups (family, colleagues, etc.).

- **Long- versus short-term orientation** is about people who think down the road (e.g. worrying about the environment for their grandchildren, when they don't even have kids yet) versus people who think about more immediate costs or benefits (e.g. yes but I want to drive a Hummer).

- **Masculinity versus femininity** is about gender roles and whether the culture prizes achievement (a masculine stereotype) or modesty, cooperation, and quality of life (a feminine stereotype).

- Finally, **indulgence versus restraint** describes cultures that tend to let people do their own thing or there are more controls and norms around proper and expected behavior.

Cultural distance
the gap or the extent of differences in values and communication styles between cultures.

Hofstede's six cultural dimensions
can be used to characterize the cultural nature of countries.

Power distance
belief about power distribution in society.

Uncertainty avoidance
level of tolerance of ambiguity.

Individualism versus collectivism
independent versus interdependent relationships between members of society.

Long- versus short-term orientation
the importance of long-term (vs. short-term) planning for the future.

Masculinity versus femininity
the division of roles between men and women.

Indulgence versus restraint
degree of desired gratification.

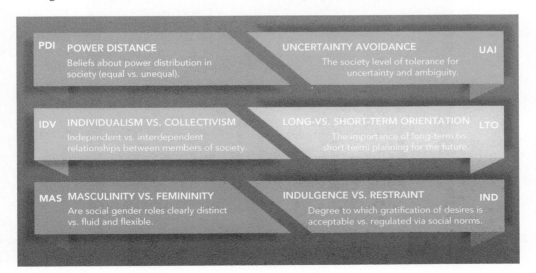

FIGURE 13.7 Hofstede's Cultural Dimensions

Dr. Geert Hofstede was a psychologist hired by IBA in the late 1960s to study the attitudes of their workers about the globe, hoping that his insights would help the company improve its productivity. Hofstede's conceptualization of cultural values is considered the standard for understanding cultural differences and the most seminal work in this area. Academic and marketing industry leaders rely on his cross-cultural dimensions.

Hofstede's theoretical framework has been used extensively so there is a great deal of information that is widely available about different aspects of global business, cultural values, and communication (Google "Hofstede Insights"). The availability of this information makes it one of this tool's greatest advantages. Figure 13.8 presents a comparison of the United States, Brazil, Germany, and China across Hofstede's dimensions.[17] You can clearly see that the United States scores the highest on individuality and indulgence and the lowest on power distance. France has the higher tolerance to ambiguity. China scored the highest on power distance, long-term orientation and the lowest on individualism.

Using those culture comparisons, a brand team is better informed. For example, if the brand is a prepared meal, imagery involving family and sharing would be important in communal (not individualistic) cultures like China or Brazil (or Mexico). If the product is insurance, marketing communications might highlight life's risks for cultures that like to avoid uncertainty such as France or Brazil but instead highlight a different aspect such as responsible decision-making for cultures like China or the United States.

China is obviously an important market given its size, and we see in Figure 13.8 that is similar to the United States in terms of masculinity (i.e. achievement-orientation) but different on just about everything else. That implies that a US brand team will have inadequate intuitions about how to enter the Chinese market with their US brand. That doesn't mean that failure is certain. It does mean that the smart brand team will do some marketing research on the Chinese consumers!

India is another extremely important market. It is similar to China on power distance, masculinity, uncertainty avoidance, and indulgence. It is more individualistic than China (though less than the United States) and has less of a long-term orientation (rates more like France in Figure 13.8).

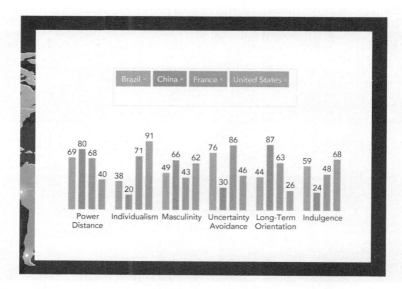

FIGURE 13.8 Country Comparison Across Hofstede's Cultural Dimensions

As if all of that isn't complicated enough, it's also important to realize that there are subcultures within countries. So once again, some preliminary marketing research on anticipated local consumer responses to the brand would be very beneficial.

Hofstede's theory highlights how influential cultural values are, not just on people's everyday behaviors, but also on their consumer behavior. As such, marketers must take cultural values into consideration when constructing their marketing mix strategies, especially with regard to their products and promotions. The greater the distance between the company's home country and its foreign target market, that is, the more different a new market is from one's home market, the greater the adaptation of the marketing mix that will be needed.

Economic Distance

Another important factor is about economics – money matters to almost all consumers everywhere! Economic distance refers to the level of similarity of the economic system and economic metrics between the brand's home country and the foreign target market.[18] Low economic distance means that both countries have fairly comparable forms of markets, wealth distribution, income levels, and GDPs. This is the situation between the United States and Canada, for example. Economic distance has a strong impact on the decision to target a specific market.

Marketers must analyze the foreign market's economic structure to evaluate the cost of entering that market. There are four basic global economies. They have a significant effect on a country's products and service needs, income levels, purchasing power, and consumer needs and behaviors.

Subsistence economies are the most basic form of economies. They are nonmonetary economies that rely mostly on the exchange of goods and simple agriculture. There is no industrialization. People in these economies struggle with everyday survival and support themselves at a minimum level (hence, subsistence). Most African countries fall into this category. Many times, marketers will avoid entering these markets because they see them as difficult to enter and not profitable enough. However, in some cases these countries provide the greatest opportunities for market development. In sports, Nike, Adidas, Puma, and Fila have been successful in several African countries.[19]

Raw material exporting economies are those that are rich in minerals and raw materials. However, they lack the production capabilities needed to convert these resources into end products. So, they rely heavily on exporting raw materials and importing finished goods. Ghana, for example, is the largest exporter of cocoa, and Indonesia is the largest exporter of nickel. These markets are very attractive to companies that sell large equipment, tools, supplies, and trucks.

Industrializing economies are countries that are experiencing rapid growth via industrialization. They have a well-educated labor force. These economies are witnessing rapid industrialization, urban growth, and wage increases. They are starting to develop a middle class and a demand for services, not just products. They are often attractive when seeking to reduce production costs. The growing buying power of the consumers in these economies also make them attractive to companies selling more sophisticated products such as electronics, products that are not considered necessities, and luxury products. Newly industrializing economies include countries such as the BRIC nations (Brazil, Russia, India, China), Venezuela, Hungary, and Mexico.

Industrial economies are the most advanced economies. They have a strong emphasis on the production of sophisticated products and R&D, as well as a large service sector. Their diverse manufacturing activities and their very large middle class make them very attractive to those selling any sort of products or materials. Countries in this category are the main exporters of manufactured finished goods and services. These countries will trade them with less developed

Subsistence economies nonmonetary economies that rely mostly on the exchange of goods and simple agriculture.

Raw material exporting economies that are rich in minerals and raw materials with no production capabilities.

Industrializing economies that are experiencing rapid growth via industrialization. They have a well-educated labor force.

Industrial economies have a strong emphasis on the production of sophisticated products and R&D, as well as a large service sector.

economies in exchange for raw materials and semifinished goods. The United States, Germany, Japan, and Israel are examples of such economies.

Think About It

"Women control 70% of global consumer spending . . . when women do better, economies do better."

Christine Lagarde, president of the European Central Bank

Political and Legal Distance

Politics and legality might not be something that consumers think about frequently, but these factors matter to the company because they affect how the brand can get into the hands of consumers in the new countries.[20] Political distance is the difference in the political systems, political stability, governmental laws, level of bureaucracy, and monetary regulations of various countries. This category also includes the international relations between countries, and any treaties, tariffs, trade quotas, restrictions on foreign direct investment, and other regulations they might have. The greater the distance between two countries, the less likelihood that extensive trade relations will develop.

It is very important to note that this element varies across industries and even with regard to specific products. For example, in the pharmaceutical industry there are restrictions about specific ingredients in medications in different countries. A medication might sell in a certain foreign market, but not another medication or not in another country.

Some regulations in the home country might affect the ability of companies to conduct business in foreign markets. For example, in the United States, there are restrictions that pertain to bribery, health, and safety as well as environmental policies that are more restrictive than in other countries. Yet US companies need to adhere to such restrictions even when conducting business in foreign markets. In some cases, countries will establish policies to regulate and minimize cross-border competition. In extreme cases, trading with specific countries will be prohibited (e.g. reflected in current embargoes between the United States and Afghanistan).

To summarize, the decision to target a specific market is a result of internal and external considerations, which will vary from company to company, and from one target market to another. The brand team must identify those elements that are critical to their success in that target market. One factor that is important is the availability of information. Without access to primary and secondary information, a company is basically blind to its target market and will not be able to assess the risks that are involved in entering that market. There is a great deal of information online, from the Global Economic Monitor[21] and the World Bank's databases[22] to Statistica[23] and Mintel.[24]

Deciding How to Enter the Market

Marketers need to think through strategy regarding how to best reach consumers and how to achieve optimal reception.[25] Marketers can't assume that what is currently working in their home country will necessarily work in a new country. Once the company has identified a foreign target market, it needs to decide how to proceed. If the brand team moves too fast (for some cultures) or too big and aggressively (for other cultures), consumers will be turned off, and the brand's international launch is doomed. So, thinking of consumers, marketers must decide on the following:

- Timing of the entry
- Scale of the entry
- Mode of entry

Timing of the Entry

The timing of the entry refers to the organization's strategic preference to be the early or the late mover in the market. Each has its own advantages and disadvantages in terms of reaching consumers and brand positioning.

Early movers enjoy novelty and frequently become the brand most associated with the product category. As a result, down the road, those brands enjoy advantages, such as brand recognition, positive brand image, stronger consumer loyalty, larger market share, market experience, and the opportunity to create high switching costs for consumers and entry barriers for future competitors to secure their market share.

However, they also take on the major and costly risks of being a pioneer, educating customers and suppliers, as well as the cost of making mistakes due to lack of knowledge. For example, Uber, which was the first mover in its category, faced regulatory resistance in many countries. Its services were suspended in Spain, and South Korea and partially banned in Germany, the Netherlands, and Thailand.

When marketers choose a late entry strategy, it normally has an improved product, lower price, or a significantly differentiated product to introduce to the market. Late entries can capitalize on the early movers' experience and the market readiness for the products. However, they risk their ability to build market share and may remain in a follower position.

As a late mover, the brand team must have a very good understanding of the factors that made the early movers a success to avoid mistakes. This was a hard lesson that Domino's Pizza learned in China. Domino's Pizza entered China five years after Pizza Hut started to serve the Chinese market. Domino's attributed Pizza Hut's success to its ability to educate the market about pizza consumption. For China and many other Asian markets, the combination of dough, tomato sauce, and cheese is an unusual one. However, Pizza Hut's success was not because of its product offering. It was because of its dining experience and the fact that it was one of the first Western brands serving China. Because of its upscale image, Chinese consumers go to Pizza Hut on special occasions. Pizza remains a rare consumption option for most Chinese consumers. Domino's lacked this element of an upscale dining experience and had nothing to offer to attract the Chinese consumers. In addition, Domino's 30-minute delivery promise is very hard to guarantee in the traffic-jammed cities of China. This is a very good example of a strategic value that is not sustainable in a specific market.

Do the Right Thing!

Sometimes brand teams are so enthusiastic about their brands that they push the brand into a new country. They think they're doing that country a favor – now those consumers can share and have this wonderful brand! Critics think that is arrogant imperialism. Do you think it's wrong? It might be naive, but is it ethically improper? The weird thing is that the brand team doesn't have to do much to ensure greater success – they can do a little bit of consumer research into values and preferences in the new country and culture and see if their brand will be successful, or must be modified, or does not stand a chance no matter what. And whether the push is naive or unethical, the recipient consumers in the new country have a voice and a monetary vote. Thus, the brand team that does not consider the new consumers has only itself to blame if sales are less than expected.

Scale of the Entry

This factor refers to the decision of the firm to enter the market on a large scale or a smaller scale. Large-scale entry involves high risks for high returns.

Big organizations often favor large-scale entry because of its advantage in securing market share and brand recognition. It's almost difficult for a big company to do something on a small scale. However, it is a very risky strategy, with long-term implications, it's very hard to reverse, and it can limit the strategic flexibility of the company. It also might trigger a reaction from local competitors.

For example, Walmart attempted to enter Germany on a large scale with 85 stores. It seemed like the perfect match, given the supposed frugal nature of the German consumer. However, cultural differences made it hard for the German consumer to embrace the giant retailer. Specifically, Walmart's smiling and greeting policy made its consumers uncomfortable because German people don't usually smile at total strangers. A similar problem occurred with its bagging policy, something that the German consumer was not used to. Finally, the strong emphasis on "green consumption" and environmental concerns in Germany did not resonate well with the perception about Walmart's brand and operations.[26]

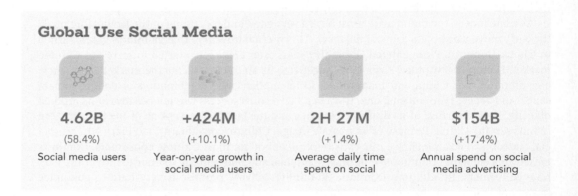

Global Use Social Media

4.62B	+424M	2H 27M	$154B
(58.4%)	(+10.1%)	(+1.4%)	(+17.4%)
Social media users	Year-on-year growth in social media users	Average daily time spent on social	Annual spend on social media advertising

Companies often use small-scale entry because it involves minimal risk, limited exposure and allows time to learn about the market. However, it makes it difficult to build market share and capture a first-mover advantage.

Mode of the Entry

The final factor in the decision about how to enter the market relates to the mode of entry. Exporting, licensing, franchising, joint ventures, and direct investments are all mode of entry options. Much of the decision depends on the company's willingness and ability to commit resources to enter the target market, as well as its level of risk tolerance, need for control, and desire for profit. As you can see from Figure 13.9, these elements vary across entry mode options, and each has its advantages and disadvantages. Choosing one mode of entry over the other often implies trading a commitment of resources and level of risk for a level of control and profit potential.[27]

ENTRY MODE	ADVANTAGES	DISADVANTAGES
EXPORTING	Commitment of minimal resources Little risk	Lack of control Lack of contact with foreign market Little profit potential
LICENSING	Little or no investment Rapid way to gain entry Means to overcome import barriers Little risk	Lack of control Risk of creating competitor Need for quality control Limits market development
FRANCHISING	Little or no investment Rapid way to gain entry Little risk	Lack of control Risk of creating competitor Need for quality control
JOINT VENTURES	Risk sharing Less demanding on resources Potential synergies	Risk of conflict with partner Risk of creating competitor Lack of control
DIRECT INVESTMENT	Full control Access to local assets Less competition	Costly High risk Cultural clashes

FIGURE 13.9   Advantages and Disadvantages of Modes of Entry

A frequent choice for a means of "going global" is to export goods made at home. In doing so, the company enjoys a low level of commitment and risk. But the level of control and profit potential are also lower. Experts say to choose to export if

- The volume of foreign business is not large enough to justify production there.
- The cost of production in a foreign market is high.
- The country has extensive political instability, a poor infrastructure, and a large global gap.

Another choice is to do a direct investment. That requires a major commitment of resources and is relatively high risk, but it will provide the company with full control and much greater potential for profit. This option is best selected if there are

- Extensive import barriers
- A small cultural gap
- Strong sales potential
- Little political risk

So which entry mode should a company choose? It should take into consideration internal and external factors when making this decision for each market it targets. In many cases, firms use multiple modes of entry in different foreign markets.

A good example of this choice is Starbucks. Starbucks is the largest coffeehouse company in the world today. It has over 33,000 stores in 83 countries worldwide. Half of Starbucks stores are in international markets. Starbucks focuses on the main markets in the Americas (Canada, Latin America, and the United States), China and the Asia Pacific (CAP), and the Middle East and Africa (EMEA). Starbucks' operations include either company-operated stores or licensed stores.[28]

Adapted from Starbucks Corporation 2022

Deciding on the Marketing Mix: How Do We Market and Communicate with These New Consumers?

After selecting the foreign market to target, the next step would be to design its marketing mix.[29] The goal here is to provide sustainable value that addresses consumers' needs in this market, and thus generates revenue and secures the brand's and company's competitive advantage.

Marketing mix gap how different is the marketing mix in the new country versus the home country of the company.

The global gap between the company's home country and the new foreign market it targets will affect the marketing mix (see Figure 13.10). Specifically, in the same manner that the marketing mix must be adjusted to address its consumers' needs domestically, the brand team will need to do so in the foreign market as well. The question is, to what extent should the marketing mix in the foreign market be different from the home market? This is the company's **marketing mix gap**.

FIGURE 13.10 Deciding on the Marketing Mix

In the past, most companies considered one of two strategic options for their marketing mix.[30] The first was the **standardization** of the marketing mix, which means implementing the same marketing mix the same way across foreign markets. The second option was the **adaptation** of the marketing mix, which means changing some or all parts of the marketing mix to better address local needs. Today organizations implement some variation of both strategies, in some or all parts of the marketing mix. This strategy is known as **glocalization**, meaning taking into consideration local culture and needs and integrating them into the brand's global strategy.

Both standardization and adaptation strategies have their benefits. A standardization strategy enables companies to save on costs when entering the market because of economies of scale, uniform products, and a shorter learning curve. An adaptation strategy, on the other hand, enables companies to address their consumers' needs more effectively and to create a more meaningful positioning for their brand. The less adaptation needed, the smaller the marketing mix gap is and the more attractive the market is.

The level of standardization or adaptation needed is determined by the company's value, its capabilities, and the global gap. Coca-Cola, for example, had a very clear standardization strategy for many years. In recent years, however, it has shifted more toward a glocalization strategy, taking into consideration local needs as part of its global brand value.[31] In particular, Coca-Cola has adapted the promotional element of the marketing mix.

Standardization implementing the same marketing mix the same way across foreign markets.

Adaptation changing some or all parts of the marketing mix to better address local needs.

Glocalization taking into consideration local culture and needs, and integrating them into the brand's global strategy.

Coca-Cola adopts the promotional element of the marketing mix in different markets.

How should we adapt the marketing mix? When it comes to products and promotions, marketers can adopt one of the following five strategies:

1. *Dual extension strategy:* Using the same product and the same message across foreign markets. Essentially, this is standardization. This strategy is very common in bustiness-to-business (B2B) or industrial products.

2. *Product adaptation strategy:* Changing some elements in the product but keeping the message similar across foreign markets. Car manufacturers often change the ventilation systems in cars sold in the Middle East because of high levels of dust in the air.

3. *Communication adaptation strategy:* Making changes in the message while keeping the product the same across foreign markets. This strategy reduces the costs of entry. Much of the spending goes toward advertising, promotions, and point-of sale materials.

4. *Dual adaptation strategy:* Making changes in both the product and the message in order to better target local markets. This strategy makes sense when there is a significant global gap.

5. *Product invention strategy:* Creating new offerings for different foreign markets. This is the most costly and risky strategy of all. It is especially effective when targeting mass markets in less industrialized countries.

In reality, most companies often implement more than one strategy when entering a foreign market. Here is an example of how McDonald's adapted both the message and the product. The dual adaptation strategy is very indicative of McDonald's global strategy.[32] As you can see from the photos, in India, you can buy a Maharaja Mac, which includes either a chicken-based patty or a vegetarian patty. None of the McDonald's in India offers beef patties because cow is considered a sacred animal. In France, you can buy wine at McDonald's, and in Germany you can buy beer. In Israel, you cannot buy a cheeseburger, as mixing cheese and meat is not kosher.

McDonald's product adaptation in India.

While adaptation of the product seeks to enhance the firm's value in a specific market, adaptation of the promotional aspects of the marketing plan tries to ensure that this value is clearly communicated to the consumers in that market.[33] Marketers must take into consideration the following elements:

- *Language:* With almost 3000 languages in the world, language is often a marketer's greatest communication challenge. Languages vary in their alphabets, sentence structure, meaning of certain words, and even the direction in which they are written (left to right, right to left, up to down). As such, navigating the language barriers is more than just translation, and there have been errors. General Motors had a car model called Nova, and when they entered the South American markets, GM learned that the translation meant "It won't go." Not the best name for a car.

- *Colors:* Colors play an important role in the formation of a brand (logo), product design, store design, and communication offline and online.[34] However, a single color can have different meanings in different cultures. This is especially challenging for marketers who are trying to maintain a uniform brand image across cultures while adapting to local perceptions.

For example, a Japanese manufacturer tried to enter the Indian market with a predominantly black-colored product. It didn't understand why sales never gained any traction. In Japan, the black color is considered having modern, sleek appeal. After doing some marketing research, the company learned that the black color represents death in India. With a simple change in the color, there was an increase in sales.

As simple as color is, it can be tricky – purple can signify royalty (e.g. the United Kingdom) or death (e.g. Brazil). White can signify purity (e.g. the United States) or death (e.g. China).

The traditional Western wedding dress color is white.
The traditional Indian wedding dress color is red.

- *Values:* While language and color are visual aspects of culture, values are a hidden aspect of it. Nevertheless, they have a profound effect on consumers' behavior. Values determine what is acceptable or unacceptable in a given society. They are shaped by our family, education, experiences, and religious beliefs. For example, in Western societies, individual aspirations and achievements are valued and encouraged. But in Eastern societies, a more collectivistic view of achievements is common.

- *Business norms:* Business norms vary across cultures. Differences in business norms present a real challenge when trying to conduct business in a foreign market. Handshaking is a very common business gesture but far from universal. In some Asian cultures, such as in Japan, a respectful bow is the traditional business greeting, though handshaking is becoming more common. In some Muslim cultures, physical contact between unrelated men and women is forbidden. In these cultures, it would be more appropriate to shake hands with a woman only if she extends her hand first.

Bow or shake
hands?
Business norms
can be confusing.

- *Religious beliefs:* In addition to values, religious beliefs have a tremendous effect on what consumers purchase or do not purchase.[35] It is critical to understand the influence religious beliefs have on consumers' behavior and to be sensitive to them. Respecting and being sensitive to religious beliefs would be appreciated by consumers. In the same way, failing to respect religious beliefs can be detrimental to the reputation of a company or brand. When Nike introduced its line of Nike Air sneakers, the Council on American-Islamic Relations protested the logo, arguing that it resembled the word *Allah* in Arabic script. Nike apologized immediately and recalled that line of shoes. You would think that the company learned a valuable lesson, right? Not exactly. Just a few years later, Nike made a similar mistake with a different line of shoes and was forced to recall that line again.

- *Customs and taboos:* Every culture has its own unique sets of customs and taboos, which vary from one country to another. Similar to respecting religious beliefs, marketers should respect cultural customs and taboos. For example, in some places the number 4 is considered unlucky, so marketers should avoid price products using this number or packing four items together. Here are some examples of other interesting cultural taboos:

  - You should never point the bottom of your shoe toward another person in Thailand and in Arab countries. It's considered a rude gesture.

  - In Spain, you should not stretch or yawn in public. It is considered extremely vulgar.

  - You should never chew gum in public in Austria, Italy, Germany, or Malaysia.

  - Do not eat food with your left hand in the Middle East, India, and parts of Africa. In these countries, the left hand is associated with bodily functions and considered dirty.

How can marketers navigate such sensitive issues in foreign markets? Seeking guidance from native experts who are familiar with the local culture and customers can help companies avoid cultural mistakes. In addition, marketing research is essential to help marketers understand and navigate these complex issues. Marketing research can also help firms identify business opportunities that may be a result of such cultural differences.

Price

Choosing the right pricing strategy for different foreign markets is a critical and complex issue in global marketing. Don't forget, price is the only revenue-generating element of the marketing mix, while all other elements involve costs. As such, a company's pricing strategy can have a detrimental effect on its overseas expansion efforts. If the firm operates in multiple foreign markets, it faces the challenge of coordinating its pricing across different countries. Different factors affect the price of the same product in global markets: manufacturing costs, transportation and distribution costs, promotional costs, competition, market conditions, and product quality. When deciding on the price in a foreign market, marketers can use three main pricing strategies:

1. *Uniform price everywhere:* This strategy entails selling the product for the same price in every market regardless of any outside factors. This strategy might make the product too expensive in some markets and too cheap in others. It also does not reflect the value of the product. Consumers may view the value of the product as higher or lower than the price. However, this strategy may be beneficial for products with high demand.

2. *Market-based pricing:* This strategy involves setting the product's price based on what the consumer can afford and is willing to pay. It reflects the customer's perceived value of the product and takes into consideration the buying power in each market and level of competition. It is a very common strategy for brands that face high levels of competition. If consumers see the product as having greater value in comparison to competitors, the company can charge more for it. If not, the company should set the price at the same level as the competition.

3. *Cost-based pricing:* This is the simplest pricing strategy. It takes into consideration the cost of the product and adds a standard markup for its costs everywhere. This strategy has several advantages. It secures the company's expected profit and enables it to estimate revenue. This strategy is especially helpful when there is little information about a customer's willingness to pay and there aren't direct competitors in the marketplace to benchmark. This strategy may also make the product too expensive in some markets.

Burgernomics: The Price of a Big Mac in Comparison

Price of a Big Mac in selected countries (in U.S. dollars)

Switzerland	6.71
United States	5.67
Brazil	4.80
United Kingdom	4.41
South Korea	3.89
Japan	3.54
China	3.12
India	2.65
Russia	2.20
South Africa	2.15

As of January 2020
Source: The Economist

Consumers often see price escalations when trying to account for costs and the risk of entering a new market. This can be offset a bit across markets when one market compensates for the cost of others. The Big Mac index reflects McDonald's market-based pricing strategy. It is an informal way of measuring the purchasing power parity (PPP) of each country, as well as a comparison between countries. It can also be used to estimate consumers' buying power in each country.[36]

Channels of Distribution

Channel of distribution considerations are critical to a successful market entry. Essentially, this is how the product gets to the end consumer. Entering foreign markets often involves a major adaptation of the channel distribution process.

Obviously, targeting foreign markets will make the supply chain from the seller to the buyer much longer. But this also means that more parties will be involved. The longer and more complex a channel of distribution is, the harder it will be for companies to control it.

KFC learned that the hard way. It recently decided to switch its distributer in the United Kingdom from a local distributer to DHL to reduce costs, "improve the efficiency and performance of supply chain," and gain a stronger advantage over their competitors. The United Kingdom is the largest foreign market KFC serves, with over 900 restaurants. What happened? Shortly after DHL took over, the company encountered operational problems that led to the closure of almost 800 restaurants due to the shortage of chicken. KFC published the ad below, apologizing for this situation. Note the way it did it. This ad was received very positively by UK consumers due to its humanistic tone. However, do you think such an ad would have been perceived in the same way by American consumers?

Finally, the distribution of the product within each market might be the most challenging of all, because formal distribution channels might not exist. Companies will need to research the distribution channels available to them in each country and how they affect their core value and competitive advantage in a specific market in terms of profit margins and transportation costs.

KFC respond to UK chicken shortage scandal.

No organization can assume that foreign distribution systems are the same as they are in their home country. For example, in many countries around the world ice cream is sold in the format in the picture below. (Ask your grandparents about Good Humor ice cream trucks here in the United States.) This form of channel distribution is extremely challenging. Similarly, vending machines are common in the United States but may not be as common in other markets, such as India.

Ice cream seller
in France.

Developing Global Brands

How is it that some brands are popular with consumers around the world? As marketers, we know that brands are the intangible aspect of every company. It's the image that brands engrave on their consumers' mind. Strong brands serve as a source of differentiation and competitive advantage for their companies. While firms can copy each other's products, they cannot copy their brands. In a global market, brands compete on three levels.

The Local Level

The lowest brand category includes **local brands**. These are brands that have achieved success in a single national market. They can pose a significant threat to new entries, because they are very much embedded in the cultural fabric of the market. Both Best Buy and Starbucks learned that the hard way. Best Buy failed when it tried to enter China due to very strong local electronic chains. Starbucks failed when it tried to enter Italy because of the strong loyalty of Italian consumers to local establishments and a coffee culture that did not resonate with Starbucks' operation. This failure is especially ironic, because the Italian coffeehouses were the inspiration for Starbucks' coffee shops.

Local brands brands that have achieved success in a single national market.

Best Buy department store at Xujiahui.

The International Level

The next level of brand category is **international brands** that are offered in several related markets. These markets are often connected geographically. One example is the Latin America brands that operate in multiple Latin America markets.

Multiple brands of herbal mate tea sold in Latin America.

The Global Level

A **global brand** is a brand that consistently delivers the same value to consumers across national borders. The products of global brands meet the wants and needs of a global market and are offered in multiple world regions. Global brands have the same name and similar image and positioning throughout the national markets in which they operate.

Proctor & Gamble is a great example of such a global brand, with over $65 billion in world-wide sales and a presence in 180 markets.[37] The company's global strategy is to develop its overall global brand as well as its 65 independent brands.

Global brand
a brand that consistently delivers the same value to consumers across national borders.

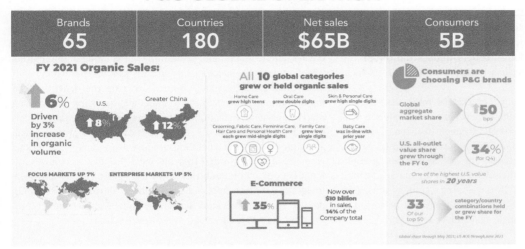

P&G GLOBAL OPERATION

Brands	Countries	Net sales	Consumers
65	180	$65B	5B

Global brands are associated with three characteristics. Consumers use these characteristics as a guide when making purchase decisions:

- *Quality signal:* Global brands often send a strong signal of quality that secures their competitive advantage.

- *Global myth:* Global brands are symbols of cultural ideals. They have a very pronounced and clear brand identity.

- *Social responsibility:* Many global brands engage in social responsibility activities and address social problems around the world.

Global Brands' Positioning

From a positioning perspective, global brands are easily recognized, consistent across markets, play on consumers' emotions and address their needs, have a unique image, are adaptable, and are well managed across markets.[38] Disney is a great example of one of the most successful global brands of all times. Millions of children around the world see Disney as part of their childhood. It is embedded in their lives, memories, experiences, and emotions.

Organizations often consider their country of origin when crafting the positioning of a global brand. A brand's country of origin affects the perceptions and attitudes consumers have toward the country from which the brand originated. They can be positive or negative and will affect the way the brand and products will be adopted in foreign markets. For example, a Chinese consumer goods company wanted people to think of its merchandise as high quality, so it adopted a German-sounding name (the Haier Group), dropping its original name (Qingdao). In France, politicians,

Global brands' positioning
the image the brand has in different markets across the globe.

nongovernmental organizations, and trade unions supported a petition calling for a Christmas boycott of the American distribution giant Amazon. Amazon was accused of unfairly profiting from the COVID-19 restrictions that have threatened small businesses and thousands of jobs in that country.

SUMMARY

Globalization is one of the driving forces behind companies seeking opportunities to expand into new markets. Marketers are tasked with the challenge of strategically developing and delivering sustainable value across multiple foreign markets by addressing diverse consumers' needs, wants, and demands to ultimately help the business generate revenue and gain a competitive advantage. This proves challenging as global consumers may have vastly different values, beliefs, and attitudes than the target segment the company has been focusing on in its local market.

To overcome this challenge, marketers must assess their current position and whether their offerings provide value to consumers on a global scale. A series of a strategic decisions that must be made in global marketing are deciding whether to go global, exploring global opportunities, deciding which markets to enter, deciding how to enter the market, deciding on the marketing mix, and developing a global brand. By developing a strategy consisting of an integrated set of choices, the brand team will be set up to achieve its objectives and compete against its competitors.

Throughout the entire process of going global or not, it is important to keep the consumer at the center. It is crucial that marketers emphasize the need to understand the target market's culture and language, as well as the environment they live in as that could impact how consumers perceive the brand or offerings. This concept of glocalization, which is a variation of both standardization and adaptation, addresses consumers' needs more effectively and creates a more meaningful positioning of the brand in that market, which impacts the success of a company's global expansion.

If done properly, global brands can reap the benefits of being a dominant player in the market, such as being easily recognized, consistently positioned across markets, able to play on consumers' emotions, and able to address consumers' needs; having a unique image; and, most importantly, being adaptable. Disney is an example of a brand that has used the diverse cultures and languages of many countries and languages to its advantage by integrating those factors. This has allowed Disney to successfully deliver sustainable value across multiple foreign markets and maintain its competitive advantage against competitors.

KEY TERMS

Globalization
Global marketing
Global marketing
strategy
Global segmentation
Pluralization of
consumption
Demographic
segmentation
(global)

PESTEL model
Global marketing
targeting
Culture
Cultural distance
Hofstede's six cultural
dimensions
Power distance
Uncertainty
avoidance

Individualistic versus
collectivistic
Long- versus short-term
orientation
Masculinity versus
femininity
Indulgence versus
restraint
Subsistence
economies

Raw material
exporting
economies
Industrializing
economies
Industrial economies
Marketing mix gap
Standardization
Adaptation
Glocalization

Local brands
International brands
Global brand
Global brands'
positioning

EXERCISES

1. List five different brands. For each brand, phrase its business in terms of a product and in terms of a solution to a problem.

2. In pairs or in small teams, pick a product, then pick a country where this product is not yet offered. What adaptations to the marketing mix of this product would you recommend

implementing when entering this foreign market? Explain your recommendations.

3. Ask your international friend for an example of a product that is well-loved back home but they suspect wouldn't be very popular over here. Share your insights in class.

4. Go to https://www.hofstede-insights.com/product/compare-countries:

    a. Choose four or five countries you wish to compare.

    b. Go over the description of dimensions of each country and their graph presentation.

    c. Write a short summary of the differences and the communalities between the countries.

    d. For each country, list five to eight products that you think would be highly successful in the country. Explain your choices.

5. Identify a US product or a brand that failed in a different country. Based on the global gap and the marketing mix gap, explain why this product or brand failed.

ENDNOTES

1. G. A. Knight, "Educator Insights: International Marketing Blunders by American Firms in Japan—Some Lessons for Management," *Journal of International Marketing* 3, no. 4 (1995): 107–29.

2. U. Beck, *What Is Globalization?* (New York: John Wiley & Sons, 2018).

3. "What Is Globalization?," 2020, https://youmatter.world/en/definition/definitions-globalization-definition-benefits-effects-examples.

4. "Perfect Market Entry Strategies to Enter International Markets," https://www.businesswire.com/news/home/20180410005826/en/Perfect-Market-Entry-Strategies-to-Enter-International-Markets%C2%A0-Infiniti-Research.

5. https://www.detroitnews.com/story/business/autos/chrysler/2016/08/31/fiat-chrysler-launches-jeep-luxury-suv-brand-india/89647586.

6. https://www.forbes.com/sites/helenwang/2012/09/03/yum-china-from-rebranding-to-reinventing/?sh=1d291ab0f722.

7. https://www.forbes.com/the-worlds-most-valuable-brands/#4be4df60119c.

8. S. S. Hassan, S. Craft, and W. Kortam, "Understanding the New Bases for Global Market Segmentation," *Journal of Consumer Marketing* 20, no. 5 (2003): 446–62.

9. T. Levitt, "The Pluralization of Consumption," *Harvard Business Review* 2, no. 8 (1988).

10. https://www.pstrassmannblogspot.org/2019/09/152-long-view-of-2020-global-economy.html.

11. https://blogs.worldbank.org/opendata/new-world-bank-country-classifications-income-level-2020-2021.

12. https://www.business-to-you.com/scanning-the-environment-pestel-analysis.

13. D. L. Alden, J. B. E. Steenkamp, and R. Batra, "Brand Positioning Through Advertising in Asia, North America, and Europe: The Role of Global Consumer Culture," *Journal of Marketing* 63, no. 1 (1999): 75–87.

14. G. Hofstede, *Culture's Consequences: Comparing Values, Behaviors, Institutions and Organizations across Nations* (London: Sage, 2001).

15. O. Shenkar, "Cultural Distance Revisited: Towards a More Rigorous Conceptualization and Measurement of Cultural Differences," *Journal of International Business Studies* 32, no. 3 (2001): 519–35.

16. https://www.hofstede-insights.com.

17. https://www.hofstede-insights.com/product/compare-countries.

18. T. G. Conley and E. Ligon, "Economic Distance and Cross-country Spillovers," *Journal of Economic Growth* 7, no. 2 (2002): 157–87.

19. https://africanbusinessmagazine.com/top-african-brands/global-brands-dominate-africa.

20. C. W. L. Hill, *International Business: Competing in the Global Marketplace* (New York: McGraw Hill, 2021).

21. https://datacatalog.worldbank.org/dataset/global-economic-monitor.

22. https://data.worldbank.org.

23. https://www.statista.com.

24. https://www.mintel.com.

25. S. Zou and S. T. Cavusgil, "The GMS: A Broad Conceptualization of Global Marketing Strategy and Its Effect on Firm Performance," *Journal of Marketing* 66, no. 4 (2002): 40–56.

26. M. Landler and M. Barbaro, "Wal-Mart Finds That Its Formula Doesn't Fit Every Culture," *New York Times,* 2006. https://www.nytimes.com/2006/08/02/business/worldbusiness/02walmart.html; https://www.toytowngermany.com/forum/topic/46198-wal-mart-pulls-out-of-germany-with-1-billion-loss/.

27. S. J. Chang and P. M. Rosenzweig, "The Choice of Entry Mode in Sequential Foreign Direct Investment," *Strategic Management Journal* 22, no. 8 (2001): 747–76.

28. https://investor.starbucks.com/press-releases/financial-releases/press-release-details/2021/Starbucks-Reports-Q2-Fiscal-2021-Results/default.aspx.

29. P. Cateora, J. Graham, and M. Gilly, *International Marketing*, 18th ed. (New York: McGraw Hill, 2021).

30. J. K. Ryans, D. A. Griffith, and D. S. White, "Standardization/Adaptation of International Marketing Strategy," *International Marketing Review* 8, no. 3 (2003): 46–60.

31. https://cocacolageoassignment.weebly.com/distribution-and-global-adaptation.html#:~:text=Coca%20Cola%20also%20adapts%20to,recycled%20up%20to%2070%20times.

32. https://www.forbes.com/sites/panosmourdoukoutas/2011/07/22/how-macdonalds-wins-through-adaptation-and-innovation/?sh=76beb9fd5faa.

33. D. Maheswaran and S. Shavitt, "Issues and New Directions in Global Consumer Psychology," *Journal of Consumer Psychology* 9, no. 2 (2000): 59–66.

34. "How Translating Colors Across Cultures Can Help You Make a Positive Impact," https://eriksen.com/marketing/color_culture.

35. https://www.bloomberg.com/news/articles/2019-01-31/nike-faces-demand-to-recall-sneakers-as-muslims-object-to-design.

36. https://www.statista.com/chart/13672/burgernomics-the-price-of-a-big-mac-in-global-comparison; D. C. Parsley and S. J. Wei, "A Prism into the PPP Puzzles: The Micro-foundations of Big Mac Real Exchange Rates," *Economic Journal* 117, no. 523 (2007): 1336–56.

37. https://www.pgcareers.com/about-us.

38. Y. Fan, "The National Image of Global Brands," *Journal of Brand Management* 9, no. 3 (2002): 180–92.

CREDITS

Social Media

14

LEARNING OBJECTIVES

After studying this chapter, you should be able to:

- Reflect and appreciate that while we tend to see social media as one thing, in reality, there are different forms and platforms of social media. Each has its unique characteristics and audience.

- Think about the many potential uses of social media. Social media is pervasive and brands must play in that space – consumers expect it. Fortunately, social media can be extremely useful for marketers.

- Understand that social media is just one marketing tool and it must be integrated into the marketing strategy and coordinated with other marketing efforts so that it appears consistent to consumers.

Social media can be great fun:

- Kellogg's Pop-Tarts has 100k Twitter followers, posts a picture of a Pop-Tart and asks, "How beautiful do I look in my new profile pic?"

- Moosejaw Mountaineering, an outdoor retailer, posts things like, "Bigfoot is the Waldo of the backcountry."

- Old Spice playfully snarked a tweet at Taco Bell upset that its "fire sauce" didn't contain fire, and Taco Bell responded, "Is your deodorant really made with old spices?"

- Chipotle's on TikTok saying "Less Tok, More Guac."

- The NBA puts its news and highlights on Twitter and Instagram, but saves its silly stuff for its 6 million TikTok fans.

Yet social media can be tricky to do well:

- For example, Adidas emailed its customers "Congrats, you survived the Boston Marathon!" Oops, well-meaning, but perhaps restate? A little sensitivity, please?

Okay, so social media can definitely be fun, and the brand team's tweeters and posters need to be careful. Does any of this matter for business? You guessed it. The answer is yes! Consumers discover new products from social media postings, they read reviews about new and existing ones, they show-off their latest purchases, they complain about failed shopping experiences, and even if ads feel annoying, yes, they also work – consumers respond to social media advertising.

So let's see more about social media. We'll begin first with the marketer's perspective – what does the brand team need to know about social media and how to do it well? In social media, everything we do is intended to interact with consumers. So then we'll flip to the consumer's perspective to gain an understanding about the underlying social network connections, what is buzz, how do influencers or opinion leaders work, how do consumers share information and their affection for a brand and form a brand community, and so forth. We'll then examine social media analytics and email marketing as a particular form of social media.

Social Media in the Context of Marketing Strategy

Marketers seem to know that social media works, and they're spending accordingly. Figure 14.1 shows the growth in marketing spending on digital advertising.[1] So let's figure out how social media works in business, how to get our money's worth, and how it all fits in the big brand picture.

Social media
any online means of communication that enables users to create and share content with others.

Social media refers to any online means of communication that enables users to create and share content with others.[2] The first thing to remember is that "social media" is just one tool in the brand manager's toolkit. Yes, it needs to be done well, but if another element of the marketing mix is wrong, say the pricing is too high, then social media won't save the brand. Pricing can take down a brand. So can social media. All of the pieces of the marketing puzzle need to be coordinated and working well to lift the brand to success. But hey, no pressure!

Second, we must remember that "social media" is not one thing. Social media comprises of a wide range of platforms, websites and apps. As we shall see, each of these means of online communication serves a different purpose and provides us with unique ways to construct and transmit information.

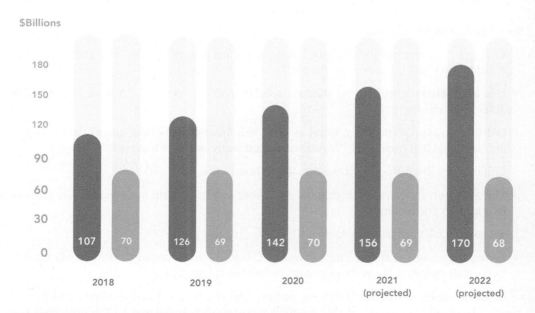

$Billions

FIGURE 14.1   US Total Media Ad Spending, by Media

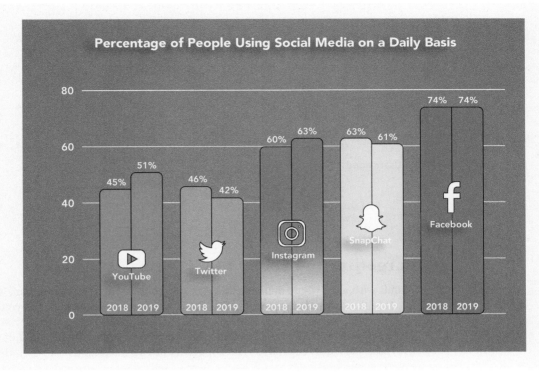

Percentage of People Using Social Media on a Daily Basis

Percentage of people using social media daily.

Marketing strategy begins with trying to understand one's current and desired customers – that is, segmentation and targeting. With that knowledge, strategy turns to questions about positioning the brand. If we were Nike and we had just developed a new, high-tech running shoe, we might hope to find a social media site that focused on jocks or, even better, specifically runners. Unfortunately, the large, familiar social media sites don't tend to be that specialized.

It's analogous to television stations – big channels like ABC, CBS, or NBC appeal to many viewers – each network hosts a variety of shows, some of which any consumer might follow. Yet consumers would be hard-pressed to describe the brand personality of any of those TV stations; they're not that focused, and the viewers are not to be targeted narrowly or precisely. But cable TV stations are very focused, specializing in men's sports, news, women's fashion, children's animation, etc. Advertising on ABC will reach many viewers. However, it will cost a lot, and the ad expenditure will be inefficient because many viewers won't be interested in our brand. Instead, if we advertise on Fox News, MSNBC, ESPN, TBS, TNT, History, Hallmark, the Food Network, Animal Planet, A&E, etc., the viewership will be smaller, so we'll reach fewer people. But those whom we reach will be closer to our target market, assuming, of course, that we choose well for our brand, like ESPN for those Nike shoes and Animal Planet for a brand of dog treats. The specialized media outlets also usually offer cheaper advertising prices as well.

The same principles hold with social media. There are numerous "small" media sites that are very focused. Brand managers need to know the ones that are most relevant to their brands, at least from the viewpoint of the customer. Big social media sites tend to appeal to large numbers of consumers (by definition), which makes the site users more heterogeneous or not as precisely fitting the ideal target customer. There are also always new sites that show aggressive growth and will likely become bigger (e.g. 18.7% of US users are on daily). There are some generalizations about the big social media, which are discussed next, but always double-check because these profiles are very fluid and dynamic.

TikTok - THE FASTEST GROWING SOCIAL MEDIA PLATFORM

68 min
Average time
spent daily

14%
Marketers will
up their spend

62%
Users aged 10–29

155
# of countries
available

1.1B
Active users
worldwide

#1
Downloaded app

$1.9B
Revenue

59%
Female users

Targeting and Social Media Profiles

Brands wish to be where their customers are. So consider, as a brand manager, who are you hoping to be speaking to and engaging, that is, who is your target market? What do you think they want?

Currently, Facebook and YouTube are by far the most popular social media sites. See Figures 14.2 and 14.3 for basic statistics on these sites.[3] Approximately 70% of US adults say they use these sites fairly regularly.[4] The popularity of Facebook holds true even though they've been experiencing some high profile issues, such as selling some personal data. The popularity of sites holds as long as consumers perceive that the social media sites provide value for them.

Over 80% of Americans today have at least one social media account (see Figure 14.4).[5] But consumers differ with respect to which social media outlets they prefer. How do different social media outlets compare? Statistics indicate that the age differences are not as big as you'd think, at least for larger social media platforms. Young people – teens and adults 18- to 24-year-olds – haven't dropped Facebook altogether, but they are driving growth with their frequent use of Instagram, Snapchat, and Twitter. On the other end of the age spectrum, YouTube is popular across most categories – there are no particular gender differences, or racial or ethnicity differences in popularity, but the one exception is that people older than 65 don't use YouTube as frequently as the other age categories.

FACEBOOK STATISTICS

155
Ave # of friends

82%
College grades

10M
# of advertisers

27.2M
Revenue

2.8B
Monthly active users

98%B
Mobile active users

57%
Annual growth rate

43.2%
Female users

FIGURE 14.2 Facebook Statistics

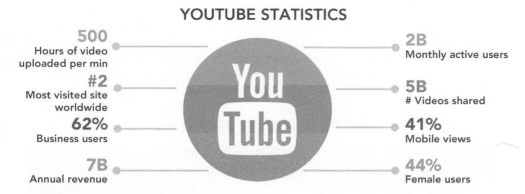

FIGURE 14.3 YouTube Statistics

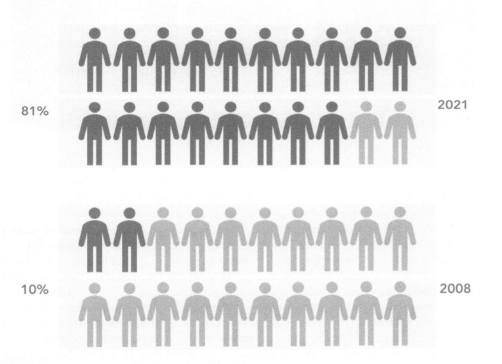

FIGURE 14.4 Social Media Over Two Decades

There aren't many gender differences, except that Pinterest appeals more to women (42%) than men (15%), and Reddit a bit more to men (15%) than women (8%).[6] The only reliable difference for level of education is that LinkedIn is more frequently used by those with higher education (51% of adults with college degrees say they use the site vs. only 9% of adults with high school or less education),[7] which makes sense given the career-oriented content that dominates LinkedIn. LinkedIn also draws the best income statistics, in that 45% of its active users make $75,000 or more a year.

In terms of frequency of usage, Facebook is typically accessed daily on average, whereas Instagram and Snapchat are accessed, on average, multiple times a day. What is the modality of that access? Typically, users are on their smartphones (180m users a month), twice the number of users accessing sites via their desktops or laptops (90m users a month).[8]

Show me the money – are there statistics on whether there are business opportunities using social media? The overall volume or presence suggests there is great potential. Globally, 40% of the world's population (about 3 billion) use social media.[9] As another indicator of the size of the consumer audience, YouTube reaches more 18- to 49-year-olds than any cable TV station in the United States,[10] and that age bracket includes big spenders in many purchase categories.

EXPRESSING YOURSELF ON SOCIAL MEDIA

SOCIAL MEDIA EXPLAINED WITH SUSHI

Once you've chosen the social media platform, what do you say? It's important to consider how to express brand content in a way that fits the media platforms. For example, the figure below is a play on a consumer endorsing coffee, and how the expressions would vary with the particular social media. So, on Twitter you'd say, "i am drinking #coffee," on Facebook you'd say, "I like coffee!," on LinkedIn you'd say, "my coffee-drinking skills have been endorsed," etc.

Facebook is considered to be more about building brand equity, brand loyalty, and enhancing relationships with customers.[11] Twitter is usually likened to PR. On YouTube, the brand team can post product demonstrations, or even use social influencers to promote the company's product.

In any of these media, it's important to play up the visual, that is, you wouldn't post a boring list of product specifications (until the consumer clicked through on a link to "learn more"). Photos get more likes, more comments, and more click-throughs than other kinds of posts.

In every piece posted (words, photos, videos), think about how to present the brand, to be consistent with the brand image that is desired. There should be different web pages for each sub-brand, and perhaps the home page might feature a rotating set of the brand line's products. Curalate.com research indicates that 30% of all shoppers and almost 80% of 18- to 34-year-old shoppers discover a new product on Facebook.[12] Pinterest and Instagram are other frequent sources (60%) of new product discovery.

What Are the Brand Goals?

As with marketing in general, or advertising more specifically, social media as part of the marketing plan needs a strategy.[13] Imagine two scenarios: first, brand team discussions are sometimes proactive, such as planning a media budget for a new product launch. Second, sometimes brand team discussions are more reactive, such as trying to diagnose possible reasons for recent sales decline in a brand line.

These motivating questions form the "situation analysis" depicted in Figure 14.5. The first question is simply, what is the situation, what are we dealing with, or what do we seek to accomplish? These strategic and planning questions are for the purposes of engaging consumers, and we discuss the consumers' experience with them in Figure 14.6.

Next, what are the strategic options we have?[14] For the new product launch, one objective might be to achieve 25% product awareness within three months of launch. For the scenario of trying to stem the sales decline, a different objective might be to reach out to former customers and encourage at least 25% of them to rebuy.

Tactics, the next phase, are the "how-to," and in this chapter, the question is whether and how social media might help achieving the marketer's goals. Think of the process that first drives

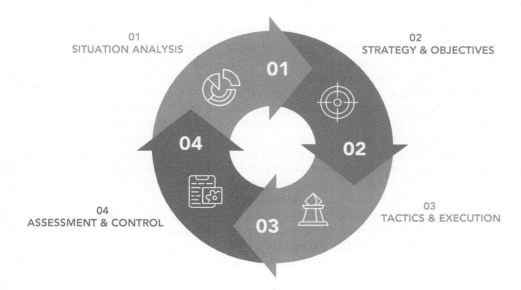

FIGURE 14.5 Social Media Marketing – Strategy and Assessment

FIGURE 14.6 When Is Social Media Most Helpful?

consumers to awareness of the brand ➔ then to positive attitudes and some interest in trying the brand ➔ next to purchase and trial ➔ and then if there is liking, repeat purchasing and perhaps loyalty, word-of-mouth recommendations, even becoming a brand ambassador, lots of likes on Facebook, etc. Some of these goals are more easily met via social media than others.

As Figure 14.6 indicates, in the early stages, social media can certainly help. For example, awareness can be enhanced by posting ads on related websites. In the later stages, social media can also be very helpful. For example, making recommendations and becoming an opinion leader or an "influential" are goals that are obviously easily attained through social media websites – both the brand's sites and the consumers' sites.[15] For the in-between stages, social media may help a little. For example, trial is helped along with social media particularly when coupled with promotions. Repeat purchasing requires that the purchase offers customer satisfaction; if the product is awful, it wouldn't matter that the social media platform rocked. So yes, social media can help achieve some marketing goals, but it is no panacea for all aspects of marketing.

What that all suggests is social media might be very helpful with the new product scenario. The brand team can post news about the impending launch and the excitement can help create **buzz**, which is an amplification of the original marketing message by consumers.[16] The team might use **email marketing** to contact its brand fans and send them reduced rates to encourage trial.

Of course, Figure 14.6 also suggests that social media might be less effective in the scenario about declining sales. Yet the brand team can look at its CRM database, searching for consumers who haven't bought in a while, and email them with a promotion. These fallen-away customers are also an opportunity if the brand team wishes to conduct some marketing research to inquire as to why the consumers are not purchasing as often as they used to—is the consumer critical of the brand, and why (and is this changeable), or perhaps the consumer's needs have simply changed (and if so, is this a new brand opportunity).

The last phase in Figure 14.5 is to step back and assess the marketing efforts. It is frequently tempting to skip this step because the brand team wants to move on to other issues. However, if no measure is taken of whether the marketing was effective, then the team will not know whether the whole undertaking had been worth it. (We'll talk more about measures and analytics later in the chapter.)

> *"Advertising is very simple in a lot of ways. Advertisers go where the users go, and users are choosing to spend a lot more time online."*
>
> Susan Wojcicki, YouTube CEO

How to Do It?

It is obvious that social media can be a very powerful strategic tool for marketers.[17] But, how should they use it effectively? There are three paths to success on social media. Using humor, being informative, and fostering engagement.

Using Humor

First, there is no question that humor dominates. Consumers, and generally social media users, enjoy humor, and it can increase the likelihood that a posting goes "viral." For many brands, humor can fit the brand positioning. Being funny or silly may not be the main feature of a brand, but it can be consistent with the brand image, and there's no question that humor can grab one's attention.

For example, Wendy's (with almost 3 million Twitter followers) uses humor very effectively. Wendy's brand team is also savvy about using humor in a timely manner, such as when they comment in real time about unfolding sports events (e.g. playfully teasing fans of a losing team). Similarly, Skittles posts pictures of a couple of their candies and says, "Quick, eat these Skittles.

Buzz
an amplification of the original marketing message by consumers.

Email marketing
promotional information delivered by email to consumers.

Wendy's uses humor effectively on social media.

There's no time to explain" (a humorous approach that is simple and goofy). Chipotle tweets out "Good morning to everyone, except people who take our Tabasco bottles" (a tweet that is playful and an informative reminder). Denny's tweets out, "If you close your eyes while holding a warm pancake it's almost like holding hands with a real human" (which is funny, and a bit pathetic!).

As much as humor can be appreciated by consumers, it isn't an answer for every brand manager. For one thing, what is seen as funny varies across cultures (e.g. internationally) and even across subcultures (e.g. men and women), so a posting that is seen as playful by one group might not even be understood by some other consumers or it could upset another group of consumers. In addition, humor might not fit all brands.

Be Informative

A second path to success is simply to be informative. For example, KLM was one of the first airlines that rose to the occasion to keep its flyers informed[18] – the precipitating event was a volcanic ash cloud over Iceland that had halted plane traffic in Europe, thereby stranding the consumers and creating great delays in their travels. Updating flight times and gate changes may seem like business as usual these days but at the time, KLM's actions showed quick thinking and their novelty earned them many fans.

Reebok is another example of a brand that excels in various social media platforms, and their main instrument is not humor. Being funny isn't something they necessarily avoid, but their main communication goal is to inform. The company can provide information about new products on Instagram, Facebook, and YouTube, and they are also known for providing useful information on LinkedIn about employment opportunities.

Examples abound showing how brand managers use social media to be informative to consumers. For example, Target shares video content and they provide customer service online. Target appears on Pinterest with suggestions for wedding registries or baby clothing. Another classic, even classy brand is Tiffany – they have more than 2 million Twitter followers, not by trying to be funny but simply by showing their latest jewelry designs. Another example is a London zoo that hosts a tiger-cub-cam so fans can watch the little cats at play or rest, inducing some moments of "aww" and perhaps good feelings toward the zoo itself.

Some brand managers think that social media is just a tool for **B2C** (business-to-consumer) brands and that it's not as useful for those who oversee **B2B** (business-to-business) brands. Yet sharing content to be informative can be a strategic element for B2B companies as well.[19]

B2C
business to consumer.

B2B
business to business.

KLM was one of the first airlines that kept its flyers informed.

In particular, LinkedIn is useful for companies, in part as an HR tool to help recruit great talent. More generally, the company can publish regular company and brand updates, it can post blurbs from executives to show leadership and confidence in the company, and generally the postings are to share knowledge (not to entertain, per se). YouTube can also be a nice B2B outlet, with its brand channels or users posting information about products more richly than is possible in a 15-second click-through ad. Cisco is an example of a B2B brand that uses social media in a smart way – its employees regularly post video content about issues that they expect would be of interest to Cisco's IT customers.

Another particular form of social media that serves B2B purposes very well is the blog. In-house experts can post information, suggestions, reveal forthcoming brand extensions, etc. Researchers at Daily Infographic say there are some 1.5 billion blogs, with over 30 million bloggers in the United States alone.[20] They also found that more than 50% of Fortune 100 companies have a corporate blog. Why? Who reads these things? Their research indicates that some 75% of internet users have said they read blogs to learn more about products prior to making a purchase; they trust the information posted in blogs. That trust is earned by the fact that bloggers are often seen as experts, and, therefore, they have some credibility. In addition, blogs just don't have the same feel as high pressure sales or ads. The blogs need to be updated, as frequently as your consumers want (which is more frequent in product categories that are exciting), so there needs to be corporate support of the social media effort. Ideally, blogs will let users post their opinions and reactions, which in turn helps keep the content fresh as well as show the company's efforts toward transparency and friendliness.

Engagement: Be Responsive and Encourage User-generated Content

The third path to success on social media is to be sure to share content and do so regularly, and you can count on your consumers to help! In social media, the key is engagement, as if the brand is truly in dialog with its consumers. Companies want consumers to be interested

Taco Bell lobbied Apple for (and got!) a taco emoji!

in their products and make purchases and recommendations, and it turns out that consumers want to know the company is engaged as well. So, communications from the company must be responsive and timely. We don't want customers wondering, "Is there really someone on the other end of their communication, does the company care?" Consumers value the interactivity, and the company's social media team members are the frontline brand reps, so it is important to be responsive to the brand fans' postings.

Consumers also like engaging by posting their opinions and experiences, verbally and in photos. These posters are often brand fans, but even consumers who are not as passionate about the brand, in this day and age, cannot resist adding their thoughts. When consumers post pictures, it's often a modern day expression of affection and liking.

Some consumers will post complaints, but if the platform is going to be democratic, the brand needs to allow everything to be posted. Norms are developing that poor language or libelous sounding expressions can be deleted, but otherwise, transparency reigns supreme.

This openness naturally makes senior executives nervous – it's all very exciting but it also feels risky. One way to stay on top of social media is to lead – take the initiative in engaging the

Dominos' "Pizza Legend" contest.

conversation. Post information and news or silly pictures (if they're appropriate), challenge consumers to a contest. For example, Domino's encourages customer involvement by having them create and order tailor-made pizzas, then name the creations, and enter them into their "Pizza Legend" contests.

These different paths to social media success – humor, being informative, and engagement, or being responsive and encouraging user-generated content – are not necessarily at odds with each other. For some brands, multiple strategies can be useful.

Tactical Execution – and How *Not* to Do It

Before a brand team switches on its social media function, it needs to have serious discussions about how to do it, who will do what, and what to do when something goes wrong. Because something *always* goes wrong.

Choosing a platform – If a brand team is just beginning its social media practices, it might be best to enter only a few platforms to get some practice before rolling out on a broader scale to play in more social media spaces. So which social media outlet(s) should they focus on? The brand team can begin by considering the demographic profiles of the users discussed earlier. Who are the target (desired) customers?

Choosing posters – The brand team needs to decide who among them will be the primary posters, or will there be an egalitarian free-for-all such that any or all employees are encouraged to post any time about anything (and give the company's legal reps a complete tizzy). How frequently should Brad tweet? How frequently should Emily post something on Facebook? The frequencies depend in part on the particular social media site (e.g. greater frequencies or less inter-post time durations at Twitter than Facebook).

Coordinating consistent voice – In addition, the brand team needs to get the posters, Brad and Emily to coordinate with each other so that the overall brand voice is consistent across the media. What will that voice be? Be clear about who you are. Try to build a brand image you can be proud of. Remember that the medium is highly visual, so emphasize posting photos and videos. Yet keep a consistent "look" for purposes of brand building. You probably don't need to use bad language or bathroom humor, and you probably don't want trashy sex or violence to be linked to your brand. Figure out your tone – will you go for professional or humorous or snarky?

When things go wrong – Another conversation worth having is preparing for something blowing up. For example, every brand team needs to be ready for negative customer posts. No matter how awesome the brand is, some customer will find some problem and want to vent. Some customers are reasonable, others are not. For that matter, some brand managers are good tweeters or posters, and others are not.

For those who doubt social media can go "bad," here are a few well-known and publicized biffs. Sometimes the brand posting or tweet is just sort of dumb, like:

- When a fan in Alaska asked if Chick-fil-A might open a restaurant nearby and the company responded that they had no plans to expand beyond North America. Um. . . Alaska is in North America Dude!

POSTING ON SOCIAL MEDIA

OPTIMAL TIMES FOR SOCIAL MEDIA POSTS

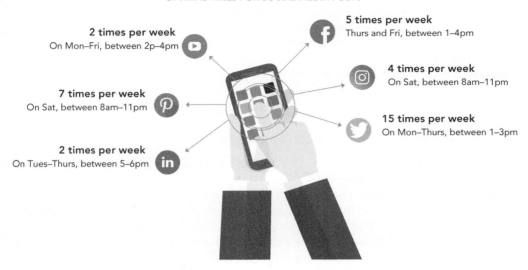

2 times per week
On Mon–Fri, between 2p–4pm

7 times per week
On Sat, between 8am–11pm

2 times per week
On Tues–Thurs, between 5–6pm

5 times per week
Thurs and Fri, between 1–4pm

4 times per week
On Sat, between 8am–11pm

15 times per week
On Mon–Thurs, between 1–3pm

Sometimes the brand posting or tweet is more problematic and controversial, which has bystanders watching the interchange doing a facepalm and wondering, "What were they thinking?" Consider these examples:

- Estée Lauder announced its new line of cosmetic on Reddit, showing a picture of all light color foundations and almost nothing for women of color.

- Benetton, no stranger to controversy, sent out a nice multicultural photo of three young boys, and says "Sorry ladies. Girls not allowed! #Benetton #kids." They were trying to be cute, but the backlash indicated potential customers were not happy. Humor is very tricky!

- Z Palette has been insensitive to its customers' economic status. Some users posted that $85 was a lot for a lipstick and the company replied with the likes of "You're in a dorm room. It may be a stretch for your budget" and "Thank God we don't need your money." Be careful with snark – your brand probably deserves better.

For such situations, the brand team needs to be prepared. What will your recovery process be? Obviously, first acknowledge the authenticity of the consumer's point of view, and if there is a real crisis (and there probably is, at least in the consumer's mind), acknowledge the problem, and try to fix it. Publicly be sure to apologize. If possible, encourage the consumer to communicate with the brand team more privately such as via email. Consider the consumer's criticisms, apologize and be authentic, do not be snarky or curt about any of it (even if you're screaming in your office!). Explain how you'll fix the problem and how you hope the fix will avoid such problems in the future.

A policy that should also be decided ahead of time is whether the company will support a brand team tweeter if the tweet is not well-received or will the firm throw the employee under the bus? If the brand team is afraid for their jobs, they will quite rationally post infrequently and only rather safe and boring content. That's no way to win brand fans.

Do the right thing!

Some marketers engage in a number of tactics that are just not cool.

One current practice is to embed popular search terms in the brand's website (that might be irrelevant to the brand) to enhance SEO (search engine optimization). Another practice is encouraging (and paying for) consumers to post fake reviews (positive for the focal brand and negative for competitor brands).

Social Networks and Influencers

How is it that social media really works? That is, what's social about these media that is different from TV, radio, billboards, and the like?

The "social" of social media plays off the notion of a social network, such as one's friends – some friends are closer to you than others, some are more like acquaintances. For marketers, when a consumer finds a new product that they want to tell people about, who do they tell? They tell people in their social networks – their friends, family, coworkers, they talk about it online, etc. That's **word-of-mouth**, people talking to others about your brand.

Word-of-mouth
transfer of information about products or brand between consumers.

Figure 14.7 shows a consumer, say it's you, at the center (the solid dot), and arrows emanating from that person to a few others, who might in turn keep the flow going.[21] There was an old shampoo commercial starring Heather Locklear in which she said she liked the shampoo so much that she "told 2 friends, and they told 2 friends, and so on and so on." That flow is the mechanism of diffusion. It is sometimes compared to medicine and called "contagion" and that's how we've come to refer to social media that goes "**viral**" (consumers are catching brand cooties!). Other times, the spread is referred to as buzz. Both buzz and viral are terms that refer to word-of-mouth, usually positive, indicating that consumers are talking about your brand.[22]

Viral
shared information that spreads quickly to millions of people online.

FIGURE 14.7   Social Network. Adapted from Catherine Park 2019.

Word-of-mouth can be extremely helpful to consumers. Seeking advice from opinion leaders provides information and helps the consumer make rational and informed decisions in product categories where the consumer might have little expertise and perhaps no time or particular motivation to search for more information. Word-of-mouth advice helps when there is no experience (say, where to buy a condo in a town that is unknown to the consumer buyer), or only a little experience (say when buying cars, given that this occurs relatively infrequently), or the information is hard to come by (so one might ask coworkers to recommend a dentist after moving in to a new town), or when the consumer is entering a new product category (such as considering buying an electric car but not knowing where to plug it in at the airport), etc.

Even advice that seems anonymous, such as consumer reviews, can be helpful. For product categories in which a consumer has expertise (say in buying books) or for which the purchase is relatively low risk (an inexpensive purchase category), then consumers might not consult others' reviews and comments. Whereas for other purchases, say visiting another city, it might be worth reading some reviews of hotels, given that they can be somewhat expensive, and the consumer might not be familiar with the town or the hotel's locations and amenities. The trip could be expensive, and, in addition to financial risk, there could be social risk, say in wanting to make good memories, and just not wanting the trip to go badly. For purchases in product categories like these, it can be helpful to see what other consumers say, even if we do not personally know those consumers. This aspect of social media is helpful.

Sometimes social networks become structured online such as **brand communities**, communities that are formed based on the emotional attachment to a brand, that can form for a brand, endorsing, say, Mercedes, on their Facebook page (see Figure 14.8), or collections of like-minded consumers who are brand fans posting their pictures in a user-generated brand-fandom space outside of the Mercedes or Facebook domains.[23] Consumers might shop on brand spaces, and watch or post videos, photos, and opinions. Consumers might "like" brands for incentives (e.g. coupons) but usually the likings are just unsolicited endorsements by fans trying to support the brand.

Brand communities communities that are formed based on emotional attachment to a brand.

Here's the thing. No brand is universally loved. When you're the brand manager, you wonder why everyone in the world doesn't love your wonderful brand. But that doesn't happen, for any

Videos

Photos (futuristic new product)

Shop (non-car paraphernalia)

Posts (upcoming events)

FIGURE 14.8 Facebook Page of Mercedes Benz

brand. So, in addition to your brand eliciting positive word-of-mouth, there will always also be negative postings, consumers who are annoyed about something, who post negative things trying to influence others not to buy the brand. Sometimes their critical comments can be informative – culling such criticisms feels discouraging, but try to have the mindset of looking for an opportunity to improve the brand or the service or whatever the consumer was complaining about. Of course, sometimes consumers are just big whiners, and there's no satisfying them. The brand team can post attempts to be conciliatory, but they can't be overly obvious in sucking up to consumers. Asking to communicate privately with the unhappy consumer is always a good idea.

So in this mix of positive and negative postings, when marketers examine social networks, what are they looking for? One indicator that marketers watch is called the Net Promoter Score (NPS). The NPS is a straight-up acknowledgment that there will be both happy and unhappy consumers. The score counts the number of positive postings and subtracts the negative postings, and that difference is the "net," and reflects the strength of consumers in their support in promoting the brand. Brands that have more positive postings, and/or fewer negative postings, will come out strongest on this index.

Opinion leaders experts in a specific consumption domain. They are highly trusted and have the power to influence other consumers' decision making.

What else do marketers look for within social networks? They're looking for **opinion leaders** – consumers who seem to be relatively more connected to many others (simply many connections in Figure 14.7), or have some extra credibility (like an expert blogger), or some other reason for leadership (such as celebrities). In social networks, such important people are referred to as "central," and they are the people that marketers like to reach out and contact because they are the **influencers** – their opinion matters to others. If the brand can hook an influential, then the brand immediately picks up many more fans.[24]

Influencers consumers who have the ability to influence the opinions and behaviors of other consumers.

The Global Mindset

 Social marketing movements in Hong Kong use online social media to vote for methods of demonstration, to reinforce their identity as a democracy.

Social media is a really exciting part of the marketer's job, in part because things are changing so quickly! Beyond encouraging consumer loyalty and purchases, social media is being used to facilitate social marketing efforts and activism goals in changing society. A dramatic example of this is when Reddit became the forum for amateur day trading consumers to mess with the big pros on Wall Street. Because they could! The movement was likened to Robinhood (taking from the rich and distributing the riches to the poor). The GameStop stocks were being traded like crazy, and then the amateur traders just stopped. Then what? The pros could hold or sell. The value of the shares dropped nearly in half. Reddit is also the venue that gives "karma" points to contributors for posting good content and comments. It's unclear whether interfering with Wall Street is good karma. But the point is that people united can achieve many goals, and social media can facilitate that (in addition to boosting branding and purchasing!).

Social Media Analytics

Recall from Figure 14.5 that social media, like any marketing tactic, begins with clear plans and goals from marketing strategy. The feedback loop requires that the brand team track and measure the results of their marketing efforts, to understand what seemed to work well and what should be improved upon in the future. Social media tactics are undertaken to reach consumers and engage them with the brand – social media analytics are measures of whether that's working. Are consumers finding you? Are they engaging and interacting with the website and other consumers? Are they clicking to directed links that lead to buying? In social media, there are numerous methods to help these assessments; in general, these measures are known as social media analytics.[25]

Social media analytics are the various measures that track consumer traffic on the social media websites to assess popularity, volume, and possible effectiveness of marketing campaigns. Figure 14.9 shows a screenshot from Google Analytics.[26] Google has done a great job of offering a user-friendly interface for managers to see various indices, such as numbers of consumers and web traffic in general, as well as popular sources of traffic, that is, what web pages consumers were on before clicking onto the company or brand page. What search terms are popular? Among what demographics of consumers? (Currently, a very popular Google search on phones is the GPS-based query, "Find a ___ near me.")

In Facebook, obviously numbers of followers and clicks on pages are immediately available. These numbers are like traditional advertising measures of "reach" (e.g. views, how many pairs of eyes saw your page, or clicks). Further engagement is also easily assessed, such as numbers of consumers who liked the page, or commented on it, or shared the content with others.

As discussed previously, most brand teams are posting content on more than one social media platform, so in addition to the site-specific statistics (e.g. Google, Facebook), other website services, like www.hootsuite.com, help to manage communications across multiple social media sites. This cross-site management is especially helpful for brand teams in planning when certain content should be posted on Twitter or Facebook or LinkedIn, and it easily captures the resulting statistics in terms of activity on those platforms.

What might these analyses reveal? When volume ticks up, pay attention. The increased interest, visits, comments can be diagnostic (good or bad news but either way, you want to be on top of it), and it can certainly predict sales.

Sentiment analysis is simply a marketer assessing the positive or negative valence of the social media around the brand, for example, counting likes and dislikes.[27] Consumer sentiment

Social media analytics various measures that track consumer traffic on the social media websites to assess popularity, volume, and possible effectiveness of marketing campaigns.

Sentiment analysis assessment of the positive or negative valence of the social media around the brand.

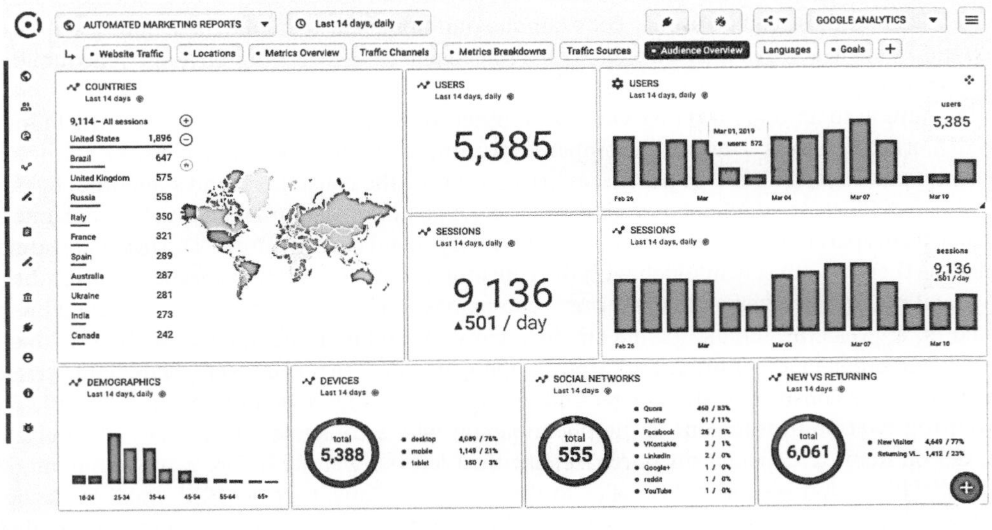

FIGURE 14.9 Google Analytics Screenshot

is also derived from text analytics methods, which are used to measure whether the posts tend to be positive and supportive, negative and critical, or just neutral (e.g. questions, information). In general, **text analyses** use linguistic parsing to look at words ("awesome"!) and word phrases ("awesome failure!") to understand the content and positivity or negativity of posts, without having to have humans read the usually extremely large databases of text.

Text analysis
uses linguistic parsing to look at words and word phrases to understand the content and positivity or negativity of posts.

Don't forget, social media is not just about telling consumers some message, they are great ways to listen to consumers as well and get a better understanding of what they want. What are consumers saying about your brands and competitor brands? Are negative comments about your brand fixable? Are there sales leads and opportunities or even new product development ideas that might come out of the consumer comments?

Search engine optimization
the process of getting websites to rank higher in search engines.

Social media analytics also help with **search engine optimization**, that is, how to make sure that consumers who are looking for you online actually find you.[28] If a consumer is searching for athletic shoes, have you paid for an online ad to pop up so that you're on the consumer's screen (that is, search engine marketing)? If not, will competitor brands scroll onto the screen before your brand? Basically, where are your consumers coming from, what are they looking at, what do they get close to buying (putting items in shopping carts), and do they buy or return to buy?

The techniques recommended for enhancing search outcomes are not rocket science, but they can seem a bit tedious – still, do a good job because the effort is worth it. The URL itself must be optimized, that is, have several common and popular key words in it. The so-called meta-data (e.g. meta-title, meta-description, meta-keywords that are inserted when the website is created and edited) should contain popular key words as well, to increase the likelihood that when a consumer is doing a fairly general search of athletic shoes, your brand makes it into the consideration set. It's simple – you want consumers to be able to find you!

Companies can also experiment with the look and feel and images and links on their websites. They can do "A/B tests" in which some consumers see version A of the website and other consumers see version B, and outcomes can be compared to see which seemed more attractive to consumers (see Chapter 3 for more details).

Email Marketing

Paid media
promotional materials that involve a paid placement.

Earned media
publicity achieved through promotional efforts other than paid media.

Marketers distinguish between **paid media** like advertising, **earned media** like fans posting on social media,[29] and **owned media**, which is the content and outlets the brand creates and maintains.[30] Each of these can be useful. For example, traditional ads (paid media) can be a source of web traffic, such as when a TV ad ends with a screenshot of "geico.com," obviously encouraging consumers to go online to learn more.

Owned media
content and outlets the brand creates and maintains.

In addition to an organization's website, another form of owned media includes the brand's email marketing efforts. These days, companies accumulate databases of their consumers' contact information, from past visits or purchases, past opt-ins by the consumers, and sometimes by purchasing email lists to supplement their own. The contact information, including the consumers' emails, forms part of the customer relationship management (CRM) efforts. The list of consumer emails is then used to stay in touch with the consumers and alert them to special opportunities.

Shopping cart abandonment
the phenomenon where consumers had been on a website, clicked on items to consider for purchase, but then left the website before actually buying the items.

Email marketing takes on many forms – companies send consumers who have signed up, or opted in, a "welcome" email.[31] Some emails revolve around e-tail commerce, such as a "thank you" for an order, or a "confirmation" as in shipping information and delivery dates. Some emails try to reengage consumers, such as reminding them of an abandoned online cart. Specifically, **shopping cart abandonment** is the phenomenon where consumers had been on a website, clicked on items to consider for purchase, but then left the website before actually buying the items.[32] This action results in lost sales to the company. Thus, part of CRM email marketing efforts is to ping those consumers from time to time with reminders that they have items in their carts still to be purchased.

Research seems to indicate that most consumers appreciate when the email is personalized, such as using the consumer's first name in the salutation as well as when the email is tailored to be relevant to the consumer's interests. When consumers have opted into receiving alerts or announcements, they indicate an interest in the brand and a willingness to learn about new products that might be relevant to them and their lifestyles, considering their own past shopping and browsing behaviors, etc. Email marketing is a very efficient means of enhancing any efforts toward CRM.

Another suggestion by email marketing gurus is to be sure that the email and links and images are easily readable on mobile phones. Given that consumers are conducting a great deal of business on their phones – from purchasing to forwarding information to friends – the email and links cannot be overly memory-saturating (slow to download or refresh) or effortful and complex. Keep the marketing communications simple and easy to read.

Just as search engine optimization is an analytic attempt to track consumer searches, there are metrics of success for email marketing also. For example, a company's own CRM database is likely to be of reasonable quality (e.g. is the email delivered vs. did the email bounce from an unknown or no longer valid address). But a company may feel like expanding the email list to garner attention by consumers who are new, as in acquisition, not just their current consumers, as in efforts for customer retention. Thus, when purchasing supplemental email lists, another metric is the list size and the quality or accuracy of the new list as well.

After assessing whether an email reaches a consumer, the next metrics evaluate open rates, that is, the percentage of emails that consumers open, mostly as a function of quickly reading the email's subject line and its source, that is, the company and brand name. Experts seem to indicate that open rates are quite good if they average around 5–10%.

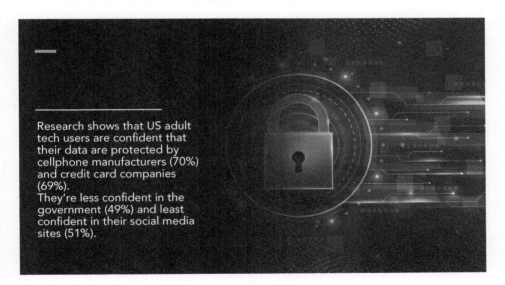

Research shows that US adult tech users are confident that their data are protected by cellphone manufacturers (70%) and credit card companies (69%).
They're less confident in the government (49%) and least confident in their social media sites (51%).

After opening an email, the next metric is whether the consumers click-through any links embedded in the email. The **click-through rate (CTR)** is the percentage of consumers who see a link contained in their email (or online at a social media site), and click on it to be sent to the brand page for further consideration (and possible later purchase). Once an email is opened, an excellent click-through rate is about 10–15%.

The next metric has to do with purchase-related activities. How long is the consumer on the website, what percentage of consumers place items for possible purchase in their shopping cart, and what percentage of those carts are bought, yielding sales, versus, does the consumer leave the website, resulting in the unfortunately frequent actions of abandoned carts mentioned previously.

Click-through rate (CTR)
the percentage of consumers who see a link contained in their email.

Lastly, a word about timing; many emails from a company feel "responsive" in that they are triggered by a consumer's actions – whether the consumer had opted in for more information, or had recently purchased or came close to purchasing items on the company's website. Other emails are scheduled to keep current, as a top-of-mind effort as consumers make decisions across numerous product categories.

In Close

To be successful and embraced by consumers, social and digital media should encourage consumer participation and interaction. Companies should also encourage consumers to post opinions and user-generated content. It is exciting and rewarding to do so, and also feels risky because the brand team is no longer 100% in charge of the marketing communications and brand message!

We'd be remiss to not mention a particular form of risk, and that is data security and privacy. Marketing researchers are working hard to help companies keep consumers' data safe. We'll say more about data privacy in Chapter 15 (when discussing companies behaving properly and ethically), but for now we note some variation in consumers' levels of comfort in sharing personal information. You can see the chart indicates that US consumers are a little bit more skeptical than the global average about trade-offs in sharing data for whatever benefits may be expected.

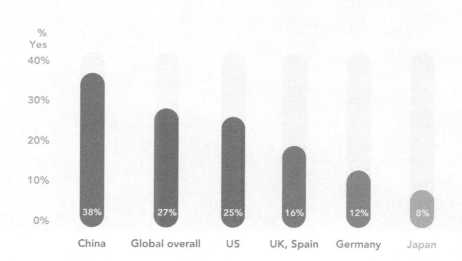

SHARING PERSONAL DATA ONLINE

Would you share personal data (financial, driving records, energy use, etc.) in exchange for rewards like lower costs or personalized service?

China	Global overall	US	UK, Spain	Germany	Japan
38%	27%	25%	16%	12%	8%

If we step back for an even broader perspective, we can see that social media is at the forefront of many new developments in the interactions between companies and brands and their consumers. Artificial intelligence will obviously play a larger role and may help make the communications from a company to the consumer more relevant than what sometimes currently feels like spam. Various forms of machines, whether robotics and drones or simply the consumers' phones, and the connections among them, as on the Internet of Things (IoT), are opportunities for brand teams to get closer to consumers and make the consumers experience better brand engagement and greater customer satisfaction and loyalty.

SUMMARY

Social media offers new and exciting channels of reaching and interacting with consumers. They need to be planned and coordinated in the context of the brand's greater strategic goals. Social media channels are strong at helping consumers learn about new products, see products in action, tell friends and coworkers about their new finds, etc. Social media doesn't particularly dictate other elements of the marketing mix, such as price, and all of the mix needs to be coordinated to express a consistent brand image. Several classes of content can be effective, including the use of humor (if appropriate), being informative, and, in general, seeking engagement such as being responsive to consumers' inquiries and posts and encouraging consumers to provide their own content.

Social media works through the underlying mechanism of social networks.

In networks, influential consumers are sought who are those most likely to be influential in other consumers' decision-making. Like any element of the marketing mix, social media efforts should be tracked and measured to understand the success of current media campaigns and try to adapt future communications for even

better success. Email marketing was also discussed as a form of owned media, which companies use to stay in touch with their consumers.

Social media marketing was once thought to be a great costless alternative to traditional media, which can be quite expensive. While social media postings, blogs, and email marketing seem relatively cheap, they are nevertheless not free, because there need to be people, members of the brand team, doing the work and overseeing the output efforts and the incoming consumer responses. Yet if the company is willing to make the time and personnel investment, what can social media do for a marketer? Social media can increase brand awareness, getting "reach" like advertising, it can drive customer engagement, such as consumer traffic to the web, whether consumers click-through on links embedded in their emails or other social media websites. Getting consumers to the brand's website is a huge step toward shopping cart conversions, that is, sales. Social medial can also keep consumers happy in that the platforms provide settings in which the company can offer quick and responsive customer service.

Popular books about social networks:
- *The Tipping Point (Malcolm Gladwell)*
- *Six Degrees (Duncan Watts)*
- *And the Band Played On (Randy Shilts)*

Movies involving social networks:
- *And the Band Played On (Matthew Modine, Alan Alda, Richard Gere)*
- *Pay It Forward (Kevin Spacey, Haley Joel Osment, Helen Hunt)*

KEY TERMS

Social media	Word-of-mouth	Social media analytics	Paid media	Click-through
Buzz	Viral	Sentiment analysis	Earned media	rate (CTR)
Email marketing	Brand communities	Text analysis	Owned media	
B2C	Opinion leaders	Search engine	Shopping cart	
B2B	Influencers	optimization	abandonment	

EXERCISES

1. Google the "Dolly Parton" meme, in which she kicked off numerous celebrities (e.g. Ellen, Jennifer Garner, Janet Jackson, Reba McEntire, Miley Cyrus, Mark Ruffalo, Will Smith, Oprah, Al Roker, and more) posing in four different pictures, one appropriate for each of LinkedIn, Facebook, Instagram, and Tinder. With your neighbor, take phone pix of each other in the four different appropriate poses. If they're not too embarrassing, share with the class.

2. Take a look at your own online social media presence across the platforms. Are there any social media where you don't have a presence and maybe should? Do you think your social media images tell the right story about who you are and how you want others to see you?

3. What are the social media platforms that you and your friends like the most? Which of those can't you use at work? Which

ones will you have to use more at work? How would you describe the "personality" of each of these social media outlets?

4. Who (or what) do you follow via any form of social media? Why? Are any (many?) of these brands or companies? How could a brand team get you to follow the brand?

5. Discuss with a classmate some ways that you believe you've gotten smarter about e-commerce. For example, do you read online reviews? Do you think reviewers are all equally valid?

How can you tell the difference? When there are many reviews versus very few, what does that tell you? If you were a brand manager, how could you entice your satisfied customers to write excellent reviews and give you a 5-star rating? For another example, when you're Googling looking for some product, do you click on the pop-up ads? Do you click on the first answers that are identified as having paid for an "Ad" to appear early in the listings? Why or why not? Do you think the information provided in those early posts is any better or worse than the results that follow? Why? How?

ENDNOTES

1. Statistics in Figure 14.1: https://www.google.com/search?rlz=1C1SFXN_enUS499US577&q=us+total+media+ad+spending,+by+media&tbm=isch&source=univ&sa=X&ved=2ahUKEwiErervhYvnAhUJnOAKHXl8Dy4Q7Al6BAgJEDc&biw=1536&bih=762#imgrc=-bSdZaB52VQc_M:; https://jubilantdigital.com/digital-marketing-facts-2020/; https://dripdigital.com/social-media-facts-and-statistics.

2. E. Butow, et al., *Ultimate Guide to Social Media Marketing* (Irvine, CA: Entrepreneur Press, 2020).

3. For Facebook, see https://www.omnicoreagency.com/facebook-statistics/. For YouTube, see https://www.omnicoreagency.com/youtube-statistics.

4. https://www.pewresearch.org/internet/2021/04/07/social-media-use-in-2021.

5. https://www.statista.com/statistics/273476/percentage-of-us-population-with-a-social-network-profile.

6. https://www.marketingcharts.com/digital/social-media-108184.

7. https://www.linkedin.com/pulse/social-media-stats-neil-horowitz.

8. A. Macarthy, *500 Social Media Marketing Tips: Essential Advice, Hints and Strategy for Business: Facebook, Twitter, Instagram, Pinterest, LinkedIn, YouTube, Snapchat, and More! (CreateSpace, 2014*, 2021).

9. https://www.statista.com/statistics/617136/digital-population-worldwide.

10. https://www.thinkwithgoogle.com/marketing-strategies/video/youtube-18-49-reach-statistics.

11. https://www.forbes.com/sites/forbesagencycouncil/2017/04/05/how-to-leverage-social-media-to-build-brand-loyalty/?sh=33199b6c2354.

12. https://lp.curalate.com/social-content-new-consumer-storefront-survey.

13. C. Diaz-Ortiz, *Social Media Success for Every Brand: The Five Story Brand Pillars That Turn Posts into Profits* (New York: HarperCollins, 2019).

14. M. Barker, et al., *Social Media Marketing: A Strategic Approach*, 2nd ed. (Cengage, 2016).

15. C. W. C. Ki and Y. K. Kim, "The Mechanism by which Social Media Influencers Persuade Consumers: The Role of Consumers' Desire to Mimic," *Psychology & Marketing* 36, no. 10 (2019): 905–22.

16. X. Luo and J. Zhang, "How Do Consumer Buzz and Traffic in Social Media Marketing Predict the Value of the Firm?," *Journal of Management Information Systems* 30, no. 2 (2013): 213–38.

17. J. McDonald, *Social Media Marketing Workbook: How to Use Social Media for Business*(JM Internet Group, 2021).

18. https://www.klm.com/travel/us_en/plan_and_book/booking/booking_status/index.htm.

19. https://blog.hubspot.com/marketing/b2b-marketing.

20. https://techjury.net/blog/blogging-statistics.

21. https://thenextscoop.com/importance-influencer-marketing-digital-age.

22. J. Berger, *Contagious: Why Things Catch On* (New York: Simon & Schuster, 2016).

23. https://www.facebook.com/MercedesBenz.

24. B. Hennessy, *Influencer: Building Your Personal Brand in the Age of Social Media*(Citadel Press, 2018).

25. J. H. Lipschultz, *Social Media Measurement and Management: Entrepreneurial Digital Analytics (Routledge,* 2019).

26. Google search images with completely open permissions: https://www.google.com/search?as_st=y&tbm=isch&hl=en&as_q=google+analytics&as_epq=&as_oq=&as_eq=&cr=&as_sitesearch=&safe=images&tbs=sur:fmc#imgrc=kKVmA7YZIbxgAM.

27. E. M. Younis, "Sentiment Analysis and Text Mining for Social Media Microblogs Using Open Source Tools: An Empirical Study," *International Journal of Computer Applications* 112, no. 5 (2015).

28. A. Clarke, *SEO 2021: Learn Search Engine Optimization with Smart Internet Marketing Strategies* (CreateSpace, 2021).

29. A. T. Stephen and J. Galak, "The Effects of Traditional and Social Earned Media on sales: A Study of a Microlending Marketplace," *Journal of Marketing Research* 49, no. 5 (2012): 624–39.

30. M. J. Lovett and R. Staelin, "The Role of Paid, Earned, and Owned Media in Building Entertainment Brands: Reminding, Informing,

and Enhancing Enjoyment," *Marketing Science* 35, no. 1 (2016): 142–57.

31. C. S. White, *Email Marketing Rules: Checklists, Frameworks, and 150 Best Practices for Business Success (CreateSpace*, 2017).

32. M. Kukar-Kinney and A. G. Close, "The Determinants of Consumers' Online Shopping Cart Abandonment," *Journal of the Academy of Marketing Science* 38, no. 2 (2010): 240–50.

CREDITS

https://www.emarketer.com/content/us-digital-ad-spending-2021

https://www.businessofapps.com/data/tik-tok-statistics

https://blog.hubspot.com/blog/tabid/6307/bid/6128/the-ultimate-list-100-facebook-statistics-infographics.aspx#:~:text=Daily%20active%20users%20(DAUs)%20on,12%25%20increase%20year%20over%20year

https://thesmallbusinessblog.net/youtube-statistics

https://www.broadbandsearch.net/blog/social-media-facts-statistics

https://mobloggy.com/why-hire-a-digital-marketing-agency/social-media-explained-with-coffee

https://www.brandchannel.com/2016/10/18/dumb-ways-to-die-101816

https://www.iphoneincanada.ca/news/klm-airlines-facebook-messenger-check-in

https://econsultancy.com/30-brands-with-excellent-social-media-strategies

https://econsultancy.com/30-brands-with-excellent-social-media-strategies

https://www.awwwards.com/sites/domino-s-pizza-legends

https://sproutsocial.com/insights/best-times-to-post-on-social-media

https://www.facebook.com/MercedesBenz

https://www.google.com/search?as_st=y&tbm=isch&hl=en&as_q=google+analytics&as_epq=&as_oq=&as_eq=&cr=&as_sitesearch=&safe=images&tbs=sur:fmc#imgrc=kKVmA7YZIbxgAM

Pew Research Center, "Americans and Cybersecurity" is source of ethics box stats. https://www.pewresearch.org/fact-tank/2018/03/27/americans-complicated-feelings-about-social-media-in-an-era-of-privacy-concerns/

https://www.shutterstock.com/image-vector/cyber-technology-security-network-protection-background-1928381819

Figure 14.2: Meta

Figure 14.8: Mercedes-Benz AG

Figure 14.9: Google LLC

Image p. 276: TikTok

Image p. 278: YARUNIV Studio/Shutterstock

Image p. 281: Twitter, Inc.

Image p. 282: KLM

Image p. 283: Twitter, Inc.; Jubilant FoodWorks Ltd.

Image p. 291: Vektor illustration/Shutterstock

15 Do Good Consumption

LEARNING OBJECTIVES

After studying this chapter, you should be able to:

- Understand how *companies* can do better at doing good.
- Understand how *consumers* can do better at doing good.
- Learn about the strategic importance and potential benefits that companies enjoy from doing good.

Some companies and brands show a lot of heart! Consider these examples of "Buy-one, GIVE-one!" or B1G1:

- Since it opened, TOMS Shoes has donated more than 95 million pairs of shoes to children in need all over the world. Every time someone buys a pair of shoes, they give away a pair of shoes to someone in need.[1]
- Warby Parker helps consumers buy prescription glasses online, and then donates a pair of glasses for each pair purchased, "Buy-A-Pair, Give-A-Pair."[2]
- At the Bombas socks company, they say "One purchased = one donated." The donated socks are given to homeless shelters because new clothing is under-donated.[3]

Why do we consider these examples of good corporate behavior? Why are such stories rare? When you think about doing business, you are probably not thinking about doing good to society, such as helping the environment. But, as we will discuss in this chapter, doing good to society or to the environment became part of doing business in the past few years. Mostly because of you, the consumer! You no longer just want to buy a product – you want to buy a product from an organization that has values and contributes back to society and to the environment. Kudus to you!

This chapter considers what constitutes good behaviors by companies and how marketers can encourage consumers to engage in good behaviors as well. We begin by defining corporate social responsibility, proceed to ethics, both in general and with respect to marketing, all with an aim to understand how to enhance prosocial behaviors by companies and consumers.

"Do Good" as a Strategic Decision

HOW a company does good to society or to the environment is (or should be) a strategic decision.[4] To succeed, the do-good value and strategy needs to be closely related to the firm's vision, products, and consumers. Recall the Unique Value Proposition (UVP) from Chapter 2 – we saw that a company should establish its competitive advantage by leveraging three elements that form its UVP: what the company does best (products or services), consumers' needs, and what the competitors do best (their products or services). By offering consumers products and services that address their needs in a way that is different from those of the competitors, a company can gain and maintain a significant competitive advantage. So how does good business strategy relate to the company's "do good" initiatives? Good question!

When a company or brand considers engaging in a "do good" initiative, they must make sure that such an initiative is authentically related to their UVP, hopefully one that will enhance the company's UVP (see Figure 15.1). Let's see what we mean by that.

Patagonia is a company that is involved in many environmental initiatives, all of which are directly related to the clothing industry – fair trade, waste, pollution. Now, you might say, "Well, great, but, they are a clothing company, so they are part of the problem." True. But everything that Patagonia does aims to address these issues. Here are a few examples[5]:

- 68% of Patagonia's fabrics are made with recycled materials.

- They use only virgin cotton that has been grown organically, which saves water and reduces CO_2 emissions by 45% compared to conventional cotton.

- About 66% of their line is Fair Trade Certified™ sewn, impacting and supporting 66,000 workers.

- They offer a "Worn Wear" program, which repairs consumers' outfits and reduces waste.

- Finally, 1% of Patagonia's sales is donated to the preservation and restoration of the natural environment. You may think 1% isn't much. But, since 1985, they've donated almost $90 million.

You can see that their every initiative is authentically related to Patagonia's values.

Maybe this all sounds like it would be better for a company to do something good rather than not doing anything, but that's not always the case. In fact, it can backfire and make some consumers resentful rather than appreciative.

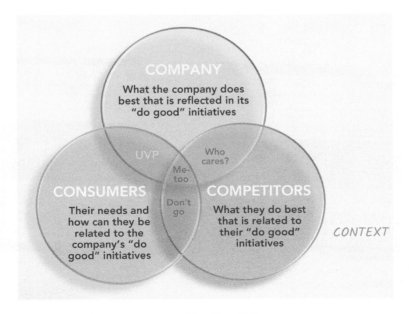

FIGURE 15.1 Unique Value Proposition – "Do Good" Strategy

For example, Gillette launched a campaign called "The Best Men Can Be." It builds on the company's original tag line "The Best A Man Can Get" and encouraged men to hold each other accountable, showing examples of positive behaviors, say the right thing, act the right way, etc. The brand seemed to be striving to be timely and do good.

The response from the consumers was mixed. While some consumers appreciated the support in this #MeToo environment, others viewed Gillette's message as inauthentic, and many men felt offended by the campaign. They viewed it as anti-male, treating all men as sexist, and denigrating traditional masculine qualities. In this one campaign, Gillette managed to alienate many of its core consumers.[6] With over 35 million viewers on YouTube, two thirds gave the commercial a "dislike."[7]

Doing good sounds like a terrific goal, but like most business decisions – we need to be smart about it. Gillette's messaging may not have fit their UVP very well. Does this mean Gillette shouldn't have launched this messaging? That is a strategic decision for the brand team. Note that with a little bit of marketing research, they'd have seen the consumers' reactions before launching the campaign. Then their decision, whether to go forward with this campaign or not, would have been made more fully informed. This story reinforces the notion of how important it is to stay in touch with your consumers, even when trying to do good!

Corporate Social Responsibility

Corporate social responsibility (CSR) incorporating social and environmental concerns into the business model and operation.

Many companies try to show leadership by striving for **corporate social responsibility (CSR)** as a guiding principle.[8] What is CSR and why do consumers care? CSR is an idea of self-governing by holding the company or brand accountable (hence "responsible") to others (hence "social") from consumers to employees to the public, or any such stakeholder. CSR can take on many forms, from basic philanthropy to fairness in labor practices to supporting volunteerism, and, of course, currently popular are efforts toward environmental conservation. Figure 15.2 shows examples of CSR initiatives.[9]

Public response to Gillett's messaging.

Levi's
Worker Well-Being Initiative

Starbucks
Coffee & Farmer Equity

Toyota
Prius: Hybrid Car

FIGURE 15.2 Examples of Companies' CSR Initiatives

Why do companies do this? A very pure reason that seems to be a driving factor in many such good-hearted companies is that they truly wish "to do the right thing." And, of course, some companies strive toward CSR proactively, whereas others are held to CSR standards driven by their customers, suppliers, or employees, sometimes in response to perceived poor corporate behavior (but fixing bad things is good too). Other companies and brands strive for CSR to please their consumers – consumers notice these engagements and many consumers appreciate it!

CSR efforts initially were thought to be just another cost of doing business, "Oh, that fussy customer segment, worried about the whales," and such. Yet a growing mantra in CSR circles is that an organization can "do well by doing good."[10] Could that be so, could it actually benefit a company to boldly engage in such beneficence? You bet! As an example, marketing researchers surveyed managers in over 4000 companies in 10 countries and showed that those companies that were more closely aligned with the UN's Sustainable Development Goals showed better corporate measures in terms of surveys and perceptions as well as indicators of financial performance and ROI.[11] Win–win! Some of the benefits of CSR are presented in Figure 15.3.[12]

Ultimately, CSR is about ethics. Thus, let us first take a look at ethics in general. Then we can be better informed and turn to the topic of ethics and marketing.

Ethics

Let's begin with a definition of **ethics**. Dictionary.com says that ethics are the "moral principles that govern a person's behavior or the conducting of an activity."[13] **Moral** is then defined as

Ethics
"moral principles that govern a person's behavior or the conducting of an activity."

Moral
being "concerned with the principles of right and wrong behavior and the goodness or badness of human character."

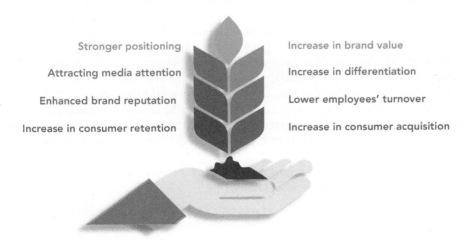

Stronger positioning

Attracting media attention

Enhanced brand reputation

Increase in consumer retention

Increase in brand value

Increase in differentiation

Lower employees' turnover

Increase in consumer acquisition

FIGURE 15.3 Benefits of CSR

being "concerned with the principles of right and wrong behavior and the goodness or badness of human character."[14] Honestly, you're an adult. You know what ethical behavior is. Do the right thing. It's not usually difficult to figure out what that is. It can be more challenging to do.

Strong, positive **ethics in business** and marketing means that you and your company need to do the right thing for all your constituents – your customers, your employees, society, the environment.[15] That's been our mantra throughout the book: do the right thing. Figure out what the right thing is, and then do it. Always.

Next, let's proceed with the philosophy of ethics. Basically, do we always behave in a certain manner that we think is right regardless of the outcomes, or do the ends essentially justify the means (all's well if everything turned out okay in the end)? There are several ways to ponder ethical dilemmas. Two of the primary litmus tests fall under the rubric of Deontological ethics or Teleological ethics.[16]

- **Deontological ethics** means a person or organization has a duty or responsibility to behave in an appropriate manner no matter what the results are (*deon* is Greek for duty).[17]
- **Teleological ethics** assess the consequences of a behavior (*teleo* is Greek for end or complete).[18]

Ethical perspectives have been debated by wise philosophers for millennia, so it should not be surprising that the reality is more complicated, but roughly speaking, these two perspectives focus on the process and outcomes of one's actions, respectively.

Deontological ethics. Immanuel Kant developed the deontological ethical perspective. The idea in this camp is that people (consumers, managers, anyone) should behave ethically and properly, without regard to any possible consequences. For example, one might hold to the principle that it is wrong to lie, even if your best friend is asking you "How do I look?" in clothing that looks ridiculous. Deontologists would say, don't lie, even if it hurts your friend's feelings.

A current manifestation of deontology is identifying people's "rights." Rights for people imply they have free will to make certain choices, and they can say or behave as they wish as long as doing so does not in turn violate rights of others. Other rights include to not be injured, to be told the truth, and to have privacy respected. It is easy to see the complexities, the shades of gray. Who decides on these rights? Are they universal? Can there be exceptions? What about conflicts – if you want to always tell the truth and you want to always be nice, especially to your friends, how do you reconcile these goals?

Teleological ethics. John Stuart Mill developed utilitarianism, a teleological view, also known as consequentialism. The idea in this perspective is to assess possible actions by the benefits and harms to others, then taking the action deemed that is most likely to provide the greatest good for the greatest number affected. To use the lying example, teleologists would say that perhaps it is acceptable to tell a little white fib to keep your friend's self-esteem intact – the process (the lie) is less important than the outcome (the friend's feelings). Who does it harm, really . . .?

The teleological perspective also has its ambiguities – who is to say what is a benefit or harm, and who will assess the severity? Would a financial harm be rendered as badly as a physical or emotional harm? How many people need to be affected before the number is too large to be acceptable? How do we know that our predictions about the various outcome scenarios are even close to accurate?

Deontology and teleology are the most pervasive ethical perspectives, but for a broader awareness, know that there are alternatives, including:

- A *fairness or justice approach*, based on Aristotle's saying, "Equals should be treated equally and unequals unequally." (Who defines "unequals"?)
- The *common-good approach* is rooted in writings from Plato to Cicero, and it says that what is good for an individual is good for the community. Thus, social systems should

Ethics in business
a company need to do the right thing for all its constituents.

Deontological ethics
a person or organization has a duty or responsibility to behave in an appropriate manner no matter what the results are.

Teleological ethics
an assessment of the consequences of a behavior.

One might say that ethics are ultimately simply about being good to one another. In the movie "Pay It Forward," Kevin Spacey plays Haley Joel Osment's teacher. He challenges his students to do something to make the world a better place. Osment's project is to do something nice for three strangers, and ask them, instead of reciprocating to him, to pay his good deed forward by also doing something nice to three strangers of their own.

benefit everybody, such as governmental taxes used to strengthen infrastructures or provide health care.

- The *virtue approach* is a form of deontology; it says that to be better people, we should behave in ways that reflect integrity, honesty, compassion, and such virtues. Faced with an ethical question, one would ask, "What would a good, virtuous person do?" Of course, there are many virtues, and it is difficult to be great at everything.

In your personal life or as a marketing manager on the job, the idea is that we should consider our problem-solving and decision-making within an ethical framework – what is the right thing to do, or which action will harm the least and benefit the most? With that basic overview, let's consider how ethics play out in marketing.

Ethics and Marketing

Let's get right to the heart of it: marketing sometimes takes a rap for bad behavior. Some critics are against the idea of marketing in principle; they say that attempts at persuasion in advertising is manipulation. Others point to specific instances, where they'll allow that marketing can be useful (trying to please the customer!) but that sometimes the particular tactics are disagreeable. There are the examples of targeting certain segments, such as advertising cigarettes or high-sugar-content drinks to children, trying to sell dicey financial investment opportunities to the elderly, creating and pushing products based on offensive stereotypes to minorities, and on and on.

Well, guess what, there are good marketers (see Figure 15.4) and bad marketers (just as there are good and bad accounting practices, good and bad financiers, etc.).[19] Marketing is a tool, and what makes marketing good or bad is the way the company uses it. **Ethical marketing** refers to the incorporation of ethics into marketing practices and processes.[20] When used right, marketing can enable companies to make a real change in society and for the environment. Let's see how to do marketing well, so marketing managers can be proud of their business activities.

The good news is that professional marketers take ethics very seriously. They know there are detractors, and to address such concerns, the American Marketing Association encourages

Ethical marketing the incorporation of ethics into marketing practices and processes.

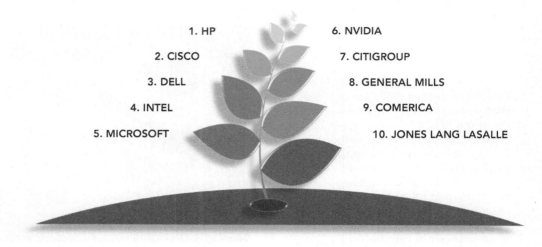

1. HP
2. CISCO
3. DELL
4. INTEL
5. MICROSOFT
6. NVIDIA
7. CITIGROUP
8. GENERAL MILLS
9. COMERICA
10. JONES LANG LASALLE

FIGURE 15.4 America's Most Responsible Companies, 2020. Adapted from Newsweek.

marketers to hold to very high standards. Its extensive *Codes of Conduct* guidelines begin with the exhortation that marketers must do no harm and avoid deception.[21] The guidelines encourage embracing ethical values of honesty (e.g. product claims), responsibility (e.g. toward kids, seniors, economically impoverished households, the environment), respect (e.g. appreciate diverse demographic groups), transparency (e.g. accepting constructive criticism from various constituencies), and being good citizens (e.g. in philanthropic activities).

That's a lot. Let's break it down by looking specifically at some things that marketing companies do and some things that consumers do.

Ethics and Marketing for Companies

Consumers and governments expect companies and marketers to behave ethically.[22] When large problems occur and persist, governmental regulations can provide more specific guidance. Three important regulatory bodies created to protect consumers are the FDA, FTC, and FCC. So let's look at each of these "alphabet" agencies.

The US Food and Drug Administration (FDA) oversees numerous concerns regarding consumer packaged goods.[23] When food labels claim that a food is low fat, just what qualifies as low fat? While fat or sugar content can be measured rather precisely, what about when a brand wants to claim it is "heart-healthy" – how does the brand substantiate that claim? The FDA protects consumers' health by monitoring the safety of food, drugs (from vaccines to vitamins and supplements to some cosmetics), and medical devices. For example, it's the FDA that protects youth from smoking ads.

The US Federal Trade Commission (FTC) promotes consumer protection in the realm of businesses and the marketplace.[24] For example, one FTC bureau focuses on busting up anticompetitive business practices, so that companies cannot collude and fix prices. Another arm of the FTC is dedicated to nailing telemarketing fraud, such as when consumers are asked for fees in advance of receiving supposed (nonexistent) contest winnings, or when consumers are called and asked to verify credit card numbers and other personal information, or when consumers are asked to donate to fake charities, which seems especially cruel given that the scam taps people's compassion

Whole Grain Versus Multigrain
If you are looking for a healthy bread and crackers option, look for the words whole grain or 100% whole wheat. It's not enough if it says multigrain or made with whole grain.

and desire to help others. Through the Children's Online Privacy Protection Act (COPPA), the FTC tries to discourage websites from being able to collect private information from children under 13.[25] The FTC also tells companies to disclose if they are using actors and not real doctors in pharma endorsement ads.

The US Federal Communications Commission (FCC) oversees communications across radio, TV, cable, satellite, internet services, and related developing technologies. The FCC supports competition and innovation and tries to keep media regulations current with all the new evolving uses and needs. On YouTube, search the (old) comedian George Carlin ranting against the seven dirty words you can't say on TV – that's due to the FCC. Currently, the FCC is trying to figure out how to limit robocalls soliciting telemarketing business.

Firms are required to disclose the use of actors as doctors in ads.

These agencies are busy, not necessarily because businesses are looking for creative ways around rules, but rather that some standards might be a bit ambiguous. For example, in advertising, companies can get busted for making false claims, but puffery or exaggeration is allowed, and the question is, where does one draw the line?

The agencies are also kept busy because the forms of problems keep morphing. A huge problem these days is how to protect consumers' privacy and identity. Companies have large databases that are very beneficial to their data-based or direct marketing efforts. For example, knowing a household's past purchases obviously helps the company in making better-suited product recommendations. But that efficacy presupposes that the firm has a great deal of information on each consumer or household, so the company needs to diligently protect its customers' data.

We might also contemplate the question as to just how far a company should take ethics responsibilities. Should Toyota make all its cars such that they cannot exceed 65 mph? Perhaps grocery stores shouldn't sell cigarettes, or gas stations that do should quadruple their price to discourage such "bad" behavior. Financial debt is a problem for many people, so maybe a person should be at least 21 years old (not just 18) to get a credit card (like voting). These actions might seem paternalistic. They are protective, but are they overstepping? Wouldn't they diminish consumers' free will? What values will a society embrace? The examples might have seemed far-fetched, but speed limits do not go to 100 mph – who decided that? Many drugs, if not alcohol or cigarettes, are illegal – why? Credit cards at 18 might be okay but driving at 12 years old is not – how did society come to each of these cutoffs?

Even if marketers are reluctant or hesitant to impose such restrictions, social marketing programs abound that encourage some behaviors and discourage others, without reaching the levels of laws and regulations. **Social marketing** refers to a systematic implementation of marketing strategies in order to influence and achieve specific consumers' behaviors that benefit society as a whole.[26] For example, many consumers say they care about the environment, and they wish to see that companies care as well. Figure 15.5 reenacts an experiment by marketing researchers[27] in which hotel customers were asked to reuse the room's towels to "help save the environment" or to "join your fellow guests in helping save the environment." The latter appeal was more successful – the social appeal made the proper behavioral norm clearer, and no one wants to be the person who doesn't do the right thing!

Social marketing
a systematic implementation of marketing strategies in order to influence and achieve specific consumers' behaviors that benefit society as a whole.

FIGURE 15.5 Which Is More Effective: A Notecard Appealing to the Individual or Social Norms? U.S Department of Agriculture / Public domain.

One environmental concern that worries some consumers is what happens after consumption, how are things disposed of, and it turns out that that angst is somewhat shared by retailers.[28] Marketing researchers interviewed store managers of both retailers and wholesalers and found that the managers expressed a great deal of anxiety about the food they had to throw away every day. Managers felt bad tossing food out when they knew that some people suffer from poverty. Employees also felt bad when they dumped food that they themselves could not have afforded to purchase. Stores are coming to the realization of providing options such as discounts (near expiration dates), upcycling (e.g. using older fruit to make juices), returning product to suppliers, or donating food to charities or plants for animal feed, providing alternatives to outright disposal.

The image on the right is part of the USDA campaign to alert consumers about the problem of wasted food and to educate them about how to minimize food waste.

Another challenge that companies face is how to "do good" consistently across their different brands and product lines. It seems reasonable to expect that a company claiming they are ethical and "doing good" would be trying to do so across all brands and product lines. However, that is not always the case. Take, for example, L'Oreal Paris, which has a portfolio of 39 brands, such as Lancôme, YSL, Maybelline, Urban Decay, and NYX.

On their website L'Oreal states that "Since March 2013, the Group has taken another decisive step: The Group no longer tests on animals, anywhere in the world, and does not delegate this task to others." But, they note a caveat – "An exception could be made if regulatory authorities required it for safety or regulatory purposes."[29] This exception refers to the Chinese market where animal testing is mandatory for foreign cosmetics. As such, some of its brands are not cruelty-free (i.e. Lancôme, YSL, Maybelline), while others are (i.e. Urban Decay and NYX). Many cruelty-free consumers who are aware of L'Oreal duality would not purchase any of its brands (even the cruelty-free ones) and will view L'Oreal's strategy as deceptive. Again, we see that firms must employ ethical practices in an authentic way to avoid negative responses from consumers.

The Global Mindset

The five UN eco-goals include: Clean water Responsible consumption and production Attending to climate concerns Ocean use Proper land use

Ethics and Marketing for Consumers

If they're given the chance, many, perhaps most, consumers will try to do the right thing.[30] Long ago, consumers learned that they can and should recycle – their paper, their glassware, their plastics, and most participate when bins are provided. Recycling requires the cooperation of the companies that manufacture the goods that are ultimately recycled, the recycling companies for pick-up and following processes, and the consumers for sorting their trash.

There are numerous ongoing efforts to help improve the world around us all. A currently dominant theme falls under the broad rubric of sustainability, or green marketing; for example, consumers have learned that it is good to purchase energy-efficient light bulbs, or hybrid and electric cars. Consumers have also learned that they can rise up and boycott companies that do things that seem objectionable, from mistreating workers, supporting questionable causes, or behaving in ways that discriminate against other groups of consumers.

Simplicity and the Sharing Economy

Sometimes consumers elect to engage in behaviors that are of their own choice and relatively independent of companies and the marketplace.[31] For example, the consumer movement that embraces voluntary simplicity is somewhat a backlash to materialism whereby consumers bought so many products for themselves and their families and households. Instead, the simplicity-value rejects the notion that more stuff leads to happiness, for oneself or for the planet. The values of voluntary simplicity are consistent with the rejection of ownership in some product categories in favor of leasing and the sharing economy, such as cars, apartments, and workspace.

Marketers can help consumers achieve their voluntary simplicity lifestyle goals as well. In a recent de-marketing program that got a lot of buzz, Patagonia ran an ad that said, "Don't buy this jacket if you don't need it" to increase consumer awareness regard textile waste. The company uses organically grown cotton to avoid pesticides, they pledge 1% of their sales to environmental preservation, and they have donated Black Friday sales to green organizations.

In a different kind of sharing, Figure 15.6 shows another way that marketers have learned how to communicate with consumers to encourage good behavior, in this case charitable giving. Turns out, not only are people not very good at math, math is too impersonal. If a marketer is trying to encourage giving to a pet shelter, show a pet! If a marketer is trying to help health benefits for newborns, show a baby! The pictures just grab consumers in ways the facts just don't.

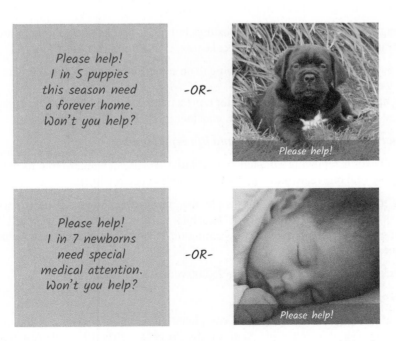

FIGURE 15.6 Which Is the More Effective Marketing Appeal: Impersonal Numbers or Overwhelming Cuteness?

"As consumers we have so much power to change the world by just being careful in what we buy."

Emma Watson, actress

Ethics and Consumer Segments

We know that smart marketers acknowledge that the marketplace is comprised of different segments of customers with different needs and lots of different opinions to satisfy them. For example, some customers are already avid brand fans, whereas others are more resistant. Companies need to think about consumer segments when they try to "do good" as well.[32]

We've talked about different kinds of consumers throughout the book, including cultures in Chapter 12. With respect to "doing good," one of the consumer segments that organizations are trying to serve better is the African American community. Yes, trying to "do good" can often be in response to consumer demand. The point here is to acknowledge *all* people, of all types, as being equally worthy of recognition, respect, and support. Consider these examples intended to support the *African American community*:

- @LEGO_Group posted "We stand with the Black community against racism and inequality. There is much to do. We will donate $4 million to organizations dedicated to supporting Black children and educating all children about racial equality."[33]

- Proctor & Gamble's Emmy-winning ad called "The Talk" depicts African American moms talking to their kids about racism, for example, one says, "There are some people who think you don't deserve the same privileges just because of what you look like. It's not fair. It's not."[34]

- In a one-minute ad posted on YouTube, Nike morphed its familiar "Just do it" brand slogan into "For once, don't do it. Don't pretend there's not a problem in America. Don't turn your back on racism. Don't accept innocent lives being taken from us. Don't make any more excuses. Don't think this doesn't affect you. Don't sit back and be silent. Don't think you can't be part of the change. Let's all be part of the change."[35]

- And changes arise not just in website postings but, for example, in changing product packaging and imagery (e.g. Aunt Jemima pancake mix, Uncle Ben's rice, etc.).

How inspirational! Those brands are trying to do something good, and pushing us all to think that way as well.

Other communities are also seeking better representation, as our society strives toward greater inclusion and enlightenment. For example, consider this variety of movements:

- *Consumer segments – demographic and life experiences:*

  - Land O'Lakes is removing a depiction of a Native American woman from its dairy products packaging. (No one really knows why it was there to begin with!)

  - Trying to be more sensitive to all people also motivates changes in sports team mascots, such as changing the Washington Redskins to the Washington Football Team, the Washington Bullets (too violent!) to Washington Wizards, or the Cleveland Indians to TBD, we'll see.

  - Starbucks launched a program to hire 25,000 veterans by 2025.[36]

- *Young people:*

  - SurveyMonkey gives $0.50 for each completed survey to a charity of the survey taker's choice; they've donated over $1m to the Boys & Girls Club of America and the Humane Society.

- Netflix is offering extended paid parental leave, to help get their employees' kiddos off to a good start in life![37]

- *People with challenges:*

  - Some companies are also trying to make versions of their products more accessible to consumers who have physical challenges with the current versions of the products, such as Microsoft creating touchpads as an alternative video game controller.

  - Procter & Gamble is bottling its Herbal Essence hair care in bottle with tactile indentations to help the visually impaired.

  - Tommy Hilfiger provides clothing with easier access, from one-handed zip-ups to magnetic closures.[38]

- *Environment:*

  - Johnson & Johnson has been working to transfer more energy consumption to renewables, especially wind, and to provide safe water to global communities.

  - The Ford Motor Company is expanding in a big way into electric vehicles.

- *Environment and people:*

  - Ben & Jerry's has long been recognized for its do-good initiatives, from opposing cow hormones (partly due to the economic impact on family farming), and their Foundation encourages their employees to give back and participate in social justice programs. B&J gives 7.5% of its pretax profits to charities.[39]

  - Levi Strauss is reducing the water used in manufacturing their blue jeans and works to support people living with HIV/AIDS.

  - Google is also noteworthy for transferring its energy consumption to renewables, and its CEO speaks up against anti-Muslim rhetoric.

- Finally, a class of consumer behavior that is tricky is various consumer addictions. An addiction can involve drugs or alcohol or gambling or shopping and extending credit card debt, etc. The ethics questions for the company are challenging because companies don't want to go too far and reduce the freedoms of nonaddicted consumers to have access to their goods and services. Yet the companies recognize that making certain products available to the marketplace contributes to some problematic behavior.

Do the Right Thing!

Businesses serve many consumer segments. Can "doing the right thing" ever cause conflict among the different needs of the different consumer groups? For example, some products that are trying to do the right thing by the environment are faced with new challenges in that they might need to modify their current supply chain. Sometimes doing so means the new method is more expensive. Companies almost always pass along those additional charges. So, now the company is offering a product that environmentally aware consumers may wish to embrace, only to find that the product is now priced well beyond their reach. Was this a good action? Was this a good outcome? What could be done better?

A "Dark Side" or "Doing Bad"?

The ideas just mentioned, about consumer addictive behaviors, take us down an interesting inquiry. Are companies responsible for consumer behavior that mishandles their products? For example, some beer consumption is acceptable and encouraged, but alcoholism is not good for anyone. Sometimes bad consumer behavior might be attributed to the consumer. It's a matter of free will and the consumer's choices. Even so, some companies and brands have tried to help consumers by messaging them to "drink responsibly," or "don't drink and drive," or "choose a designated driver," and so on.

Yet of course there have been exceptions, such as when companies willingly behave in a questionable manner. We've discussed brands that make false or exaggerated claims, whether in false advertising (e.g. Dannon's Activia having "special" bacteria), or false packaging (e.g. Kellogg's Rice Krispies supposedly boosting your immune system or Kellogg's Mini-Wheats supposedly could make you smarter), or in slogans even if the slogan was not intended to be literal (e.g. Red Bull's "RB gives you wings"). Today's concerns often revolve around data privacy and security; consumers trust companies enough to provide quite a bit of personal information, and most don't read the data privacy and usage agreements, and many consumers really don't want their data sold to a company's partners.

Is CSR and Doing Good Actually Valued by Consumers?

Finally, let's be sure we're being practical (we're a business, after all).[40] One question a brand team will frequently raise is whether consumers have willingness to pay more for "do-good" products and an organization's CSR efforts. When surveyed or interviewed, the majority of consumers say yes, they will pay more and choose brands that are aligned with their values. But do they? See the responses in Figure 15.7.

Consumers buying a $4.00 cup of coffee at Starbucks might indeed pay $5.00 instead if told the extra $1 goes to support a worthy cause. Take that 25% markup to more expensive items, and car dealerships don't tend to see consumers buying a $40,000 car paying $50,000 for it with the promise that the extra $10k goes to a worthy cause. The consumer's heart might wish to support the causes, but the difference between $1 and $10,000 reduces participation.

And on this issue of willingness to pay, not surprisingly there are segment differences. For example, while the news seems to tell us that younger consumers are the drivers of many social justice and environmental issues, this figure indicates that older consumers are those who do so (but be patient, younger consumers simply don't control as much money, yet!)

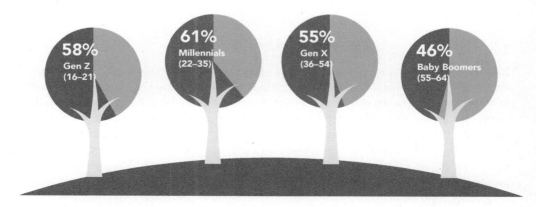

FIGURE 15.7 Percentage of Consumers Who Will Pay More for Eco-friendly Products

As you can see, brands, marketers, and companies are starting to be more enlightened and inclusive. It's a good start that hopefully will lead to more "doing good" and even "doing *great*!" Nevertheless, it is clear that marketing communication not only reflects society trends, it can actually enhance them and even lead them in the right direction. With your help, of course. You can be part of these initiatives in supporting certain brands, and by being a socially aware marketer, trying to do good for our society, all our people, and our environment!

SUMMARY

This chapter discussed CSR and how consumer behavior is affected by ethical concerns. Deontological and teleological ethics are frameworks within which marketing managers can decide whether their company is doing the right thing, on behalf of its customers and the world. Try to use one or both of these frameworks as a lens through which to view and evaluate your brand team's proposals. Consumers and governments should hold companies to high ethical standards, and there are similar concerns for ethical behaviors by consumers themselves.

KEY TERMS

Corporate social responsibility (CSR)
Ethics
Moral

Ethics in business
Deontological ethics
Teleological ethics

Ethical marketing
Social marketing

EXERCISES

1. In the sense of deontological ethics, write down a virtue that you try to live by. Give an example of when being true to that guiding principle was actually difficult to do. Share your story with your class teammate. After you exchange virtues and stories, try to challenge each other in describing circumstances where you could imagine an exception to the rule, or should there never be an exception to the rule?

2. With a friend in class, take a teleological ethics perspective and imagine you're both on a new product development team at a pharmaceutical company. Your decision is whether to recommend that the company launch a new drug. The company's research has shown that the drug could boost health outcomes in some patients but it also has serious side effects for some others. How big and what kind of health benefit would be "worth it"? How serious and extensive would the side effects have to be before it was not worth it? (In evaluating "doing as much good and as little harm as possible," does there have to be zero tolerance for harm?) Does it matter who is helped or who is hurt? Who gets the meds, when and why?

3. What are the companies and brands that you're proud to purchase because, not only do you like their stuff, but you know they try to "do good" (for people, the environment, etc.)? What brands would you not buy because they are known to "do bad"? Think about two or three brands that are your favorites but they don't really have a reputation for "doing good" (they don't "do bad" either). What could each of these brands do to enhance their public perception of corporate social responsibility?

4. Most companies hold the belief that "doing good" is good for business. Search the website of your favorite brand for all the social responsibility activities they are involved in. Were you aware of these activities? Are they a factor in your decision to purchase a product from this company? Would you recommend the company to continue their social responsibility initiatives?

5. In pairs or small groups, list five companies. For each company, suggest three social responsibility initiatives that the company should get involve in based on its UVP – "do good" strategy (Figure 15.1). Explain your recommendations.

6. Find an ad or a commercial that you find to be unethical. What makes it unethical in your view? How should the company address this issue?

ENDNOTES

1. https://www.toms.com/us/impact-report.html.2. https://www.warbyparker.com/buy-a-pair-give-a-pair.

3. https://bombas.com/pages/giving-back#:~:text=Bombas%20was%20founded%20on%20the,One%20purchased%20%3D%20one%20donated.

4. W. MacAskill, *Doing Good Better: How Effective Altruism Can Help You Help Others, Do Work That Matters, and Make Smarter Choices About Giving Back* (New York: Avery, 2016).

5. https://www.patagonia.com/activism.

6. https://www.bbc.com/news/newsbeat-46874617.

7. https://www.youtube.com/watch?v=koPmuEyP3a0.

8. J. Moon, *Corporate Social Responsibility: A Very Short Introduction* (Oxford University Press, 2015).

9. Google with open copyrights: Worker well-being initiatives Levi's: https://www.google.com/search?q=Worker+Well-Being+Initiative+levis&source=lnms&tbm=isch&sa=X&ved=2ahUKEwjQ2ozSifznAhXnQ98KHYlzDTEQ_AUoA3oECAwQBQ&biw=1280&bih=579#imgrc=jRnqFmxGr0OlCM; Coffee Farm: https://www.google.com/search?as_st=y&tbm=isch&hl=en&as_q=coffee+farm&as_epq=&as_oq=&as_eq=&cr=&as_sitesearch=&safe=images&tbs=sur:fmc#imgrc=Zv3sNj-ENv2CsM; Hybrid, Toyota: https://www.google.com/search?as_st=y&tbm=isch&hl=en&as_q=hybrid+car&as_epq=&as_oq=&as_eq=&cr=&as_sitesearch=&safe=images&tbs=sur:fmc#imgrc=dKRrcMmWUNWHlM.

10. T. Usnik, *The Caring Economy: How to Win with Corporate Social Responsibility (CSR)* (Amazon Kindle, 2018).

11. G. Hult, et al., "A Ten Country-Company Study of Sustainability and Product-Market Performance: Influence of Doing Good, Warm Glow, and Price Fairness," *Journal of Macromarketing* 38, no. 3 (2018): 242–61.

12. https://www.forbes.com/sites/csr/2012/02/21/six-reasons-companies-should-embrace-csr/?sh=106b4a513495.

13. https://www.dictionary.com/browse/ethics.

14. https://www.dictionary.com/browse/moral#.

15. J. J. Quinn, "Personal Ethics and Business Ethics: The Ethical Attitudes of Owner/Managers of Small Business," *Journal of Business Ethics* 16, no. 2 (1997): 119–27.

16. B. MacKinnon, *Ethics: Theory and Contemporary Issues*, 9th ed. (Cengage, 2017).

17. S. Chakrabarty and A. E. Bass, "Comparing Virtue, Consequentialist, and Deontological Ethics-based Corporate Social Responsibility: Mitigating Microfinance Risk in Institutional Voids," *Journal of Business Ethics* 126, no. 3 (2015): 487–512.

18. K. H. Brunk, "Exploring Origins of Ethical Company/Brand Perceptions—A Consumer Perspective of Corporate Ethics," *Journal of Business Research* 63, no. 3 (2010): 255–62.

19. https://www.newsweek.com/americas-most-responsible-companies-2020.

20. G. R. Laczniak and P. E. Murphy, "Fostering Ethical Marketing Decisions," *Journal of Business Ethics* 10, no. 4 (1991): 259–71.

21. https://www.ama.org/codes-of-conduct.

22. O. C. Ferrell and J. Fraedrich, *Business Ethics: Ethical Decision Making & Cases*, 12th ed. (Cengage, 2018).

23. https://www.fda.gov/consumers/consumer-updates/it-really-fda-approved.

24. https://www.ftc.gov/about-ftc/what-we-do.

25. https://www.ftc.gov/enforcement/rules/rulemaking-regulatory-reform-proceedings/childrens-online-privacy-protection-rule.

26. A. R. Andreasen, ed., *Social Marketing in the 21st Century* (Sage, 2006).

27. N. J. Goldstein, R. B. Cialdini, and V. Griskevicius, "A Room with a Viewpoint: Using Social Norms to Motivate Environmental Conservation in Hotels," *Journal of Consumer Research* 35, no. 3 (2008): 472–82; hotel bathroom pic via Google with extended rights: https://www.google.com/search?as_st=y&tbm=isch&hl=en&as_q=hotel+bathroom&as_epq=&as_oq=&as_eq=&cr=&as_sitesearch=&safe=images&tbs=sur:fmc#imgrc=79jTQad1mqcASM.

28. V. Gruber, C. Holweg, and C. Teller, "What a Waste! Exploring the Human Reality of Food Waste from the Store Manager's Perspective," *Journal of Public Policy & Marketing* 35, no. 1 (2016): 3–25.

29. https://inside-our-products.loreal.com/our-approach/our-alternative-methods-animal-testing.

30. O. M. Freestone and P. J. McGoldrick, "Motivations of the Ethical Consumer," *Journal of Business Ethics* 79 (2008): 445–67; T. Newholm and D. Shaw, "Studying the Ethical Consumer: A Review of Research," *Journal of Consumer Behaviour* 6, no. 5 (2007): 253–70.

31. A. Stephany, *The Business of Sharing: Making It in the New Sharing Economy* (Springer, 2015).

32. F. S. McIntyre, J. L. Thomas, Jr., and F. W. Gilbert, "Consumer Segments and Perceptions of Retail Ethics," *Journal of Marketing Theory and Practice* 7, no. 2 (1999, 2015): 43–53; A. Nairn and P. Berthon, "Creating the Customer: The Influence of Advertising on Consumer Market Segments—Evidence and Ethics," *Journal of Business Ethics* 42 (2003): 83–100.

33. https://twitter.com/LEGO_Group/status/1268216876498399237?ref_src=twsrc%5Etfw%7Ctwcamp%5Etweetembed%7Ctwterm%5E1268216876498399237%7Ctwgr%5E%7Ctwcon%5Es1_&ref_url=https%3A%2F%2Fwww.latestly.com%2Fsocial-viral%2Flego-donates-4-million-to-support-education-on-racial-equality-black-children-pulls-advertising-for-police-related-toys-netizens-praise-companys-decision-1800744.html.

34. https://www.youtube.com/watch?v=ovY6yjTe1LE&t=1s.

35. https://www.cnn.com/2020/05/30/business/nike-dont-do-it-message-trnd/index.html.

36. https://www.foxbusiness.com/markets/starbucks-military-veteran-spouse-hiring.

37. https://money.cnn.com/2015/08/04/technology/netflix-parental-leave.

38. https://usa.tommy.com/en/tommy-adaptive.

39. https://www.benjerry.com/about-us/sear-reports/2019-sear-report.

40. A. B. Thompson, *Do Good: Embracing Brand Citizenship to Fuel Both Purpose and Profit* (New York: AMACOM, 2017).

CREDITS

https://luissfuturemakers.wordpress.com/2019/03/22/gillette-the-best-man-can-be-flop-or-top-disasters-could-arise-from-the-noblest-intentions

https://www.google.com/search?as_st=y&tbm=isch&hl=en&as_q=coffee+farm&as_epq=&as_oq=&as_eq=&cr=&as_sitesearch=&safe=images&tbs=sur:fmc#imgrc=Zv3sNj-ENv2CsM

https://www.google.com/search?as_st=y&tbm=isch&hl=en&as_q=hybrid+car&as_epq=&as_oq=&as_eq=&cr=&as_sitesearch=&safe=images&tbs=sur:fmc#imgrc=dKRrcMmWUNWHlM

https://www.google.com/search?q=Worker+Well-Being+Initiative+levis&source=lnms&tbm=isch&sa=X&ved=2ahUKEwjQ2ozSifznAhXnQ98KHYlzDTEQ_AUoA3oECAwQBQ&biw=1280&bih=579#imgrc=jRnqFmxGr0OlCM

https://www.newsweek.com/americas-most-responsible-companies-2020

https://www.shutterstock.com/image-photo/pay-forward-concept-illustrated-on-white-68373865

https://www.shutterstock.com/image-photo/slices-finest-organic-bread-decorated-natural-49768897 https://www.multivu.com/players/English/8163851-cigna-americas-tv-doctors-go-know-take-control

https://www.google.com/search?as_st=y&tbm=isch&hl=en&as_q=hotel+bathroom&as_epq=&as_oq=&as_eq=&cr=&as_sitesearch=&safe=images&tbs=sur:fmc#imgrc=79jTQad1mqcASM

https://universe.byu.edu/2017/11/27/confusion-abounds-over-how-to-make-food-donations-in-utah-1

https://www.shutterstock.com/image-photo/brussels-belgium-15-may-2018-un-1091235845

https://www.google.com/search?q=baby&tbm=isch&ved=2ahUKEwjwoIbq6pfmAhUMTFMKHZ5YBo0Q2-cCegQIABAA&oq=baby&gs_l=img.3..0i13l2j0l2j0i131j0i3j0i131j0l2j0i131.59080.60478..60709...1.0..1.304.601.6j3-1......0....1..gws-wiz-img.....0..0i10.td3AuUXLi3o&ei=MXjlXbDEH4yYzQKesZnoCA&safe=images&tbs=sur%3Afmc&hl=en#imgrc=r33I4s1VVJn_UM

Figure 15.2: Levi Strauss & Co.; jbntt/Pixabay; Toyota Motor Corporation/Wikimedia Commons/CC BY 2.0

Figure 15.5: Nicor/Wikimedia Commons/CC BY-SA 3.0

Figure 15.6: Petr Kratochvil/CC0 1.0

Image p. 298: Procter & Gamble

Image p. 301: marekuliasz/Shutterstock

Image p. 303: Smileus/Shutterstock; Cigna

Image p. 305: Anne Taylor

Image p. 306: Alexandros Michailidis/Shutterstock

THEORY GLOSSARY

A

Activities, Interests, Opinions (AIO) model a helpful tool in lifestyle psychographic segmentation.

Apostle model identifies different types of consumer loyalty.

B

Balance theory looks at connections between a consumer and other consumers and brands to see if the links are consistent.

Behavioral learning theories see learning as a behavioral response to external events or cues.

Big five theory focuses on five personality traits that combine to create the individual's unique personality.

Brand personality archetype connects the brand value proposition to consumers' basic desires, motivations, and needs.

Brand personality framework includes five brand personalities: excitement, sincerity, ruggedness, competence, and sophistication.

C

Categorization theory storing information in the memory by categorizing it.

Classical conditioning pairing two independent stimuli to each other to generate a new learned response.

Cognitive appraisal theory posits that all emotions are generated from a cognitive evaluation process.

Cognitive dissonance theory studies situations in which consumers question whether their buying decision is the right one.

Cognitive learning theories focus on internal mental processes as a central part of learning.

Cognitive processing systems include system 1 and system 2 processing styles.

Compromise effect a situation in which consumers will be more likely to choose a middle option of a selection set and avoid choosing extreme options.

Consumer decision-making process reflects the stages that consumers go through before, during, and after they purchase a product or service.

Customer lifetime value (CLV) the total revenue that a business can expect a single customer to generate over the entirety of his or her relationship with the business.

D

Diffusion of innovation the rate at which consumers adopt innovations and their spread within the market over time.

E

Elaboration likelihood model   proposes two approaches to persuade people or change their attitude: the central route and the peripheral route.

Extended-self theory   posits that our possessions are a direct extension of our self-identity.

F

Four stages of memory   attention, encoding, storage, and retrieval.

Framing effect   the interpretation of information, which depends in part on how it is presented.

Functional theory of attitudes   posits that attitudes and beliefs are significant to various psychological functions.

H

Heuristics   simplifying strategies that provide shortcuts in decision-making.

Hofstede's six cultural dimensions   can be used to characterize the cultural nature of countries.

Humanistic perspective   emphasizes that individuals have free will and that people are basically good and have a need to live to their full potential.

I

Involvement theory   posits that we will engage in less information processing in low-involvement situations and extensive information processing in high-involvement situations.

M

Marketing mix   a set of strategies that companies use to sell products or services to their target customers, including product, price, place, and promotion strategies.

Marketing mix gap   how different is the marketing mix in the new country versus the home country of the company.

Marketing research process   a systematic multistage effort of collecting, analyzing, and interpreting information about the consumers, the market, a product, or any other marketing-related element.

Maslow's hierarchy of needs   Maslow's theory of human motivation.

Maslow's elaborated hierarchy of needs   includes three additional levels to the original hierarchy: cognitive needs, aesthetic needs, and transcendence needs.

McClelland's needs theory   a trio theory of needs that include a need for achievement, a need for affiliation, and a need for power.

Multi-attribute theory   recognizes that there are many features of a brand, and consumers might like some of those attributes more than others.

O

Operant conditioning   alteration of a behavior based on rewards or punishments.

P

PAD emotional state model   asserts that all emotional responses have three dimensions: pleasure, arousal, or dominance.

Persuasion knowledge model   acknowledges that people use their persuasion knowledge to deal with persuasion attempts.

PESTEL model   a strategic framework used to gain a macro picture of an industry environment.

Prospect theory   examines people's perceptions of their prospects or expected outcomes.

Psychoanalytic perspective   highlights the important role of early childhood experiences and the influence of the unconscious mind and sexual instincts in the formation of personality.

S

Segmentation, targeting, and positioning (STP)   a three-step process that enables companies to be more effective and efficient in delivering their value through their offerings.

Structure of self-concept   consists of the individual self, the relational self, and the collective self.

T

Theory of planned behavior   predicts a person's intention to engage in a specific behavior.

Theory of reasoned action   suggests that what determines people's intention to perform a behavior is what drives their behavior, which is a function of a person's attitude toward the behavior.

Tricomponent attitude model   predict intentions of engaging in the behavior, which in turn will lead to our actual behavior.

U

Unique value proposition   a statement that articulates the promise the company makes to its customers to be delivered in a unique and differentiated way.

KEYWORD GLOSSARY

A

A/B testing   a type of an experiment in which participants are exposed to one of two conditions.

Absolute threshold   the lowest level of stimulus intensity required from us to experience a sensation.

Acculturation   adoption of the values of a different culture.

Acquired needs   psychological in nature.

Activities, Interests, and Opinions (AIO) model   a helpful tool in lifestyle psychographic segmentation.

Actual personal self   the benchmark by which we assess what we have achieved so far.

Actual social self   how we think others perceive us.

Actual state   the state that consumers are currently experiencing.

Adaptation   changing some or all parts of the marketing mix to better address local needs.

Adoption of innovation   reflects the level of receptiveness consumers have to new ideas, behaviors, or products.

Advertising wearout   a decline in the effectiveness of the message due to repetition overload.

Aesthetic needs   the human need for beauty and aesthetically pleasing imagery, music, objects, and experiences.

Affective component of attitude   reflects feelings, emotions, and sentiments toward an object.

Affirmative action   a set of policies and practices within a government or organization seeking to increase the representation of particular groups based on their gender, race, sexuality, creed, or nationality in areas in which they are underrepresented, such as education and employment.

Amplified word-of-mouth   consumption-related communication that is strategically solicited and promoted by companies as part of a planned marketing effort.

Anchor and adjust   early information that consumers see helps to set the context against which new information is compared.

Apostle model   identifies different types of consumer loyalty.

Aspirational groups   groups that consumers identify with and would like to be associated with.

Attention   the process by which we choose which information we will devote resources to process it and which information we will screen out.

Attitudes   overall evaluations, positive or negative, of a given object, such as a brand, or another person.

Awareness set   a set of brands that consumers are familiar with and are able to recall or recognize.

B

B2B   business to business.

B2C   business to consumer.

Balance theory   looks at connections between a consumer and other consumers and brands to see if the links are consistent.

Basic emotions   those that we all experience such as happiness, sadness, disgust, fear, surprise, and anger.

Behavioral component of attitude   behaviors toward an object.

Behavioral influence purchases   purchases that are influenced by others or by environmental cues.

Behavioral learning theories   see learning as a behavioral response to external events or cues.

Behavioral segmentation   categorizing consumers based on behavioral patterns of interaction with the company or the brand.

Beliefs   convictions that are formed based on previous experiences and may not necessarily be based on logic or fact.

Benefit   a favorable outcome that is the result of a feature. It is closely related to the value the product provides the consumers.

Big data   large, hard-to-manage volumes of structured or unstructured data.

Big five theory   focuses on five personality traits which in different variation of intensity create the individual's unique personality.

Brand communities   communities that are formed based on the emotional attachment to a brand.

Brand extension   leveraging the familiarity and reputation of an existing brand when incorporating a new product.

Brand personality   a set of human characteristics and traits that are associated with a specific brand.

Brand personality archetype   connects the brand value proposition to consumers' basic desires, motivations, and needs.

Brand personality framework   includes five brand personalities: excitement, sincerity, ruggedness, competence, and sophistication.

Buyers   see "Consumers".

Buyer's remorse   see "Regret".

Buzz   an amplification of the original marketing message by consumers.

C

Cash back   offers customers the option to earn money back from their purchases, normally in the form of a percentage of their total purchases during a certain period.

Categorization theory   storing information in the memory by categorizing it.

Causal research   a research method in which the marketer aims to identify a cause-and-effect relationship between two variables by manipulating the independent variable.

Certainty and uncertainty   being sure (or unsure) about an outcome.

Chasm   the strategic challenge companies face when trying to move from a small segment of the market (innovators and early adopters) to the mainstream and broader segments of the market.

Choice set   often includes two or three best brand options.

Churn rate   reflects the percentage of consumers that stop purchasing products or services from a business during a certain period.

Classical conditioning   pairing two independent stimuli to each other to generate a new learned response.

Click-through rate (CTR)   the percentage of consumers who see a link contained in their email.

Cognitive appraisal theory   posits that all emotions are generated from a cognitive evaluation process.

Cognitive bias a systematic error in the way we think and process information when making a decision.

Cognitive component of attitude thoughts and beliefs about an object based on information or direct experience.

Cognitive dissonance a situation in which consumers question whether their buying decision is the right one.

Cognitive learning theories focus on internal mental processes as a central part of learning.

Cognitive needs reflect the desire to satisfy our curiosity by increasing our intelligence, knowledge, and understanding of the world around us.

Collective self the part of our self-concept that reflects our membership in various social groups.

Compensatory decision rule choosing the brand option that gets the highest score.

Competitor-based positioning positioning that makes an implicit or explicit reference to the company's competitors.

Complaints expressions of dissatisfaction with a product or service made to the provider of that product or service.

Compromise effect a situation in which consumers will be more likely to choose a middle option of a selection set and avoid choosing extreme options.

Compulsive shopping behavior an excessive preoccupation with shopping that has an adverse effect on their lives.

Conditioned stimulus a previously neutral stimulus that produces the same behavior as unconditioned stimulus, after repeated association with it.

Conjoint analysis a technique that allows a marketer to test tradeoffs that consumers are willing to make when considering brand choices.

Conjunctive rule choosing a product only if its attributes are equal to or exceed the minimum cutoff level of all criteria.

Consumer behavior how buyers (individuals, groups, or organizations) make decisions prior to, during, and after acquiring a product (goods, services, experiences, etc.) to satisfy their needs, wants, and demands.

Consumer doppelganger mimicking a person's consumption behavior if we regard him/her as expert in this domain.

Consumer insights the knowledge derived by studying consumers' behavior. It builds on the data gathered via marketing research, which is analyzed and interpreted in a way that guides companies' strategic decisions.

Consumer loyalty reflects consumers' attitudes and behaviors that indicate they real like and are loyal to a product, service, brand, or business.

Consumers those who acquire products to satisfy their needs.

Consumers' decision-making process reflects the stages that consumers go through before, during, and after they purchase a product or service.

Consumers' involvement the extent to which a product or purchase is relevant and of interest to the individual consumer.

Context dependence context in which learning occurs.

Core values the most central things consumers care about.

Corporate social responsibility (CSR) incorporating social and environmental concerns into the business model and operation.

Cross-tabs tables of numbers displayed to examine the relationship between rows and columns.

Cultural distance the gap or the extent of differences in values and communication styles between cultures.

Culture a set of values, beliefs, and traditions that are held by a specific social group and handed down from generation to generation.

Culture-based positioning　positioning that highlights the country of origin of the product or brand or relating it to a cultural symbol that enhances its value.

Customer acquisition cost (CAC)　the cost of acquiring a single consumer.

Customer benefit-based positioning　positioning that is based on the product's features or benefits, especially if they are unique and differentiated.

Customer lifetime value (CLV)　the total revenue that a business can expect a single customer to generate over the entirety of his or her relationship with the business.

Customer Satisfaction Score (CSAT)　rates consumers' level of satisfaction on a scale of 1 to 3, 1 to 5, or 1 to 7, ranging from "not satisfied at all" to "completely satisfied," or use a 5-star rating system.

Customer-centric companies　companies with a marketing orientation view.

D

Database marketing　using CRM data to reach out consumers.

Decoy effect　a situation in which consumers are more likely to change their preference between two options when a third option is presented to them that makes one of the options more attractive.

Defectors　unsatisfied consumers who will never purchase from the business again but still have negative opinions about it.

Deficiency needs　arise when needs in levels 1–4 are not fulfilled.

Demand　an economic principle reflecting consumers' willingness and ability to pay a certain price for the desired product.

Demographic segmentation　dividing the market based on the demographic characteristics of the consumer.

Demographic segmentation (global)　dividing the market based on the demographic characteristics of the consumers in different countries.

Deontological ethics　a person or organization has a duty or responsibility to behave in an appropriate manner no matter what the results are.

Dependent variable　the measured response.

Descriptive research　a research method that take the insights drawn from the exploratory phase and test them out on a larger, random, more representative sample of consumers.

Desire for conformity　a motivation for consumers to fit in with others.

Desire for uniqueness　motivation to stand out as special, and not just one in the crowd.

Desired state　a future state consumers want to achieve, which will motivate them to seek a product that will satisfy their need or solve their problem.

Detractors (with a rating of 0 to 6)　the least valuable consumers for a business who may damage the reputation of the business by spreading negative word-of-mouth or writing negative reviews.

Differential threshold　the minimum level of difference between two stimuli that consumers can detect at least half of the time.

Diffusion of innovation　the rate at which consumers adopt innovations and their spread within the market over time.

Diminishing marginal utility　the increase in value or utility is rather small after the initial boost.

Direct marketing　see "Database marketing".

Discount programs　offer consumers a fixed discount on the retail price of any given item.

Disjunctive rule　choosing a product with the attribute that is equal to or exceed the minimum cutoff level of at least one criterion.

Disposal of products　reflects the process of getting rid of unwanted or used products, or any waste that is associated with them (e.g. their packaging).

Dissatisfaction   see "Satisfaction".

Dissociative groups   groups with whom consumers do not share similar opinions, values, or attitudes.

E

Early adopters   consumers who will typically wait for a more finalized and reliable version of the product before purchasing it.

Early majority   consumers who want to make sure that if they spend their money on a product, it will function properly.

Earned media   publicity achieved through promotional efforts other than paid media.

Effective frequency   the number of times a message needs to be repeated in order to generate the desired behavior from consumers.

Ego   governs personality in a more rational way.

Ego-defensive function of attitude   helps consumers protect themselves from feeling threatened, or from experiencing feelings of low self-esteem or insecurity.

Elaboration likelihood model   proposes two approaches to persuade people or change their attitude: the central route and the peripheral route.

Elimination-by-aspects rule   choosing a product based on ranked criteria as well as a cutoff level.

Email marketing   promotional information delivered by email to consumers.

Emotion   an affective response to an external stimulus.

Emotional advertising   a purposeful use of images and slogans in marketing messages to evoke consumers' emotions in a way that will make them notice, remember, share, and buy the products or services.

Emotional branding   a marketing practice of forming meaningful connections between brands and consumers by arousing their emotions.

Encoding   involves how consumers receive the information, start thinking about it, and possibly storing it in memory.

Enculturation   understanding and adoption of values.

Endowment effect   seeing more value in things that we own.

Engagement rate   the percentage of consumers who use the program out of the total number of consumers a business has.

Esteem needs   our desire to feel good about who we are. We want to feel self-confident and be valued by others.

Ethical marketing   the incorporation of ethics into marketing practices and processes.

Ethics   moral principles that govern a person's behavior or the conducting of an activity.

Ethics in business   a company need to do the right thing for all its constituents.

Ethnic group   a grouping of people who identify with each other on the basis of shared attributes that distinguish them from other groups.

Ethnography   a combination of interviews and observations to study a specific phenomenon.

Evaluation of alternatives   consumers' assessment of all product and brand options in terms of their ability to deliver the benefits that they are looking for.

Evoke set   a set of specific brands that consumers are familiar with and will consider purchasing.

Exchange   the process by which buyers and sellers negotiate over something of value (i.e. a product).

Experiential purchases   purchases that are hedonically motivated; they operate heavily on emotions.

Experiment   a research method that provides sights into cause-and-effect by demonstrating what response occurs when a particular variable is manipulated.

Explicit and implicit attitudes   the way internal drives and motivations interact with external stimuli to form attitudes.

Exploratory research methods   those used when the marketing question is still being formed.

Extended self   our possessions are a direct extension of our self-identity.

Extensive problem-solving   a situation where consumers have little or no information about or experience with the product or brand options that can solve their problem.

External factors   factors such as the consumers' sociocultural environment, their family and friends, their reference groups, and the people they interact with online and offline.

External search   acquiring information that is beyond consumers' direct experience with a product or brand.

Extraversion attitudes   attitudes that are predominantly motivated by external factors.

F

Familiarity   feelings of knowing something.

Feature   a characteristic of a brand or product that is related to its performance.

Figure-ground relationship   separating stimuli into either figure elements or ground elements.

Financial risks   the relationship between costs and benefits.

Fixed interval   reinforcing a behavior after a specific (predictable) amount of time.

Fixed ratio   reinforcing a behavior only after a specified number of responses.

Focus group   a data collection technique used to collect information through group interaction.

Formal groups   groups that have formal structure and roles.

Framing   the interpretation of information, which depends in part on how it is presented.

Frequency   the number of items that consumer buys in a specific time frame.

Frequency programs   simple programs that reward consumers for a certain amount of purchases.

Functional risks   concerns about product failure or underperformance.

Functional theory of attitudes   posits that attitudes and beliefs are significant to various psychological functions.

G

Gain   when the outcome looks better than the current reference level.

Generic goals   desired outcomes that consumers pursue in order to satisfy physiological and psychological needs.

Geographic segmentation   dividing the market based on the geographic location of the consumer.

Gestalt principles of organization   posits that the whole of a stimulus is different than the sum of its parts.

Global brand   a brand that consistently delivers the same value to consumers across national borders.

Global brands' positioning   the image the brand has in different markets across the globe.

Global marketing   the company's commitment of resources to strategically develop and deliver sustainable value across multiple foreign markets by addressing consumers' needs, wants, and demands to generate revenue and gain a competitive advantage.

Global marketing strategy   the adaptation of the marketing strategy to foreign markets.

Global marketing targeting   choosing which markets to enter across the globe.

Global segmentation   the process of identifying specific segments of consumers, on a country, regional, or consumer level, that will have similar needs or attributes and will response similarly to the same marketing mix.

Globalization the proliferation of products, technology, information, and business opportunities across national borders and cultures.

Glocalization considering local culture and needs and integrating them into the brand's global strategy.

Growth needs arise when needs in levels 5–8 are not fulfilled.

H

Hedonic motivation reflects the drive to experience a sensory pleasure, meaning something that is emotionally gratifying and satisfying.

Heterogeneity level of individual differences.

Heuristics simplifying strategies that provide shortcuts in decision-making.

High-involvement purchases purchases that are infrequent, costly, very important to consumers, and regarded as risky.

Hoarding disorder the excessive accumulation of items, regardless of their value or the consumer's need for them.

Hofstede's six cultural dimensions can be used to characterize the cultural nature of countries.

Homeostasis the motivation to maintain our current desirable state.

Hostages consumers who are unsatisfied with the brand or business even though they are repeat consumers.

Humanistic perspective emphasizes that individuals have free will and that people are basically good and have a need to live to their full potential.

I

Id the primitive, unconscious component of personality.

Ideal personal self a driver for self-improvement.

Ideal self what we aspire to become in the future.

Ideal social self how we would like other people to view us.

Independent variable the variable that is being manipulated.

Individual self the personality traits that make us unique

Individualism versus collectivism independent versus interdependent relationships between members of society.

Indulgence versus restraint degree of desired gratification.

Industrial economies economies that have a strong emphasis on the production of sophisticated products and R&D, as well as a large service sector.

Industrializing economies economies that are experiencing rapid growth via industrialization. They have a well-educated labor force.

Influencers consumers who have the ability to influence the opinions and behaviors of other consumers.

Informal groups groups that are formed around joint interests of their members.

Innate needs physiological in nature and are required to sustain our body.

Innovators consumers who are actively searching for the next new product.

Internal factors factors that are intrinsic to the consumer.

Internal search retrieval of information from long-term memory.

International brands offered in several related markets. These markets are often connected geographically.

Interview   a data collection method aimed to obtain information via a list of questions or unstructured conversation.

Introversion attitudes   attitudes that are predominantly motivated by internal factors.

Involvement theory   posits that we will engage in less information processing in low-involvement situations and extensive information processing in high-involvement situations.

Irrational attitudes   formed without any grounded reason, and they are more intuitive in nature.

J

Just noticeable difference (JND)   see "Differential threshold".

K

Knowledge function of attitudes   forming an attitude based on knowledge and information.

L

Laggards   consumers who either come to the marketplace late or might not ever buy in to a trend.

Late majority   consumers who are very skeptical when it comes to new products and ideas and will adopt new products only after average consumer has adopted them.

Learning   the gain of information.

Lexicographic rule   choosing a product based on ranked criteria from the most to the least important criterion.

Lifestyle   broadly covers how consumers live, particularly how they spend their time and money.

Limited problem-solving   situations where consumers have prior experience with the product or brand options that can solve their problem but are unfamiliar with different variants of the product.

Local brands   brands that have achieved success in a single national market.

Long- versus short-term orientation   the importance of long-term (vs. short-term) planning for the future.

Loss   when the outcome looks worse than the current reference level.

Loss aversion   the idea that, relative to the status quo or reference point, nobody wants to suffer a loss.

Loss of other opportunities   concerns about losing an option to buy a product.

Love and belonging   consist of ties to family members and friends as well as romantic relationships.

Low-involvement purchases   small, mundane, routine purchases, inexpensive, relatively unimportant to consumers, those are made automatically without really thinking about them and those that carry very low risk.

Loyal customer rate   the number of repeat consumers divided by the total consumers the business has.

Loyalists or apostles   consumers who are very satisfied and very loyal to the brand or business.

Loyalty rewards programs   a structured marketing tool for fostering long-term relationships with consumers by rewarding them for repeat purchases and loyal buying behavior.

M

Marketers   individuals or organizations that offer goods or services.

Marketing mix   a set of strategies that companies use to sell products or services to their target customers, including product, price, place, and promotion strategies.

Marketing mix gap how different is the marketing mix in the new country versus the home country of the company.

Marketing myopia defining the company's business in terms of a product instead of a need or a solution to a problem.

Marketing orientation defining the company's business as a solution to their consumers' problems, which reflects a long-term view of the business.

Marketing research a systematic multistage effort of collecting, analyzing, and interpreting information about the consumers, the market, a product, or any other marketing-related element.

Marketing strategy the process by which companies create and deliver unique value to their consumers.

Marketplace the environment, physical or nonphysical, where buyers and sellers engage in the process of exchange.

Masculinity versus femininity the division of roles between men and women.

Maslow's hierarchy of needs Maslow's theory of human motivation.

Maslow's elaborated hierarchy of needs :includes three additional levels to the original hierarchy cognitive needs, aesthetic needs, and transcendence needs.

McClelland's needs theory a trio theory of needs that include a need for achievement, a need for affiliation, and a need for power.

Membership groups groups that consumers currently belong to or are associated with.

Memory recall retrieval of information from the past.

Memory recognition the ability to identify a stimulus that has been previously encountered as a familiar one.

Memory retrieval the cognitive process that involves accessing information that we've stored in memory.

Memory storage putting the coded information into memory.

Mercenaries consumers that are also satisfied with the brand or business. However, they will switch between brands.

Mere exposure effect establishing familiarity via repetitive exposure.

Modeling the process of mimicking and imitating the behavior of others.

Monetary value the worth or price points of the items the consumer typically buys.

Moral being concerned with the principles of right and wrong behavior and the goodness or badness of human character.

Motivation the driving force behind our actions.

Multi-attribute theory recognizes that there are many features of a brand, and consumers might like some of those attributes more than others.

N

Need for achievement our motivation to excel. People with a high need for achievement usually seek feedback to monitor their progress.

Need for affiliation our desire to be loved and accepted by others. To do so, we actively seek social interactions.

Need for avoidance our desire and motivation to avoid unpleasant or risky situations, either consciously or unconsciously.

Need for power our desire to impact or influence the behavior of others.

Need for uniqueness an acquired need to express individuality and distinctiveness from others.

Needs basic human requirements that are essential for an individual to survive, to function in a social context, and to achieve complete development and self-actualization.

Net Promoter Score (NPS) asks consumers to rate their likelihood of recommending the business to others on a scale from 1 to 10.

Netnography   observing the online behaviors and interactions of consumers mostly on social media.

Neuromarketing research   uses the tools of neuroscience to study the behavior of consumers and their decision-making processes.

Neutral stimulus   stimulus that initially does not result in any particular behavior.

Noncompensatory decision rule   a high score on one attribute will not offset a low score on another attribute of the brand or product.

O

Observation   directly watching the behavior and interaction of consumers in their natural environment.

Observational learning   learning by watching others, then changing our own attitudes or behaviors accordingly.

Operant conditioning   alteration of a behavior based on rewards or punishments.

Opinion leaders   experts in a specific consumption domain. They are highly trusted and have the power to influence other consumers' decision-making.

Opt in or opt out   encourages consumers to enroll (or unenrolled) in various programs.

Organic word-of-mouth   unsolicited communication between individuals about a product or service.

Owned media   content and outlets the brand creates and maintains.

P

PAD emotional state model   asserts that all emotional responses have three dimensions: pleasure, arousal, and dominance.

Paid media   promotional materials that involve a paid placement.

Pain of paying   experienced by consumers when they pay for a product.

Participant-observer   a way of conducting an ethnographic research.

Participation level   the percentage of consumers from the total consumers of a business who enroll in loyalty rewards programs.

Passives (with a rating of 7 or 8)   satisfied customers who will switch between brands if they find a better deal.

Perceived risk   the sense of uncertainty that we experience every time we make a purchase.

Perception   the process through which we make sense of the world around us.

Perceptual anomaly   breaking a similarity pattern that can highlight the dissimilar object or objects.

Perceptual blocking   actively blocking out stimuli.

Perceptual closure   the tendency of the brain to perceive a stimulus as a whole even in the absence of one or more of its parts, which might be hidden or totally absent.

Perceptual defense   ignoring or distorting stimuli that view as conflicting, threatening, or unacceptable.

Perceptual distortions   mistakes that are made when interpreting stimuli.

Perceptual interpretation   the meaning embedded in a stimulus.

Perceptual map   a visual representation of customers' perceptions about the specific attributes of a brand or product.

Perceptual overload   receiving too many stimuli to process.

Perceptual proximity   the brain's tendency to group together stimuli that are in close proximity to each other and recognize them as part of the same object.

Perceptual selection   filtering out irrelevant or less significant information.

Perceptual similarity   perceiving objects that are visually similar as a single group rather than individual items.

Personality   the individual's unique characteristics and distinct patterns of thoughts, feelings, and behaviors.

Personality-based marketing   the use of consumers' underlying psychological profiles as drivers of marketing strategies.

Persuasion knowledge model   acknowledges that people use their persuasion knowledge to deal with persuasion attempts.

PESTEL model   a strategic framework used to gain a macro picture of an industry environment.

Physical risks   concerns about the outcomes of product failure.

Physiological needs   the basic needs that are necessary for human survival, such as food and water.

Placement strategy   the way the product will be provided to the customer, or the point of sale or service.

Pluralization of consumption   the pursuit of similar segments with the same needs across multiple national markets.

Points of difference (PODs)   benefits that the company offers that are desirable to its consumers and are NOT being offered by its competitors.

Points of irrelevance (POIs)   offerings that do not address any of the needs or problems the consumers have.

Points of parity (POPs)   benefits that the company offers that are desirable to consumers, but they are also offered by competitors.

Points programs   reward consumers with points, usually proportional to the amount they spent.

Positioning   the utilization of the marketing mix to influence consumer perceptions regarding a brand or product relative to competitors.

Post-purchase behavior   refers to all the behaviors consumers engage in after a transaction is completed.

Post-purchase emotions and attitudes   refers to any emotions or attitudes that consumers have and additional actions that they may take after paying for their purchase.

Power distance   belief about power distribution in society.

Prepurchase search   a search that is directly related to the recognition of the need or problem, to find the optimal product or service.

Prevention-focused motives   our desire for safety and security, when we want to avoid negative outcomes and meet our responsibilities and duties.

Price anchoring   providing consumers with a price point that they can refer to when setting their reference point.

Price strategy   the cost of purchase for consumers.

Price-based positioning   positioning that is based on the product's price.

Primacy effect   information that is encountered first will be remembered better or the best.

Primary data   data the brand team decides it must go out and collect.

Primary membership groups   groups that consumers interact with frequently and regularly.

Primary needs   see "Innate needs".

Problem recognition   a discrepancy between consumers' current state and a desired future state.

Product line extension   introduction of a product that is a slight variation of a well-established product line.

Product strategy   refers to what the company is selling.

Product use-based positioning   positioning that associates the product with a specific use.

Products   goods, services, experiences, activities, ideas, information, or anything offered to a market to satisfy a need.

Product-specific goals   desired outcomes that are associated with specific products and services.

Promoters (with a rating of 9 or 10)   those who give the highest ratings are the most valuable customers.

Promotion strategy   includes any activity designed to connect with a company's target market.

Promotion-focused motives   reflect our desire for growth, accomplishment, and the achievement of positive outcomes.

Prospect theory   examines people's perceptions of their prospects or expected outcomes.

Psychoanalytic perspective   highlights the important role of early childhood experiences and the influence of the unconscious mind and sexual instincts in the formation of personality.

Psychographic segmentation   dividing the market based on consumers' lifestyle and interests.

Psychological risks   concerns about the values brands stand for and the image their brands convey.

Pull goals   goals that motivate an individual to work toward desirable outcomes.

Pull motivation   brings an individual toward a desired end state. For example, think about your first job.

Punishment   reinforcing a behavior by observing another's being reinforced or punished.

Push goals   goals that motivate one to avoid negative or undesirable consequences.

Push motivation   an internal disposition that pushes an individual toward a desired end state.

Q

Qualitative data   a nonnumerical descriptive information.

Quality-based positioning   positioning that is based on the product's quality.

R

Race   a grouping of humans based on shared physical or social qualities into categories generally viewed as distinct by society.

Rational attitudes   formed based on objective values, normally established through practical experience.

Raw material exporting economies   that are rich in minerals and raw materials with no production capabilities.

Rebate programs   see "Cash back".

Recency   the most recent time a consumer purchased the company's product or services.

Recency effect   information that is encountered last will be remembered better or the best.

Redemption rate   the percentage of rewards that were cashed in from all the rewards that were issued.

Reference dependence   using a reference point when evaluating options or outcomes.

Reference group   a person or group of people that consumers think about and make comparisons to.

Reference price   the price consumers think is a reasonable and fair price for a product.

Regression analysis   a statistical model in which the marketer tries to predict an outcome (dependent variable), as a function of an independent variable (a variable that is independent of the outcome).

Regret   happens when consumers make unfavorable comparisons between a chosen option and an unchosen option.

Regulatory focus theory   centers on the way people self-regulate their behaviors when attempting to achieve their goals.

Reinforcement   a procedure, negative or positive, that alters a response to a stimulus.

Relational self   highlights elements that we have in common with others.

Repetition   a recurrent exposure to the same stimulus.

Retail atmospherics   the store atmosphere that marketers create to attract customers.

Routinized purchases   purchases that consumers have made multiple times.

S

Safety needs   reflect the fundamental needs for feeling safe and secure.

Satisfaction   a subjective assessment of the gap between consumers' initial expectations of the product or the purchasing process (pre-purchase) and their perceptions about the actual performance of the product or their actual purchase experience (post-purchase).

Schedule of reinforcement   setting up a rule indicating on which instances a behavior will be reinforced.

Schemata   mental models used to organize information in a way that allows our brain to interpret it more efficiently.

Search engine optimization   the process of getting websites to rank higher in search engines.

Seasonality   establishing familiarity via repetitive exposure.

Secondary data   data that already exist that might be useful in shedding light on the current marketing questions facing the brand team.

Secondary membership groups   groups that consumers have infrequent and irregular interaction with.

Secondary needs   see "Acquired needs".

Segmentation   the division of a broader consumer market into subgroups of consumers based on shared characteristics or needs.

Segmentation, targeting, and positioning (STP)   a three-step process that enables companies to be more effective and efficient in delivering their value through their offerings.

Selective attention   being selective in the attention given to the marketing messages we are exposed to.

Selective exposure   active exposure to marketing messages that are pleasant and enjoyable, and avoidance of upsetting messages.

Self-actualization needs   our motivation to live up to our potential, to be the best we can be, and to make the most of our abilities.

Self-concept   the way people view themselves.

Self-congruence   consistency between our actual and ideal selves.

Self-esteem   how much we value ourselves.

Self-image   the way we see ourselves.

Self-improvement   involves a wide range of behaviors aimed at changing our current state to a more desirable one.

Self-monitoring   the ability to regulate and monitor self-presentations, attitudes, emotions, and behaviors.

Sellers   see "Marketers".

Sensation   input that our sensory receptors obtain from the physical world.

Sentiment analysis   assessment of the positive or negative valence of the social media around the brand.

Share of wallet   percentage of disposable income that customers spend with one business.

Shopping cart abandonment   the phenomenon where consumers had been on a website, clicked on items to consider for purchase, but then left the website before actually buying the items.

Shrinkflation   offering smaller size packages or smaller quantities of the product while maintaining the same price or even increasing it.

Social class   a group of people who share the same socioeconomic status.

Social cognitive theory   posits that learning happens in a social context and is reflected in the interaction between a person, the environment, and behavior.

Social marketing   a systematic implementation of marketing strategies in order to influence and achieve specific consumers' behaviors that benefit society as a whole.

Social media   any online means of communication that enables users to create and share content with others.

Social media analytics   various measures that track consumer traffic on social media websites to assess popularity, volume, and possible effectiveness of marketing campaigns.

Social models   the people we choose as models. They don't have to be celebrities.

Social risks   concerns about what others think about us.

Socioeconomic status   a combined measure of a person's social status and economic standing.

Standardization   implementing the same marketing mix the same way across foreign markets.

Status quo bias   the notion that we'd rather do nothing than make a change that could go bad.

Stimulus discrimination   occurs when only the original stimulus elicits a response, and it is not transferable to other stimuli.

Stimulus generalization   occurs when a new stimulus that is similar to a previously associated stimulus evokes the same response as the previously associated prompt.

Subculture   a group of people who share some traits or preferences.

Subliminal message   a message that consumers are not consciously aware of, but it still might affect their behavior.

Subsistence economies   nonmonetary economies that rely mostly on the exchange of goods and simple agriculture.

Sunk cost fallacy   the tendency to continue a behavior because we already invested time, effort, or money into it, regardless of whether or not the current costs outweigh the benefits.

Superego   regulates a person's ideals and morals, which are shaped by family and society.

Survey   a list of questions used for collecting data from a predefined group of respondents about a specific topic of interest.

System 1   the information-processing style that operates when consumers are using heuristics.

System 2   the cognitive rational processing style of decision-making.

T

Target market   a group of consumers with similar characteristics or needs that the company can serve successfully with its products or services.

Targeting   identifying which segment or segments provide the company with the best business opportunity.

Teleological ethics   an assessment of the consequences of a behavior.

Temporal risks   concerns about the time invested in searching for a product, repairing it, or replacing it.

Test market   a research method used by companies to explore consumers' response to their new products or marketing campaigns, by testing it on a small group of consumers before launching it to the general market.

Text analysis   uses linguistic parsing to look at words and word phrases to understand the content and positivity or negativity of posts.

Theory of planned behavior   predicts a person's intention to engage in a specific behavior.

Theory of reasoned action   suggests that what determines people's intention to perform a behavior is what drives their behavior, which is a function of a person's attitude toward the behavior.

Tiered programs   programs that incentivize consumers to stay engaged on a consistent basis over time.

Total set   a broader set of brands that include options that consumers are not aware of.

Transaction   the end result of a successful exchange process, when the buyer pays the seller and in return receives the desired product.

Transcendence needs   address our desire to help others self-actualize.

Tricomponent attitude model   predict intentions of engaging in the behavior, which in turn will lead to our actual behavior.

U

Uncertainty avoidance   level of tolerance of ambiguity.

Unconditioned behavioral response   a natural reaction to an unconditioned stimulus.

Unconditioned stimulus   a stimulus that leads to an automatic response.

Unique value proposition (UVP)   a statement that articulates the promise the company makes to its customers to be delivered in a unique and differentiated way.

Utilitarian function of attitudes   reflects subjective assessment of the benefit an object can provide.

Utilitarian motivation   our drive to acquire products or services that will help us solve a problem or accomplish a specific task.

V

VALS (Values, Attitudes, and Lifestyles)   one of the most widely used psychographic tools that profiles US consumers based on their motivations and their recourses.

Value-expressive function of attitude   enables consumers to convey their core values, self-concept, and beliefs to others.

Variable ratio   reinforcing a behavior after an unknown or random number of responses.

Vicarious learning   see "Observational learning".

Vicarious reinforcement   see "Punishment".

Viral   shared information that spreads quickly to millions of people online.

W

Wants   refer to specific products and brands consumers choose to satisfy their needs based on their culture and individual personality

Word-of-mouth   an exchange of information between consumers about products, services, brands, experiences, promotions, deals, and anything that is consumption related.

Word-of-mouth marketing (WOMM)   see "Amplified word-of-mouth".

INDEX